DESIGN THINKING PROCESS & METHODS 4th Edition

Robert A Curedale
Copyright © 01 December 2017 by Robert A. Curedale
All rights reserved. Published by Design Community College Inc.

Design Community College Inc.
PO Box 1153
Topanga CA 90290 USA
info@dcc-edu.org
Designed and illustrated by Robert Curedale
Cover color graphic and artwork designed by Robert Curedale
ISBN-10: 1-940805-35-X
ISBN-13: 978-1-940805-35-1

DESIGN THINKING

Process & Methods Guide
4th edition

Robert Curedale

Published by Design Community College Inc.
Los Angeles https://dcc-edu.org

CONTENTS

INTRODUCTION

THINKING FROM DESIGN TO DESIGN THINKING

Design thinking is a human-centered approach for finding innovative real solutions to tough problems. Design thinking combines the approaches of design, management and science to solving a wide range of challenges. Design thinking can be used to develop products, services, experiences as well as design and business strategy. After decades working in and managing design offices in Europe, Asia, Australia and North America, I focused my attention on what I think is most important about design.

For a century the practice of design has followed the rules set down at the dawn of the industrial age in the Bauhaus. The emphasis of design during the 2oth century was mostly on creating a more beautiful world. It was not about form follows function. Early in my career as a designer I believed that the primary goal of design was to create beautiful things as did my peers.

"

Beauty will save the world."

Prince Myshkin
in Feodor Dostoevsky's
novel, "The Idiot"

Now we are at the sunset of the industrial age in the West there are good reasons to rethink the purpose of design in the world. The purpose of beauty in design has been to create attachment to objects. Beautiful objects have been necessary for advertising to create brand promise. If objects are designed and created for their utility alone then there would be no attachment to those objects. If there was no beauty in the world we would not be motivated to live and make the world a better place Beauty provides optimism like the American dream. Beauty sold things. The optimism of a red Ford Mustang styling promised the fulfillment of the American dream.

Beauty alone cannot save the world. Design can do more than provide beauty.

"

Making things people want is better than making people want things."

John V Willshire

Enter design thinking. Design thinking focusses on delivering solutions to unmet human needs. It is about, innovation, creating a better future for complex or problems. It is a holistic, more ethical, more businesslike, more inclusive, a more satisfying and ultimately better way to design things. Designers are not artists. We have different responsibilities.

It is about delivering better real solutions rather than [brand] promises.

In the 20th-century, design inspiration came from magazines and web sites of a small gang of perhaps 20 famous designers in each field of design. There was an emphasis on making more things rather than better things. This century, design inspiration will come through value networks which each will customize to their own needs, social networks, crowd sources, the Internet of things and this will facilitate innovation and customization on a level never before possible. Design will be about filtering information and curating the best holistic solutions with new digital hybrid skills.

Design thinking has become the new design doing and is sweeping the globe. Design thinking is a way of enabling designers and others to think beyond creating beautiful things towards making the deeper changes that are needing to happen in a complex world. Design Thinking has the power to transform nearly everything.

"

Design thinking is about creating intelligent change."

CONNECTIONS

Of the many elements of change affecting design practice and education this century, the one I find most interesting and the element of change which may be most far-reaching is the influence of global networks.

Design originated millennia ago, when humans started to live in small communities and began collaborating and to share knowledge and to trade. Over the last three decades Internet has facilitated a level of collaboration that is unprecedented in human history. Innovation has always happened when people from different cultures have been brought together in a space and today that space is a virtual space. Networks are changing the skills that designers need to practice.

In 2008 I established a number of social networks for working designers. These groups have grown to over one and a quarter million active design practitioners across every field of design. This network of designers and architects is about half the nightly audience of Fox News.

During this ten year period, I have been actively involved in tens of thousands of conversations with diverse global designers.

This extraordinary network has placed me at a gateway in a stream of information hat has had no parallel in history of design.

An opportunity is presented with this large cross section of the world's designing power

**" **

When patterns are broken, new worlds emerge. "

Tuli Kupferberg,
Countercultural Poet

Combining this unparelleled access to what is current in design practice, with my long experience with the practical problems of implementing design perhaps I could do something that no design school or corporation, acting alone could do. I could plant the seeds of awareness and skills needed to change the culture of design towards something more positive, towards something based on need.

**" **

Many ideas grow better when transplanted into another mind than the one where they sprang up. "

Oliver Wendell Holmes

In 2013 I wrote the first Design thinking process and methods manual. I have now created 28 publications related to design thinking, service design

and user-centered design and presented hundreds of face-to-face workshops and on line classes in design thinking to thousands of mid-career working designers and corporate managers. I have distributed more than 100,000 copies of my publications to every country on earth.

DESIGN THINKING IS NOT A FAD

Design thinking is no longer a buzzword, it is a necessary strategy to remain competitive if you create products and services for people.

Design thinking's impact on how organizations go about solving problems, has been profound. Its influence has expanded far beyond design into business, education, national development and science.

**" **

The theme of the story is shifting from "What is design thinking?" to Look at what we did using design thinking.", from design thinking to design doing. "

Andy Hagerman

Design thinking is one of the most important ideas of the 21st century. It has become a required skill for working designers and managers. Thousands of companies of all sizes throughout the world have adopted the key skills and practices associated with design thinking. Large corporations including Pepsi, Linksys, and IBM have invested tens of millions of dollars to train their staff and adopt design thinking practices.

DESIGN THINKING IS A CORE BUSINESS PRACTICE

Design thinking drives repeatable innovation and business value. Innovation is now seen as a core competence and requirement for businesses. Design, engineering, and business management students need to be equipped with design thinking to manage and lead innovation in organizations.

There is a growing body of evidence demonstrates that the application of design thinking to business provides greater ROI, increases employee and customer satisfaction, and creates differentiated products and services.

The list of world's leading brands that are using design thinking has grown considerably from the introduction in my first book and now includes organizations such as GE, Pepsico, Target, Deloitte Innovation, SAP, Singapore And Australian Governments, Procter And Gamble, Whirlpool, Bayer, BMW, DHL, Daimler, Deutsche Bank, Philips Electronics, Infosys, AirBnB, and Autodesk. It is being taught at leading universities including Stanford, Yale, and Harvard.

THIS EDITION

This book is written for the learning style of practicing designers. The descriptions of methods are brief and condensed.

GROWING INTEREST IN DESIGN THINKING

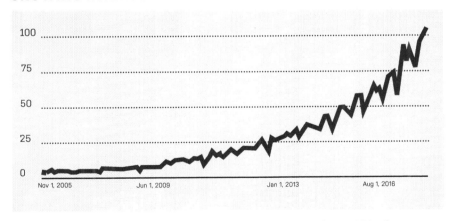

100
75
50
25
0

Nov 1, 2005   Jun 1, 2009   Jan 1, 2013   Aug 1, 2016

Data sourced from Google trends Google index data to 100, where 100 is the maximum search interest. Google Trends is a public web facility of Google Inc., based on Google Search, that shows how often a particular search-term is entered relative to the total search-volume across various regions of the world, and in various languages.

We have added methods that designers tell us they are using and removed methods found in the last edition that have proved less popular. Designers like to understand the basic concept quickly then adapt and blend the approach creatively to their own application. The referencing isn't intended for academic research. We are working to make this edition and future editions the most useful references for design thinking for design practice available.

In this edition I have removed much of the white space to create a condensed layout and a reduced page count in order to minimize the shipping costs and make maximum use of the paper so I can help bring design thinking to as many designers and managers as possible throughout the world.

My goal was to make this fourth edition the deepest dive available into Design Thinking practice. It is an approach that can be applied by anyone. Design thinking can also be fun. I hope that you will find this 4th edition an essential reference.

"

The implications of globalization are that corporations are facing extreme competition; the pace of innovation is faster today; you have to quickly develop your ideas and innovate faster than your competitors,"

"You have to be open to new ideas and be willing to learn new ideas and unlearn outdated ideas. You have to learn new cultures and paradigms."

Narayana Murthy
Infosys co-founder

"

We use DT at Home Depot to bring cross-functional teams together to gain alignment. Through the process, individual expertise help form a well-rounded view of the problem space and introduce new solutions. To facilitate, scale and push design thinking, the role of design is paramount."

Brooke Creef
Product Design Lead
Design Thinking Facilitator
Home Depot
Source: Linkedin

01
HISTORY

HISTORY OF DESIGN THINKING

WHERE DID IT ALL START?

Design Thinking has evolved over a period of twenty to thirty years and incorporates ideas from a number of design methodologies and movements. The term Design Thinking first emerged in the 1980s with the rise of human-centered design

In the 1960s efforts were made to develop the field that has become known as Design Research to better inform the practice of design. The notion of design as a "way of thinking" was explored by Herbert A. Simon in his 1969 book The Sciences of the Artificial. It was further explored in Robert McKim's 1973 book Experiences in Visual Thinking. Rolf Faste expanded McKim's work in the 80s and 90s in his teaching at Stanford, defining and popularizing the idea of "Design Thinking"as a way of creative action that was adapted for business purposes by IDEO through his colleague David M. Kelley.

Peter Rowe's 1987 book Design Thinking was the first popular usage of the term "Design Thinking" in the literature on design. The 1992 article by Richard Buchanan titled "Wicked Problems in Design Thinking"

expressed a broader view of Design Thinking.

Through the 1980s it was recognized that design needed to focus on understanding the needs and designs of people as well as business. Design Thinking incorporates some ideas from the user centered design movement that developed during this period. By the 1990s David Kelley of IDEO, Larry Leifer and Terry Winograd were amongst the founders of what is now known as the Design Thinking movement.

In 2005, SAP co-founder Hasso Plattner made a personal donation of U.S. $35 million to fund the d.school, which is officially named "Hasso Plattner Institute of Design at Stanford. that has pioneered the teaching of Design Thinking. The approach is now taught at a number of leading business schools such as the Rotman School in Toronto and at Harvard as well as many design schools.

I have listed here some of the important contributions to the field with dates and those people responsible. In this chapter I also give a brief history of the emergence of service design. Design Thinking is in part a response to the requirements of designing services. Services are

RELATED DESIGN MOVEMENTS

Year	Design movement	Design approaches	People
2010s	Design Thinking	Experience design	David Kelley
		Creative class	Tim Brown
			Roger Martin
			Bruce Nussbaum
			Rolf Faste
2000s	Service Design	Human Centered Design	Lucy Kimbell
1990s	Process Methods	Meta Design	Ezio Manzini
			William Rause
			Richard Buchanan
1980s	Cognitive Reflections	User Centered Design	Don Norman
			Donal Schon
			Nigel Cross
			Peter Rowe
			Bryan Lawson
1970s			Robert McKim
1960s	Design Science	Participatory Design	Horst Rittel
		Design Methods	Herbet Simon
			Bruce Archer
1950s	Creativity Methods	Brainstorming	Alex Osborn

more complex than physical objects to design. Cross disciplinary teamwork is a requirement of service design as is are the mindsets of Design Thinking. 90% of employment in the United States is now in service industries.

380BC

Plato's Republic contains some of the roots of participatory design.

300BC

Porphry of Tyros develops mind maps.

100BC

Hermagoras of Temnos, Quis, quid, quando, ubi, cur, quem ad modum, quibus adminiculis. (Who, what, when, where, why, in what way, by what means)

1300

Ockham's razor is a principle attributed to the fourteenth-century English philosopher and Franciscan friar, William of Ockham, and it forms the basis of methodological reductionism. The principle states that the elements that are not really needed should be pared back to produce something simpler and in doing so, the risk of introducing inconsistencies, ambiguities and redundancies will be reduced. Ockham's razor is also referred to as the principle of parsimony or law of economy.

1637

Rene Descartes (in 1637) wrote his Discourse on Methodology in which he focused on the importance of objectivity and evidence in the search for truth. A key idea in his writing: researchers should attempt to distance themselves from any influences that might corrupt their analytical capacity

1600s Isaac Newton and Francis Bacon asserted that knowledge about the world could be acquired through direct observation (induction) rather than deduced from abstract propositions.

1711-76

David Hume is associated with the founding of the empirical research tradition suggested that all knowledge about the world originates in our experiences and is derived through the senses. Evidence based on direct observation and collected in an objective and unbiased way are fundamental tenets of empirical research.

1781

Immanuel Kant's (1781) Critique of Pure Reason. He argued that there are ways of knowing about the world other than direct observation and that people use these all the time. He proposed that: perception relates not only to the senses but to human interpretations of what our senses tell us
our knowledge of the world is based on 'understanding' which arises from thinking about what happens to us, not just simply

from having had particular experiences

1798-1857
Auguste Comte (1798-1857) asserted that the social world can be studied in terms of invariant laws just like the natural world. This belief is the basis of a school of thought (or paradigm) known as 'positivism' which was a major influence in social research throughout the twentieth century.

1860s and 1870s
Wilhelm Dilthey. His writing (during the 1860s-70s) emphasized the importance of 'understanding' and of studying people's 'lived experiences' which occur within a particular historical and social context. He proposed that social research should explore 'lived experiences' in order to reveal the connections between the social, cultural and historical aspects of people's lives and to see the context in which particular actions take place.

1864- 1920
Max Weber (1864-1920) was very influenced by Dilthey's ideas and particularly his views on the importance of 'understanding' He emphasized that the researcher must understand the meaning of social actions within the context of the material conditions in which people live. He proposed two types of understanding: direct observational understanding, and explanatory or motivational understanding.

He argued: difference in the purpose of understanding between the natural and social sciences. In the natural sciences, the purpose is to produce law-like propositions whereas, in the social sciences, the aim is to understand subjectively meaningful experiences.

1877
Georg von Mayr invents radar charts.

1879
Louis Emile Javal develops eye tracking.

1880
John Venn invents Venn Diagrams

1890s
Credit Agricole pioneer co-creation methods. From the late nineteenth century and throughout the twentieth-century qualitative research methods developed and became more widely adopted.

1909
E.B. Titchener invented the word empathy in an attempt to translate the German word "Einfühlungsvermögen".

1921
Robert Bruere first uses the terms primary research and secondary research.

1928
Margaret Mead develops ethnographic field studies.

1929
Bonislaw Malinowski develops
ethnographic field studies.

Research of Malinowski in
ethnography and the Chicago
School in sociology. During
this period, foreign cultures
were the issue in ethnography,
and outsiders within one's own
society in sociology.

Ethnography: Within sociology
and anthropology, early
qualitative research often took
the form of ethnographic
work which flourished in both
America and Britain

Early examples of ethnographers
include Malinowski, Radcliffe
Brown, Margaret Mead, Gregory
Bateson and Franz Boas, all
of whom studied 'native'
populations abroad, and Robert
Park and the work of the Chicago
school where the focus was
on the life and culture of local
groups in the city.

1940s
2nd World War from which came
operational research methods
and management decision-
making techniques

1940
Robert Merton develops focus
groups.

Harold van Doren published
"Industrial Design – A Practical
Guide to Product Design and
Development",covering design
methods and practices.

1942
Gordon Allport, may have been
the first to describe diary studies.

1943
Kelly Johnson invents the term
Skunkworks.

1944
Alex Bavelas develops Fly on the
wall method.

1948
Edward Tolman invents
Cognitive Maps.

1950s
Development of creativity
techniques.

Structured interviews began to
dominate the research landscape
during and after World War II
(Fontana and Frey 2000: 648–49)

1950
Herman Kahn Rand develops
Scenarios method.
1953
Term brainstorming was
popularized by Alex Faickney
Osborn in the 1953 book Applied
Imagination

1957
Walt Disney Corporation
develop activity maps method.

1958
Michael Polanyi uses the term
Tacit Knowledge.

1960s
Designers explore models
for design methodology, and

"design research" to better understand and improve design processes and practices This movement marked the beginning of a debate over the process and methodology of design.

1960
Affinity diagram was devised by Jiro Kawakita

Allan Collins, Northwestern University USA develops mind maps.

1961
Gordon The first creativity books start to appear.

1962
The First 'Conference on Design Methods,.

1962
Archer, L. Bruce. Systematic Method for Designers.

Ernest Becker Behavioral Maps

1963
Osborn, Alex F. Applied Imagination: Principles and Procedures of Creative Thinking. New York: Scribner,

1964
Christopher Alexander The first design methods or methodology books start appearing.

1965
Bruce Archer professor of Design Research at the Royal College of Art is arguably the first author to use the term Design Thinking in

his book "Systematic Method for Designers" London: Council of Industrial Design, H.M.S.O. Archer, L. Bruce. Systematic Method for Designers. Council of Industrial Design, H.M.S.O.

1965
SWOT Analysis developed by Albert Humphrey Stanford University

1967
Francis J Aguiler develops PEST Analysis.

1968
Kaoru Ishikawa develops fishbone diagram.

Professor Bernd Rohrbach pioneers 635 Brainstorming Method

1969
Herbert A. Simon establishes a "science of design" which would be "a body of intellectually tough, analytic, partly formalizable, partly empirical, teachable doctrine about the design process."

Simon, Herbert (1969). The Sciences of the Artificial. Cambridge: MIT Press. Bill Gaver Royal College of Art cultural probes

Visual psychologist Rudolf Arnheim publishes his book Visual Thinking, which inspires the teaching of ME101: Visual Thinking, by Robert McKim, in the School of Engineering at

Stanford University

1970s
John Chris Jones, "In the 1970s I reacted against design methods. I dislike the machine language, the behaviorism, the continual attempt to fix the whole of life into a logical framework."

1970
Jones, John Christopher. Design Methods. New York: John Wiley & Sons.

1971
Victor Papanek published Design for the Real World. Papanek applied the principles of socially responsible design.

1972
Horst Rittel and his counterpart Melvin M. Webber first coined the term Wicked problems.

1973
Robert McKim's publishes Experiences in Visual Thinking The class McKim creates, "ME101: Visual Thinking,"in the design program at Stanford University.

Combined the Qualitative & Quantitative data by S.D. Sieber.

1979
Bruce Archer "There exists a designerly way of thinking and communicating that is both different from scientific and scholarly ways of thinking and communicating, and as powerful as scientific and scholarly methods of inquiry when applied to its own kinds of problems."

1980s
The term Design Thinking first emerged prominently in the with the rise of human-centered design.

Rolf Faste building on McKim's work in his teaching at Stanford,

Systemic engineering design methods are developed, particularly in Germany and Japan.

1980s sees the rise of human-centered design and the rise of design-centered business management.

Service design adopts ideas of interaction design and usability design. "The term interaction design was first proposed by Bill Moggridge and Bill Verplank in the late 1980s. To Verplank, it was an adaptation of the computer science term user interface design to the industrial design profession. To Moggridge, it was an improvement over soft-face, which he had coined in 1984 to refer to the application of industrial design to products containing software."

1980
Bryan Lawson, "How Designers Think: The Design Process Demystified" and "How Designers Think about design cognition in the context

of architecture and urban planning."

1981
George Doran develops Smart Goals Method.

Koberg, Don, and Jim Bagnall. The All New Universal Traveller: a Soft-systems Guide To: Creativity, Problem-solving and the Process of Reaching Goals. Los Altos, CA: Kaufmann

The American Society of Mechanical Engineers conference on Design Theory and Methodology. The rise of human-centered design and the rise of design-centered business management.

1982
Cross, Nigel. "Designerly Ways of Knowing." Design Studies 3.4 (1982): 221-27.

"

Everyone canand does design. We all design when we plan for something new to happen, whether that might be a new version of a recipe, a new arrangement of the living room furniture, or a new lay tour of a personal web page. So design thinking is something inherent within human cognition; it is a key part of what makes us human."

Nigel Cross

1982
G. Lynn Shostack proposed design that integrates material components (products) and immaterial components

1983
Schön, Donald. The Reflective Practitioner: How Professionals Think In Action. New York: Basic Books, 1983.

Donald Schön With a background in philosophy and urban planning much of Schön's work argues against the technical-rationality of design profession seen in the 1960's.

"

The reflective practitioner allows himself to experience surprise, puzzlement, or confusion in a situation which he finds uncertain or unique. He reflects on the phenomenon before him, and on the prior understandings which have been implicit in his behaviour. He carries out an experiment which serves to generate both a new understanding of the phenomenon and a change in the situation."

Donald Schön

1983
Lyn Shosack develops service blueprinting method. In early contributions on service design (Shostack 1982; Shostack 1984), the activity of designing

service was considered as part of the domain of marketing and management disciplines. Shostack (1982), for instance proposed the integrated design of material components (products) and immaterial components (services). This design process, according to Shostack, can be documented and codified using a "service blueprint" to map the sequence of events in a service and its essential functions in an objective and explicit manner.
Source: wikipedia

1984
Jay Conrad Levinson guerrilla ethnography

1985
Edward de Bono Six Thinking Hats.

1986
Six Sigma emerges to streamline the design process for quality control and profit.

1987
Peter Rowe professor at the Harvard Graduate School of Design, book Design Thinking was the first significant usage of the term "Design Thinking" in literature. Rowe, G. Peter (1987). Design Thinking. Cambridge: The MIT Press. ISBN 978-0-262-68067-7.

1988
Rolf Faste, director of the design program at Stanford, publishes "Ambidextrous Thinking," Whiteside, Bennet, and

Holtzblatt Contextual Inquiry.

Rolf Faste, director of the design program at Stanford, creates "Ambidextrous Thinking", a required class for graduate product design majors that extends McKim's process of visual thinking to design as a "whole-body way of doing.

1990s
Human-centered design evolves from a technology driven focus to a human one.

1991
Rowe popularized the phrase "Design Thinking" referring to the ways in which designers approach design problems,

Mood boards first used by Terence Conran. IDEO combines from three industrial design companies. They are one of the first design companies to showcase their design process, which draws heavily on the Stanford University curriculum. IIT Institute of Design establishes the first PhD program in Design in the United States.

1991
IDEO forms. They invite experts from fields like anthropology, business strategy, education or healthcare to guide their design teams and processes.

1992
Richard Buchanan's article "Wicked Problems in Design Thinking," Design Issues, vol.

8, no. 2, Spring 1992. adopts a broader view of Design Thinking

1994
Rolf Faste, "Ambidextrous Thinking", Innovations in Mechanical Engineering Curricula for the 1990s, American Society of Mechanical Engineers,

Matthew Van Horn invents the term Wireframe in New York.

1995
Ikujiro Nonaka expands the ideas of Michael Polanyi on tacit versus explicit knowledge.

1997
David Kelley contributed to the book the article The Designer's Stance through an interview by Bradley Hartfield, "It might help to pose two caricatures two hypothetical extremes. One is engineering as problem solving; the other is design as creating. "

"

The designer wants to create a solution that fits in a deeper situational or social sense." "design is messy. Engineering ... is not supposed to be messy. The designer can handle the messiness and ambiguity and is willing to trust intuition." Successful design is done in teams."

David Kelley.

1999
The term Critical Design was first used in Anthony Dunne's book "Hertzian Tales"
IDEO Design Thinking approach was the featured on ABC's Nightline in 1999 in an episode called "The Deep Dive."

1999
Liz Sanders The founder of MakeTools, is a pioneer in applied design research. Liz invents many tools used in design thinking.

"

This human-centered design revolution is causing us to rethink the design process. In order to drive the human-centered design revolution, we need to tap into the imaginations and dreams not only of designers, but also of everyday people. New design spaces are emerging in response to everyday people's needs for creativity."

Liz Sanders

2000s
Debate about the hijacking and exploitation of Design Thinking by business educators.

2000
Brandt and Grunnet develop Empathy Tools.

The Rotman School of

Management develops a new model for business education based on Dean Roger Martin's integrative thinking for solving wicked problems.

2002
Florida, Richard L. The Rise of the Creative Class: and How It's Transforming Work, Leisure, Community and Everyday Life. New York, NY: Basic, 2002.
William McDonough Cradle to Cradle.

2000
Bodystorming Buchenau and Fulton.

2003
Misuse Scenario method developed by Ian Alexander.

Ezio Manzini One of the founders of DESIS and supporters of slow design, Manzini's works are grounded in participatory design for sustainability. Utilising many service design tools his books and projects including Sustainable Everyday and Design.

Engine, initially founded in 2000 as an Ideation company, positioned themselves as a Service Design consultancy.

2004
The Service Design Network was launched by Köln International School of Design, Carnegie Mellon University, Linköpings Universitet, Politecnico di Milano, and Domus Academy in order to create an international network for Service Design academics and professionals. Nowadays the network extends to service design professionals worldwide as well as design consultancies who have started offering service design."

2005
The Hasso Plattner Institute of Design or the d.school is established at Stanford.
2005, SAP co-founder Hasso Plattner made a donation of U.S. $35 million to fund the d.school, which is named the "Hasso Plattner Institute of Design" at Stanford."

2006
Lawson, Bryan. "How Designers Think." Oxford UK: Architectural Press Elsevier, 2006

Jeff Howe uses the term Crowd Sourcing.

2007
Cross, Nigel. Designerly Ways of Knowing. London UK and Boston MA: Birkhauser Verlag AG, 2007.

Hasso Plattner Institute for IT Systems Engineering in Potsdam, Germany establishes a Design Thinking program

Martin, Roger L. The Opposable Mind: How Successful Leaders Win through Integrative Thinking. Boston, MA: Harvard Business School, 2007.

2008

HPI at Potsdam and Stanford University launched a joint research program on innovation, which is jointly led by Leifer and Christoph Meinel.
Deborah Szebeko founded British-based social design agency of ThinkPublic who specialises in design and innovation within the public sector and NGO's.

.

"

We use a mixture of design processes. We've got a diversity of designers, including service designers, graphics designers, information designers, programmers, marketers, social scientists, positive psychologists, and even anthropologists. This diversity of experts bring different techniques related to their disciplines, and this mixture creates a unique design process—we call it a co-design process—whereby we capture public views."

Deborah Szebeko

2009
Tim Brown of IDEO, and is the author of Change by Design: How Design Thinking Transforms Organizations and Inspires Innovation
Roger Martin, Dean of the Rotman School of Management in Toronto, authors The Design of Business: Why Design

Thinking is the Next Competitive Advantage

Brown, Tim. "The Making of a Design Thinker." Metropolis Oct. 2009: 60-62. Pg 60: "David Kelley... said that every time someone came to ask him about design, he found himself inserting the word thinking to explain what it is that designers do. The term Design Thinking stuck." The MMM Program at Northwestern University is the first MBA program to incorporate Design Thinking into its core curriculum.

2010
Lockwood, Thomas. Design Thinking: Integrating Innovation, Customer Experience and Brand Value. New York, NY: Allworth, 2010

2011
Faste, Rolf. "The Human Challenge in Engineering Design." International Journal of Engineering Education, vol 17, 2001.
A number of schools begin teaching Design Thinking in classrooms and community projects

Cross, N (2011) Design Thinking: Understanding How Designers Think and Work, Berg, Oxford and New York.

CHAPTER SUMMARY

Design Thinking has evolved over a period of twenty to thirty years and incorporates ideas from a number of design methodologies and movements including.

1. Service design
2. Experience design
3. Participatory design
4. Design Science
5. Design research
6. Human-centered design

The term Design Thinking first emerged in the 1980s with the rise of human-centered design

In the 1960s efforts were made to develop the field that has become known as Design Research to better inform the practice of design. The notion of design as a "way of thinking" was explored by Herbert A. Simon in his 1969 book The Sciences of the Artificial. It was further explored in Robert McKim's 1973 book Experiences in Visual Thinking. Rolf Faste expanded McKim's work in the 80s and 90s in his teaching at Stanford, defining and popularizing the idea of "Design Thinking"as a way of creative action that was adapted for business purposes by IDEO through his colleague David M. Kelley.

CHAPTER REVIEW

1. Name three design movements related to design thinking.
2. What was Rolf Faste's contribution to the development of design thinking?
3. What was Don Norman's contribution to the development of design thinking?
4. What was John Chris Jone's contribution to the development of design thinking?
5. Where was the term "Design Thinking" first significantly used and who used it?
6. Who popularized the use of the term "Design Thinking"?
7. Who donated funds to establish the d.school at Stanford university to teach design thinking?
8. Who popularized the use of brainstorming in the United States?
9. What do IDEO do and where are they located?
10. What was the contribution of David Kelley to design thinking?
11. Who is Tim Brown and what did he contribute to design thinking?
12. What did Roger Martin contribute to design thinking?

02

TRENDS

20TH CENTURY DESIGN	21ST CENTURY DESIGN THINKING

INDIVIDUAL DESIGNERS

DESIGN TEAMS

PRODUCTS

SYSTEMS OF PRODUCTS, SERVICES AND EXPERIENCES

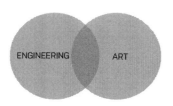

ENGINEERING   ART

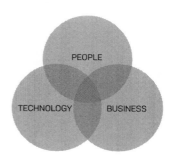

PEOPLE

TECHNOLOGY   BUSINESS

DESIGN INSPIRATION FROM IMAGES OF THE WORK OF ABOUT 20 FAMOUS DESIGNERS IN EACH DESIGN DISCIPLINE

DESIGN INSPIRATION FROM RESEARCH AND THE UNMET NEEDS OF-END USERS

DESIGN THINKING, INNOVATION, AND COMPETITIVE ADVANTAGE

The rate of change is accelerating. Business disruptors like social media, the cloud, mobile and 3d printing are leading to companies changing, growing and dying faster than ever before. Innovation is now necessary for survival in the global marketplace. With innovation, a company may be able to increase their business by 1000%. With optimization perhaps only 10%. Most operational businesses are not structured for innovation.

Corporations need startups for innovation. Many markets and systems have become complex.

You've gotta start with the customer experience and work backwards to the technology."

Steve Jobs

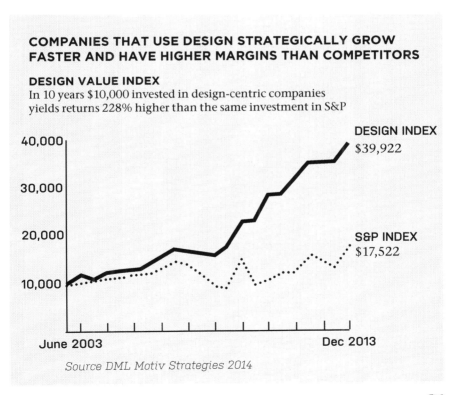

COMPANIES THAT USE DESIGN STRATEGICALLY GROW FASTER AND HAVE HIGHER MARGINS THAN COMPETITORS

DESIGN VALUE INDEX
In 10 years $10,000 invested in design-centric companies yields returns 228% higher than the same investment in S&P

DESIGN INDEX
$39,922

S&P INDEX
$17,522

June 2003   Dec 2013

Source DML Motiv Strategies 2014

DESIGN THINKING

1. Helps you understand what is important to customers and your business.
2. Helps you make good decisions.
3. Tells you which problems you need to solve.
4. Helps differentiate you in a competitive market.
5. Gains new customers
6. Retains customers
7. Allows you to charge more
8. Lower costs
9. Less wasted effort building things no one needs.

Source: Adapted from Phil Barrett Associate director, Deloitte Digital

THE CURRENT STATE OF DESIGN THINKING PRACTICE IN ORGANIZATIONS

In 2015 Hasso-Plattner-Institut Für Softwaresystemtechnik An Der Universität Potsdam in Germany undertook the first large scale study of companies using design thinking This study provided the first clear evidence that design thinking is a strategy that can provide measurable and substantial support for innovation in organizations.

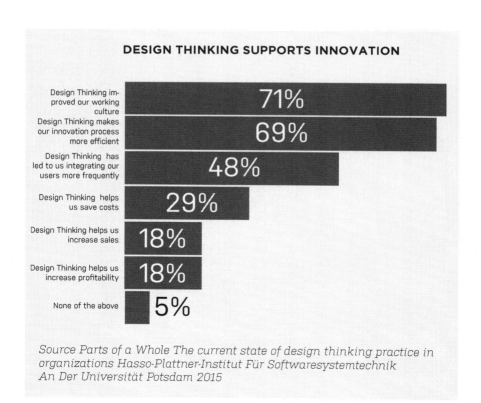

DESIGN THINKING SUPPORTS INNOVATION

Design Thinking improved our working culture — 71%
Design Thinking makes our innovation process more efficient — 69%
Design Thinking has led to us integrating our users more frequently — 48%
Design Thinking helps us save costs — 29%
Design Thinking helps us increase sales — 18%
Design Thinking helps us increase profitability — 18%
None of the above — 5%

Source Parts of a Whole The current state of design thinking practice in organizations Hasso-Plattner-Institut Für Softwaresystemtechnik An Der Universität Potsdam 2015

WHAT SKILLS WILL CHILDREN NEED TO DRIVE INNOVATION?

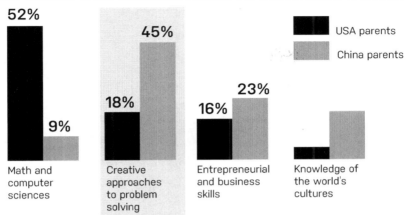

Source: Newsweek Intel global Innovation Survey

AGILE AND DESIGN THINKING

Agile software development has many points of overlap with design thinking. It seems likely that agile approaches were part of the inspiration for design thinking at IDEO.and Stanford coming through those organizations strong connections to software engineering. I cover here some basic information about agile for your information and possible cross fertilization at your organization with design thinking methods and approaches.

WHAT IS AGILE?

Agile software development is based on an incremental, iterative approach. Instead of in-depth planning at the beginning of the project, Agile methodologies are open to changing requirements over time and encourages constant feedback from the end users. Cross-functional teams work on iterations of a product over a period of time, and this work is organized into a backlog that is prioritized based on business or customer value. The goal of each iteration is to produce a working product.

LEAN VS AGILE

Lean development focuses on eliminating and reducing waste (activities that don't add any value). Lean development takes the principles from Lean manufacturing and applies them to software development. These principles are very similar to Agile, however Lean takes it one step further. In the development phase, you select, plan, develop, test, and deploy only one feature before you repeat the process for the next feature.

In Agile methodologies, leadership encourages teamwork, accountability, and face-to-face communication. Business stakeholders and developers must work together to align the product with customer needs and company goals.

Agile refers to any process that aligns with the concepts of the Agile manifesto.

THE AGILE MANIFESTO

In February 2001, 17 software developers met in Utah to discuss design development methods. They published the Manifesto for Agile Software Development, which covered how they found "better ways of developing software by doing it and helping others do it" The Agile Manifesto lists 12 principles. These are the principles:

1. "Our highest priority is to satisfy the customer through early and continuous delivery of valuable software.
2. Welcome changing requirements, even late in development. Agile processes harness change for the customer's competitive advantage.
3. Deliver working software frequently, from a couple of weeks to a couple of months, with preference to the shorter timescale.
4. Business people and developers must work together daily throughout the project.
5. Build projects around motivated individuals. Give them the environment and support they need, and trust them to get the job done.
6. The most efficient and effective method of conveying information to and within a development team is face-to-face conversation.
7. Working software is the primary measure of progress.
8. Agile processes promote sustainable development. The sponsors, developers, and users should be able to maintain a constant pace indefinitely.
9. Continuous attention to technical excellence and good design enhances agility.
10. Simplicity -- the art of maximizing the amount of work not done -- is essential.
11. The best architectures, requirements, and designs emerge from self-organizing teams.
12. At regular intervals, the team reflects on how to become more effective, then tunes and adjusts its behavior accordingly."

ADVANTAGES OF AGILE

Agile focuses on flexibility, continuous improvement, and speed. Here are some of the top advantages of Agile:

1. Change is embraced.
2. End-goal can be unknown.

3. Faster, high-quality delivery: iterations.
4. Strong team interaction.
5. Customers are heard.
6. Continuous improvement.

DISADVANTAGES OF AGILE
It can be hard to establish a solid delivery date, documentation can be neglected, or the final product can be very different than originally intended.

Here are some of the disadvantages of Agile:
1. Planning can be less concrete.
2. Team must be knowledgeable.
3. Agile is most successful when the development team is completely dedicated to the project.
4. Documentation can be neglected:
5. The initial Agile project might not have a definitive plan, so the final product can look much different than what was initially intended.

AGILE PROCESS PHASES
Phases are flexible and always evolving. Many of these phases happen in parallel.
1. Planning.
2. Requirements analysis.
3. Design.
4. Implementation.
5. Testing.
6. Deployment.

APPROACHES
There are a number approaches within the Agile movement. They could be considered flavors of agile.

Extreme Programming
Also known as XP, Extreme Programming is a type of software development intended to improve quality and responsiveness to evolving customer requirements.

Feature-driven development
There are five basic activities in FDD: develop overall model, build feature list, plan by feature, design by feature, and build by feature.

Adaptive system development
Adaptive system development represents the idea that projects should always be in a state of continuous adaptation. ASD has a cycle of three repeating series: speculate, collaborate, and learn.

Dynamic Systems Development
1. The eight principles are:
2. Focus on the business need, deliver on time,
3. Collaborate,
4. Never compromise quality, build incrementally from firm foundations,
5. Develop iteratively.
6. Demonstrate control.
7. Communicate continuously and clearly.

Lean Software Development
Lean Software Development takes Lean manufacturing and Lean IT principles and applies them

to software development. Seven principles.
1. Eliminate waste.
2. Amplify learning.
3. Decide as late as possible.
4. Deliver as fast as possible. Empower the team.
5. Build integrity in.
6. See the whole.

Kanban
Kanban, is a visual framework to implement Agile. It was developed in Japan.
Its principles include:
1. Small, continuous changes to your current system.
2. Visualize the work flow.
3. Limit work in progress. Manage the flow.
4. Make policies explicit.
5. Continuously improve.

Crystal Clear:
Crystal Clear is part of the Crystal family of methodologies. It can be used with teams of 6 to 8 developers and it focuses on the people, not processes or artifacts.

Crystal Clear requires the following:
1. Frequent delivery of usable code to users,
2. Reflective improvement.
3. Osmotic communication preferably by being co-located.

Scrum
Scrum is one of the most popular approaches of agile. It is an iterative software model that follows a set of set roles,

responsibilities, and meetings.

Sprints, lasting one to two weeks, allow the team to deliver software on a regular basis.

Source: Adapted from https://www. smartsheet.com/agile-vs-scrum-vs-waterfall-vs-kanban

"

Agile practices focus on giving teams and individuals ownership of their work and accountability to the team"

"Agile is about doing as opposed to being paralyzed by over-planning; in agile you get the minimal necessary requirements and start working."

"As agile organizations, teams and team members, we must constantly question what could be better in order to continually improve."

"Agile is all about adapting to change; it was built on the foundational principle that business drivers will change and the development teams must be ready to adapt."

https://blog.versionone.com

SOME DISRUPTIVE "WICKED PROBLEMS" REQUIRING NEW DESIGN SKILLS

1. Being human in a digital world.
2. Entrepreneurship.
3. Focus on regional/ local characteristics
4. Growth of Asian markets
5. Information society
6. Internet of things. Connected devices.
7. Less predictable world.
8. Looking at the creative community holistically to tackle larger societal issues.
9. Massive data sets.
10. Move from transaction to experience society.
11. Multidisciplinary collaboration
12. Outsourcing.
13. Storytelling.
14. Tiny moments of value rather than big wow delight.
15. Urgency for innovation
16. Wearables.
17. a never- ending cycle of decisions and choices.
18. Design automation.
19. Service design in the public sector.
20. Data + Design
21. Brands will become less branded.
22. Design as a discipline becomes more accepted in the business world. Elevation of design.
23. Design Research is expanding to use intelligent tools such as machine learning.
24. The death of short-termism.
25. T-shape designers. Designers are specialist in one area, while generalists in related fields.
26. Design metrics.
27. The war for talent. Growing challenges in talent recruitment.
28. Digital experiences have democratized luxury and elevated our standard of living.
29. Digital trust.
30. Continuing education. Education doesn't happen in college only, people get trained all their life.
31. Networking. "Everything is networked now," says Pinterest co-founder Evan Sharp, whom I interviewed for my project on designer founders. "All of culture, all of communications, it all is going through networks."
32. Artificial intelligence.
33. Machine learning.
34. Fortune 500 Design firm acquisitions.
35. Digital design.
36. Advertising and marketing budgets will be diverted to design.
37. Wisdom of crowds. Many individuals provide content and make decisions rather than a few experts.
38. Mobile technology becomes an integrated part of communication.
39. Health monitoring. Consumers are now routinely using wearable health monitoring devices.
40. Telework. More employees enjoy flexibility in working

hours and locations.
41. Design focus moves from styling to human centered design.
42. Neuroscience and Design Research. Now when we test prototypes, we can measure behavior, cognition, emotional reactions, physiological markers, and brain activity.
43. Transit culture. People ive and work in many cultures.
44. Social networking. People share interests and activities in on-line communities.
45. Personalization of content, products and services.
46. Digital trust. The robustness, clarity and visibility of organizations trustworthiness and security will become a primary part of the customer proposition and a constant draw on organizations resources.
47. Digital security.
48. Luxury
49. Service Economy. Service industry now employ 90% of Americans.
50. Smaller organizations. Small organizations and startups have the opportunity to enter the market and compete with large organizations.
51. Wellbeing.
52. Strategic contribution of Design is expected.
53. Brands That Focus on Customer Experience.
54. Active Listening.
55. App integration.
56. Micro co-creation
57. Growth of user experience design.
58. User generated content & open sharing. User generated content & open sharing People provide information and share their information on-line.
59. Virtual reality.
60. Privacy by design

❝

Design today is no longer about designing objects, visuals or spaces; it is about designing systems, strategies and experiences."

Gjoko Muratovski
Professor in design and innovation. Tongji University, Shanghai

❝

We need to invent a new and radical form of collaboration that blurs the boundaries between creators and consumers. It's not about "us versus them"or even"us on behalf of them."For the design thinker,it has to be "us with them."

Tim Brown IDEO

NETWORKS MAY DISRUPT AND TRANSFORM DESIGN AND DESIGN EDUCATION THIS CENTURY

MANUFACTURING AGE TO 1960

1. Inspiration comes through famous designers and magazines
2. Limited ability to address complex problems.
3. Limited ability to design intangible experiences.
4. Limited ability to consider non-visual senses and experiences. Smell, touch, sound,
5. Advertising and marketing creates design based on brand promise.
6. Expectations of the design industry's social responsibility low

SERVICE EXPERIENCE AGE +1965

1. Cross disciplinary teams
2. Increasing complexity of design
3. Inspiration comes through research
4. Dematerialization
5. Blurring of boundaries of traditional design disciplines.
6. Designing systems of products experiences and services.
7. Difficult challenges businesses face in this new, and complex environment.

NETWORKED AGE +2010

How value is generated. Maker movement

1. Decreasing value of brand due to customization and iminishing power of marketing and advertising.
2. Budgets move from maketing to design.
3. Changing relationship of designers to users as users create content.
4. Internet of things
5. Social networks
6. Crowd funding
7. Inspiration comes through custome value networks
8. Trend to hybrid design design skills.

"

Everything is now subject to innovation, not just physical objects, but also political systems, economic policy, ways in which medical research is conducted, and even complete "user experiences."

Laura Weiss, IDEO

ECONOMIC EVOLUTION

SOCIETY	PREINDUSTRIAL ECONOMY	INDUSTRIAL ECONOMY	POST-INDUSTRIAL ECONOMY
Game	Against Nature	Against fabricated nature	Among Persons
Time-line	To 1850	1850 to 1950	from 1950
Use of Human Labor	Raw Muscle Power	Machine tending	Artistic, Creative, Intellectual
Unit of Social Life	Extended Household	Individual	Community
Standard of Living Measure	Subsistence	Quantity of Goods	Quality of life in terms of health, education, recreation
Structure	Routine, Traditional, Authoritative	Bureaucratic, Hierarchical	Interdependent, Global
Technology	Simple hand tools	Machines	Information
View	Local	Local	Global
Quest	Surviving	Modernizing	
Effect		Productivity & family life	
Skills		Specialization	
Approach		Follow cultural norm	
Focus		Product function	
Qualities		Products	
Value		Commodities	

DESIGN THINKING IS A BETTER APPROACH WHEN DESIGNING IN POST-INDUSTRIAL ECONOMIES

SOCIETY	SERVICE ECONOMY	EXPERIENCE ECONOMY	NETWORKED ECONOMY
Game	Against Nature	Against fabricated nature	Among Persons
Activity	To 1950	From 1980	From 2010
Use of Human Labor	Service production & delivery	Machine tending	Artistic, Creative, Intellectual
Unit of Social Life	Network	Individual	Individual
Standard of Living Measure	Service experience	Quality of the experience	Quality of life in terms of health, education, recreation
Structure	Routine, Traditional, Authoritative		
Technology	Simple hand tools		
View	Global	Contextual	Systematic
Quest	Brand identity	Lifestyle Identity	Individual empowerment
Effect		Productivity & family life	
Skills		Eperiment	Creativity
Approach		Follow cultural norm	Persue Aspirations
Focus	Service Experience	Brand Experience	Enabling creativity
Qualities	Prodcut service mix	Prodcut service mix	Value networks
Value	Service experience	Targeted experiences	Enable self development

This framework was first proposed by Brand & Rocchi (2011)

HYBRID DESIGN SKILLS

These are the new skills being adopted by designers working across traditional boundaries of design disciplines.

SKILLS FOR 21ST CENTURY COMPETITIVENESS

1. Global awareness
2. Critical thinking
3. Adaptability
4. Collaboration
5. Media fluency
6. Innovation
7. Synthesis
8. Effective speaking
9. Problem solving
10. Information literacy
11. Creativity
12. Analytical skills
13. Entrepreneurship
14. Curiosity
15. Effective writing

Identified by numerous international governmental and industry studies

DESIGN THINKING MINDSETS

1. Show don't tell
2. Be experiential visual and a story gatherer and teller
3. Focus on human values
4. Empathize with your end user
5. Craft clarity
6. Define the problem
7. Embrace experimentation
8. Iterative low fidelity prototyping
9. not continued discussions
10. Be mindful of the process
11. Bias towards action
12. Radical collaboration
13. Diversity rules

EXPERIENCE DESIGN CORE SKILLS

1. Research techniques.
2. Brainstorming. Concept elicitation, managing participatory design.
3. Ethnography and discovery. Contextual inquiry, user interviews, user goals, motivations, and work patterns.
4. User modeling. Persona and scenario creation. Methods for representation of archetypal and target user needs.
5. Domain modeling. Task analysis, work-flow diagrams, card sorts. Stakeholder interviews.
6. Role-playing.
7. Product design. Product-level interaction principles and concepts.
8. Interaction design.
9. Interface design component-level interaction principles and concepts.
10. Information architecture.
11. Studio critiques.
12. Usability testing.
13. Directional testing.
14. Data analysis.
15. Prototyping. High fidelity, medium and low fidelity representations of solutions
16. Storyboarding.
17. Context scenarios, use cases, storytelling and other narrative ways of defining

solutions.

18. Competitive analysis. Stakeholder interviews.

BUSINESS UX SKILLS

1. Project management.
2. Time management. Managing concurrent projects, meeting deadlines, managing content and managing resources.
3. Stakeholder or client management.
4. Basic business writing— letters, email messages, meeting notes, and summaries.
5. Communications skills
6. Rhetoric and persuasive writing.
7. Expository writing and composition.
8. Technical writing.
9. Public speaking and presenting.
10. Visual communication.
11. Interpersonal skills.
12. Mediation and facilitation.
13. Active listening.
14. Team-building.
15. Collaboration.
16. Managing resources.
17. Meeting deadlines.
18. Facilitating and moderation of groups
19. Creative briefs.
20. Usability skills.
21. Knowledge of usability. testing principles and methods.
22. Knowledge of principles of cognitive psychology.

MEDIA UX SKILLS

1. Managing color palettes.
2. Graphic user interface
3. Page layout and composition
4. Animation.
5. Sound design.
6. Prototyping.
7. Knowledge of file formats and trade offs.

TECHNICAL UX SKILLS

1. Understanding of basic computer programming principles, tools, and technologies.
2. Gui development principles, tools, and technologies.
3. Database principles, tools, and technologies.
4. Understanding of software and hardware development processes—specification, coding, and testing.
5. Knowledge of existing and new technologies and constraints.
6. Knowledge of mechanical engineering and manufacturing—for hardware devices.

TOOLS UX SKILLS

1. Powerpoint or keynote.
2. Adobe creative suite.

PERSONAL ATTRIBUTES

1. Empathy.
2. Passion.
3. Humor.
4. Skepticism.
5. Abductive thinking.
6. Analytical thinking.
7. Ability to synthesize.

Adapted from sources including: "The Skills of UX Professionals" By Robert Reimann

THE GROWTH OF SERVICES

WHAT

A.G.B. Fisher proposed a model for economies of primary, secondary, and tertiary industries. Primary production was defined as agriculture, fishing, forestry, hunting, and mining. He concluded that as income rises demand shifts from the primary to secondary and then to tertiary sectors. Sociologist Daniel Bell proposed a model in three general stages. Preindustrial, industrial and post-industrial societies.

PREINDUSTRIAL SOCIETY

The principal activities are agriculture, fishing, forestry, and mining. Technology is simple, and productivity is low. People depend on their own bodies to get things done. Success depends on nature, the climate and on soil quality. The social unit is the family and extended household. People seek only enough to feed themselves. A large number of people are employed in household services.

Before 1900 in the US.

1. More than 80% workforce in Agriculture sector
2. Service occupations mostly were domestic servants and sailors
3. Family relationships and tradition important.
4. Education and innovation are not important
5. Quality of life dependent on nature

INDUSTRIAL SOCIETY

The dominant activities are associated with the production of goods. Economic and social life has become mechanized and more efficient. Productivity is improved. Focus on optimization. Division of labor is further extended. Technological advancements support constant improvement of machines. The workplace is where men, women, materials, and machines are organized for efficient production and distribution of goods. The unit of social life is the individual in a free market society. Quantity of goods possessed by an individual is an indicator of his standard of living

1900 TO 1950

1. Important activity goods production.
2. Quality of life measured by goods.

3. Focus on maximizing the productivity of labor and machines.
4. Extreme division of labor
5. Dehumanizing jobs.
6. "Manual workers" outnumber "white collar workers."

POSTINDUSTRIAL SOCIETY

Activities focused on service production, information and knowledge. Networks of people. The central character of economic life is the professional. Higher education a prerequisite to entry into postindustrial society. The quantity and quality of services such as health, education, and recreation that an individual can afford are indicators of standard of living. The inadequacy of the market mechanism in meeting service demands leads to the growth of government.

Expansion of services such as transportation and public utilities is needed for the development of industry and distribution of goods. Expansion of wholesale and retail services, as well as services such as finance, real estate, and insurance. The percentage of money devoted to food declines. Increments in income are first spent for durable consumer goods, such as housing, automobiles, and appliances. Further increases in income are devoted to services such as education, healthcare, vacations, travel, restaurants, entertainment, and sports.

AFTER 1950

1. Service producing industries increased from 50% to 80% of GDP in US.
2. Health, education, & recreation measures of quality of life.
3. Service experiences dominate economic value.
4. Workers value based on judgment, creativity & theoretical reasoning
5. Increase in efficiency of agriculture and manufacturing releases labor to services.
6. Workers move from rural locations to cities.
7. A decrease in investment as a percentage of gross domestic product in high-income industrialized countries.
8. A rise in per capita income.
9. Deregulation.
10. Demographic shifts.
11. An increase in international trade.
12. Symbiotic growth of services with manufacturing.
13. Advances in information and telecommunication technologies.
14. People pursue more sophisticated needs (Maslow "hierarchy of needs)

Source: Adapted from: Service Management: An Integrated Approach to Supply Chain Management and Operations Cengiz Haksever and Barry Render 2013

THE EVOLVING FOCUS OF DESIGN PRACTICE

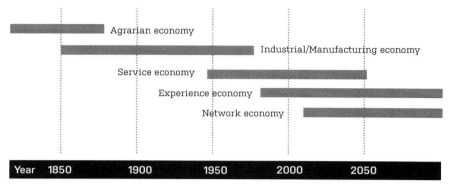

Adapted from a framework proposed by Brand and Rocchi 2011 in a Philips Design
document entitled "Rethinking Value in a Changing Landscape".

BELLS STAGES OF ECONOMIC DEVELOPMENT

SOCIETY	PRE-INDUSTRIAL	INDUSTRIAL	POST-INDUSTRIAL
Game	Against Nature	Against fabricated nature	Among Persons
Predominant Activity	Agriculture, Mining	Goods, Production	Services
Use of Human Labor	Raw Muscle Power	Machine tending	Artistic, Creative, Intellectual
Unit of Social Life	Extended Household	Individual	Community
Standard of Living Measure	Subsistence	Quantity of Goods	Quality of life in terms of health, education, recreation
Structure	Routine, Traditional, Authoritative	Bureaucratic, Hierarchical	Interdependent, Global
Technology	Simple hand tools	Machines	Information

Framework was first proposed by sociologist Daniel Bell

SERVITIZATION

WHAT

Servitization is a shift from selling product to selling product service systems.

The growth of Design Thinking is closely linked to the growing economic importance of service industry. Design Thinking with its emphasis on team collaboration and user experience is the best approach for designing services and product service systems

A study of 50,000 servitized and non-servitized French firms between 1997 and 2007 concluded that servitized firms are more profitable, employ more workers and have higher total sales than non-servitized firms. "Firms that start selling services increase their profitability by 3.7% to 5.3%, increase their numbers of employees by 30%, and boost their sales of good by 3.6% on average."

Source: Matthieu Crozet & Emmanuel Milet The effect of servitization on manufacturing firm performance 2015 Universite de Geneve

TYPES OF PRODUCT SERVICE SYSTEMS

1. Product Oriented: This is a where the consumer has a tangible product, and services, such as maintenance contracts, are provided.
2. Use Oriented: This is where the service provider owns the product, and sells services, such as sharing, pooling, and leasing.
3. Result Oriented: This is a where products are replaced by services, such as, for example, voice-mail.
4. Solution oriented: For example, selling a promised level of heat transfer instead of radiators.
5. Effect oriented: For example, selling a promised temperature level instead of selling radiators
6. Demand-fulfillment oriented: For example, selling a promised level of thermal comfort for building occupants instead of radiators."

WHY SERVITIZE?

1. Manufacturing firms in developed economies cannot compete on cost.
2. Technology is allowing the development of new services.
3. Competitive opportunities.
4. Installed base. For ever new car there are 13 existing. 4

chairs for every person in the world. 15 aircraft for each new aircraft.
5. Services have a large potential for growing profits. Grows revenue streams Additional revenue from existing customers.
6. On average manufacturers report a growth in services revenue of 5 to 10% per year. *Source Aston Centre For Servitization Research.*
7. Better cash flow.
8. Environmental benefits. De-materialization and investment in cleaner technologies.
9. Selling a Solution, in Addition to a Product:
10. Greater Financial Stability:
11. Stronger Customer Retention Rate:
12. Industrial Internet of Things growing in Importance.

STRATEGIC RATIONAL
1. Lock in customers.
2. Lock out competitors.
3. Increase differentiation.
4. Customers want services.

Source: Professor Andy Neely University of Cambridge

CHALLENGES FOR SERVITIZATION
Challenges include:
1. Leadership support
2. investments to develop and implement services and solutions.
3. Mind-set and capabilities of the organisation to selling and delivering services and solutions
4. Defining and creating a clear strategy.
5. Creating organizational infrastructure.
6. Develop capabilities for designing and delivering services.
7. Creating an organizational culture with the values supporting service design and delivery, including customer orientation, flexibility and innovation.
8. Coordinate and align the development of new products. integrated with new services
9. Involve customers in the process.
10. Create the necessary flexibility and adaptability to enable customization.
11. Formulate attractive value propositions through better understanding of customer needs.
12. Ensure that the quality of service provision lives up to customer expectations.
13. Develop trustful relationships to support the investment in customer specific competencies.
14. Manage the geographical and cultural distances in a globally distributed network of service partners.
15. Lock out competitors.
16. Increase differentiation
17. Customers want services.

Source: Driving Competitiveness Through Servitization A Guide For Practitioners Avlonitis, Frandsen, Hsuan & Karlsson

IMPLEMENTING SERVITIZATION FROM GOODS-CENTERED TO CUSTOMER-CENTERED SOLUTIONS

	Manufacturing Solution	Service Customer-centered Solution
Underlying Business logic	Products	Solutions
Customization	Standard product	Customizable
Integration	Low	High
Scope	Narrow	Wide
Delivery process	Transactional	Relationship
Outcome	Functioning product	Value for customers
Design driven	From manufacturer forward	From customer backward
Physicality	Tangible	Intangible
Output	Goods	An experience
Production	Produced	Co-produced
Consumption	Transferred and used	Consumed as produced
Dimensions	Length breadth height	Experience and time

Source: adapted from Filippo Visintin Aalto University 2012

INDUSTRY % SHARE OF TOTAL EMPLOYMENT

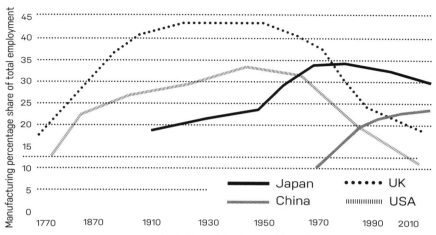

Adapted from "China's Future in the Knowledge Economy" by Peter Sheehan
ANote: scale condensed before 1900

DISTRIBUTION OF US LABOR FORCE
1840 TO 2010 % OF TOTAL WORKFORCE

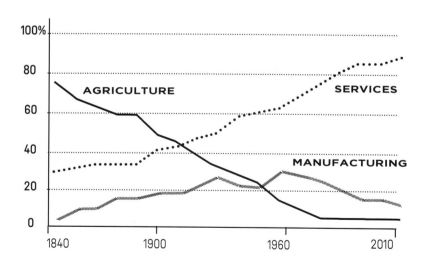

LARGEST US PRIVATE EMPLOYERS

1960

GOODS PRODUCING

GM
Ford
General Electric
US Steel
Esso
Bethlehem Steel
ITT
Westinghouse
General Dynamics
Chrysler
Sperry Rand
International Harvester

SERVICE PROVIDING

Bell System
Sears Roebuck
AP

2010

GOODS PRODUCING

HP
PepsiCo
General Electric

SERVICE PROVIDING

Walmart
Kelly Services
IBM
UPS
McDonald's Corp
Yum
Target
Kroger
Home Depot
Sears
Bank Of America
CVS Pharmacy

Source: New York Times

CHINA SERVICE INDUSTRY GROWTH

SERVICES NOW ACCOUNT FOR A HIGHER PERCENTAGE OF GDP THAN MANUFACTURING

In the first 11 months of 2015, China registered 3.9 million new companies, up 19 percent, with more than four-fifths in services, according to the State Administration for Industry and Commerce.

China's service sector now employs more than 300 million people, the largest share of the country's 775 million workers. The fastest growth has been in low-end jobs in retail, restaurants, hotels, and real estate. Over the last five years, education and government jobs, most of which are filled by college graduates, have fallen from a little less than half of total service employment to a third or so. Finance's share has also fallen, says Albert Park, professor of economics at Hong Kong University of Science and Technology. "The higher-skilled sectors—telecoms, information technology, computers, finance, and business services—are still not a large share of the total service industry," he says. "And while some are growing, they aren't growing very quickly."

Source: Bloomberg

PERCENTAGE OF CHINA'S GDP FROM SERVICES

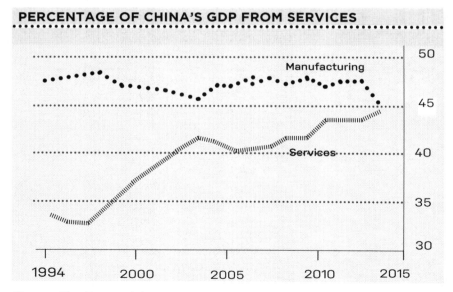

Source: The Economist

03

WHO IS USING DESIGN THINKING?

FIND LINKS TO OVER 100 DESIGN
THINKING CASE STUDIES ON OUR
WEB SITE WWW.DCC-EDU.ORG

WHO IS USING DESIGN THINKING?

FIND LINKS TO OVER 100 DESIGN THINKING CASE STUDIES ON OUR WEB SITE WWW.DCC-EDU.ORG

3M
Accenture
AdaptAir
Adobe
Ahold
AirBnB
Airbus
Amway
ANZ Bank
Anzisha (Center for Entrepreneurial Leadership at African Leadership Academy)
Arup
Australian Center for Social Innovation
Center for Entrepreneurial Leadership at African Leadership Academy
Apple
Arup
Australian Taxation Office
AutoDesk
Bank of America: Keep the Change
Bayer
Bayteq
BBVA Bancomer
Bertelsmann
BMW
Bristol Maids
Celfinet
CERN IdeaLab
Charité Berlin, BCRT/BSRT
Creuznacher
Biothinking Program
Charité: Onkolizer
Chick-fil-a
Cincinnati Children's Hospital

Medical Center
Cisco
Citrix
Clorox Company
Condair: JS Humidifiers
Creuznacher
CurioSchool
D.Light
Daimler
Datascope Analytics
Deloitte digital
Deloitte Innovation
Derdack
Design City Kolding
Deutsche Bahn
Deutsche Bank
DHL
D-Lab: Charcoal
D-Rev: ReMotions's JaipurKnee
EBS Business School
Electrolux: Design Lab
Embrace Infant Incubator
Everest
Flad Architects
Framework
Fraport
Future Balloons
FutureGov
GE
GE: GE Adventure Series
GE: Healthcare
Georgia Tech
GlaxoSmithKline
Godrej: Chotu Kool
Google: Google Ventures
GoPro
IBM
IKB

Innsbrucker Kommunal Betriebe
IKEA + IDEO
Infosys
Intuit Inc.
IPCRI (Israel Palestine Center for Research)
Janssen-Cilag
JetBlue
JLL-Jones Lang LaSalle
Juntos Finanzas
Kaiser Permanente
Kickstart
Lambeth Council
Mappy
Marriot 4 Seasons
Mattel: Platypus
Mayfieldrobotics
Mayo Clinics
Metro AG
Metropolitan Group
MeYouHealth
Microsoft
Miele
Miraclefeet Brace
Nasdaq
Naval Undersea Warfare Center (NUWC) Newport
Nestle?
New York Times
NIKE
Novabase
Onclaude
P&G
P&G früher)/ Blackberry
P&G: Consumer Products: Swiffer
Panasonic: Oxyride
PwC Australia
Pedigree Tracks
PepsiCo
Pfizer: Nicorette
Philips Electronics (PHG)
Pillpack
Ploom
PRODAP - IT Public Agency
Project Thinking

Pulse
PwC Australia
RadBoud REshape
Ravel
San Francisco's Department of Emergency Management
SAP
SAP CSR + Sankara eye care
Schröder und Partner
Sennheiser
Sense Consulting Ltd. Croatia
Shell Innovation Research
Shimano
Siemens
SMS Management and Technology
St. Joseph Health
Stanley Works: Black & Decker
Steelcase
Sternin Positive Deviance Initiative
SunCorp
Swisscom
Telekom
THALES
The Australian Center for Social Innovation
Toyota
The Good Kitchen
Three Twins Organic Ice Cream
Toyota
Unilever
University of Pittsburgh Medical Center
US - Presidential Innovation Fellows Program
VF Corporation
VisioSpring
Vlisco
VW
Whirlpool
WikiMedia
Xing
Yanmar
ZOO Hannover

SOME PUBLIC SERVICE ORGANIZATIONS USING DESIGN THINKING

Americas
  Brazil
  Brazilian Innovation Agency, www.finep.gov
  Canada
  Mars Discovery District, www.marsdd.com/
  Mexico
  Laboratorio para la Ciudad, http://labplc
  Panama
  Autoridad Nacional para la Innovación Guber (AIG), www.innovacion.gob.pa/
  USA
  Code for America, http://codeforamerica.org/
  Launch, www.launch.org/
  Public Policy Lab, http://publicpolicylab.org/

Asia-Pacific
  Australia
  Australian Government Public Sector Innovation, https://innovation.govspace.gov.au/
  DesignGov, http://design.gov.au/
  Hong Kong, China
  Efficiency Unit, www.eu.gov.hk/eindex.html
  India
  National Innovation Council, www.innovationcouncil.gov.in/
  South Korea
  Korean Institute of Design Promotion,

www.kidp.or.kr/kmain/
  Thailand
  Future Innovative Thailand Institute
  Singapore
  Human Experience Lab

Europe
  Denmark
  MindLab Denmark, www.mind-lab.dk/en
  France
  Region 27, http://la27eregion.fr/
  Finland
  Helsinki Design Lab, http://helsinkidesignlab.org/
  Sitra, www.sitra.fi/en/
  Tekes, www.tekes.fi/
  Norway
  Innovation Norway, www.innovasjonnorge.no/
  Sweden
  VINNOVA, www.vinnova.se/en/
  United Kingdom
  Design Council, www.designcouncil.org.uk/
  The Innovation Unit, www.innovationunit.org/
  Nesta, www.nesta.org.uk/
  Technology Strategy Board, www.innovateuk.org/
  PolicyLabUK
  Policy Lab, https://twitter.com
  Northern Ireland Innovation Laboratory

Source: Design Thinking for Public Service Excellence. Global Center for Public Service Excellence. Singapore.

WHERE IS THE MOST INTEREST IN DESIGN THINKING?

Top Google searches by city 2012 to 2017 on the term "design thinking" as a proportion of all searches

Google index data to 100, where 100 is the maximum search interest for the time and location selected. If you're getting an interest index of 100 in Singapore and an index of 32 in Boston, that means that the concentration of Singaporeans searching your keyword is higher than the concentration of residents of Boston searching your keyword.

Source: Google Trends
Google Trends is a public web facility of Google Inc., based on Google Search, that shows how often a particular search-term is entered relative to the total search-volume across various regions of the world, and in various languages.

1. Singapore 100
2. Cambridge 89
3. Porto Alegre 82
4. Chiyoda 72
5. Brasília 66
6. Berlin 65
7. Diadema 62
8. Gurgaon 56
9. São Paulo 51
10. Sydney 50
11. Stuttgart 48
12. San Francisco 47
13. Cope hagen 47
14. Curitiba 46
15. Rio de Janeiro 44
16. Melbourne 41
17. Lisbon 41
18. Munich 41
19. Belo Horizonte 41
20. Da'an District 38
21. Frankfurt 37
22. Bengaluru 36
23. San Jose 36
24. Toronto 35
25. Auckland 35
26. Zürich 34
27. Seoul 34
28. Medellin 34
29. Santiago 34
30. Boston 32
31. Bogotá 32
32. Hamburg 31
33. Barcelona 31
34. Monterrey 29
35. Austin 29
36. Cologne 28
37. Washington 28
38. Vancouver 26
39. Amsterdam 25
40. Minato 24
41. Shinjuku 23
42. Mumbai 23
43. Brisbane 23
44. Dublin 22
45. New York 22
46. Paris 22
47. Mexico City 22

48. Madrid 21
49. Seattle 21

**Google searches
By country 2017 on the
term "design thinking" as a
proportion of all searches**

1. Singapore 100
2. China 73
3. Peru 67
4. St. Helena 51
5. Switzerland 42
6. Germany 39
7. Australia 36
8. Denmark 36
9. New Zealand 35
10. Hong Kong 33
11. Brazil 32
12. Colombia 31
13. Netherlands 29
14. Taiwan 28
15. United Arab Emirates 28
16. Ireland 27
17. Chile 26
18. Austria 25
19. South Korea 25
20. Norway 24
21. Portugal 23
22. Guatemala 23
23. Costa Rica 23
24. Canada 21
25. Ecuador 21
26. Spain 21
27. Mexico 20
28. Finland 19
29. Malaysia 19
30. France 18
31. South Africa 16
32. United Sates 16
33. Uruguay 15
34. India 15
35. Philippines 14
36. Japan 13
37. Kenya 13

38. Sweden 13
39. Poland 11
40. Belgium 11
41. Argentina 10
42. Croatia 10
43. United Kingdom 10
44. Thailand 9
45. Czechia 8
46. Israel 8
47. Romania 7
48. Italy 7
49. Hungary 6
50. Morocco 6
51. Nigeria 6
52. Pakistan 6
53. Saudi Arabia 5
54. Ukraine 5
55. Greece 5

*Until Design Thinking
came to the Mayo
Clinic we were better
at poking holes in new
concepts than filling
them."*

Alan Duncan
Mayo Clinic

IBM
DESIGN THINKING CASE STUDIES
FIND LINKS TO OVER 100 DESIGN THINKING CASE STUDIES ON OUR WEB SITE WWW.DCC-EDU.ORG

THE COMPANY
International Business Machines Corporation is an American multinational technology company located in Armonk, New York, United States, with operations in over 170 countries.

IBM manufactures and markets computers hardware, and software, and offers hosting and consulting services in areas ranging from mainframe computers to nanotechnology. IBM is also a major research organization, holding the record for most patents generated by a business (as of 2017) for 24 consecutive years. Inventions by IBM include the automated teller machine (ATM), the PC, the floppy disk, the hard disk drive, the magnetic stripe card, the relational database, the SQL programming language, the UPC barcode, and dynamic random-access memory (DRAM).

IBM has continually shifted its business mix by commoditizing markets focusing on higher-value, more profitable markets.

IBM is one of the world's largest employers, with (2016) nearly 380,000 employees. IBM employees have been awarded five Nobel Prizes, six Turing Awards, ten National Medals of Technology and five National Medals of Science.

Source:Wikipedia

The design program allows the $143 billion company to be more strategic and shift away from the engineering-driven "features-first" ethos towards a more "user first" mentality. Design, Gilbert explains, has become a kind of overlay to IBM's business and engineering practices. "If you don't have all three [departments] you won't have a good outcome reliably, at least not at scale."

WHO ARE IBM'S CLIENTS?
Corporate clients that have been revealed publicly by IBM include:
- Oracle
- Microsoft
- Jet Blue Airways
- Dell
- HP
- Kenexa
- Intel
- Amazon
- Cisco
- SAP
- Google

"

At IBM, we think the systems of the world should work in service of people. At the heart of our human-centered mission is IBM Design Thinking: a framework to solve our users' problems at the speed and scale of the modern digital enterprise."

HOW

In 2012, IBM, the 105-year old information technology company, set out a bold vision: To flood its ranks with hundreds of designers and train its entire workforce—some 377,000 employees worldwide—to think, work, feel like designers. Like it did 60 years ago, IBM is looking to bolster its bottom line through a design-minded culture, but this time at a more ambitious scale involving the entire company. IBM has been working to reinvent itself as a design-led business. In 2012, the computing behemoth employed just one designer for every 80 coders. Today, that ratio stands at 1:20. By the end of 2016, the company hopes to narrow it to 1:15. All-told, the company is investing more than $100-million in an effort to become a design-centered corporation.

"

IBM Studios is a global network of studios where business outcomes are achieved using design and IBM Design Thinking

Spontaneous meetings anywhere and everywhere. Workspaces that move and shift as teams need them to. Comfy couches for quiet concentration. And thousands of linear feet of white boards. In spaces built for co-creation, our designers learn, practice and teach new ways of thinking about user-centered design."

The goal is to have design thinking infuse every aspect of how IBM does business.

Asked what she tells large shareholders, Rometty replied:

"

The key message" is that IBM is the only technology company that is more than a century old because it has reinvented itself repeatedly in the past, and it is doing so again today."

Ms. Rometty
IBM

Source New York times November 14 2015

Design Thinking is now in wide use at IBM.

- 70+ software projects
- 68+ project teams have participated in Designcamp
- 500 leaders have participated in two leadership summits in

2014.

IBM DESIGN EDUCATION
Designcamps
IBM Design created and deliver what they call Designcamps to educate and activate teams by teaching them how to deliver great experiences together.

IBM has, at this point, held over 100 Designcamps for product teams, product managers, IBM executives, new-hires, and more. IBM's development model focuses on three shared values:
1. Market outcomes for users
2. Continuous learning
3. Radical collaboration

Source Todd Wilkens 2015

Designcamp for Product Teams
- 1–2 times per month
- 4–6 teams, 40–50 attendees

Designcamp for Product Managers
- 1–2 times per month
- 60–80 attendees

Designcamp for Executives
- Once per month
- 20–30 attendees

Designcamp for New Hires
- 3 months
- Summer: 60–80 designers
- Winter: 30–40 designers

Source: IBM Design Thinking Field Guide http://www.ibm.biz/fieldguide-public

More than 10,000 employees

have gone through the IBM Bootcamp where they learn about the loop and other tenets of IBM's design thinking framework. The company has developed more than 100 products using design thinking including Bluemix, its cloud platform for developing apps.

THE PRINCIPLES
1. Focus on user outcomes:
2. Diverse empowered teams:
3. Restless reinvention

THE IBM DESIGN THINKING PROCESS
The loop
The loop represents the entire product-creation process, beginning with user-centered research all the way through prototyping

The plan is to completely overhaul IBM's corporate ethos. For years, he says, "our teams had a very engineering-centric culture." But in 2012, everything changed. "We wanted to shift that culture towards a focus on users' outcomes."

Charlie Hill, chief technology officer of IBM Design

PROCESS STAGES
Observe
Immerse yourself in the real world to get to know your users, uncover needs, learn the landscape, and test ideas.

Reflect

Come together and form a point of view to find common ground, align the team, uncover insights, and plan ahead.

Make

Give concrete form to abstract ideas to explore possibilities, communicate ideas, prototype concepts, and drive real outcomes.

TEAM RATIOS

- 1:8 Managers to Engineers
- 1:8 Designers to Engineers
- 1:1 Designers to Managers

SOME IBM DESIGN THINKING TERMS

Backlog

A document used to align the team on the user stories to deliver, their priority, and their status.

Client Playbacks

A series of ad hoc Playbacks delivered to clients under NDA that demonstrate the market drivers and user experience of the offering in development.

Playback 0

A milestone Playback at which the team commits to delivering a particular user experience and begins refining and delivering the design in parallel.

Delivery Playbacks 1-N

A series of milestone Playbacks at which the team demonstrates end-to-end scenarios it is delivering using live code and/or high-fidelity mockups.

Design Thinking

A process for envisioning the user experience that involves diverging and converging on solutions.

Epic

A codable grouping of user stories that spans scenarios so user stories do not repeat across epics. For example, "As a user, I want to manage my email."

Persona

A user archetype based on role and other characteristics that influence how a user interacts with the offering. Housed within the Release Blueprint Application and linked to from the Release Blueprint.

Playback

A demo of the user experience of the offering in development, used to collect feedback from and align the team, stakeholders, and go-to-market

Hill

A business goal for your release, framed around user experience. A project usually has three Hills and a technical foundation.

Hills Playback
 A milestone Playback at which the team commits to the outcomes, or Hills, it wants to achieve in the project and begins envisioning the user experience.

Project
 A set of team activity scoped by a Release Blueprint and a set of Hills. A project might have one or more releases of code.

Release Blueprint
 A wiki documenting a project's progress from Hills to user stories. It also contains strategic thinking behind the Hills and links to personas and design documents.

Scenario
 A single workflow through an experience, decomposable into steps. Each step should translate to a codable user story.

Sponsor Users
 Users engaged throughout the project to represent target personas for a project. Sponsor Users are often expected to lead Playbacks. We recommend having at least one Sponsor User per Hill.

Anatomy of a Sponsor User
1. Are they representative of your target user?
2. Are they personally invested in the outcome?
3. Are they available to collaborate?

UI Spec
 A design document that communicates user interface requirements. Housed within the Release Blueprint Application and linked to from the Release Blueprint.

User Story
 A codeable requirement expressed in terms of user experience. For example, "As a user, I want to search for my customers by their first and last names.

TOOLS
1.   Hopes and fears
2.   Stakeholder maps
3.   Empathy maps
4.   Scenario maps
5.   Big Idea vignettes
6.   Prioritization grid
7.   Needs statements
8.   Storyboarding
9.   Assumptions and questions
10. Feedback grid
11. Experience-based road-map

IBM DESIGN THINKING PROJECT

In a recent project, an airline approached IBM to improve its kiosks to speed up passenger gate check-ins.

While the engineers started by improving the kiosk's software, designers went straight to gate agents to ask why the check-in kiosks weren't used more effectively.

Designers found out that female gate agents struggled to keep kiosks charged because their constricting uniforms prevented them from reaching electrical plugs behind the machines. By finding the root of the problem, IBM delivered a mobile app that significantly eased the boarding process and reduced airline costs. Constricting uniforms prevented them from reaching electrical plugs behind the machines. By finding the root of the problem, IBM delivered a mobile application that significantly eased the boarding process and reduced airline costs.

Some IBM engineering and business teams are startled to encounter designers who speak in terms of sociological data rather than pretty prototypes. "Design used to be form and color, but understanding a user ... in that sense it could appear to be threatening," he says. "It's hard and messy, but you get much richer outcomes."

"The design researcher has been the most disruptive of the all design disciplines we've brought in—and by far the most transformative."

"IBM is intentionally filling two-thirds of its design ranks with new graduates. Gilbert says this strategy helps invigorate established processes. "We're building this [design] program for the long term and we wanted people with very fresh perspectives on the world, on the profession, on what a design culture should be."

Phil Gilbert, General Manager Of Design for IBM software

Source: Quartz "IBM is gearing up to become the world's largest and most sophisticated design company" Anne Quito. September 11, 2016

INFOSYS LTD.
DESIGN THINKING CASE STUDIES
FIND LINKS TO OVER 100 DESIGN THINKING CASE STUDIES
ON OUR WEB SITE WWW.DCC-EDU.ORG

THE COMPANY
Founded:
July 7, 1981, Pune, India
CEO:
UB Pravin Rao (Aug 2017–)
Revenue:
10.21 billion USD (2017)
Number of employees:
200,364 (March 2017)
Founders:
Nandan Nilekani, N. R. Narayana Murthy,
Subsidiaries include:
Panaya, Infosys BPO, EdgeVerve, Skytree, Inc, Skava

Infosys Limited is an Indian multinational corporation that provides business consulting, information technology and outsourcing services. It has its headquarters in Bengaluru, India. Infosys is the third-largest Indian IT company. On June 30, 2017, its market capitalization was $34.33 billion. Infosys had 84 sales and marketing offices and 116 development centers across the world as at March 31, 2017, with major presence in India, United States, China, Australia, Japan, Middle East and Europe.

As the world's largest corporate university, the Infosys global education centre in the 337 acre[campus has 400 instructors and 200 classrooms, with international benchmarks at its core. Established in 2002,

it had trained around 125,000 engineering graduates by June 2015.

Infosys had a total of 200,364 employees at the end of March 2017, of which 36% were women. Its workforce consists of employees representing 129 nationalities. In 2016, 89% of its employees were based in India.

Source:Adapted from Wikipedia

CUSTOMERS
Corporate clients that have been revealed publicly by Infosys include:
- Royal Bank of Scotland
- Bank of America
- Apple
- Nike
- Cisco
Walmart
- Victoria Secret
- Kellogg Company
- Dansk Supermarket
- Clariant
- ABB
- Kodak
- J P Morgan
- Microsoft
- Telstra
- American Airlines
- Boeing
- Adidas

"

Our answer is Zero Distance: a ground-up, grassroots approach to ensure that every developer, project manager, analyst and architect is at "Zero Distance" – to the end user, to the underlying technology and therefore to the value. Whether working side by side with the customer's customer or thousands of miles away, each of us must close the psychological distance and become personally invested and empowered to find the right problems and even better solutions."

Infosys

HOW

Infosys is using Design Thinking workshops to empower and change the mindset of its employees. The firm has trained more than 135,000 employees [March 31, 2017}, including more than 500 senior executives on Design Thinking principles. The Design Thinking training has been delivered to client teams, leadership teams, employees and fresh recruits.

1. Design Thinking drives Infosys' internal culture change. With Design Thinking, the company created Zero Distance and Zero Bench, two complementary endeavors that focus on innovation in every project (Zero Distance) and engagement of every employee (Zero Bench).

2. Design Thinking has already shown significant results for Infosys' clients. Infosys offers "Do,"one of a trio of services (Aikido) that has already engaged more than 150 customers in the methodology, which helps uncover true problems and has created stronger strategic partnerships.

3. Design Thinking is key to the company's strategy. The company uses the methodology to empower its employees and engage them in higher levels of work as it begins to use greater automation.

4. Design Thinking is a CEO-led focus within the company. With its methodology, the company has reconsidered everything from its performance evaluation system to its software and services.

"

Design Thinking is a natural extension to the Infosys DNA, where we have always valued lifelong learning and delivering value to clients. This is reflected in our rapid progress along every dimension of Design Thinking maturity and is truly at the heart of everything we do. We can see this in our Zero Distance initiative, which empowers our delivery teams to drive grassroots innovation in every project. In new areas and disruptive innovation, we see the maturity of our efforts in more than 150 Design Thinking engagements with clients, helping them to find and explore the most important problems to solve as part of our design-led service offerings. And, we see it in the very fabric of our company, in our employees. Beyond the numbers trained, it is about creating a culture, a movement, to drive innovation. I am very happy to see the tremendous work and passion of our leaders, and every Infoscion, recognized in the HfS winners circle and recognized as #1 on execution.

Dr. Vishal Sikka
Chief Executive Officer and Managing Director Infosys

PEPSI

PepsiCo is the latest company to come out in support of "Design Thinking" and to make a case for investment in design. In the September 2015 issue of the Harvard Business Review, PepsiCo CEO Indra Nooyi describes using Design Thinking to "rethink the entire experience, from conception to what's on the shelf to the post-product experience." Nooyi describes that, although early days, she believes her approach has "delivered great shareholder value while strengthening the company for the long term."

"

First, I gave each of my direct reports an empty photo album and a camera. I asked them to take pictures of anything they thought represented good design. After six weeks, only a few people returned the albums. Some had their wives take pictures. Many did nothing at all. They didn't know what design was"

Indra Nooyi
PepsiCo CEO

For companies like PepsiCo, encouraging, and even mandating, a perspective that insists on customer experience and empathy can lead to richer insights, more on-point products and clearer strategies to deliver them by helping brands connect to what customers find compelling.

Source: brandchannel.com

AIRBNB

In 2009, Airbnb was close to going bust. Like so many startups, they had launched but barely anyone noticed. The company's revenue was flatlined at $200 per week. Split between three young founders living in San Francisco, this meant near indefinite losses and zero growth. One of the founders, Joe Gebbia, had given up computing to enroll in the Rhode Island School of Design. He there heard about design thinking and he thought that they had to put themselves in the shoes of their customers to find out what they needed. Visiting the homes solved what the three founders had been unable to solve in front of their computers for months. Meeting customers in the real world was the best way to deal with the problems and come up with smart solutions. They skipped codes they had learned at school for a business to work and followed the rules of design thinking: empathize, define, design, prototype and test. A little over a year later the company had a billion dollar turnover.

Having designer founders and being design-centered from day one makes you

[as an organization] pay attention to those details. A lot of Design Thinking is about being creative [but it is also] about looking at what we know and triangulating information that we have and having that inspire creativity."

AirBnB's Head of User Research (2012-2014)

All those joining the company have to make a trip the first week and document it. The idea is for them to make a number of questions, for the employees to see with their own eyes the problems that may arise, and then be creative. Airbnb has gone from making 200 euros a week to revolutionizing tourism: more than 1,500,000 ads in 192 countries and 34,000 cities with a total number of roomers in excess of 40 million in 2015.

"

There are engineers who care about their engineering problems and maybe the users are less relevant. We just don't hire these kind of engineers here. Every engineer cares about the user and has a respect for design."

Source: AirBnB a design thinking suvccess story. https://www.bbva.com/en/airbnb-design-thinking-success-story/ Accessed November

2017

ERICSSON

Ericsson apply Design Thinking process and methods through Innova, a startup incubator within the company to assess existing ideas and turn them into marketable concepts.

"It was one unit introducing Design Thinking in their organizational structure and it became an innovation practice. A practice that they now share with the whole company."

Innova aims to support an entrepreneurial spirit amongst Ericsson's employees. After its third year, the Innova platform had 6.000 users. More than 4.000 ideas were submitted to the platform, with more than 450 ideas receiving first round funding and 45 receiving second round funding.

Source : thisisdesignthinking.net

SINGAPORE GOVERNMENT

The Ministry of Manpower's Work Pass Division used Design Thinking to develop better ways to support foreigners who choose Singapore as a destination to live, work and set up businesses.

Design Thinking methods were applied. Work Pass Division began to consider services through the eyes of their users the employers, employment agencies and foreign workers. Between 2005 and 2009, the EPOL was redesigned to increase the information flow to users of the system. This has helped to shift the perception of WPD from a high-handed regulator to a responsive and transparent facilitator of employment.

PROCTOR & GAMBLE

Clay Street Project @ Procter & GambleIn 2004, Procter & Gamble (P&G) established an internal innovation program, which incorporated Design Thinking. In the program teams from multiple disciplines and units within P&G gather for a period of 10 to 12 weeks to develop user-centered solutions. Since Clay Street produced numerous internal success stories P&G decided to provide their setup as a service for other business partners. The oferings range from one-day workshops to project support over a period of several weeks. The Clay Street initiative and a Design Thinking Network now serve as a foundation to spread Design Thinking in the organization.

http://www.theclaystreetproject.com

INTUIT

Design for Delight (D4D) Design Thinking program was established in 2007. Its mandate is to foster more entrepreneurial behavior throughout the whole organization. So far, over 200 innovation catalysts have been trained and support teams from multiple disciplines in the design of financial service experiences for Intuit's customers. They are allowed to dedicate a minimum of ten percent of their working time to training and helping others in their projects. Catalysts were enabled by a massive internal change program, which integrated a redefinition of the company's core values and major changes into the spatial working environments.

http://intuitlabs.com

PULSE

Ankit Gupta and Akshay Kothari develop Pulse with Design Thinking and empathy. They took a 10 week class called launchpad course at the d school at Stanford where rule number one is start with empathy. Students must start a business and have customers by week 5. Students must talk to customers from day one.

Ankit had a software company in india before coming to the United States. He says that we never talked to a customer and as a result we never had a customer. To develop the class project they set up shop in a coffee shop in Palo Alto for ten hours a day for several weeks.

They see everyone reading a newspaper so decide to do a news aggregator for iPad. At first they used post it notes because they had no software. First week everyone did not like it by week 3 everyone asking whether it shipped

with the iPad. They made 100 changes a day based on customer feedback.
At Ian iPad developers conference Steve jobs showed an iPad with their software. Pulse had soon developed 20 million users and Linkedin bought their company for 90 million dollars.

1. Service provision, which is sold to customers for better solution finding or as a program for internal change
2. New product and service development/improvement
3. Better alignment, collaboration and knowledge transfer
4. Empathy for the customer: gaining a better understanding of the customer and user
5. Improving own internal business processes and organizational structures
6. Commercial innovation and more efficient insight-driven marketing campaigns
7. Internal staff training for human/customer-centered mindset.
8. Toolbox. Adapting specific tools and methods to fit an individual purpose
9. Development of better teaching and training formats
10. Increasing creativity in teams
11. Customer engagement and co-creation
12. Public relations and reputation management vehicle
13. Service and experience design improvement
14. Test assumptions and iterate solutions

15. New business models and go-to-market strategies
16. Attractive recruiting tool
17. Means for more efficient meetings and arrangements
18. Generating demand and better customer acquisition via workshops
19. Improving the innovation process
20. Means for improving the style of design outcomes

2015 study by Hasso-Plattner-Institut für softwaresystemtechnik an der Universität Potsdam, September 2015

SIEMENS CT CHINA

Siemens has developed the program "Industrial Design Thinking in China (i.DT)" to train the creativity of Research & Development teams through real projects for need driven innovation with disruptive potential. The i.DT lab ran in the spring of 2015, with large workshop room, several dedicated project rooms, and an advanced machine shop with 3D printer, Computerized Numerical Control (CNC) and laser cutter to take the low resolution prototypes to the next professional level.

The process of i.DT, which can last for several months and include a number of workshops, starts from the definition of the innovation target and ends with a sales pitch. It uses extreme users and low resolution prototypes as stimuli, to satisfy unmet needs by integrating multiple technologies or businesses through fast iterations of needfinding, brainstorming, prototyping, and testing. The method has been successfully used in China for the past three years, in more than 20 development projects to date. Now i.DT is also coming to Germany to support business.

Source: Siemens Press release 2015

GE HEALTHCARE

The challenge was how to create a more child friendly CT, X-Ray and MRI scanning experience. Diagnostic imaging procedures are an unpleasant experience for patients. Doug Dietz is an industrial designer, working for GE healthcare since more than 20 years. He saw a little girl who was crying on her way to a scanner that was designed by him. Doug Dietz tried to find inspiration for this project through Design Thinking. "I started to imagine how powerful this tool could be if I brought it back and got cross-functional teams to work together." He started by observing and gaining empathy for young children at a day care center. Next, he created the first prototype of what would become the "Adventure Series" scanner and was able to get it installed as a pilot program in the children's hospital at the University of Pittsburgh Medical Center."

The patient satisfaction scores went up 90 percent. Children do not suffer of anxiety anymore. Instead some of them even ask their parents if they can come back tomorrow.

EMBRACE

Students at the Stanford d. school were challenged to design a less expensive incubator for babies born prematurely in Nepal. The students traveled to Nepal to meet with families and doctors and see the problem for themselves.

Based on the data collected, the design team reframes the design problem.

They used pictures, videos and storytelling of their experiences to brainstorm solutions. The students who undertook this project didn't stop with a prototype. They formed a company called Embrace and started manufacturing the product, which sells for $25. Embrace now has programs in 11 different countries and has helped over 50,000 premature and low birth weight infants. And all it started with the Design Thinking process. It has estimated that the product has saved 20,000 lives.

It has been so successful that the product is being purchased by US health providers where the cost of incubation using traditional methods in hospitals may be more than $100,000 per child.

Source: http://blog.triode.ca/

CHAPTER SUMMARY

Design Thinking has evolved over a period of twenty to thirty years and incorporates ideas from a number of design methodologies and movements including.
1. Service design
2. Experience design
3. Participatory design
4. Design Science
5. Design research
6. Human-centered design

The term Design Thinking first emerged in the 1980s with the rise of human-centered design

In the 1960s efforts were made to develop the field that has become known as Design Research to better inform the practice of design. The notion of design as a "way of thinking" was explored by Herbert A. Simon in his 1969 book The Sciences of the Artificial. It was further explored in Robert McKim's 1973 book Experiences in Visual Thinking. Rolf Faste expanded McKim's work in the 80s and 90s in his teaching at Stanford, defining and popularizing the idea of "Design Thinking"as a way of creative action that was adapted for business purposes by IDEO through his colleague David M. Kelley.

CHAPTER REVIEW

1. Name four corporations using design thinking.
2. Which country had the most Google searches on the term design thinking in 2017?
3. Name three international governmental organizations applying design thinking.
4. What was Ankit Gupta and Akshay Kothari's project and how was it successful?
5. Where are Infosys based?
6. How many staff has Infosys trained in design thinking by the end of 2017?
7. What is a Design Sprint?
8. How long is a Design Sprint?
9. Which company in the accommodation and toursim industry used design thinking to successfully turn around their failing organization?
10. Which two design thinking students at Stanford used design thinking to create a computer application that the sold to Linkedin for 90 million dollars and what is the app called?

04

WHAT IS
DESIGN THINKING?

DESIGN THINKING

WHAT
Design Thinking is or approach to designing that supports innovation and intelligent change. Design Thinking is a human-centered approach which is driven by creative and analytical thinking, customer empathy and iterative learning.

It involves a toolkit of methods that can be applied to different problems by cross disciplinary groups or by individuals. Anyone can use Design Thinking. It can be fun.

> **"**
> *Design thinking can be described as a discipline that uses the designer's sensibility and methods to match people's needs with what is technologically feasible and what a viable business strategy can convert into customer value and market opportunity."*

Tim Brown
IDEO

WHY USE DESIGN THINKING?
Design Thinking is useful when you have:
1. A poorly defined problem.
2. A lack of information.
3. A changing context or environment
4. It should result in consistently innovative solutions.

Design Thinking seeks a balance of design considerations including:
1. Business.
2. Appropriate application of technology
3. Empathy with people.
4. Environmental consideration.

Design Thinking seeks to balance two modes of thinking:
1. Analytical thinking
2. Creative Thinking

WHAT CAN IT BE APPLIED TO?
1. Products
2. Services
3. Experiences
4. Interactions
5. Systems of the above

DESIGN THINKING PROCESS
Design Thinking has a particular process
1. Define intent
2. Through ethnographic research develop empathy for

the point of view of the user.
3. Synthesize the research
4. Frame insights
5. Explore Concepts
6. Synthesize the concepts generated
7. Prototype the favored ideas
8. Test the prototypes with users
9. Incorporate changes
10. Iterate prototype and testing till a workable design is reached
11. Implement
12. Deliver Offering

RESOURCES

Multidisciplinary team of 4 to 12 people
A project space
Post it notes
Dry erase markers
White board
Digital camera
Copy paper
Chairs
Large table

WHO CAN USE DESIGN THINKING?

Design Thinking is a technique for everyone and any problem. Design Thinking process involves many stakeholders in working together to find a balanced design solution. The designer is a member of a type of design orchestra. The customer is involved throughout the design process and works with the design team to communicate their needs and desires and to help generate design solutions that are relevant to them.

The many methods used help

anyone to understand the diverse perspectives of the many stakeholders. It takes some courage to listen and recognize the point of view of the stakeholders. Managers, designers, social scientists, engineers marketers, stakeholders customers and others can collaborate creatively to apply Design Thinking to everyone's benefit.

The process is one of co-creation and the designer is a listener and a facilitator. Everyone adds value to the design. Design Thinking is not just for professional designers. Everyone can contribute. Many schools are now teaching Design Thinking to children as an approach that can be applied to life.

The methodology commonly referred to as design thinking is a proven and repeatable problem-solving protocol that any business or profession can employ to achieve extraordinary results."

Fast Company
Editorial staff

THE DESIGN LADDER

Companies often start at stage one then progress to higher levels. At the beginning of the 5 year study 36% of 1,000 companies were at stage 1 by the end of the study only 15% of companies remained at stage 1. Companies that were using design only as styling were growing slower on average than companies not using design at all.

Stage 4

Design as Strategy

Design is a key strategic means of supporting innovation. These companies have VPs of Design. Design connected to all business decisions. The cross disciplinary approach of Design thinking helps place a organization at this level of the ladder.

Stage 3

Design as Process

Design is integral to the development process. Design is often a sub department of marketing or engineering. Companies may have cross disciplinary teams.

Stage 2

Design as Styling

Design focuses on and aesthetics. Traditional design education can deliver designers whose primary goals are creative and artistic self-fulfilment, fame and awards rather than team business goals, technological innovation and user needs.

Stage 1

No design

Design plays no role in product and service development

Source: Danish Design Center study of 1,000 companies 2003

COMPANIES ON THE DESIGN LADDER IN RELATION TO SUCCESS IN EXPORT

| | EXPORT IN % OF TURNOVER | |
	AVERAGE	NUMBER OF COMPANIES
STEP 4 DESIGN AS INNOVATION	26.34%	131
STEP 3 DESIGN AS PROCESS	22.67%	330
STEP 2 DESIGN AS STYLING	16.48%	125
STEP 1 NON-DESIGN	12.21%	342
TOTAL	18.5%	927

"There are marked differences regarding exports according to the step on the design ladder. The export share of turnover is considerably larger in companies on the highest level than for those companies that do not employ design – and the share rises progressively according to the design-ladder level. The largest increase in export share of turnover is achieved where a systematic approach to design has been adopted, namely companies that employ professional designers and purchase design externally. The increase in exports is twice the size in companies that employ designers and purchase design externally (33.5%) compared to companies that neither employ designers nor purchase design externally (17.6 %). *Source: "The Economic Effects of Design" 2003 Denmark*

AVERAGE GROWTH IN TURNOVER
Based on study of 1000 companies and their position on the Design Ladder Danish Design Center study 2003

Stage 4. Design Thinking is a strategic approach to design and so is more likely to support faster organizational growth. **9.0%**

Stage 3. Design is integral to the development process. Companies may have cross disciplinary teams. **8.9%**

Stage 2. Companies using design only for styling in the Danish study grew slower than companies not using design at all. **6.5%**

Stage 1. Design plays no role in product service development **7.4%**

0   10   20   30   40   50   60   70   80   90   100

20 WAYS DESIGN THINKING IS BEING USED

1. Service provision, which is sold to customers for better solution finding or as a program for internal change.
2. New product and service development/improvement.
3. Better alignment, collaboration and knowledge transfer.
4. Empathy for the customer: gaining a better understanding of the customer and user.
5. Improving own internal business processes and organizational structures.
6. Commercial innovation and more efficient insight-driven marketing campaigns
7. Internal staff training for human/customer-centered mindset..
8. Toolbox. Adapting specific tools and methods to fit an individual purpose.
9. Development of better teaching and training formats.
10. Increasing creativity in teams.
11. Customer engagement and co-creation.
12. Public relations and reputation management vehicle.
13. Service and experience design improvement.
14. Test assumptions and iterate solutions.
15. New business models and go-to-market strategies.
16. Attractive recruiting tool
17. Means for more efficient meetings and arrangements.
18. Generating demand and better customer acquisition via workshops.
19. Improving the innovation process.
20. Means for improving the style of design outcomes.

2015 study by Hasso-Plattner-Institut für softwaresystemtechnik an der Universität Potsdam

Design thinking is, then, always linked to an improved future. Unlike critical thinking, which is a process of analysis and is associated with the 'breaking down' of ideas, design thinking is a creative process based around the 'building up' of ideas. There are no judgments in design thinking. This eliminates the fear of failure and encourages maximum input and participation. Wild ideas are welcome, since these often lead to the most creative solutions. Everyone is a designer, and design thinking is a way to apply design methodologies to any of life's situations.

Herbert Simon
Sciences of the Artificial MIT Press,

CHARACTERISTICS OF DESIGN THINKERS

D.SCHOOL BOOTCAMP BOOTLEG 2009	D.SCHOOL BOOTCAMP BOOTLEG 2010	TIM BROWN 2008)	BAECK & GREMETT 2011	COMMENT
Focus on human values	Focus on human values	Empathy	Empathy	"Focus on human values" includes empathy for users and feedback from them.
Create clarity from complexity	Craft clarity	Integrative thinking	Ambiguity, Curiosity, Holistic, Open mindset	All these items refer to styles of thinking. "Clarity" refers to producing a coherent vision out of messy problems. Baeck & Gremett focus on attitudes of the Design Thinker.
		Optimism		Only mentioned by Tim Brown, but seems to be regarded as a universal characteristic of Design Thinkers.
Get experimental and experiential	Embrace experimentation	Experimentalism	Curiosity, Open mindset	Experimentation is an integral part of the designer's work.
Collaborate across boundaries	Radical collaboration	Collaboration	Collaborative	Refers to the collaboration between people from different disciplines (having different backgrounds and viewpoints).
Show, do not tell, Bias toward action	Show, do not tell, Bias toward action			Emphasizes action, for example, by creating meaningful prototypes and confronting potential users with them.
Be mindful of process	Be mindful of process			Emphasizes that Design Thinkers need to keep the overall process (which is regarded as a core element of Design Thinking, in mind with respect to methods and goals.

Source: Gerd Waloszek, SAP AG, SAP User Experience – September 1, 2013

ATTRIBUTES OF DESIGN THINKING

Attribute	Description	Comment
Ambiguity	Being comfortable when things are unclear or when you do not know the answer	Design Thinking addresses wicked ill-defined and tricky problems.
Collaborative	Working together across disciplines	People design in interdisciplinary teams.
Constructive	Creating new ideas based on old ideas, which can also be the most successful ideas	Design Thinking is a solution-based approach that looks for an improved future result.
Curiosity	Being interested in things you do not understand or perceiving things with fresh eyes	Considerable time and effort is spent on clarifying the requirements. A large part of the problem solving activity, then, consists of problem definition and problem shaping.
Empathy	Seeing and understanding things from your customers' point of view	The focus is on user needs (problem context).
Holistic	Looking at the bigger context for the customer	Design Thinking attempts to meet user needs and also drive business success.
Iterative	A cyclical process where improvements are made to a solution or idea regardless of the phase	The Design Thinking process is typically non-sequential and may include feedback loops and cycles (see below).
Non judgmental	Creating ideas with no judgment toward the idea creator or the idea	Particularly in the brainstorming phase, there are no early judgments.
Open mindset	Embracing Design Thinking as an approach for any problem regardless of industry or scope	The method encourages "outside the box thinking"; it defies the obvious and embraces a more experimental approach.

Core Attributes of Design Thinking from Baeck & Gremett, 2011

BENEFITS OF DESIGN THINKING

1. A people-centered perspective;
2. Reduced risks of partial approaches;
3. A comprehensive, holistic problem perspective;
4. Reduced duplicated efforts, policy inconsistencies or overlaps;
5. Enhanced synergies and better addressed trade-offs;
6. Integrated and better-targeted solutions;
7. Stronger reality-checks at earlier stages;
8. Reduced risks of unintended consequences; and
9. Higher chances to deliver more complete and
10. Resilient solutions.

Source: Design Thinking for Public Service Excellence. Global Center for Public Service Excellence. Singapore.

ORGANIZATIONS YEARS OF DT EXPERIENCE IN 2015

Number of companies

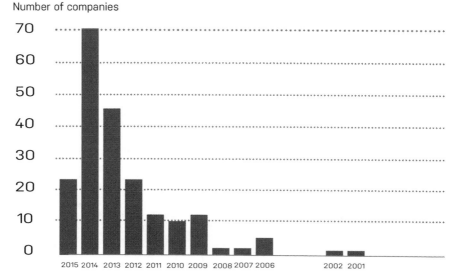

Year implemented Design Thinking

Data from 2015 study by Hasso-Plattner-Institut für softwaresystemtechnik an der Universität Potsdam, September 2015 of 235 German and international companies of all sizes

DESIGN THINKING MINDSETS

TOOLBOX

Design Thinking process is facilitated by a large number of design methods or tools. Usually more than one tool can be used.

The tools allow a designer to make informed design decisions that are not only about physical things but also about complex interfaces, systems, services and experiences. They will enable you to design products, systems buildings, interfaces and experiences with confidence that you have created the most informed design solutions for real people that is possible. These tools help designers think in four dimensions instead of three.

The methods contained in this book will help you close the gap between your clients and organizations and the people that you are designing for to help you create more considered, informed, repeatable, innovative, empathetic design solutions that people need but may not yet know that they want. Different design practitioners can select different methods for their toolkit and apply them in different ways. There is no best combination.

CONTEXT

Context is external elements that influence a design. These elements are physical and non-physical. Roads, buildings, and land contour are examples for physical elements related to the context of architecture while non-physical elements are weather conditions, local culture, as well as political and economic constraints.

The environmental context relates to the time, the day, the location, the type of place and any other physical aspect that could influence your design.

The user context is about how people are different. It's about what every user likes, and dislikes. It's also about the user's state of mind their habits and their state of mobility. The surrounding context influences the success of a design.

FRESH EYES

Outside people have a different perspective that may allow them to contribute new ideas and see problems with existing ideas and directions. Outsiders may have experiences from other industries that can help solve problems

Outside people may be aware of other people who can contribute something valuable. They may ask different questions. They may have relevant experiences that are lacking in your design team. At several points in your design process invite outsiders to review your design and give you feedback.

BALANCED DESIGN

Design Thinking seeks to find an optimal balance between four factors.

1. Business needs, including return on investment, growth, price point, competitive advantage cash flow.
2. Technology. Selection of appropriate manufacturing methods and processes, materials and engineering approaches.
3. People's needs and desires. This includes the usability, and aesthetics.
4. Environmental factors. This includes environmental sustainability.

Designers have often in the past oriented designs towards people's needs and desires but been less successful balancing business, environmental and technological factors. Many businesses have oriented their goals towards business factors. Companies that find a sustainable balance between these factors develop a competitive advantage over companies that tend to be oriented towards one factor.

CULTURE OF PROTOTYPING

Design Thinking involves embodied learning learning to "think with your hands." Prototypes can be anything from a storyboard, to a role play, to an actual physical object.

Prototypes of creative ideas are built as early as possible so the design team can learn just enough to generate useful feedback, determine an idea's strengths and weaknesses, and decide what new directions to pursue with more refined prototypes.

The important point is to learn by doing by giving form to an idea, evaluating it against other ideas, and ultimately improving upon it. "Fail early, fail often" is the motto, so prototyping is "quick, cheap, and dirty."
Make simple physical prototypes of your ideas as early as possible. Constantly test your ideas with people. Do not worry about making prototypes beautiful until you are sure that you have a resolved final design. Use the prototypes to guide and improve your design. Do a lot of low cost prototypes to test how your ideas physically work using cardboard, paper, markers, adhesive tape, photocopies, string and popsicle sticks. The idea is to test your idea, not to look like the final product. Expect to change it again. Limit your costs to ten or twenty dollars. Iterate, test and iterate. Do not make the prototype jewelry. It can stand

in the way of finding the best design solution. In the minds of some a high fidelity prototype is a finished design solution rather than a tool for improving a design. You should make your idea physical as soon as possible. Be the first to get your hands dirty by making the idea real.

UNRECOGNIZED AND UNMET NEEDS

The methods of Design Thinking are capable of identifying and developing design solutions to meet human needs sometimes even before people know that they have needs. Testing prototypes with real people and observing their interactions and responses can lead designers to innovative solutions that are not yet recognized.

6 key principles that will ensure a design is user centered:
Some Questions to ask:

1. Who are the users?
2. What are the users' tasks and goals?
3. What are the users' experience levels?
4. What functions do the users need from the design?
5. What information will be needed by end-users?,
6. In what form do they need it?
7. How do users think the design should work?

CURIOSITY

Curiosity is having an interest in the world. Curiosity is related to exploration, learning and innovation. Curiosity is one of the main driving forces behind human progress such as a caveman experimenting with fire. High levels of curiosity in adults are connected to greater analytic ability, problem-solving skills and overall intelligence. Creativity is about exploring the unknown and curiosity can be the entry point into this exploration. Children learn about the world through curiosity. A curious mind dives beneath the surface to understand the process. Curious people look at a challenge from multiple perspectives. Curious people find new paths to solutions.

“

But, one of the characteristics of our diverse team, one of the most profound things that unites us is that sense of curiosity and inquisitiveness, and taking such delight in being surprised – and being wrong – and then learning. And there is something very special about learning as a community and learning as a group. It's sort of like when you walk past something and think 'goodness that's beautiful', 'that's a nice tree isn't it!? – it's so cool if you can be with three other people

*and you can all agree
'that's a lovely tree'! So
there is something very
special about learning as
a group – having a shared
curiosity, going hand in
hand with a sense of
really wanting to make
things better."*

Sir Jonathan Ive
Apple VP of Design
2017 Soundcloud Interview

https://www.realisedesign.co.uk

CONTINUOUS FEEDBACK FROM ALL STAKEHOLDERS

Stakeholders include any individuals who are influence by the design. Specifically, the project team, end users, strategic partners, customers, alliances, vendors and senior management are project stakeholders.

Possible stakeholders include:
1. Employees
2. Shareholders
3. Government
4. Customers
5. Suppliers
6. Prospective employees
7. Local communities
8. Global Community
9. Schools
10. Future generations
11. Ex-employees
12. Creditors
13. Professional associations
14. Competitors
15. Investors
16. Prospective customers
17. Communities

Stakeholder analysis helps to identify:
1. Stakeholder interests
2. Ways to influence other stakeholders
3. Risks
4. Key people to be informed during the project
5. Negative stakeholders as well as their adverse effects on the project

HUMAN-CENTERED DESIGN

Unlike the traditional approach to design, Design Thinking does not start with the technology or a product or a service. Design Thinking starts with the people who need the product, process, or service and innovates for them.

Design Thinking identifies and addresses human needs. Design Thinking attempts to balance business requirements, human needs, the application of technologies and environmental sustainability.
Designers research how the end user has adapted their environment with their own designs or workarounds.

Human needs are investigated throughout the design process and the solution is refined through repetitive iterative steps with physical prototypes.

Design Thinking adapts the solution to the end user through understanding the end user.

OPTIMISM

Design Thinking is driven by

the optimistic belief that we can create positive change. Creativity requires optimism, believing that all problems have a solution. A willingness to try new things, experiment, prototype, give up on old ideas or ways of doing things. It is a generative activity. The word is derived from the Latin word optimum, meaning "best." Being optimistic, means that you believe that you will discover the best possible solution to a design problem. To create anything new requires a belief that there is a better way. Some people will tell you why your idea will not work.

BE VISUAL

Design Thinking is an effective approach for solving ambiguous, complex and changing problems. The solving of such problems often involves communicating ideas which are hard to describe in words. Visual mapping methods, images and sketches can help make complex ideas easier to understand and share.

You can use visual techniques even if you are not good at drawing. Take pictures of user interactions with your camera or phone. Explore some of the mapping methods described in the Methods chapter of this book. Use Venn diagrams, experience journeys, perceptual maps and radar charts to make information easier to comprehend. These visual methods are good ways of communicating connections and relationships.

CONTINUOUS LEARNING

Design Thinking is an ongoing learning process that seeks to incorporate the lessons learned into a continuous improvement of design. It incorporates ideas drawn from the Japanese management philosophy of Kaisen, Japanese for "improvement", or "change for the better" which focus upon continuous improvement of products and processes

INEXPENSIVE MISTAKES

Design Thinking makes successful designs by making mistakes early in inexpensive prototypes and learning through end user and stakeholder feedback. Prototypes are conceived and constructed in order to learn. We retain the features that are working and discover areas where the design can be improved. A process built around prototyping is an effective way of reaching an effective design solution in the most efficient way.

Designers must be willing to make mistakes in order to reach a successful solution. The environment should not punish exploration and iterative failures. Design Thinkers are searching for validity. They are problem solvers. The price of failures rises as the project proceeds. It saves cost to fail early. Abductive thinking which is the style of reasoning most likely to develop new innovative ideas and solutions makes reasonable assumptions based on incomplete information.

With this mode of thinking it is inevitable that some experiments directions will result in unexpected results. These unexpected results may be viewed as mistakes or as part of a learning process to find the best solution.

EVIDENCE-BASED DESIGN

Design Thinking uses both intuitive and evidence based design. Evidence-Based Design is the process of basing design decisions on credible research to achieve the best possible outcomes. Evidence based design emphasizes the importance of basing decisions on the best possible data for the best possible outcomes

1. Evidence Based Design provides real evidence that improves outcomes and help with the clients bottom line.
2. The design is no longer based just on the designer's opinion
3. Define the problem that you are trying to solve.
4. Start with people. Identify the group of people that the design solution will be useful for.
5. Use an integrated multidisciplinary approach.
6. Use a human centric approach
7. Consider the business case and return on investment.
8. Design to measurable outcomes and to involve end users.
9. Use strategic partnerships to accelerate innovation,
10. Use simulation and testing

to understand the end user's perspective
11. Communicate with and involve the stakeholders in the design process.

WICKED PROBLEMS

Design Thinking focuses on solutions to problems, It may be better than traditional design processes at addressing what have been called "Wicked Problems". Wicked problems are ill-defined or tricky problems, not necessarily wicked in the sense of evil. The iterative prototype and testing based approach does not assume a solution from the outset but experiments and tries alternative solutions and proceeds to refine the designs on the basis of successful testing.

Super wicked problems

K. Levin, proposed an additional type of problem called the "super wicked problem"He defined super wicked problems as having the following additional characteristics:
1. There is limited time.
2. No central decision maker.
3. The people who are trying to solve a problem are the same people who are causing the problem.
4. Policies discount the future irrationally.

Rittel and Webber specified ten characteristics of wicked problems:
1. "There is no definitive formulation of a wicked problem
2. Wicked problems have no

stopping rule.
3. Solutions to wicked problems are not true-or-false, but better or worse.
4. There is no immediate and no ultimate test of a solution to a wicked problem.
5. Wicked problems do not have an enumerable set of potential solutions,
6. Every wicked problem is essentially unique.
7. Every wicked problem can be considered to be a symptom of another problem.
8. The existence of a discrepancy representing a wicked problem can be explained in numerous ways. The choice of explanation determines the nature of the problem's resolution.
9. The planner has no right to be wrong
10. Wicked problems have no given alternative solutions."

Source: Rittel and Webber

ANALOGOUS SITUATIONS

"Bring your staff together in a large room and put up a big white board. Create two columns, one for emotions and activities involved in your customer experience and a second one for similar situations which incorporate the same emotions and activities. Once you start filling in the first column, people will naturally start to brainstorm the analogous situations. When those are noted on the white board, people will start adding new emotions and activities to the first column based on their own experiences with the analogous situations. At the end of the process, choose the most vital pain points and use them as the basis of a brainstorming session to look for solutions and methods of improving the overall customer experience.

RE-FRAMING THE PROBLEM

Re-frame to create different perspectives and new ideas.

How to re-frame:
1. Define the problem that you would like to address.
2. There is more than one way of looking at a problem. You could also define this problem in another way as:
- What if a male or female used it?
- What if it was used in China or Argentina?
- "The underlying reason for the problem is."
- "I think that the best solution is."
- "You could compare this problem to the problem of."
- "Another, different way of thinking about it is"

FUTURE ORIENTED

Design Thinking is a future oriented approach to designing. Most organizations base their new designs on what exists. Design Thinking allows an organization to change for the better. It allows an organization to move from being a follower to being a leader in the market.

PEOPLE FIRST

Design is more about people than it is about things. Stand in those people's shoes, see through their eyes, uncover their stories, share their worlds. Start each design by identifying a problem that real people are experiencing. Use the methods in this book selectively to gain empathy, understanding, and to inform your design. Good process is not a substitute for talented, motivated and skilled people on your design team.

GET PHYSICAL

Make simple physical prototypes of your ideas as early as possible. Constantly test your ideas with people. Do not worry about making prototypes beautiful until you are sure that you have a resolved design direction. Use the prototypes to guide and improve your design. Do several low cost prototypes to test how your Ideas physically work using cardboard, paper, markers, adhesive tape, photocopies, string and popsicle sticks. The idea is to test your idea, not to look like the final product. Expect to change it again. Limit your costs to ten or twenty dollars. Iterate, test and iterate. Do not make the prototype jewelry. It can stand in the way of finding the best design solution.

CONSIDERED RISKS

Taking considered risks helps create differentiated design. Many designers and organizations do not have the flexibility or courage to create innovative, differentiated design solutions so they create products and services that are like existing products and services and compete on price.

LISTEN

Reach out to understand people. Interpret what you see and hear. Read between the lines. Make new connections between the things you see and hear.

COMBINE ANALYTICAL AND CREATIVE THINKING

Effective collaboration is part of effective design. Designers work like members of an orchestra. We need to work with managers, engineers, salespeople and other professions. Human diversity and life experience contribute to better design solutions.

COLLABORATION

Design today is a more complex activity than it was in the past. Business, technology, global cultural issues, environmental considerations, and human considerations all need careful consideration. Design Thinking recognizes the need for designers to be working as members of multidisciplinary multi skilled teams.

STORYTELLING

WHAT

A powerful story can help ensure the success of a new product, service or experience. Storytelling can be an effective method of presenting a point of view. Research can uncover meaningful stories from end that illustrate needs or desires. These stories can become the basis of new designs or actions and be used to support decisions. Research shows that our attitudes, fears, hopes, and values are strongly influenced by story. Stories can be an effective way of communicating complex ideas and inspiring people to change. Characters are a good way to express human needs and generate empathy from your audience

AN EFFECTIVE STORY

1. Answer in your story: What, why, when, who, where, how?
2. Offer a new vantage point
3. Share emotion
4. Communicate transformations
5. Communicate who you are.
6. Show cause and effect Describe conflicts and resolution.
7. Speak from your experience.
8. Describe how actions created change
9. Omit what is irrelevant.
10. Reveal meaning
11. Share your passion
12. Be honest and real
13. Build trust
14. Show connections
15. Transmits values
16. Share a vision
17. Share knowledge
18. Your story should differentiate you.
19. Meets information needs for your audience
20. Offer a new vantage point
21. Tell real world stories
22. Evoke the future
23. Share emotion
24. Communicate transformations.
25. Communicate who you are.
26. Describe actions.
27. Show cause and effect
28. Speak from your experience.
29. Describe how actions created change
30. Omit what is irrelevant.
31. Share your passion
32. Be honest and real
33. Build trust
34. Transmit values
35. Share a vision
36. Share knowledge
37. Use humor
38. Engage the audience
39. Craft the story for your audience.
40. Pose a problem and offer a resolution
41. Use striking imagery
42. The audience must be able to act on your story.

PLAN YOUR STORY

Plan what you are going to say and how you are going to say it. Describe the the the transformation of your character in one sentence. Start with a dozen bullet points describing what you want to say.

Your story should have
1. Action,
2. Conflict
3. Transformation

What is your character trying to do? What stands in the way? What is the insight of your story? What does your character learn?

"

A character who sees things the way we'd see them gets to a strange place, observes things that interest him (or her), is transformed by what he sees, and fantastic new product or service that we're designing and realize how it can help make their life just that little bit better."

Chelsea Hostetter

STRUCTURE
Give your story a beginning, middle and end.

AUDIENCE
Think about the elements – plot, setting, characters, conflict, and resolution in relation to the audience. What is going to resonate with your audience? include a bit of yourself.

CONTEXT
Think about the context of where your audience are hearing the story and what they are doing there. When you introduce your characters outline the context that surrounds them and what led them to this place.

HOW
How are you going to tell your story? How much back story will you need to give? Are you going to need any artifacts, such as storyboards?

BE AUTHENTIC
Describe how one of your personas will experience the design.

FOCUS ON WHAT'S IMPORTANT
Focus on what is most important to your audience and how the design will meet their unmet needs.

BE VISUAL
Use photos, video, prototypes, storyboards or sketches to support your story.

Source: Adapted from Chelsea Hostetter, Austin Centre for Design

ASK FOR FEEDBACKFROM YOUR AUDIENCE
Engage your audience. Ask them for feedback.

CHALLENGES
1. A story with too much jargon will lose an audience.
2. Not everyone has the ability to tell vivid stories.
3. Stories are not always generalizable.

LOOK FOR BALANCE

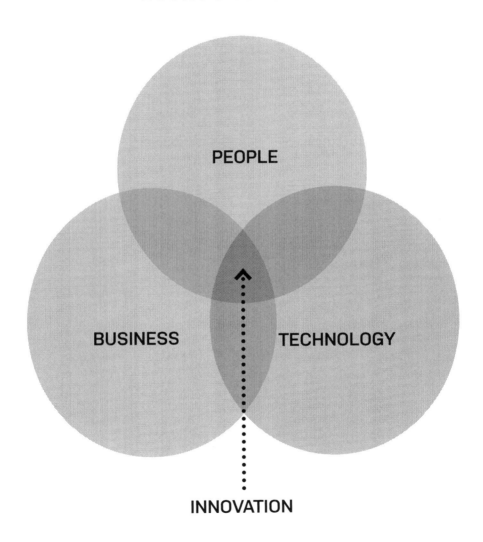

WHY USE DESIGN THINKING?

CRAFT A BETTER USER EXPERIENCE

1. Understand your customer's point of view.
2. Deliver a seamless, useful experience.
3. Bring more humanity to your business.
4. Designing the moments of truth
5. Identify those moments of a user experience that leave a lasting impression both positive or negative.
6. The entire company can focus on the vision of creating an exceptional customer experience.
7. Compare what your customers want with what your competitors are providing.
8. Understanding the ideal experience
9. Reveal the truth through your customer's eyes
10. Understand what customers think about your products and services rather than what you think they think.
11. Identify opportunities
12. When you understand where a customer experience is poor, it is an opportunity to improve your competitiveness and make your business more profitable. Evolve and stay competitive. Adapt to changing customer needs and expectations.
13. Empathize with your customers

14. Lack of understanding your customer's point of view is the number one reason new
15. Products and services fail. More than 50% of new goods and services fail in the market.
16. Get connected to your customers or end users
17. 80% Of service companies believe they offer superior services. Only 8% of their customers agree.
18. Develop more relevant products services and experiences for your customers or end users
19. Balance the needs of stakeholders more efficiently.
20. Diagnose experience problems.

IMPROVE YOUR BUSINESS PERFORMANCE

1. Strategic and tactical innovation.
2. Help all your employees and external stakeholders to contribute to the change process.
3. Improve business systems
4. Ensure systems are efficient,
5. And customer-focused.
6. Take cost & complexity out of the system.
7. Develop a better road map. Decide where you should be going with your business, what products and services you can and should be delivering and when it is best to introduce them. Build

strategic advantage against competitors.

8. Identify duplicated touchpoints and position people and other resources where they are most needed.
9. Prioritize competing deliverables
10. Plan how to allocate resources. Decide what should be the top priorities for your business to grow and generate the best returns on investment. Your decisions are guided by real customer data and feedback.
11. Plan for hiring. Plan strategically and select the best employees and skills for long-term expansion of your business.
12. Bring your whole organization together around the common goal of customer experience.
13. Understand the role that each department plays in a customer-focused strategy. Overcome silo thinking. Help different groups identify common ground.
14. Build and share knowledge. Build a common understanding both internally and externally.
15. Understand competitive positioning.
16. Knowledge of Customer behaviors and needs across channels. Customers commonly access a number of different channels when engaging an organization. Understand complex processes across channels.
17. Drive ideation and innovation
18. Decide how to allocate resources to improve best current offerings or to build whole new sets of deliverables based on what customers need and want rather than what your employees think that they want, benchmark your current performance against competitors and help you plan future initiatives.
19. Make intangible services tangible
20. Understand where friction exists between the needs of different market segments
21. Various interested parties commonly have conflicting needs and desires.
22. Tailor your experiences more efficiently to different segment's needs
23. Understand the differences in their expectations and experience.
24. Introduce metrics for what matters most for your customers
25. Plan strategically to achieve long-term organizational goals and to measure progress towards those goals
26. Align your offerings to brand promise
27. Understand where your current business supports or conflicts with your brand promise.
28. Eliminate potential failure points
29. See where your customer experience is most likely to fail and to plan to reduce the

risk and cost of failure.
30. Improve efficiency
31. Break down organizational silos
32. Reduce duplication. Prioritize between competing requirements. Identify cheapest 'cost to serve', and set performance indicators that you can measure.
33. Imagine future product and service experiences
34. Plan and implement future product and service offerings.
35. Holistic thinking
36. Balance the competing needs of your customers, your business, and technology.
37. Improve your whole organization's performance
38. Work towards one goal of the best possible customer experience rather than multiple departmental goals
39. A living strategy
40. Improve and evolve your strategy as your business changes and your customer needs and expectations evolve.
41. Make better decisions
42. Ethnographic methods used by design thinking practitioners reduce the risk of design development by validating designs as they are being designed with end users.

"

It's taken years of slogging through Design = high style to bring us full circle to the simple truth about design thinking. That it is a most powerful tool and when used effectively, can be the foundation for driving a brand or business forward."

Fast Company

"

Making things people want is better than making people want things."

DESIGN ETHNOGRAPHY

WHAT

Design ethnography is a collection of methods that helps create better more compelling and meaningful design. It helps a designer understand the points of view of people who will use the designs. Ethnographers study and interpret culture, through fieldwork.

WHO INVENTED IT?

Bronisław Malinowski 1922

WHY

1. To inform the design and innovation processes rather than basing your designs on intuition.
2. To ensure that your design solutions resonate with the people that you are designing for.
3. Ethnography helps designers see beyond their preconceptions.

CHALLENGES

1. People may behave different-ly when they are in groups or alone.
2. Researchers need to be aware of the potential impacts of the research on the people and animals they study.

HOW

There are many different ethnographic techniques. Some of the general guidelines are:

3. Listen.
4. Observe.
5. Be empathetic and honest.
6. Do research in context, in the environments that the people you are studying live or work.
7. Influence your subject's behavior as little as possible with your presence.
8. Beware of bias.
9. Take photos and notes.
10. Have clear goals related to understanding and prediction.
11. Study representative people.

RESOURCES

Notepad computer
Pens
Post-it-notes
Video camera
Camera
Voice recorder
White-board
Dry-erase pens.

Source: Publication bias: raising awareness of a potential problem

DIVERSITY

Diversity means different genders, different ages, be from different cultures, different socioeconomic backgrounds and have different outlooks to be most successful.

WHY
1. To attract good people
2. It broadens the customer base in a competitive environment.
3. Diversity brings benefits including better decision making and improved problem solving, creativity and innovation, which leads to enhanced product development, and more successful marketing to different types of customers.
4. Diversity provides organizations with the ability to compete in global markets

HOW
1. Treat everyone fairly.
2. Creating an inclusive culture.
3. View employees as individuals.
4. Ensure equal access to opportunities.
5. Compliance with statutory duties and requirements.
6. everyone staff with the skills to challenge inequality and discrimination in their environment.
7. Ensure policies, procedures and processes promote equality and diversity.
8. Seek the commitment from key participants.
9. Engage with communities.
10. Recognize, and encourage employees to see that their cultures are of value to the organization.
11. Articulate the benefits more diverse organization.
12. Develop a definition of diversity that is linked to organizational mission.
13. Identify models locally and internationally, that might serve as models for diversity efforts.
14. Develop a realistic action plan.
15. Develop metrics for success.
16. Create a safe environment for participation.
17. Set goals for bringing about organizational diversity.
18. Articulate goals.
19. Become culturally competent.
20. Commit to continuous improvement

EMPATHY

WHAT

Empathy is defined as 'standing in someone else's shoes' or 'seeing through someone else's eyes'. It is The ability to identify and understand another's situation, feelings, and motives. In design it may be defined as: identify with others and, adopting his or her perspective. It is different to sympathy. Empathy does not necessarily imply compassion. Empathy is a respectful understanding of other people's point of view.

WHO INVENTED IT?

The English word was coined in 1909 by E.B. Titchener in an attempt to translate the German word "Einfühlungsvermögen". It was later re-translated into the German language as "Empathie".

WHY

1. Empathy is a core skill for de-signers to design successfully for other people.
2. Empathy is needed for busi-ness success and for designs to be accepted and used by those people we are design-ing for.
3. Empathy builds trust.

CHALLENGES

1. Increasing use of teams.
2. Rapid pace of globalization.
3. Global need to retain talent.

HOW

1. Put yourself in contact and the context of people who you are designing for.
2. Ask questions and listen to the answers.
3. Read between the lines.
4. Observe.
5. Don't interrupt.
6. Listen.
7. Ask clarifying questions.
8. Restating what you think you heard.
9. Recognize that people are individuals.
10. Notice body language. Most communication is non-verbal
11. Withhold judgment when you hear views different to your own.
12. Take a personal interest in people.

EXPERIENCE DESIGN

Experience design is the practice of designing products, processes, services, events, and environments with a focus placed on the quality of the user experience. Experience design is concerned with moments of engagement, or touchpoints, between people and brand. Experience design requires a cross-disciplinary approach.

Source: On Point Creative, http:// opcatl.com/ (accessed July 03, 2016)

WHO INVENTED IT?
Donald Norman 1990s

WHY
A user experience can be more valuable than an individual product or service.

CHALLENGES
1. Research methods are necessary to understand another person's experiences
2. Observations can be subjective.

HOW
1. Experience evaluation. methods include:
2. Diary Methods.
3. Experience sampling method.
4. Day reconstruction method.
5. Laddering interviews.

RESOURCES
Cameras
Video cameras
Notepad computer
Digital voice recorder
Cell phones
Tablets

HUMAN NEEDS

The greatest single cause of failure of design projects according to many studies is a lack of understanding of the what is most important to the customer or end user

This really comes down to a lack of identification of what are unmet user needs. Unmet needs represent market opportunities. customers struggle to get a job done.

Identifying and addressing those unmet needs is the key to success.

Many managers do not have a process for identifying what is most important to their customers. Knowing which customer needs to address in priority order is a key requirement of the innovation process.

"

Human needs are a powerful source of explanation of human behavior and social interaction. All individuals have needs that they strive to satisfy, either by using the system, 'acting on the fringes.' or acting as a reformist or revolutionary. Given this condition, social systems must be responsive to individual needs, or be subject to instability and forced change."

Preface," in The Power of Human Needs in World Society, ed. Roger A.Coate and Jerel A. Rosati, ix. Boulder, CO: Lynne Rienner Publishers.

WHAT WE ALL NEED

PHYSICAL SUSTENANCE
1. Air
2. Food
3. Health
4. Movement
5. Physical Safety
6. Rest / sleep
7. Shelter
8. Touch
9. Water

SECURITY
1. Consistency
2. Order/Structure
3. Peace
4. Peace of mind
5. Protection
6. Safety
7. Stability
8. Trusting

LEISURE/RELAXATION
1. Humour
2. Joy
3. Play
4. Pleasure

AFFECTION
1. Appreciation
2. Attention
3. Closeness
4. Companionship
5. Harmony
6. Intimacy
7. Love
8. Nurturing
9. Sexual Expression
10. Support
11. Tenderness
12. Warmth

UNDERSTANDING
1. Awareness
2. Clarity
3. Discovery
4. Learning

"

Our real goal, then, is not so much fulfilling manifest needs by creating a speedier printer or a more ergonomic keyboard; that's the job of designers. It is helping people to articulate the latent needs they may not even know they have, and this is the challenge of design thinkers."

Tim Brown
IDEO

"

The most secure source of new ideas that have true competitive advantage, and hence, higher margins, is customers' unarticulated needs."

Jeanne Liedtka
Darden School of the University of Virginia

AUTONOMY
1. Choice
2. Ease
3. Independence
4. Power
5. Self-responsibility
6. Space
7. Spontaneity

MEANING
1. Aliveness
2. Challenge
3. Contribution
4. Creativity
5. Effectiveness
6. Exploration
7. Integration
8. Purpose

MATTERING
1. Acceptance
2. Care
3. Compassion
4. Consideration
5. Empathy
6. Kindness
7. Mutual Recognition
8. Respect
9. To be heard, seen
10. To be known, understood
11. To be trusted
12. Understanding others

COMMUNITY
1. Belonging
2. Communication
3. Cooperation
4. Equality
5. Inclusion

1. Mutuality
2. Participation
3. Partnership
4. Self-expression
5. Sharing

SENSE OF SELF
1. Authenticity
2. Competence
3. Creativity
4. Dignity
5. Growth
6. Healing
7. Honesty
8. Integrity
9. Self-acceptance
10. Self-care
11. Self-knowledge
12. Self-realization
13. Mattering to myself

TRANSCENDENCE
1. Beauty
2. Celebration of life
3. Communion
4. Faith
5. Flow
6. Hope
7. Inspiration
8. Mourning
9. Peace (internal)
10. Presence

Sources: Marshall Rosenberg, ManfredMax-Neef, Miki and Arnina Kashtan

HUMAN NEEDS

	BEING (PERSONAL OR COLLECTIVE ATTRIBUTES)	HAVING (INSTITUTIONS. NORMS, TOOLS)
SUBSISTENCE	Physical health, mental health, equilibrium, sense of humor. adaptability	Food., shelter. work
PROTECTION	Care, adaptability, autonomy, equilibrium. solidarity	Insurance systems, savings, social security. health systems. rights. family, work
AFFECTION	Self-esteem,solidarity, respect, tolerance, generosity, receptiveness. passion, determination, sensuality, sense or humor	Friendships. partners, family. partnerships. relationships with nature
UNDERSTANDING	Critical conscience, receptiveness, curiosity,discipline intuition, rationality	Literature, teachers. method. educational and communication policies
PARTICIPATION	Adaptability, receptiveness. solidarity, willingness, determination, respect, passion, sense of humor	Rights, responsibilities, duties, privileges. work
LEASURE	Curiosity, receptiveness, imagination. recklessness. sense of humor, lack of worry, tranquility, sensuality.	Games. spectacles. clubs. parties. peace of mind
CREATION	Passion, determination. intuition, imagination. boldness. rationality, autonomy, inventiveness, curiosity	Abilities, skills, methods, work
IDENTITY	Sense of belonging, consistency, differentiation, self-esteem, assertiveness	Symbols, language, religions, habits, customs. reference groups, roles, groups, sexuality, values. norms, historic memory. work
FREEDOM	Autonomy. self-esteem. determination. passion. assertiveness, open mindedness. boldness. rebelliousness, tolerance	Equal rights

	DOING (PERSONAL OR COLLECTIVE ACTIONS)	INTERACTING (SPACES OR ATMOSPHERES)
SUBSISTENCE	Feed, procreate, rest, work.	Livmg environment, social setting.
PROTECTION	Co-operate. prevent. plan, take care of, cure. help.	Living space, social environment, dwelling.
AFFECTION	Make love, express emotions. share, .take care of. cultivate, appreciate.	Privacy, intimacy, home, Spaces of togetherness.
UNDERSTANDING	Investigate, study, educate, experiment, meditate, interpret.	Settings of formative interaction, schools and universities academies groups. communities. family.
PARTICIPATION	Become affiliated, cooperate, propose. share, dissent. obey, interact, agree on, express opinions.	Settings of participative Interaction, parties. associations, communities, neighborhoods, family.
LEASURE	Day-dream, brood, dream recall old times, give way to fantasies, remember. relax, have fun, play.	Privacy, intimacy, spaces of closeness, free time, surroundings, landscapes.
CREATION	Work, invent, build. design, compose, interpret.	Productive and feedback settings, workshops, cultural groups, audiences, spaces for expression, temporal freedom.
IDENTITY	Commit oneself, integrate oneself. confront, decide on, get to know oneself, rec-ognize oneself, actualize oneself, grow.	Social rhythms, every day belongs to. maturation stages
FREEDOM	Dissent, choose to be different from, run risks, develop awareness. commit oneself, disobey, meditate	36/ Temporal/special plasticity

Adapted from Matrix of needs and satisfiers. I. Cruz. A. Stahel . M. Max-Neef 2009

SHOSHIN: THE BEGINNER'S MIND

WHAT

The phrase shoshin means beginner's mind. It refers to having an attitude of full of openness, enthusiasm, and fresh perspectives in learning something new, eagerness, and lack of preconceptions even at an advanced level, like a child.

Shoshin also means "correct truth" and is used to describe a genuine signature on a work of art. It is used to describe something that is perfectly genuine.

WHERE DID IT ORIGINATE?

1. Shoshin is a term from Zen Buddhism and Japanese martial arts.

HOW TO USE SHOSHIN

1. Withhold judgment. Do not suggest that an idea will not work or that it has negative side-effects. All ideas are potentially good so do not judge them until afterwards.
2. Observe and Listen
3. Ask why
4. Be curious
5. Look for new connections

WHY USE SHOSHIN

1. Sometimes expertise can create closed mindedness.

2. Our assumptions can stand in the way of creating new ideas. A beginner is not aware of biases that can stand in the way of a good new idea.
3. Our experience is an asset but our assumptions may be misconceptions and stereotypes.
4. Innovation often requires looking at a problem in a new way.
5. Beginner's minds can help make breakthroughs
6. Observe and engage users without value judgments.
7. Question your assumptions. Ask why?
8. Be curious and explore.
9. Search for patterns and connections no one else has seen.
10. Be open and listen

Source : http://blog.triode.ca

The older you get as a designer, the more you realize that you just don't know anything . If you can embrace that you don't know, but you know how to go find out, that makes you very effective."

Daniel Burka
Google Ventures

DESIGN THINKING SPACES

WHAT

An adequate office helps concentrate the energy of the team and build connections between team members.

HOW

PHYSICAL ENVIRONMENT FOR DESIGN THINKING

1. Flexibility of space
2. Personalization of space
3. Interaction stimulation.
4. Size of working space in design thinking office should be adequate in relation to amount of workers.
5. According to Kelley and Littman (2001) large and empty, as well as, small and crammed offices suppress the creative work
6. All employees have an equal workplace.
7. Each person has an access to an individual, personal working area
8. The space allows project teams to come together for group work within seconds.
9. Space devoted only to the particular team for the whole length of their project.
10. There design team can keep and access all of project related materials
11. Space is customizable.
12. Every employee has to be able to create a personally most suiting and stimulating space (Kelley & Littman 2001, 123–125).
13. Personalization is done through group decisions of furniture setting.
14. Every employee has a say in how the overall office space looks like.
15. Furniture and people are flexible and easily movable to insure the best setting for each project and team (Brown 2009, 34–35; Kelley & Littman 2001, 123–125).
16. Common areas are designed to increase human interaction.

SPACES FOR CREATIVE WORK HAWORTH RECOMMENDATIONS

1. Lightweight, comfortable, readily movable chairs perhaps on wheels can maximize a relatively small footprint and be arranged in multiple configurations
2. Show your work in progress and let people comment.
3. Surround yourself with the material that your team is working on.
4. Mobile large White-boards 6 ft x 4 ft and pin boards.
5. Mobile boards can have a magnetic White-board on one side and a pin board on the reverse side.
6. A laptop-sized surface for

each attendee

7. Walls can be used for projection, writing, or pinning up information in areas visible to everyone

8. Acoustic privacy should be ensured.

9. Large walls can be used as display spaces.

10. Use work tools that are easily accessible

11. Think of every vertical surface as a potential space for displaying work

12. Use flexible technologies such as wi-fi that allow relocation of services such as Internet and power connections.

13. Have a projector and screen

14. Seating should allow all participants to see one another and read body language

15. Select furniture with wheels that can be easily moved

16. Small tables can be used for breakouts or grouped into a common surface

17. Ample writing and display areas, as well as surfaces for laying things out, support the need for visual cues and reference materials

18. Provide a large area of vertical displays such as walls White-boards, pin boards, foam core boards, projection surfaces, that allow users to actively and flexibly interact with the information

19. Build spaces that support different types of collaboration.

20. Consider physical and virtual collaboration.

21. Spaces should be flexible for unplanned collaboration.

22. Provide comfortable group areas for informal interactions and information sharing.

23. The spaces need to be large enough to accommodate all the research materials, visuals, and prototypes in order to keep them visible and accessible all of the time.

Collaborative Spaces - media. haworth.com, http://media.haworth. com/asset/28519/Collaborative%20 Spaces Whitepaper_C2.pdf

TACIT KNOWLEDGE

WHAT

Tacit knowledge is the knowledge that is gained through personal experience. Examples of tacit knowledge are the ability to ride a bicycle or recognizing someone's face. Tacit knowledge is difficult to pass on to another person by writing it down or describing it. Tacit knowledge is a form of intellectual property. Tacit knowledge includes best practices, stories, experience, wisdom, and insights.

WHO INVENTED IT?
Michael Polanyi 1958

WHY
1. Tacit knowledge is valuable to any organization.

CHALLENGES

1. Mapping tacit knowledge needs immersion in context.
2. A researcher can map behavior and perceptions.

HOW
The methods of capturing tacit knowledge include:
1. Interviews
2. Observation

RESOURCES
Camera
Notepad computer
Digital voice recorder

RESEARCH

WHAT
Qualitative or ethnographic research is a core part of the approach of Design Thinking. It seeks to understand people in the context of their daily experiences. Uses ethnographic methods including observation and interviews. Aims to understand questions like why and how. Obtains insights about attitudes and emotions. Often uses small sample sizes. Seeks to see the world through the eyes of research subjects. Methods are flexible. Used to develop an initial understanding.

WHO INVENTED IT?
The Royal Statistical Society founded in 1834 pioneered the use of quantitative methods. Early examples of ethnographers include Malinowski 1922, Radcliffe Brown, Margaret Mead, Gregory Bateson and Franz Boas, all of whom studied 'native' populations abroad, and Robert Park and the work of the Chicago school where the focus was on the life and culture of local groups in the city.

WHY
1. High level of reliability
2. Minimum personal judgment.
3. It is objective.

CHALLENGES
1. Concerned with validity
2. Subjective
3. Hard to recreate results
4. People may behave differently to the way they say they behave
5. Experiences can not be generalized.
6. Methods are static. Real world changes.
7. Structured methods
8. Difficult to control the environment
9. Can be expensive if studying a large number of people.

HOW
1. Define research question
2. Select research subjects and context to study.
3. Collect data
4. Interpret data.
5. Study data for insights
6. Collect more data
7. Analyze data

QUESTIONS TO CONSIDER

PEOPLE

1. What user group does this product, service or experience target?
2. What problems or needs does our product help with for this group?
3. When and how and where is our product, service or experience used?
4. What features are most important to end users?
5. How should our product, service or experience look and work?
6. Who should we employ?
7. What external partners do we need?
8. What does the customer need?
9. What does the customer want?
10. How does the customer learn to use this product or service?
11. What is the experience when the customer enters this experience?
12. How does the customer purchase or initiate this experience?
13. How does the customer interact with each touchpoint?
14. How are customers retained?
15. What are the barriers to a customer returning?

What is the process if a customer has an unsatisfactory experience?
16. We will know this assumption is true when we see:
- What market feedback?
- What quantitative measure?
- What qualitative insight?

BUSINESS

1. We will make money by:
2. Our customers will find our product service or experience valuable because:
3. We will acquire customers through:
4. It will cost how much to establish these products or services. It will cost how much per month/year to offer these products or services and maintain our business.
5. Establishing these products or services will be funded by:
6. My primary competition of brand and products in the market will be:
7. We will eat them because:
8. Our biggest business risk is:
9. We will reduce this risk by:
10. What could cause our business to fail?

TECHNOLOGY

Why do particular technologies/ materials/ processes/ finishes offer strategic advantage?

THINKING STYLES

ABDUCTIVE THINKING

Abductie reasoning is the core thinking approach in design thinking. With abductive reasoning, unlike deductive reasoning, the premises do not guarantee the conclusion. Abductive reasoning can be understood as "inference to the best explanation" Abductive reasoning typically begins with an incomplete set of observations and proceeds to the likeliest possible explanation. It's goal is to explore what could possibly be true. Abductive thinking allows designers to find solutions in ambiguous, changing situations. It is the thinking approach necessary for innovation. Abductive thinking finds solutions by creating prototypes and testing and improving the designs. This modee of thinking wasn't taught in management, science and engineering schools. It doesn't start with clearly defined evidence.

"

A person or organization instilled with that discipline is constantly seeking a fruitful balance between reliability and validity, between art and science, between intuition and analytics, and between exploration and exploitation. The design-thinking organization applies the designer's most crucial tool to the problems of business. That tool is abductive reasoning."

Roger Martin

Charles Sanders Peirce originated the term and argued that no new idea could come from inductive or deductive logic.

1. **Abductive logic**: The logic of what might be.
2. **Deductive logic** reasons from the general to the specific.
3. **Inductive logic** reasons from the specific to the general.

DEDUCTIVE THINKING

The process of reasoning from one or more general statements (premises) to reach a logically certain conclusion. Deductive reasoning is one of the two basic forms of valid reasoning. It begins with a general hypothesis or known fact and creates a specific conclusion from that generalization.

Described by Aristotle 384-322bce, Plato 428-347bce, and Pythagoras 582-500 BCE

INDUCTIVE THINKING

Inductive thinking is a kind of reasoning that constructs or evaluates general propositions that are derived from specific examples. Inductive reasoning contrasts with deductive reasoning, in which specific examples are derived from general propositions.
Described by Aristotle 384-322bce,

CRITICAL THINKING

"The process of actively and skillfully conceptualizing, applying, analyzing, synthesizing, and evaluating information to reach an answer or conclusion. disciplined thinking that is clear, rational, open-minded, and informed by evidence, willingness to integrate new or revised perspectives into our ways of thinking and acting"
Critical thinking is an important element of all professional fields and academic disciplines."

DESIGN THINKING

The Design Thinking is not a style of thinking. Design Thinking is a formal method for practical, creative resolution of problems and creation of solutions, with the intent of an improved future result. In this regard it is a form of solution-based, or solution-focused thinking

Source: Deductive, Inductive and Abductive Reasoning - TIP Sheet.

Design Thinking taught forward looking businesses the value of bringing creative inventiveness aka, abductive thinking to the center of modern innovation practice. Design Thinking taught modern institutions that human life should be the primary springboard of 21st century innovation."

Farenheit 212
Rethinking design thinking
Historically most organizations were managed by divergent or analytical thinkers. Over the last ten years this has changed.

Silicon Valley didn't think a designer could build and run a company. They were straight up about it. We weren't MBAs, we weren't two PhD students from Stanford."

Brian Chesky
Co-founder of AirBnb
Graduate of the Rhode Island School of Design

CREATIVE & ANALYTICAL THINKING

CREATIVE THINKING
Right Brain
Traditional training of designers and artists

Explore
Generate ideas
Imagine possibilities
Re-frame
Build ideas
"Yes and what if?
Try different perspectives
Imagine extreme cases
Increase ideas

DIVERGENT THINKING

CONVERGENT THINKING

Make decisions
Clarify
Make sense
Decrease
Create hierarchies
Refine
Cluster
Connect
Test

ANALYTICAL THINKING
Left Brain
Traditional training of managers and
engineers

Source: Adapted from the center for Creative Emergence

DIVERGENT AND CONVERGENT THINKING

DIVERGENT THINKING

Divergent thinking is a thought process or method used to generate creative ideas by exploring many possible solutions.Divergent thinking occurs in a spontaneous, free-flowing, 'non-linear' manner.

During the divergent phase of design the designer creates a number of choices. The goal of this approach is to analyze alternative approaches to test for the most stable solution. Divergent thinking is what we do when we do not know the answer, when we do not know the next step. Divergent thinking is followed by convergent thinking, in which a designer assesses, judges, and strengthens those options.

A study by J.A. Horne,and a separate study by Ullrich Wagner and his colleagues in Germany have shown that sleep loss can significantly impair creativity.

Left brain people are said to be more rational, analytic, and controlling, while right brain people are said to be more intuitive, creative, emotionally expressive and spontaneous. There is evidence that regions of the right hemisphere have a role in what is called divergent thinking and creative problem solving.

CONVERGENT THINKING

The psychologist J.P. Guilford first coined the terms convergent thinking and divergent thinking in 1956. The design process is a series of divergent and convergent phases.

This process is systematic and linear. This kind of thinking is particularly appropriate in science, engineering, maths and technology. Convergent thinking is opposite from divergent thinking in which a person generates many unique, design solutions to a design problem.

The design process is a series of divergent and convergent phases. During the divergent phase of design the designer creates a number of choices. The goal of this approach is to analyze alternative approaches to test for the most stable solution. Divergent thinking is what we do when we do not know the answer, when we do not know the next step. Divergent thinking is followed by convergent thinking, in which a designer assesses, judges, and strengthens those options.

On his account, the left brain is specialized for convergent thinking, while the right brain is specialized for divergent thinking.

TRIANGULATION

Denzin (1978) defined triangulation as "the combination of methodologies in the study of the same phenomenon".

Triangulation is a powerful technique that facilitates validation of data through cross verification from two or more sources. to see if the different methods give similar findings. The researcher looks for patterns to develop or support an interpretation by comparing the results from two or more different research methods. The researcher looks for patterns of convergence to develop or corroborate an overall interpretation One example of triangulation is to compare observed behavior with the responses of a survey.

The term originates in surveying land where triangulation is used to create a map.

Denzin (1978) and Patton (1999) identify four types of triangulation:

1. Methods triangulation - checking out the consistency of findings generated by different data collection methods.
   - It is common to have qualitative and quantitative data in a study.
   - These elucidate complementary aspects of the same phenomenon.
   - Often the points were these data diverge are of great interest to the qualiatitive researcher and provide the most insights.

2. Triangulation of sources - examining the consistency of different data sources from within the same method. For example:
   - at different points in time
   - in public vs. private settings
   - comparing people with different view points.

3. Analyst Triangulation - using multiple analyst to review findings or using multiple observers and analysts
   - This can provide a check on selective perception and illuminate blind spots in an interpretive analysis.
   - The goal is not to seek consensus, but to understand multiple ways of seeing the data.
   - Theory/perspective triangulation - using multiple theoretical perspectives to examine and interpret the data. *Source: qualres.org*

THINKING STYLES

Business Thinking	Design Thinking	Creative Thinking
Left Brain	Uses whole brain	Right brain
Rational	Both rational and intuitive	Emotional
Structured	Structured and intuitive	Intuitive
Analytical	Analytical and creative	Creative
Likes well defined problems	Works with defined and ill defined problems	Works with ill defined complex problems
Does not tolerate mistakes	Mistakes are inexpensive and a learning opportunity	Tolerates mistakes during exploration
Analyse then decide	Prototype test decide	Ideate then decide
Focuses on parts of a problem	Focuses on parts and on whole iteratively	Holistic diffuse focus
Convergent	Convergent and divergent	Divergent
Vertical	Vertical and Lateral	Lateral
Objective	Objective and subjective	Subjective
Linear	Linear and associative	Associative
Yes but	Yes and yes but	Yes and
Verbal and mathematical	Visual, verbal mathematical	Visual
The answer	Explores, tests iterates	One possible answer
Judges	Withholds judgment until tested	Withhold judgment
Probability	Possibility and probability	Possibility
Improve	Improves and innovates	Innovate
Sequential	Sequential and synthesizing	Synthesizing
Analyze and evaluate	Imagines, synthesizes and tests	Imagine
Parts and details	Parts and the whole	Whole and big picture
Observe	Imagines and observes	Imagine
Numeric models	Numeric and experiential	Experiential models
Phases	Phases and dimesions	Dimensions
Sort and separate	Sorts infuses and blends	Infuse and blend
Independent	Independent and interdependent	Interdependent
Successive	Successive and simultaneous	Simultaneous
Safe	takes risk but minimizes the cost of failure	Risk taking
Knows	Believes, tests and knows	Believes

PRIMARY RESEARCH

WHAT

Primary research also called as field research involves collecting data first hand created during the time of the study. Primary research methods can include, including questionnaires and interviews and direct observations.

WHO INVENTED IT?

Robert W. Bruere of the Bureau of Industrial Research 1921 may have been the first to use the term

WHY

You can collect this information yourself. There may be no secondary research available. It may be more reliable than secondary research. It may be more up to date than secondary research

CHALLENGES

1. May be more expensive than secondary research.
2. Information may become obsolete
3. Large sample can be time-consuming

HOW

Methods such as:
1. Diaries
2. E-mail
3. Interviews
4. News footage
5. Photographs
6. Raw research data
7. Questionnaires
8. Observation

RESOURCES

Camera
Notebook
Pens
Digital Voice recorder
Diaries
E-mail

SECONDARY RESEARCH

WHAT
Research data that conveys the opinions and experiences of others. Secondary research is as the most widely used method of data collection. Secondary research accesses information that is already gathered from primary research.

WHO INVENTED IT?
Robert W. Bruere of the US Bureau of Industrial Research 1921 may have been the first to use the term secondary research.

WHY
1. Ease of access
2. Low cost
3. May be the only resource, for example historical documents
4. Only way to examine large scale trends

CHALLENGES
1. Possible bias in sources
2. May be out of date
3. May not be aligned with research goals
4. Lack of consistency of perspective
5. Biases and inaccuracies
6. Data affected by context of its collection

HOW
1. Define goals.
2. Define the context of the problem to be researched.
3. Frame research questions.
4. Develop procedure.
5. Select and retrieve appropriate data.
6. Proceed with analysis and interpretation
7. Compare your findings and interpretations with other relevant studies.
8. Draw conclusions.

RESOURCES
Books
Internet
On-line search engines
Magazines
E-books
Bibliographies
Biographical works
Commentaries, criticisms
Dictionaries, Encyclopedias
Histories;
Newspaper articles
Website

Steps in the research process - University of Hong Kong, http://www4.caes.hku.hk/acadgrammar/report/resProc/steps.htm (accessed July 03, 2016).

CHAPTER SUMMARY

Design thinking can be applied to
1. Products
2. Services
3. Experiences
4. Interactions
5. Systems

Design thinking is useful when you have:
1. A poorly defined problem.
2. A lack of information.
3. A changing context or environment
4. It should result in consistently innovative solutions.

Design thinkers seek to balance
1. Business.
2. Appropriate application of technology
3. Empathy with people.
4. Environmental consideration.

Abductie reasoning is the core thinking approach in design thinking.With abductive reasoning, unlike deductive reasoning, the premises do not guarantee the conclusion. Abductive reasoning can be understood as "inference to the best explanation" Abductive thinking allows designers to find new solutions in ambiguous, changing situations. It is the thinking approach necessary for innovation. Abductive thinking finds solutions by creating prototypes and testing and improving the designs.

ANYONE CAN USE DESIGN THINKING

REVIEW QUESTIONS

1. What are four reasons to use design thinking?
2. What type of design areas can you apply design thinking to?
3. How many people is optimum for a Design Thinking team?
4. Who can use design thinking?
5. What are the four stages of the design ladder?
6. Which design thinking is being used?
7. What are the nine attributes of design thinking?
8. What are four benefits of design thinking?
9. Name four typical types of design stakeholders.
10. What are "wicked problems".
11. What are the three factors that design thinking balances to seek a design solution?
12. What is convergent thinking?
13. What is divergent thinking?
14. What is abductive reasoning?
15. Name five basic human needs.

Design thinking can be described as a discipline that uses the designer's sensibility and methods to match people's needs with what is technologically feasible and what a viable business strategy can convert into customer value and market opportunity."

Tim Brown IDEO

05

APPLYING DESIGN THINKING IN YOUR ORGANIZATION

APPLYING DESIGN THINKING IN YOUR ORGANIZATION

Here is some advice to help you introduce design thinking into your organization.

FIRST LEARN ABOUT DESIGN THINKING

Arrange for several leaders in your organization representing the main cross functional departments to do a substantial course in design thinking together.

GIVE EVERYONE A VOICE

Invite everyone to a series of meetings to discuss the introduction of design thinking in your organization.

LEAVE YOUR OFFICE AND EXPERIENCE YOUR CUSTOMER'S WORLD

Listen to your customers to understand what their problems are. Don't solve the wrong problem because you are remote from your customers.

COLLABORATE

Define the goals together as a team withe everyone's input.

WHEN YOU HAVE A PRELIMINARY DESIGN GET FEEDBACK FROM CUSTOMERS

Share the designs as widely as possible with internal and external stakeholders and invite their feedback.

LEARN BY FAILING AND TRYING AGAIN

It is important to understand that if you are trying new things not every design idea will be successful. Use the methods in this book to minimize the cost of inevitable failures during prototyping and experimentation.

INVITE ALL DEPARTMENTS AND EXTERNAL STAKEHOLDERS TO YOUR WORKSHOPS

You should have one team composed of stakeholders with different perspectives.

CHOOSE THE TEAM MEMBERS IN YOUR GROUPS CAREFULLY

Four to eight people is an optimum groups size. If you have a larger group break it into smaller groups. Consider diversity and personalities when forming groups. Don't put several people with strong personalities into the same group. Create space for discussion where people feel safe.

START WITH A MANAGEABLE DESIGN PROBLEM

Run several small scale design thinking exercises before taking on a larger project.

> **"** *Because we invested in building innovation skills into our employee base, we are not only a design-thinking company, we're a design-driven company. Meaning, we're going from creating a culture of design thinking to building a practice of design doing, where we relentlessly focus on nailing the end-to-end customer experience. This means that before anything gets built, the whole team engineers, designers, marketers, product managers are interfacing with the customers to ensure they understand the problem well, and together, they design the best solution.* **"**

Suzanne Pellican,
Vice President Of Experience
Design at Intuit

EMPATHY IS NOT THE SAME AS HUMAN FACTORS

Design thinking tools consider not just usability issues but also people's emotions, attitudes and values.

THINK HOLISTICALLY

Analytical thinkers can sometimes focus on the small details rather than the bigger issues. The process of design thinking will allow you to consider both. Think about design problems systematically, products, services and experiences. How are these things connected?

LOOK FOR UNMET NEEDS

Consider and involve the customer at every stage.

BUILD UP YOUR SOLUTIONS

Prototype early and learn and build up the solution by asking questions.

CONSIDER THE CUSTOMER JOURNEY NOT JUST THE DESTINATION

The customer journey consists of a series of micro experiences. Design thinking tools allow you to consider and optimize each of these moments to build a better overall experience.

BUILD A WAR ROOM

Place all your research and all your ideas on a wall where everyone in tour team can see it and think about and discuss what may be relevant and connected. Keep one space dedicated to your project for the entire project. Pick a large space with natural light.

GIVE PEOPLE DEFINED TIMES FOR EACH ACTIVITY

Don't give them too much time. 30 minutes to generate ideas, 15 minutes for discussion, 20 minutes to make a fast prototype. Keep the activities focused and moving. Have clear goals with each team activity.

MODERATING GROUPS

If you have the resources have two people moderate. The moderator can facilitate the group discussion while the assistant moderator takes notes and looks after the video camera. Moderating a team activity successfully is a skill which is partly a talent and partly developed through experience

ROLES

1. **Facilitator.** The person who moderates the group.
2. **Recorder.** The person who captures the discussion
3. **Data Analyst.** The person who analyses the notes or recordings of the group discussion
4. **Report Writer.** The person who writes executive summary of the discussions.
5. **Scheduler.** The person who schedules the meetings.
6. **Manager of Logistics.** The person who manages the room and other logistics.

ASSISTANT MODERATOR

1. Manages the equipment and refreshments
2. Arranges the room
3. Manages video camera and other recording equipment
4. Welcome participants as they arrive
5. Has good listening skills
6. Has good observation skills
7. Has good writing skills
8. Acts as an observer, not as a participant
9. Can remain impartial
10. Take notes throughout the discussion
11. Notes should include observation of non verbal behavior
12. Notes should include themes, follow-up questions, body language, confusion, nonverbal communication, facial expressions, gestures, signs of agreement, disagreement, frustration, and participant concerns, head nods, physical excitement, eye contact between participants, or other clues that would indicate level of support, or interest.
13. Notes follow-up questions that could be asked
14. The assistant moderator does not get involved in the group discussion.
15. Assistant should be a "fly on the wall" and only observe the discussion.
16. Should not influence the discussion by their presence.
17. Provides participant seating arrangement
18. Operate recording equipment
19. Do not participate in the discussion
20. Ask questions when invited
21. Give an oral summary
22. Debrief with moderator
23. Give feedback on analysis and reports
24. Can Handle logistics & refreshments
25. Collects signed informed

consent (if required)
26. Takes careful notes
27. Does not participate in discussion
28. Can recap major themes at end of discussion (used before wrap-up question)
29. Monitors recording equipment
30. Liaison between moderator and observers/clients
31. Debriefs with moderator after session
32. Assist with analysis and reports
33. Not required, but can be useful in some situations
34. Balance out strengths/weaknesses in moderator
35. Use to match moderator (without being obvious)
36. Switch leading discussion (good for long or intense discussions)
37. Support leader by keeping on track, recapping major themes, etc.

MODERATOR

Select the moderator carefully.
1. Someone who is culturally like the people participating.
2. Manages the process of the discussion rather than the content.
3. The moderator should have empathy with the group but also have authority.
4. Does not need to be an expert on the discussion topic but needs to show skill in managing discussion.
5. Should not share views,
6. Probes the discussion points to reveal the underlying

reasons.
7. Should 'Warm up' the group to help participants feel at ease,
8. Should develop rapport with the participants.
9. Needs to stay focused.
10. Should ensure that all participants are involved in the discussion.
11. Spends the minimum time necessary speaking.
12. Should not show bias.
13. Directs the discussion in real time
14. Follows the question guide.
15. Have an assistant to take notes and manage equipment and time.
16. The moderator should have good listening skills.
17. Use an experienced moderator.
18. A person able to create and manage a friendly and participatory environment.
19. Use pauses and probes
20. Probes:
    - "Can you explain further?"
    - "Could you give an example?"
21. Manage participants
    - Verbal and nonverbal communication
    - Short responses
    - Experts
    - Dominant talkers
    - Shy participants
    - Ramblers
22. The moderator should remain neutral and not show extremes of emotion such as surprise or anger during the conversation.
23. The moderator should be

diplomatic.
24. The moderator prevents some participants from dominating the conversation.
25. Can clearly summarize and articulate the views expressed.
26. Do not let the discussion stray into areas that are emotionally charged.

GROUP BEHAVIOR

CONSTRUCTIVE GROUP BEHAVIORS

1. Collaboration. The members of the group are interested and listen to the views of other participants.
2. Clarifies points. Asks questions in order to understand ambiguous ideas.
3. Inspires the group with relevant examples.
4. Harmony. Works to build group cohesion
5. Takes risks. Sticks their neck out to achieve the goals.
6. Reviews the process so they properly understand the goals, agenda, schedule and other points.

DESTRUCTIVE GROUP BEHAVIORS

1. Dominates the conversation with one opinion.
2. Wants to move on before the discussion is complete.
3. Does not participate in the discussion.
4. Discounts or ridicules other opinions.
5. Loses focus on the topic or goals.
6. Blocks unfamiliar ideas.
7. Self-Appointed Experts. Thank them for their knowledge and redirect question to the rest of the group
8. If one participant tries to dominate the session, the moderator should invite each person to speak in turn.
9. Shy Participants. Respect someone's right to be quiet, but do give them a chance to share their ideas
10. Ramblers. Intervene, politely summarize and refocus. Use nonverbal cues; redirect.
11. Side Talking/Side Conversation. Remind the group or individuals about the ground rules

INTERVENTION

A good moderator will intervene in the discussion when necessary Establish the ground rules in the introduction. This gives common expectations so that the team members can help manage people who exhibit destructive behavior. Listen to each person's ideas. Ask questions to clarify points or reveal bias.

1. Break a large group into smaller groups of 4 people.
2. Remind the group of the task.
3. Take a break and speak to a disruptive participant about the goals.
4. Break the problem into smaller parts.

5. Define a way to make decisions.
6. List the areas of agreement.

TIME MANAGEMENT

It is important that time is planned and managed well so that all the topics can be covered.

KEEP THE INTERVIEW ON TRACK

One of the important skills for a moderator is to steer the conversation back to the topic if it strays and to move on from question to question.

USE THE INTERVIEW GUIDE

Write in prompts to remind you to check the time at several points during the discussion.

DO NOT RUSH THE DISCUSSION

Interrupt as little as possible and not rush them.
1. Have good listening skills
2. Have good observation skills
3. Have good speaking skills
4. Can foster open and honest dialogue among diverse groups and individuals
5. Can remain impartial (i.e., do not give her/his opinions about topics, because
6. this can influence what people say)
7. Can encourage participation when someone is reluctant to speak up
8. Can manage participants who dominate the conversation
9. Are sensitive to gender and cultural issues
10. Are sensitive to differences in power among and within groups.

MODERATOR SKILLS
BUILDING RAPPORT

1. Building rapport is important.
2. Show the participants that you are a person who is prepared and willing to listen to them with interest.
3. Let the participants know that you are there to learn from them.
4. It is important to present yourself as someone facilitating rather than as a friend.
5. Balance rapport and professionalism.

LISTENING TO INTERVIEW AND DISCUSSION PARTICIPANTS

The guidelines to conducting interviews and discussions are closely connected to building rapport. These guidelines include communicating to the participants that you are listening to them as well as these strategies: neutrality, silence, and guidance.
1. Show participants that you are listening.
2. Stay neutral.
3. You want to gather information that is as honest as possible.
4. Silence is acceptable. Asking clarifying questions. Guidance includes giving
5. Monitor time carefully.

TEAMS

History demonstrates that great projects and products are often the result of great teams.

start with a clear goal and a serious deadline.
A hot group is infused with pur pose and personality.
If you distrust the power of teamwork, consider this fact. Even the most legendary individual inventor is often a team in disguise. In six scant years, for example, Thomas Edison generated an astounding four hundred patents. producing: innovations in the teleg:raPh. telephone phonograph, and lightbulb-with the help of a fourteen-man team. As Francis Jehl, Edison's longtime assistant, explained, "Edison is in reality a collective noun and means the work of many men."
The same is often true of the lone genius within a company. We've found that loners are so caught up in their idea that they are reluctant to let it go, much less allow it to be experimented with and improved upon.

The right kinds of specializations are important, but specialization is not the only quality required. To make a Design Thinking project successful, we need T-shaped people. T-shaped people have a depth of knowledge and experience in their own fields but they can also reach out and connect with others horizontally and create meaningful collaborations.

DIVERSITY

Each team member brings their unique perspective and expertise to the team, widening the range of possible outcomes. If you want a breakthrough idea, you're more likely to get it with a diverse team. Diverse teams see the same problem from many angles. They have a better understanding of any given situation and generate more ideas, making them more effective problem solvers. While it takes effort to harness and align such different perspectives, it's at the intersection of our differences that our most meaningful breakthroughs emerge.
Cross-disciplinary teams will provide you with the best results. Teams may consist of people unfamiliar with each other, with external members brought on board either as specialists or facilitators depending on the availability of skills.

Identity
1. Age and ability
2. Gender identity
3. Race and ethnicity

Experience
1. Cultural upbringing
2. Geography
3. Language

Expertise
1. Education
2. Organization
3. Discipline

The right kinds of specializations are important, but specialization is not the only quality required. To make a Design Thinking project successful, we need T-shaped people. T-shaped people have a depth of knowledge and experience in their own fields but they can also reach out and connect with others horizontally and create meaningful collaborations.

A Design Thinking team should ideally be a cross/multi-disciplinary team consisting of a mix of specializations, including specialists associated with problem areas contributing but not dominating the journey. While specialists may have vast knowledge on a technical level, they are working towards solutions targeted towards non-specialists in many cases and require outside perspectives in addition to what they already know.

EMPOWERMENT

empowered teams have the agency to make everyday operational decisions on their own. They're equipped with the expertise and authority to deliver outcomes without relying on others for leadership or technical support. By pushing operational decisions down to the lowest level, we give our teams the ability to achieve the rapid iteration our users and clients demand.

.

For each Hill team, you'll also want to assign core leadership team. These leadership teams should be composed of functional leads from each discipline. Grant them the authority to handle day-to-day triage on the team and hold them accountable for achieving their assigned outcome.

FACILITATION

1. Start with a clear goal and a serious deadline
2. Explain the five stages in the Design Thinking Process.
3. Provide your team members with printed out models of the Design Thinking process and modes to help them understand and recognize the benefits of the Design Thinking work process.
4. Explain how Design Thinking builds a third way – combining the analytical and information-driven approach of science with the holistic, empathic and creative ways of thinking in ethnography and design.
5. Explain that there are lots of proven methods
6. Knowing the background and underlying structure will help your team members to feel safer as they know that there's a solid background
7. Bring together a diverse team with different thinking styles and specializations.
8. Develop an innovative team culture, which embraces inclusiveness, collaboration, and co-creation.
9. Level the playing field to allow for a diverse set of

perspectives to influence the process.

10. Ensure the right person is in charge.
11. Break the ice with some creative exercises to loosen things up.

One must still have chaos in oneself to be able to give birth to a dancing star."

Friedrich Nietzsche

CONFLICT

1. Instinct often leads us to avoid conflict and seek out those who think alike.
2. Diversity invites conflict—and conflict is a wellspring of creativity. Harnessing this creativity requires us to listen to understand, not just argue, with those who may disagree. When you listening to understand, you uncover brand new ideas together and contribute to a more open and collaborative culture.
3. At minimum, critical team conversations should include representatives from every discipline affected. It would be unwise for engineering to make time-line decision without engaging offering management in a conversation, or for product designers to make brand decisions without consulting the marketing team.

4. This kind of radical collaboration requires a foundation of trust, respect, and shared ownership across the team.

Edison is in reality a collective noun and means the work of many men."

Francis Jehl
Edison's assistant

Which skills and mindsets do team players need for a design project?

1. *Openness: smell, touch, taste, observe, listen, ask, hear, feel...*
2. *Able to find the right questions.*
3. *Able to suspend your judgment and look beyond the obvious.*
4. *Able to understand different points of view,*
5. *See the big picture and create common grounds.*
6. *Able to imagine and build solutions haven't seen before.*
7. *Able to create cheap experiments in order*

to learn faster."

D Osterwalder,
Anna Ploskonos

COLLECTIVE INTELLIGENCE

Collective intelligence is a type of shared intelligence that emerges from the collaboration of many people and is expressed in consensus decision making.

Collective intelligence requires four conditions to exist.
1. Openness Sharing ideas, experiences and perspectives
2. Peering people are free to share and build on each other's ideas freely.
3. Sharing knowledge, experiences ideas.
4. Acting globally

CROSS POLLINATION

Use cross disciplinary teams. Share ideas and observations with people outside your organization. Travel can help your design team get exposed to new ways of looking at a problem. Read outside your field. Talk to people in different industries.

CROSS DISCIPLINARY COLLABORATION

Depending on the design challenge, design teams can engage anthropologists, engineers, educators, doctors, lawyers, scientists, etc. in the innovative problem solving process.

Design Thinking draws on the creative and analytical talents of the design team to reframe the design problem as needed. Design Thinking combines the wisdom and skills of many disciplines working in close and flexible collaboration. Each team member requires disciplinary empathy allowing them to work collaboratively with other discipline members.

EVERYONE CAN CONTRIBUTE

The Design Thinking process involves many stakeholders in working together to find a balanced design solution. The designer is a member of the orchestra. The customer is involved throughout the design process and works with the design team to communicate their needs and desires and to help generate design solutions that are relevant to them.

The process is one of co-creation and the designer is a listener and a facilitator. Everyone adds value to the design. Design thinking is not just for professional designers. Everyone can contribute. Many schools are now teaching Design Thinking to children as an approach that can be applied to life.

INNOVATION DIAGNOSTIC

An innovation diagnostic is an evaluation of an organization's innovation capabilities. It reviews practices by stakeholders which may help or hinder innovation. An innovation diagnostic is the first step in preparing and implementing a strategy to create an organizational culture that supports innovation. Before you start to research your audience. Do a diagnostic of your organization to find out how you can remove obstacles to innovation. Do an exercise to help get your team up to speed working.

WHY

1. It helps organizations develop sustainable competitive advantage
2. Helps identify innovation opportunities
3. Helps develop innovation strategy.
4. Evaluate structural weaknesses in an organization that may be limiting that organization's ability to innovate.

HOW

An innovation diagnostic reviews organizational and stakeholder practices using both qualitative and quantitative methods including

1. The design and development process
2. Strategic practices and planning
3. The ability of an organization to monitor and respond to relevant trends.
4. Technologies
5. Organizational flexibility
6. Ability to innovate repeatedly and consistently

SELF-QUESTIONNAIRE

Answer these questions and score yourself to understand to what degree your organization OR your client's organization supports innovation.

DOES MANAGEMENT COMMUNICATE THE NEED FOR INNOVATION?

1. There is no innovation in our organization
2. Innovation is not a high priority
3. Our managers sometimes talk about innovation
4. Our managers discuss innovation but not why it is needed
5. Managers regularly state the compelling need for

innovation

WHAT IS YOUR ORGANIZATIONAL STRATEGY?

1. We make low cost goods or services
2. Efficient operations
3. We are a customer focused organization
4. Fast Follower
5. Market leaders

IS THE BUSINESS THAT YOU ARE IN UNDERSTOOD BY EMPLOYEES?

1. We are not sure
2. We may get different answers from different managers
3. The definition changes in
4. We have some clarity
5. We are very clear about what business we are in

IS YOUR ORGANIZATION INNOVATIVE?

1. No
2. Probably not
3. We would like to be
4. There is some innovation
5. We are clearly an innovative organization

HOW DOES YOUR COMPANY INNOVATE?

1. We react to market forces without innovation
2. There is little innovation
3. We do some incremental innovation
4. We do mainly incremental innovation but would like to do some breakthrough innovation

5. We manage a portfolio of incremental and more substantial innovation and manage risks

DOES YOUR MANAGEMENT SUPPORT INNOVATION?

1. No
2. No resources are allocated to innovation
3. Some resources are allocated
4. We have some resources and some involvement from managers in innovation
5. We have clearly defined resources allocated and senior management is actively involved in planning and managing innovation

DO YOU HAVE CROSS-DISCIPLINARY DESIGN TEAMS?

1. Never
2. Rarely
3. Sometimes
4. Usually
5. Always

DO YOU USE OUTSIDE EXPERTS TO ASSIST IN YOUR INNOVATION PROCESS?

1. Never
2. Rarely
3. Sometimes
4. Usually
5. Always

HOW OFTEN DOES YOUR ORGANIZATION ENGAGE CUSTOMERS TO IDENTIFY THEIR UNMET NEEDS?

1. Never
2. Rarely

3. Sometimes
4. Usually
5. Always

HOW WOULD YOU DEFINE THE RISK TOLERANCE AT YOUR COMPANY?

1. We don't take any risks
2. We rarely take risks
3. Sometimes we take substantial risks
4. We manage our risk portfolio actively and take big risks when appropriate.

HOW ARE NEW IDEAS RECEIVED IN YOUR ORGANIZATION?

1. We fire people with new ideas
2. We rarely adopt new ideas
3. We sometimes adopt new ideas but they are mostly not considered
4. We regularly consider new ideas
5. We actively generate and adopt new ideas

Add up the numbers of each answer that you selected and calculate a total for all the questions

HOW WELL DID YOU SCORE?

SCORE 0 TO 15

Small changes, low investment, low risk and low return. Changing the color of a product. Every company is capable of gaining this score.

SCORE 15 TO 25

You are integrating new features into existing products and services to build differentiated versions of the same new product to sell to various demographic groups. These new features require what can be considered a medium level of investment and risk. Advancement of existing products, medium investment and risk, medium payoff.

SCORE 25 TO 35

INNOVATIVE ORGANIZATION

The second level is the beginning of large financial and product risk, but it is also where the rewards are potentially larger. This level also requires that the business devote resources to monitoring progress and actively assessing risk throughout the development process. Evolutionary products, large investment, medium risk, some payoff.

SCORE 35 TO 45

HIGHLY INNOVATIVE ORGANIZATION

Your company has the innovation skills to change people's lives. Companies in this category have the highest level of risks you are creating products or services that are new and original. Revolutionary products and services, large investment, big risks high payoff

CHAPTER SUMMARY

INTRODUCING DESIGN THINKING AT YOUR ORGANIZATION

1. First learn about design thinking
2. Give everyone a voice
3. Leave your office and immerse yourself in your customer's world
4. Collaborate
5. When you have a preliminary design get feedback from customers
6. Do not punish failure
7. Invite all departments and external stakeholders to your workshops
8. Choose the team members in your groups carefully
9. Start with a manageable design problem
10. Empathy is not the same as human factors
11. Think holistically
12. Look for unmet needs
13. Build up your solutions
14. Consider the customer journey not just the destination
15. Build a war room
16. Give people defined times for each activity

MODERATING ROLES

1. Facilitator. The person who moderates the group.
2. Recorder. The person who captures the discussion
3. Data Analyst – the person who analyses the notes or recordings of the group discussion
4. Report Writer. The person who writes executive summary of the discussions.
5. Scheduler. The person who schedules the meetings.
6. Manager of Logistics. The person who manages the room and other logistics.
7. Assistant moderator. Person who schedules the meetings.

REVIEW QUESTIONS

1. What should you do before you introduce design thinking to your organization?
2. How should you deal with failures on the project?
3. What should you look for from customers as part of the design thinking process?
4. What is a war room?
5. What are four roles when moderating groups?
6. What does an assistant moderator do?
7. What are four things you should consider when selecting a moderator?
8. What are four constructive group behaviors?
9. What are four destructive group behaviors?
10. How can a moderator build rapport with the group?
11. What is an innovation diagnostic?
12. When could you use an innovation diagnostic?

06

DESIGN SPRINTS

GOOGLE SPRINT

THE COMPANY
Industry
- Internet
- Software
- Computer hardware

Founded
September 4, 1998
Menlo Park, California, U.S.

Founders
Larry Page
Sergey Brin
Headquarters
Googleplex, Mountain View,
California, U.S.[3]

Key people
Sundar Pichai (CEO)
Ruth Porat (CFO)

Revenue
89.46 billion USD
December 31, 2016

Number of employees
73,992[4] (2017)

Parent
Alphabet Inc. (2015–present)

Source:Wikipedia

WHAT IS A GOOGLE SPRINT?

A design sprint is a five-phase framework based on design thinking that helps answer critical business questions through rapid prototyping and user testing. Sprints let your team reach clearly defined goals and deliverables and gain key learnings, quickly. The process helps spark innovation, encourage user-centered thinking, align your team under a shared vision, and get you to product launch faster.

Source: Adapted from Google design sprint kit

WHO INVENTED THE GOOGLE SPRINT?

❝

The Google design sprint framework was created in 2010. Over the years, working alongside Google Ventures, we've studied and tested 300 different business strategy, design thinking, and user research methods from places like IDEO and Stanford d.school. We took the most effective ones and evolved them, arranging them into a framework that supports both divergent thinking (creative brainstorming that results in multiple possible solutions) and convergent thinking (using defined, logical steps to arrive at one solution). The methodology has evolved over time and continues to be refined and tested."

THE PROCESS

UNDERSTAND
1. Who are the users?
2. What are their needs?
3. What is the context?
4. Competitor review.
5. Formulate strategy.
6. invite stakeholders to share: business goals, technology capability, and user need. The goal of this stage is to expand the understanding of the product/project.

DIVERGE
1. Envision
2. Develop lots of solutions.
3. Ideate
4. Anything is possible. Participants in the Design Sprint should explore all possible solutions to their user's problems.

DECIDE
1. Choose the best idea.
2. Storyboard the idea.
3. Review all ideas and vote for the best options

PROTOTYPE
1. Build something quick and dirty to show the users.
2. Focus on usability not making it beautiful.
3. Prototype and test without investing a lot of time, money, or resources.

VALIDATE
1. Show the prototype to real users outside the organization.
2. Learn what doesn't work.

WHEN TO USE IT
1. You can use it at the beginning of a project to define what your product is offering, or to create a shared vision;
2. When you are stuck and not making progress.
3. To speed up the design development process.

BENEFITS OF RUNNING A DESIGN SPRINT
1. It is fast.
2. User validation;
3. It is agile.
4. Collaboration tool.

1. WRITE A SPRINT BRIEF
What are the
1. Deliverables
2. Resources
3. Logistics

4. Time line?

THE SPRINT CHALLENGE:
Validate the challenge with managers. Common challenges are to redesign something, to explore something to improve something.

2. DO RESEARCH
Audit existing research. Review the gaps. Fill the gaps with new research.
Types of Research:
1. Participant Observation
2. User Interviews
3. Surveys
4. Diary Study

3. ASSEMBLE YOUR TEAM
A cross-functional team. The ideal working size is 5-7 people per team. If you have a larger group you can break up into smaller sub-groups.

The team usually include a UX designer, a User Researcher, a Product Manager, an Engineer and or a UX writer. Ideally you would also have any key leadership who have the ability to reject the outcomes of the sprint.

Roles
Sprinters Knowledge Experts User Research Participants Sprint Master Stakeholder

4. LIGHTNING TALKS
Invite team members and external stakeholders and experts to be speakers. Having key team members hold lightning talks Include the users.

5. CREATE A DECK

6. FIND THE SPACE

7. GET SUPPLIES
1. Sharpies
2. Post-it-notes
3. Paper
4. Tape
5. Scissors
6. 2 Large white boards
7. White-board markers

8. CHOOSE AN ICE BREAKER

9. SET THE STAGE
Lay out the ground rules and schedule.

GROUND RULES:
1. Ask for people's full attention
2. Laptops closed until they are needed
3. Mobile phones away

SPRINT BRIEF
1. What is the sprint challenge?
2. Something real
3. Something that there is a defined need for
4. Something inspiring.
5. Something clear and concise
6. Includes a time frame.

DELIVERABLES:
1. List the deliverables

LOGISTICS
1. Who?
2. When?
3. Where?
4. Who is the Sprint Master?

GOOGLE SPRINT SCHEDULE-3 DAYS

DAY 1
9:00   Arrival and registration
9:30   Introductions
- Overview of Sprint and rules (5 min)
- Ice Breaker/Meet the team (15 min)
- Introduce the Challenge (3 min)
- Directions for HMW's (2 min)

10:00   Understand: Lightning Talks
Business Perspective - Voice of the User -
User Journeys and Pain Points
Design Evolution/Product
Audit Competitive Landscape
Technological Opportunities
11:30   HMW's and Affinity Mapping
12:30   Lunch
13:30   Review existing User Journey Map out an improved journey Success Metrics
14:30   Comparable Problem in Parallel Space
15:00   Boot up
Crazy 8's Sketching
16:00   Solution Sketch
17:00   End of day Team check-in

DAY 2
9:30   Open with a Daily Inspiration & Recap of Day 1
Present Solution Sketches
Assumptions & Sprint Questions
Vote and decide on what to Prototype
11:00   Begin Storyboarding
12:30   Lunch
13:30   Finish Storyboard
14:00   Assign tasks & Start Prototyping
17:00   End of Day Check in

DAY 3
9:30   Opening with Recap of Day 2
Finish Prototype
Prepare script for user sessions
12:15   Lunch
13:00   User testing session 1/2
13:45   Debrief
14:00   User testing session 3/4
14:45   Debrief
15:00   User testing session 4/5
16:00   Debrief & Share back to the team
17:00   End of Sprint

Source: Adapted from Google design sprint kit. https://designsprintkit. INithgcogle.com'planning/

DESIGN AND ARCHITECTURAL CHARRETTES

WHAT

A design charrette is a collaborative design workshop usually held over one day or several days. Charrettes are a fast way of generating ideas while involving diverse stakeholders in your decision process. Charrettes have many different structures and often involve multiple sessions. The group divides into smaller groups. The smaller groups present to the larger group

WHO INVENTED IT?

The French word, "charrette" spelled with two r's means "cart" This use of the term is said to originate from the Ecole des Beaux Arts in Paris during the 19th century, where a cart, collected final drawings while students finished their work.

"

During the 19th century, students of l'Ecole des Beaux Arts in Paris would ride in the cart sent to retrieve their final art and architecture projects. While en route to the school in the cart, students frantically

worked together to complete or improve these projects. The meaning of the word has evolved to imply a collection of ideas or a session of intense brainstorming. An intensely focused activity intended to build consensus among participants, develop specific design goals and solutions for a project, and motivate participants and stakeholders to be committed to reaching those goals. Participants represent all those who can influence the project design decisions."

Source: A Handbook for Planning And Conducting Charrettes for High-Performance Projects August 2003 • NREL/ BK-710-33425 Gail Lindsey, FAIA Design Harmony, Inc. Joel Ann Todd Environmental Consultant Sheila J. Hayter National Renewable Energy Laboratory.

WHY
1. Fast and inexpensive.
2. Increased probability of implementation.
3. Stakeholders can share information.
4. Promotes trust.
5. Charrettes can save time and

money and improve project performance.
6. Provide a voice for diverse stakeholders.
7. Begin planning the project.
8. Motivate participants.
9. identify key short-, mid-, and long-term priority goals.
10. Save time and money by soliciting ideas, issues, and concerns for the project design to help avoid later iterative redesign activities.
11. Establish a multidisciplinary team that can set and agree on common project goals.
12. Develop early consensus on project design priorities.
13. Provide early understanding of the potential impact of various design strategies.
14. Identify project strategies to explore with their associated costs, time considerations, and needed expertise to eliminate costly "surprises" later in the design and construction processes.
15. Identify partners that can provide expertise.
16. Set a project schedule and budget that all team members feel comfortable following.

Source: A Handbook for Planning And Conducting Charrettes for High-Performance Projects August 2003 • NREL/ BK-710-33425 Gail Lindsey, FAIA Design Harmony, Inc. Joel Ann Todd Environmental Consultant Sheila J. Hayter National Renewable Energy Laboratory.

HOW

1. Definition of the problems.
2. Analysis of the problem
3. Alternative possible solutions.
4. Small groups to clarify issues.
5. Research
6. Concepts for alternative solutions.
7. Presentation and analysis of final proposal.
8. Discussion and conscensus.

CHALLENGES
1. Managing workflow can be challenging.
2. Stakeholders may have conflicting visions.

WHEN
1. Define intent
2. Know context and user
3. Frame insights
4. Explore concepts
5. Make Plans

RESOURCES
Large space
Tables
Chairs
White-boards
Dry-erase markers
Camera
Post-it-notes

1.5 DAY MINI-CHARRETTE

HOW DAY 1
1. Evening mixer night before event.
2. Breakfast 30 minutes.
3. Moderator introduces participants expectations and goals.
4. Overview of project 30 mins
5. Break 15 minutes
6. Individual presenters present

information about aspects of
project 1 hour
7. Lunch 1 hour
8. Further presentations related
to aspects of project 1 hour
9. Question and answer session
15 minutes
10. Multi disciplinary breakout
groups 2.5 hours
11. Group size preferred 4 to 8
participants.
12. Groups explore strategies
and issues.
13. Groups present strategies
and goals to larger group
30 minutes. Larger group
brainstorms goals.
14. Site tour 1 hour - for urban or
architectural projects.

DAY 2
1. Breakfast 30 minutes
2. Review of Day 1, 30 minutes.
3. Breakout groups explore
concept solutions as sketches
2.5 hours.
4. Groups present to larger
group 30 minutes.
5. Larger group brainstorms
next steps 30 minutes
6. Lunch 1 hour

2.0 DAY DESIGN CHARRETTE

HOW
DAY 1
1. Evening mixer night before
event.
2. Breakfast 30 minutes.
3. Moderator introduces
participants expectations
and goals.
4. Overview of project 30 mins
5. Break 15 minutes

6. Individual presenters present
information about aspects of
project 1 hour
7. Lunch 1 hour
8. Further presentations related
to aspects of project 1 hour
9. Question and answer session
15 minutes
10. Multi disciplinary breakout
groups 2.5 hours
11. Group size preferred 4 to 8
participants.
12. Groups explore strategies
and issues.
13. Groups present strategies
and goals to larger group
30 minutes. Larger group
brainstorms goals.
14. Site tour 1 hour - for urban or
architectural projects.

DAY 2
1. Breakfast 30 minutes
2. Review of Day 1, 30 minutes.
3. Breakout groups explore
concept solutions as sketches
2.5 hours.
4. Groups present to larger
group 30 minutes.
5. Lunch 1 hour
6. Breakout groups refine
concept solutions as sketches
2.5 hours.
7. Groups present to larger
group 30 minutes.
8. Wrap up and next steps 30
minutes

4.0 DAY ARCHITECTURAL CHARRETTE

HOW TO USE THIS METHOD
1. Define problem
2. Public meeting Vision
3. Brief group

4. Alternative concepts generated
5. Small groups work
6. Small groups present.
7. Whole group discussion
8. Public meeting input
9. Preferred concepts developed
10. Small groups work
11. Small groups present.
12. Whole group discussion
13. Open house review
14. Small groups work
15. Small groups present.
16. Whole group discussion
17. Further plan development.
18. Public meeting confirmation of final design.

0.5 DAY PRODUCT CHARRETTE

HOW

1. Choose a problem to focus on.
2. Select moderator.
3. Select and invite participants.
4. Team size of 4 to 20 participants preferred representing users, managers, design and diverse group of stakeholders.
5. Break down teams over 8 into smaller groups of 4 or 5 participants.
6. Brief participants in advance by e-mail.
7. Allow one hour per problem
8. Use creative space such as a room with a large table and whiteboard.
9. Brief participants allow 15 minutes to one hour for individual concept exploration.
10. Give participants a goal such as 5 concepts.
11. Output can be sketches or simple models using materials such as cardboard or toy construction kits.
12. Each individual presents their concepts to the group.
13. In larger groups each group of 4 can select 3 favored ideas in smaller group to present to larger group. Each smaller group selects a presenter.
14. Moderator and group can evaluate the concepts using a list of heuristics.
15. Put all the sketches or post it notes on a wall.
16. Group concepts into categories of related ideas.
17. Dot vote each category to determine best ideas to carry forward.
18. Do another round of sketching focusing of 3 best ideas.
19. Iterate this process as many times as necessary.
20. Record session with digital images.
21. Smaller group can take preferred ideas and develop them after the session.

0.5 DAY UX CHARRETTE

HOW

1. Choose a problem to focus on.
2. Select moderator.
3. Select and invite participants.
4. Team size of 4 to 20 participants preferred

representing users, managers, design and diverse group of stakeholders.
5. Break down teams over 8 into smaller groups of 4 or 5 participants.
6. Brief participants in advance by email.
7. Allow one hour per problem
8. Use creative space such as a room with a large table and white board.
9. Brief participants allow 15 minutes to one hour for individual concept exploration.
10. Give participants a goal such as 5 concepts.
11. Output can be wireframes or storyboards.
12. Each individual presents their concepts to the group.
13. Moderator and group can evaluate the concepts using a list of heuristics.
14. Put all the sketches or post it notes on a wall.
15. Group concepts into categories of related ideas.
16. Dot vote each category to determine best ideas to carry forward.
17. Do another round of sketching focusing of 3 best ideas.
18. Iterate this process as many times as necessary.
19. Record session with digital images.
20. Smaller group can take preferred ideas and develop them after the session.

APPLICATION OF MULTIPLE
DESIGN SPRINTS ON A PROJECT

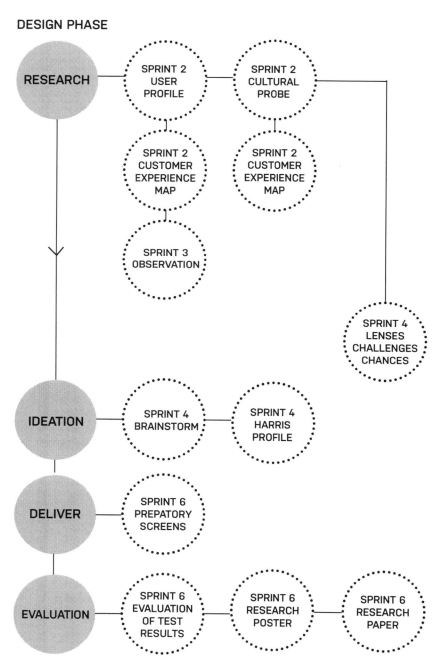

DESIGN PHASE

CHAPTER SUMMARY

A design sprint is a five-phase framework based on design thinking that helps answer critical business questions through rapid prototyping and user testing. Sprints let your team reach clearly defined goals and deliverables and gain key learnings, quickly. The process helps spark innovation, encourage user-centered thinking, align your team under a shared vision, and get you to product launch faster.

The French word, "charrette" spelled with two r's means "cart" This use of the term is said to originate from the Ecole des Beaux Arts in Paris during the 19th century, where a cart, collected final drawings while students finished their work.

Charrettes can save time and money and improve project performance.

REVIEW QUESTIONS

1. What is a design sprint?
2. How long is a design sprint?
3. How big is a design sprint team?
4. What are four benefits of a design sprint?
5. What areas of design use design sprints?
6. What is a charrette?
7. Where was the term charrette first used?
8. What is the literal translation into English of the word charrette?
9. What types of stakeholders are typically involved in charrettes?
10. What does Google use design sprints to design?

07
PROCESS
OVERVIEW

DESIGN THINKING PROCESS OVERVIEW

PLANNING
What are our goals?
1. Meet with key stakeholders to set vision and intent.
2. Assemble a diverse team
3. Explore scenarios of user experience.
4. Document stakeholders performance requirements
5. Define the group of people or user segment that you are designing for. What is their gender, age, and income range? Where do they live? What is their culture?
6. Define your scope and constraints
7. Identify a needs that you are addressing. Identify a problem that you are solving.
8. Identify opportunities.
9. Consider project risks
10. What are the main hurdles that your team will need to overcome?
11. What information do you not have that will be necessary for a successful design?
12. Create a budget and plan.
13. Create tasks and deliverables.
14. Create a schedule.

DISCOVER EMPATHIZE
What does the research tell us?
1. Identify what you know and what you need to know.
2. Document a research plan
3. Benchmark competitive products.
4. Explore the context of use
5. Understand the risks.
6. Observe and interview individuals, groups, experts.
7. Develop design strategy.
8. Undertake qualitative, quantitative, primary and secondary research.
9. Talk to vendors.

SYNTHESIZE
What have we learned?
1. Review the research.
2. Make sense out of the research.
3. Develop insights.
4. Cluster insights.
5. Create a hierarchy.

HAVE A UNIQUE POINT OF VIEW
What is the design brief?

IDEATE
How is this for as a starting point?
1. Brainstorm
2. Define the most promising ideas.
3. Refine the ideas.
4. Establish key differentiation of your ideas.
5. Investigate existing

DESIGN THINKING PROCESS

PLAN	WARM UP	DISCOVER/ RESEARCH/ EMPATHIZE	SYNTHESIS/ POINT OF VIEW

ACTIVITIES

PLAN Develop a deep understanding of your customers or end users through engaging them and using ethnographic research methods	**WARM UP** Some fast exercises to get the team up to speed and working productively with each other.	**DISCOVER** Develop a deep understanding of your customers or end users through engaging them and using ethnographic research methods	**SYNTHESIS POV** Make sense from your research. What are the insights? What is connected? What are the unmet needs and of your audience? What problem will you solve?

METHODS

Innovation Diagnostic Smart goals Blue ocean Goal grid Reframing matrix Warming up WWWWWH Interviews Observation Focus Groups Day in the life Perceptual maps	Desert island Milestones Common Ground Hobby Barney Difficult experience Observe Compliment Free association Zombie cats	Interviews Observation Focus Groups Day in the life Diary studies Benchmarking Competitors Camera journals Empathy tools	Affinity diagrams 5 Whys Mind Maps Personas Perceptual Maps Empathy Maps Experience Maps Service blueprints

OUTPUT

PROJECT PLAN	PRODUCTIVE TEAM	RESEARCH DATA/NEEDS FINDING	UNIQUE INSIGHTS/ POINT OF VIEW

MAKING CHOICES	MAKING CHOICES	CREATING CHOICES	MAKING CHOICES

DIVERGENT OR CONVERGENT

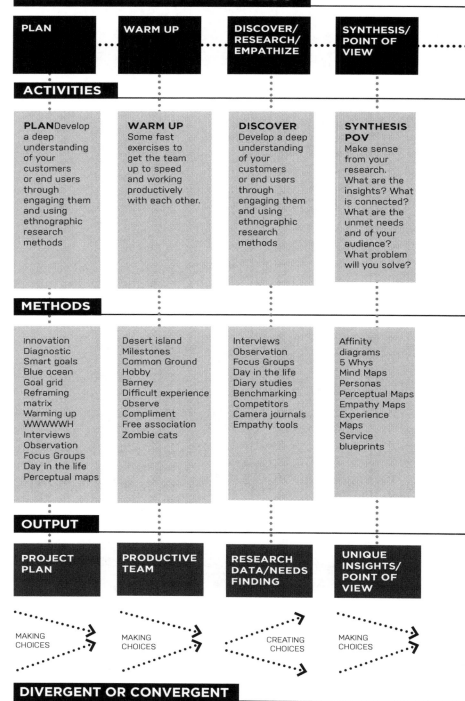

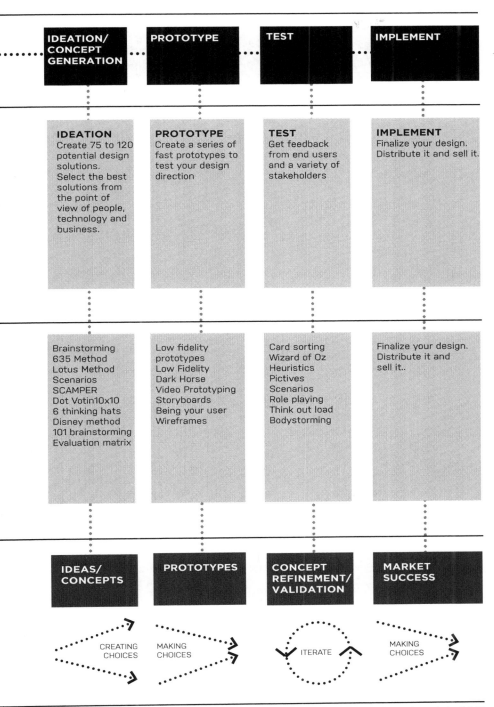

IDEATION/ CONCEPT GENERATION	PROTOTYPE	TEST	IMPLEMENT

IDEATION
Create 75 to 120 potential design solutions.
Select the best solutions from the point of view of people, technology and business.

PROTOTYPE
Create a series of fast prototypes to test your design direction

TEST
Get feedback from end users and a variety of stakeholders

IMPLEMENT
Finalize your design. Distribute it and sell it.

Brainstorming
635 Method
Lotus Method
Scenarios
SCAMPER
Dot Votin10x10
6 thinking hats
Disney method
101 brainstorming
Evaluation matrix

Low fidelity prototypes
Low Fidelity
Dark Horse
Video Prototyping
Storyboards
Being your user
Wireframes

Card sorting
Wizard of Oz
Heuristics
Pictives
Scenarios
Role playing
Think out load
Bodystorming

Finalize your design. Distribute it and sell it..

IDEAS/ CONCEPTS	PROTOTYPES	CONCEPT REFINEMENT/ VALIDATION	MARKET SUCCESS

CREATING CHOICES

MAKING CHOICES

ITERATE

MAKING CHOICES

Copyright © Robert Curedale 2017

intellectual property.

PROTOTYPE TEST ITERATE
How could we make it better?
1. Make your favored ideas physical.
2. Create low-fidelity prototypes from inexpensive available materials.
3. Develop question guides
4. Develop test plan.
5. Test prototypes with stakeholders.
6. Get feedback from people.
7. Refine the prototypes.
8. Test again.
9. Build in the feedback.
10. Refine again.
11. Continue iteration until design works.
12. When you are confident that your idea works make a prototype that looks and works like a production product.

IMPLEMENT AND DELIVER
Let's make it. Let's sell it.
1. Create your proposed production design.
2. Test and evaluate.
3. Review objectives.
4. Manufacture your first samples.
5. Review first production samples and refine.
6. Launch.
7. Obtain user feedback
8. Conduct field studies.
9. Define the vision for the next product or service.

CHAPTER SUMMARY

The stages of the design thinking process are:

1. Planning
2. Discovery
3. Synthesis
4. Point of view
5. Ideate
6. Prototype and test
7. Implement and deliver.

REVIEW QUESTIONS

1. What are the stages of the design thinking process?
2. Describe the activities in each stage of the design thinking process.
3. What are four methods that can be used in the discovery phase?
4. What are four methods that can be used in the Synthesis phase?
5. What are four methods that can be used in ideation?
6. What are four prototyping methods used in design thinking?
7. What is iteration?
8. What phase of the process is idea brainstorming usually done?
9. What are four things you do during the planning phase?
10. During which phase do you benchmark competitors?

08

THE PLANNING PHASE

THE PLANNING PHASE

One of the most critical factors for project's success is having a good project plan. The plan is a roadmap for the project. The project plan is created by the project manager and team through a process of discussion with stakeholders. Good planning is most important when the task is complex.

HOW TO PLAN A DESIGN PROJECT

1. Study the project assignment carefully.
2. Think about what your final result will look like. Will it be a physical product, or a digital one? Will it involve a service?
3. Select you team.
4. Define a project space.
5. Define team roles and responsibilities.
6. Develop project vision and strategy
7. Determine the activities
8. How team makes decisions
9. Develop team communication plan.
10. Develop a scope statement.
11. Plan the activities in time.
12. Identify important milestones
13. Determine and identify interdependencies between your activities
14. Develop the schedule and cost estimates.
15. Create management plan.
16. Analyze project risks.
17. Develop reporting plan.
18. Plan how project information will be stored and how different stakeholders can access it.

SMART GOALS
Your project goals should be:

1. **Specific.** The desired results should be formulated specifically, and not too generally.
2. **Measurable.** The results should be formulated in a way that it is possible to measure whether they have been completed. 'I will produce minimal 5 ideas' instead of 'I will produce several ideas'
3. **Acceptable.** Be sure that there is consensus (among the members of your team or with your tutor) on what the results entail or try to accomplish.
4. **Realistic.** Results should be feasible; they can be completed in the scope of the project.
5. **Time.** When will the results will be completed

Source: wikid.eu

SERVICE PLANNING & STRATEGY

HOW CUSTOMERS SELECT A SERVICE PROVIDER

1. Price
2. Availability
3. Speed
4. Convenience
5. Dependability
6. Personalization
7. Quality
8. Reputation
9. Safety

GUIDELINES FOR SUCCESSFUL SERVICE DESIGN

1. Define the service package in detail
2. Focus on customer's perspective (expectation and perception)
3. Recognize that designer's perspective is different from the customer's perspective
4. Define quality for tangible and intangibles elements
5. Make sure that recruitment, training, and rewards are consistent with service expectations
6. Establish procedures to handle exceptions
7. Establish systems to monitor service

SERVICE STRATEGY DIFFERENTIATION

Differentiation in service means being unique in brand image, technology use, features, or reputation for customer service.

1. Making the intangible tangible
2. Customizing the standard product
3. Reducing perceived risk
4. Giving attention to personnel training
5. Controlling quality

SERVICE STRATEGY FOCUS

Cost and differentiation for a particular target market, not the entire market.

1. Buyer Group
2. Service Offered
3. Geographic Region

SERVICE PACKAGE

1. Spaces
2. Physical evidence
3. Web sites
4. Channels
5. Touchpoints
6. Back stage interactions
7. Front stage interactions
8. Support processes
9. Information
10. Training

Source: NKFUST

ACTION PLAN

WHAT

An action plan is a document that summarizes action items, due dates and other related information.

WHY
1. To focus team effort.
2. To monitor progress towards a goal.

CHALLENGES
1. Start with the final delivery date required and work backward to assign delivery dates for individual actions.
2. The action plan should be displayed where it is accessed by all team members.

HOW
1. Team brainstorms actions needed to reach a goal and the times when each action should be completed.
2. The moderator draws the action plan on a White-board.
3. Team members are assigned responsibility for individual actions.
4. The plan is reviewed by the team to ensure that there are no conflicts.
5. The plan is signed off on by the team.
6. The plan is posted in the project room for future reference.

BHAG

WHAT

BHAG stands for Big Hairy Audacious Goal. It is a type of goal that is bigger than a usual mission statement.

Some examples of BHAGs are:
1. Google BHAG is to make all digital information in the world accessible to people everywhere
2. Nokia BHAG is to connect one billion people to the Internet. For the first time.

WHO INVENTED IT?
J Collins and J Porras,1996

WHY
1. Bold visions stimulate bold steps
2. BHAGs encourage you to set your sights high and long term.

HOW
1. It needs to motivate people and get them excited.
2. It shouldn't be in your comfort zone
3. It should take a herculean effort to achieve.
4. It should not be possible to achieve with incremental change.
5. BHAGs have time frames of 10-30 years.
6. The BHAG should be aligned to the organization's core values.

BLUE OCEAN

CREATE AND CAPTURE NEW DEMAND.

Know that "customers dispositions are complex, counter-intuitive and paradoxical" (Liebl 2011) and that new demand, respectively new market proposals, can only be created when recognizing the complex and interdependent dimensions of what actually constitutes or may constitute value to them. Acknowledge that user-centric means orienting the user. That is, people only know what they want, once they are confronted with it, what requires to develop a permanent learning attitude, whose main subgoal is to develop anticipative empathy in interaction. Accept furthermore that new customers and new value in the prospective services-era will only be created in permanent exchange with users themselves and other key interpreters

ALIGN THE WHOLE SYSTEM OF A FIRM'S ACTIVITIES

Use the above gained knowledge about max. value creation for the user vs. max. value capture for the company to find the best sustainable equilibrium by knowing how to construct business models which are capable of profitably delivering an optimum of the value, i.e. the conceived ideal customer experiences. Those configurations should facilitate and take advantage of the permanent value negotiation processes in terms of a SD-logic.

CREATE UNCONTESTED MARKET SPACE.

Disrupt existing or create new markets by crafting the above-stated business models and services in such a way that they provide superior value relatively to the next best alternative solutions. This can be done by either solving or creating new customer functions (i.e. latent needs), or by addressing existing ones differently. Alternative solutions needn't be just technology, but may also be new (service-supported) practices or reinterpretations of old industry paradigms into a new meaning.

Source: Kim & Mauborgne 2005, p.18

BOUNDARY EXAMINATION

WHAT
Boundary examination is a way of refining the definition of a problem.

WHO INVENTED IT?
Rickards (1974) and VanGundy (1981) Edward de Bono 1982

WHY
1. The boundary setting may be part of the problem.
2. The boundary may reflect biases.

HOW
1. Define the problem with a written statement.
2. Divide the group into small groups of 2 or 3 people.

3. Have each group underline key words
4. Analyze each key word for underlying assumptions.
5. Have each group examine each key word for hidden assumptions. Have each small group share their assumptions.
6. Having explored how the particular choice of key words affects the meaning of the statement, see if the small groups can redefine the problem in a better way.
7. Redefine the problem boundary by substituting new keywords.
8. Come to an agreement about the definition of the problem.

Source:: af-methods.org

BUSINESS MODEL CANVAS

WHAT
The Business Model Canvas is a strategic tool for developing new or documenting existing business models. The headings can be drawn on a white board so groups of people can jointly discuss business model elements with post-it notes or board markers. It is a hands-on tool that fosters understanding, discussion, creativity, and analysis.

WHO INVENTED IT?
The Business Model Canvas was initially proposed by Alexander Oswalder in 2008.

WHY
1. It is a hands-on tool that fosters understanding, discussion, creativity, and analysis.
2. It assists firms in aligning their activities by illustrating potential trade-offs.

HOW
1. Start by creating a set of personas, humanized portraits of the customers, be the buyer and/or user of the company's product.
2. Personas are average customers in each segment not extreme or fringe end users. Which customers are you creating value for? Who is your most important customer?
3. What is the value proposition for each persona?
4. What are the customer's current alternatives?
5. Your Value Proposition has to be better than those alternatives for you to get traction so your customer will buy your product or service.
6. What core value do you deliver to the customer?
7. Which customer needs are you satisfying?
8. Once you get a list of value propositions, sort them in order of most to least compelling and record them

GOOGLE TRENDS SHOWS THE GROWING POPULARITY OF THE BUSINESS MODEL CANVASS

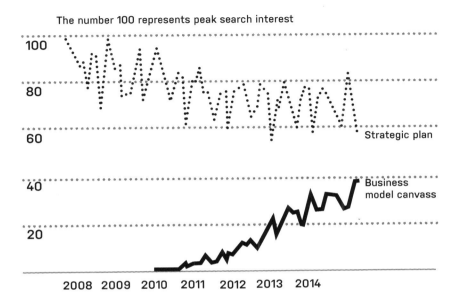

The number 100 represents peak search interest

Strategic plan

Business model canvass

2008 2009 2010 2011 2012 2013 2014

Source: Adapted from http://blog.strategyzer.com

on the Canvas.

9. What channels will you use to reach your customers? For example on line, in-store.

10. Storyboard the customer journey to think through customer relationships and segments.

11. Revenue streams. For what value are your customers willing to pay? What and how do they recently pay? How would they prefer to pay? For example in one payment or by subscription. How much does each revenue stream contribute to the overall revenues?

12. Activities. What key

activities does your value proposition require? What activities are most important in distribution channels, customer relationships, and revenue stream?

13. Resources. What resources does your value proposition require? What resources are most important in distribution channels, customer relationships, and revenue stream?

14. Partners. Who are your key partners? What are the motivations for the partnerships?

15. Costs. What are the greatest costs in running your

business
16. Which resources or activities are most expensive?

COMMUNICATIONS MAP

WHY
1. It may show where there are gaps in communications which need to be addressed.
2. Assists the project team to provide timely and accurate information to all stakeholders.

HOW
1. Identify stakeholders.
2. Identify those with whom your organization needs the strongest communications linkages to.
3. Identify Internal audiences.
4. Identify peer groups or sub groups.

5. Identify strong and frequent communications
6. Identify connectivity needed to a primary audience.
7. Identify less frequent communications connectivity needed to a secondary audience.
8. Determine stakeholder needs.
9. Identify communication methods and resources.
10. Prepare communication map showing existing and desired communications.
11. Distribute to stakeholders for feedback.
12. Incorporate Changes
13. Implement.

GOAL GRID

"The Goals Grid provides a structure for analyzing patterns in goals and objectives and for detecting potential conflict with the goals and objectives of others."

Fred Nickols

WHO INVENTED IT?
Ray Forbes, John Arnold and Fred Nickols 1992

GOAL GRID

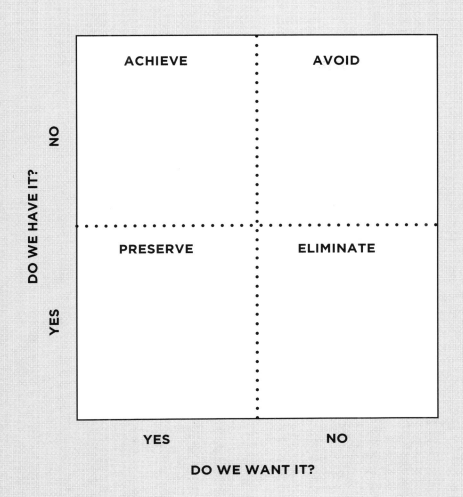

WHY

A goal grid is a method for clarifying goals.

HOW

1. The team brainstorms a list of goals.
2. The moderator asks the team these questions:
   - "Do we have it?"
   - "Do we want it?"
   - "What are we trying to achieve?"
   - "What are we trying to preserve?"
   - "What are we trying to avoid?"
   - "What are we trying to eliminate?"

OBJECTIVES TREE

WHAT

Objective Tree method, also known as decision tree, is a tool for clarifying the goals of a project. The objective tree method shows a structured hierarchy of goals with higher level goals branching into related groups of sub-goals.

WHY

1. An objectives tree is a visual way of mapping your design objectives so that you can discuss and refine them.
2. Building a better understanding of the project objectives.
3. It is a way to refine vague goals into more concrete and achievable goals.
4. Build stakeholder consensus.

5. Identify potential constraints

HOW

1. Prepare a list of design objectives. This can be done by brainstorming within your team and by undertaking research of your customers, their needs, and desires. You can also create an objective tree from a problem tree. Convert each problem into an objective.
2. Create lists of higher and lower level objectives by sorting your original list of objectives. This can be done with an affinity diagram.
3. Create an objectives tree, showing hierarchical relationships and interconnections
4. Place each task in a box.
5. Connect the boxes with lines that show associations.
6. Iterate.
7. Make the task descriptions as simple as possible

RESOURCES

White-board
Dry-erase markers.

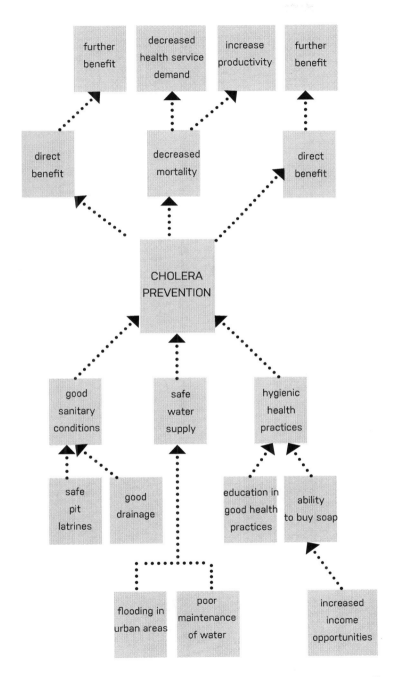

Source: Adapted from Water Supply and Sanitation Collaborative Council

PROBLEM TREE

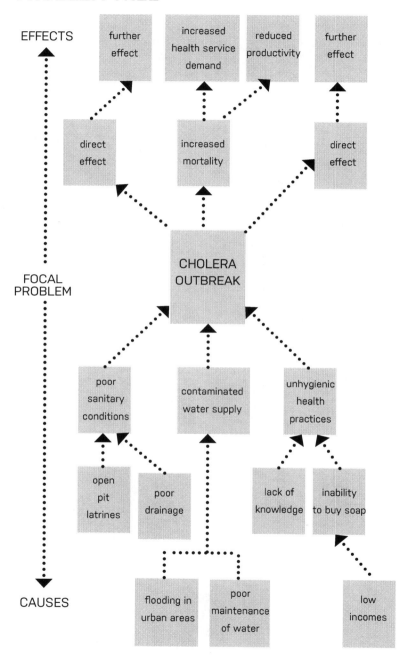

EFFECTS

further effect

increased health service demand

reduced productivity

further effect

direct effect

increased mortality

direct effect

FOCAL PROBLEM

CHOLERA OUTBREAK

poor sanitary conditions

contaminated water supply

unhygienic health practices

open pit latrines

poor drainage

lack of knowledge

inability to buy soap

CAUSES

flooding in urban areas

poor maintenance of water

low incomes

Source: Water Supply and Sanitation Collaborative Council

PROBLEM TREE

WHAT
A problem tree provides an overview of all the known causes and effect to an identified problem. The problem tree shows a structured hierarchy of problems being addressed with higher level problems branching into related groups of sub-problems.

WHY
1. A problem tree is a visual way of mapping your design problems so that you can discuss and refine them.
2. It is useful for identify a core problem and it's and root causes
3. It is a way to refine vague problems into more concrete and solvable goals.
4. The problem tree often helps build a shared sense of understanding, purpose and action.
5. Address the real needs of the users.
6. Helps the planning of a project.
7. Provides a guide as to the complexity of a problem by identifying the multiple causes

HOW
1. Imagine a large tree with its trunk, branches, leaves, primary and secondary roots.
2. Write the main problem/ concern in the center of a large flip chart (trunk).
3. Add the causes of the main problem onto the chart below the main problem, with arrows leading to the problem (primary roots).
4. For each of the causes, write the factors that lead to them, again using arrows to show how each one contributes (secondary roots).
5. Draw arrows leading upwards from the main problem to the various effects/consequences of that problem (branches).
6. For each of these effects, add any further effects/ consequences (leaves).
7. All stakeholders should participate. This way, their commitment can be obtained and, they will have understanding for the choices made.

Source: Adapted from Water Supply and Sanitation Collaborative CouncilAdvocacy A PLP Toolkit Final Draft 231013

REFRAMING A PROBLEM

WHAT
This method helps develop innovative solutions with a number of questions.

WHO INVENTED IT?
Tudor Rickards 1974 Manchester Business School

CREATING A PROBLEM TREE

STEP 3   Secondary effect

What is the effect of this?

STEP 2   Immediate effect

What is the effect of this?

STEP 1   CORE PROBLEM

What is the cause of this?

STEP 2   Immediate cause

What is the cause of this?

STEP 3   Secondary cause

WHY
To create different perspectives and new ideas.

RESOURCES
1. Pen
2. Paper
3. White-board
4. Dry Erase markers

HOW
Define the problem that you would like to address.

Complete these sentences while considering your problem. There is more than one way of looking at a problem. You could also define this problem in another way as."
1. "The underlying reason for the problem is."
2. "I think that the best solution is."
3. "If I could break all laws of reality I would try to solve it by."
4. "You could compare this problem to the problem of" "Another, different way of thinking about it is"

Design Thinking is an approach to problem finding that assumes people often work on the wrong problems and can leverage and improve outcomes by reframing them."

Bill Burnett
Director Stanford Design

REFRAMING MATRIX

WHAT
The reframing matrix is a method of approaching a problem by imagining the perspectives of a number of different frames and exploring the possible solutions that they might suggest.

WHO INVENTED IT?
Michael Morgan 1993

WHY
1. This is a method for assisting in empathy which is an important factor in gaining acceptance and creating successful design.

CHALLENGES
The reframing is not done with stakeholders present or in context so may be subjective

HOW
1. Define a problem.
2. On a White-board or paper draw a large square and divide it into four quadrants.
3. Select 4 different perspectives to approach the problem. They could be four professions or four people or four other perspectives that are important for your problem.

REFRAMING MATRIX

PRODUCT PERSPECTIVE	PLANNING PERSPECTIVE
1. Is there something wrong with the product or service? 2. Is it priced correctly? 3. How well does it serve the market? 4. Is it reliable?	Are our business plans, marketing plans, or strategy at fault? 1. Could we improve these?
POTENTIAL PERSPECTIVE	**PEOPLE PERSPECTIVE**
1. How would we increase sales? 2. If we were to seriously increase our targets or our production volumes, what would happen with this problem?	1. What are the people impacts and people implications of the problem? 2. What do people involved with the problem think? 3. Why are customers not buying the product?

4. With your team brainstorm a number of questions that you believe are important from the perspectives that you have selected.
5. The moderator writes the questions in the relevant quadrants of the matrix.
6. The group discusses each of these questions.
7. The answers are recorded and the perspectives are incorporated into the considerations for design solutions.

SWOT ANALYSIS

WHAT

SWOT Analysis is a useful technique for understanding your strengths and weaknesses, and for identifying both the opportunities open to you and the threats you face.

SWOT may be used to
- Understand your business better
- Address weaknesses
- Deter threats
- Capitalize on opportunities
- Take advantage of your strengths
- Develop business goals and strategies for achieving them.

WHO INVENTED IT?
Albert Humphrey 1965 Stanford University

WHY
1. SWOT analysis can help you uncover opportunities that you can exploit.
2. SWOT analysis does not require special training or technical expertise.
3. Multi-level analysis
4. Access to a range of data from multiple sources enhances decision-making.
5. You can analysis both your own organization, product or service as well as those of competitors.
6. Helps develop a strategy of differentiation.
7. SWOT can be performed in a short time.

CHALLENGES
1. No Weighting Factors
2. SWOT may be subjective.
3. May reflect the bias of individuals who participate in the brainstorming session.
4. May be hrd to identify threats.

HOW
1. Explain basic rules of brainstorming.
2. Ask questions related to the four SWOT categories.
3. Address Opportunities category after the other three categories.
4. Record answers on a white board or video
5. Categorize ideas into groups

SAMPLE SWOT QUESTIONS

STRENGTHS
1. Advantages of proposition
2. Capabilities
3. Competitive advantages
4. Marketing - reach, distribution
5. Innovative aspects
6. Location and geographical
7. Price, value, quality?
8. Accreditation, certifications
9. Unique selling proposition
10. Human resources
11. Experience,
12. Assets
13. Return on investment
14. Processes, IT, communications
15. Cultural, attitudinal, behavioral

WEAKNESSES
1. Value of proposition
2. Things we cannot do.
3. Things we are not good at
4. Perceptions of brand
5. Financial
6. Own known vulnerabilities
7. Time scales, deadlines and pressures
8. Reliability of data, plan predictability
9. Morale, commitment, leadership
10. Accreditation,
11. Cash flow, start-up cash-drain
12. Continuity, supply chain robustness

OPPORTUNITIES
13. Market developments
14. Competitors' vulnerabilities
15. New USP's
16. Tactics - surprise, major contracts
17. Business and product development
18. Information and research
19. Partnerships, agencies, distribution
20. Industrial trends
21. Technologies
22. Innovations
23. Global changes
24. Market opportunities
25. Specialized market niches
26. New exports or imports
27. Volumes, production, economies
28. Seasonal, weather, fashion influences

THREATS
1. Political effects
2. Legislative effects
3. Obstacles faced
4. Insurmountable weaknesses
5. Environmental effects
6. IT developments
7. Competitor intentions
8. Loss of key staff
9. Sustainable financial backing
10. Market demand
11. New technologies, services, ideas
12. Regulations
13. Internal processes

EXERCISE ONE
BUSINESS MODEL CANVAS

BACKGROUND
Are you trying to find innovative ways of creating new services to replace old, outdated ones? The Business Model Canvas is a strategic template for developing new or documenting existing business and service models. It is a visual template with elements describing a firm's or product's value proposition, infrastructure, customers, and finances. A business model describes the rationale of how an organization creates, delivers, and captures value.

GOALS
To become more aware of critical aspects that supports a successful service business.

TASKS
Choose a service which you have consumed recently and set out the underlying business model. What value is created, for whom, by whom and how? Using the BM Canvas framework, map out how this value is created and 'revenue stream', cost structure, key networks, channels, etc.

1. How have business models for your chosen product/service changed? How might they change?
2. How could you provide different ways of creating the core value proposition?
3. Could you expand the target market segments?
4. Which alternative channels might you use to reach them?
5. Which new technologies might you take advantage of?
6. Which new partners might you link with to improve the way value is delivered?
7. How can you cut costs?
8. How can you add or improve revenue streams?
9. Using these and other questions develop business model which represents a better way of delivering value.
10. Prepare a short presentation to 'pitch' your idea to potential investors.

DELIVERABLES
One Business Model Canvas of a service that you have used recently. One business model canvas of an improved service

CONSIDER THE FOLLOWING WHEN BUILDING YOUR CANVAS

Customer Segments
1. Who is the customer?
2. What's the customer's major need?
3. What job has he to accomplish?
4. Total Market Size
5. Segmented by
• Geography
• Age

- Income
- Substitutes
6. Competitors
7. Early Adopters
8. Large base free / small base?
9. Niche community
10. Mass Market
11. Regulatory approved product

Value Proposition
1. New product category
2. Enabler
3. Highest performance
4. Ease of Customization
5. Best design
6. Disruptive price
7. Cost Reduction
8. Risk Reduction
9. Convenience
10. Security and Safety
11. Rent or lease instead of sell
12. Disruption in service
13. What unmet need is being met?

Channels
1. How you contact the customer?
2. Deliver the value
3. Promote the value
4. Improve his position and more...
5. Direct versus Indirect
6. Direct:
7. Sales force
8. Web
9. Retail store
10. Key Opinion Leaders
11. Mobile platforms
12. Direct email/mailings/spam
13. Franchise
14. Indirect:
15. Partner
16. OEM / embedded
17. Wholesale
18. Mobile Platform

Customer Relationships
1. What is the customer retaining cost?
2. Acquisition cost?
3. Lifetime value?
4. Switching cost?
5. Personal assistance
6. Dedicated Personal Assistance
7. Self Service
8. Automated Services
9. Communities Co-creation
10. Revenue Streams
11. Why will customers pay?
12. How do customers prefer to pay?
13. What's the retail price?
14. How many paying customers will there be?

Key Resources
1. What resources required to maintain the business model
2. Platform
3. Infrastructure
4. People
5. Skills
6. Patents
7. Specialists
8. Content creators
9. Software rights
10. Content library

Key Activities
1. Key activities necessary to build the business
2. Maintaining the platform
3. Brand building
4. Reducing cost
5. Innovation
6. R&D
7. Selling
8. Regulatory approval
9. Reimbursement

10. Signing Partnerships
11. Acquiring content
12. Logistics
13. Managing inventory
14. Managing a community/ niche

Key Partners

1. Strategic partner needed to build the business model
2. Outsourced coding
3. Reseller of software
4. Social Networking Platform
5. OEM Partner
6. Research Partner
7. Manufacturer
8. Retailer
9. Crowds

Cost Structure

1. How much it costs to build the business
2. Fixed Costs
3. Variable costs
4. Engineering cost
5. Manufacturing cost
6. HR cost
7. Revenue Streams
8. Channels
9. Customer Relationships Customer Segments
10. Key Partners Key Activities Value Propositions
11. Key Resources
12. Cost Structure

CHAPTER SUMMARY

One of the most critical factors for project's success is having a good project plan. The plan is a road-map for the project. The project plan is created by the project manager and team through a process of discussion with stakeholders. Good planning is most important when the task is complex.

Planning
1. Study the project assignment carefully.
2. Think about what your final result will look like. Will it be a physical product, or a digital one? Will it involve a service?
3. Select you team.
4. Define a project space.
5. Define team roles and responsibilities.
6. Develop project vision and strategy.
7. Determine the activities.
8. How team makes decisions
9. Develop team. communication plan.
10. Develop a scope statement.
11. Plan the activities in time.
12. Identify important milestones.
13. Determine and identify interdependencies.
14. Develop the schedule and cost estimates.
15. Create management plan.
16. Analyze project risks.
17. Develop reporting plan.
18. Plan how project information will be stored and how different stakeholders can access it.

Smart goals
Your project goals should be:
1. Specific.
2. Measurable.
3. Acceptable.
4. Realistic.
5. Time. When will the results will be completed?

REVIEW QUESTIONS

1. What are four possible activities during the planning phase?
2. What are the five things to consider when framing SMART goals?
3. What is a business model canvas?
4. Who invented the Business model Canvas?
5. Name 14 elements to consider when building a Business Model Canvas.
6. What is reframing.
7. What do the letters in SWOT stand for?
8. What is the purpose of SWOT analysis?

09
WARMING UP

INTRODUCTION

WHAT

A warming up exercise is a short exercise at the beginning of a design project that helps the design team work productively together as quickly as possible. The duration of an icebreaker is usually less than 30 minutes.

They are an important component of collaborative or team-based design. The Design Thinking approach recognizes the value of designers working productively as members of a diverse cross-disciplinary team with managers, engineers, marketers and other professionals.

There are many types of warming up exercises. On following pages are some exercises that have been used for design teams. Select an exercise that suites the culture of your group.

RESOURCES ALL EXERCISES

White-board
Dry erase markers
Large table
Chairs
Post-it-notes
A comfortable space
Digital camera

POINTS TO CONSIDER

1. Be aware of time constraints.
2. Should limit the time to 15 to 30 minutes
3. Make it simple
4. It should be fun
5. You should be creative
6. Be enthusiastic
7. If something isn't working, move on.
8. Consider your audience
9. Chairs can be arranged in a circle to help participants read body language.
10. Select exercises appropriate for your group.

WHY USE WARMING UP EXERCISES?

When a designer works with others in a new team it is important that the group works as quickly as possible in a creative constructive dialogue. An icebreaker is a way for team members to quickly start working effectively together. Ice-breakers help start people thinking creatively, exchanging ideas and help make a team work effectively.

WHEN TO DO WARMING UP EXERCISES

1. When team members do not know each other
2. When team members come from different cultures
3. When team needs to bond quickly
4. When team needs to work to a common goal quickly
5. When the discussion is new or unfamiliar
6. When the moderator needs to know the participants

SOME EXAMPLES OF WARMING UP EXERCISES

COMMON GROUND
HOW
1. The moderator asks the group to divide into pairs of participants
2. Each participant should select a group member that they do not know if possible.
3. Each person should interview the other person that they are paired with and make a list of 5 to ten things that they have in common.
4. One person from each pair should then present the list to the larger group.

DESERT ISLAND
HOW
1. The moderator introduces the warming up exercise.
2. Break a larger group down int smaller groups of 4 or 5 people.
3. Each person has 30 second to list all of the things that they would take to a deserted island. Each person should list at least 3 things.
4. Each person should defend why their 3 items should be one of the chosen items selected by their team.
5. Each team can vote for three items preferred by their team.
6. Each of the teams presents the three items that they have agreed upon to the larger group.

EXPECTATIONS
HOW
1. Each team member introduces themselves
2. Each team member outlines what are their expectations of the project.
3. Each team member shares their vision of the best possible outcome for the project.
4. Allow about 2 minutes per person

HOPES AND HURDLES
WHAT
Hopes and Hurdles is a brainstorm that identifies factors that may help or hinder the success of a project:

1. Business drivers and hurdles
2. User and employee drivers and hurdles
3. Technology drivers and hurdles
4. Environmental drivers and hurdles.
5. Vendors
6. Competitive benchmarking

POINTS TO CONSIDER
1. It provides a tangible focus for discussion.
2. It draws out tacit knowledge from your team.
3. It helps build team consensus.
4. It drives insights
5. Do not get too detailed
6. Some information may be sensitive.

HOW
1. Select a moderator

2. Define the problem.
3. Brainstorm hopes and hurdles
4. What are our strategic strengths?
5. What are we able to do quite well?
6. What strategic resources can we rely upon?
7. What could we enhance?
8. What should we avoid doing?
9. What are we doing poorly?
10. Collect the ideas on a Whiteboard or wall with post-it-notes.
11. Organize the contributions into two lists. Hopes in one list and hurdles in a second list.
12. Prioritize each element
13. Use the lists to create strategic options.

JUMPSTART STORYTELLING

WHO INVENTED IT?
Seth Kahan 2001

HOW
1. Divide the participants into groups of 5
2. Ask each person to describe to their group a story that is related to the objective of the workshop
3. Each person gets 90 seconds
4. Ask the participants to remember the story that resonated the most with them;
5. Reform the groups of 5 with different people
6. Ask everyone to retell their story.
7. Note how the story improves with each retelling.
8. 90 seconds per story
9. Ask each participant to reassess which story resonates with them the most
10. Ask everyone to remember the person who told the most powerful, relevant, engaging story.
11. Each group should select the most compelling stories within their group and invite the people the group favored to retell their story to the larger group

MILESTONES

WHO INVENTED IT?
Ava S, Butler 1996

HOW
1. The moderator creates a milestone chart on a Whiteboard.
2. The moderator estimates the age of the oldest members of the group and on a horizontal line write years from the approximate birth year of the older members to the present at five year intervals.
   1960 1965 1970 1975.
3. Using post-it notes each participant adds three personal milestones to the chart. One milestone per post-it-note under the year that the milestone occurred.
4. During the break participants read the milestones.

DIFFICULT EXPERIENCE
HOW

1. Break the team group down into pairs.
2. Tell your partner about one difficult experience you have had.
3. "I think my partner may benefit if they think about their experience from the perspective of ...."
4. "My partner could learn more about this new perspective by................"
5. Share your assumptions with your partner and discuss.

5 FRAMES
HOW

1. Break the team group down into pairs.
2. On a piece of paper write down five frames through which you view the world.
3. An example of a frame could be your age, your gender, your nationality etc.
4. Share your lenses with a partner, discussing how they shape your world.

OBSERVE
HOW

1. Break the team group down into pairs.
2. Each person observe your partner for two minutes then write five observations about your partner. For each observation write down one conclusion you have about your partner.
3. Share your assumptions with your partner.

Sources: Difficult Experience, 5 Frames and Observe adapted from three exercises developed by Emi Kolawole in collaboration with Amy Lazarus of Inclusion Ventures.

ZOMBIE CATS
HOW

1. Divide large groups into two equal sized groups.
2. Challenge the groups to find two things they all have in common with one another.
3. This stage should be done where each group cannot hear the conversation of the other group.
4. The two things become their team name.
5. After 5 minutes discussion, have each group act out their team name to the entire room and have others guess the team's name.

Source: Smashing Magazine.

1000 USES
HOW
1. Divide participants out into equal sized groups.
2. Select a random object such as a a paper clip, and challenge each group to come up with 1,000 uses for the object.
3. All uses must be unique with no repeats.
4. Each participant will take turns in a circle coming up with new ideas.
5. Appoint a note taker to capture how many ideas their group comes up with.
6. After 5 minutes have each group share how many ideas they generated.
7. The group with the most ideas wins.

Source: Smashing Magazine.

BARNEY
HOW
Each person uses the next letter of the alphabet and fills in the phrase ____ sells ____ in ____. For example, Peter sells potatoes in Poland. The outcome of this exercise is improved focus.

PHOTO
HOW
The moderator finds a photo. Each player in turn makes up a caption for the photo.

Source: Matt Drenstein

COMPLIMENT
HOW
1. Form a circle.
2. Turn to the person on your left and pay them a compliment. An alternative is to have each team member select another team member rather than the person next to them.

FREE ASSOCIATION
HOW
The first person says a word. The next person says a word that has some connection to the previous word.

HOBBY
HOW
Each person names one of their hobbies. Explain
1. Why you like it,
2. How you became interested in it,
3. Something most people don't know about it.

Source: teamfirstdevelopment.com

CHAPTER SUMMARY

A warming up exercise is a short exercise at the beginning of a design project that helps the design team work productively together as quickly as possible. The duration of an icebreaker is usually less than 10 to 30 minutes.

Icebreakers are an important component of collaborative or team-based design. The Design Thinking approach recognizes the value of designers working productively as members of a diverse cross-disciplinary team with managers, engineers, marketers and other professionals.

There are many types of warming up exercises.

REVIEW QUESTIONS

1. What are four benefits of warming up exercises?
2. Who should participate in warming up exercises?
3. Describe four different warming up exercises?

EXERCISE ONE
WARMING UP

INSTRUCTIONS
Break your team into groups of two people.
Each person should partner with someone they do not know if possible. Warming up exercises help stimulate constructive interaction, help people get to know each other and contribute effectively. Do one of the following exercises or select your own exercise from those listed in this chapter.

WHO AM I?
Duration: 3 minutes
Draw or write a one sentence description of something that represents yourself.
Duration 2 minutes per person
Each person introduces themselves to the group using their sketch or description.

COMMON GROUND
Duration: 5 minutes
Each person should interview their partner and make a list of 3 things that they have in common.

DESERT ISLAND
Duration: 3 minutes
Each person should list 3 things that they would take if that was all they could take to a desert island.
Duration 2 minutes per person
Introduce yourself to the group using your list.

OUTCOMES
Duration: 5 minutes
Each person should sketch or write what they believe could be the best possible outcome for the project.
Duration 2 minutes per person
Each person introduces themselves to the group using their sketch or description.

RESOURCES
Copy paper
Markers
White board

10

THE DISCOVERY PHASE

DISCOVERY PHASE

Before you start designing you need to understand whether various stakeholders feelings, thoughts, and attitudes and whether other similar designs already exist.

Studies show that greatest single reason for failure of new designs of products and services is a lack of within the design team of the perspectives of the stakeholders. Over 75% of new product initiatives fail in the market and lack of empathy is the number one reason that they fail so this stage will significantly improve the return on investment of your project if done diligently.

During this phase we investigate our users unmet needs and develop a deep understanding understand the way they think, what they feel, the behaviours they engage in and the values they hold through engaging them observing and listening to them explain their point of view, their problems and their underlying needs.

In order to create a design effectively we need to understand the context that surrounds the end users. We use a variety of research techniques to investigate the user needs and the design context.

By the end of this phase we will have an overview of user needs, existing services and their effectiveness and have a foundation to explore many possible design directions. We will investigate the business requirements of the design. We explore user unmet needs through.

1. Workshops
2. Interviews
3. Observation
4. Focus groups
5. Affinity diagrams
6. Discovery methods

DISCOVER
1. Who your users are.
2. Your users' needs and how you're not meeting them.
3. The people you need on your team.
4. What the stakeholder journey or experience looks like.

"

When you talk, you are only repeating what you know, but when you listen then you learn something new."

Dalai Lama

HOW?

1. Develop empathy for your stakeholders.
2. Develop and implement a research plan.
3. Assume a beginner's mindset.
4. Carry out user research
5. Imagine yourself in that person's situation.
6. Adopt a beginner's way of thinking. Withhold judgement and preconceived bias.
7. Identify gaps in knowledge.
8. Set Aside Your Beliefs, concerns and personal agenda and try to see things from the stakeholders points point of view.
9. Question everything. Be curious.
10. Listen.
11. Talk to users to uncover underlying needs.
12. Immerse yourself in your customer's reality.
13. Walk in your user's shoes.
14. Look for your end user's workarounds for their problems.
15. Learn what the stakeholder would do.
16. Immerse yourself in the problem. Walk in your user's shoes, observe what's not

being said.
17. Capture your learnings.

OUTPUTS

Outputs of this phase could include:

1. A list of user needs
2. A list of user unmet needs
3. A hierarchy of user needs
4. A plan for the resources required to complete the project.
5. the ability to scope and plan an alpha
6. a decision to progress to next phase
7. Perhaps a low fidelity prototype or several low fidelity prototypes.
8. Four to six personas is an optimum number to cover an organization's customer segments.
9. A list of the most important stakeholders both internally in your organization and externally.
10. A benchmarking of existing or competitive services and a SWOT analysis of these services.
11. A definition of the target audience.

Adapted from Discovery phase Government Service Design Manual, https://www.gov.uk/service manual/phases/discovery (accessed July 03, 2018).

THE DISCOVERY PROCESS

ASSEMBLE YOUR TEAM

You will need different skills and

the team roles and team size may evolve during the different development phases.

Select a diverse cross disciplinary group of people. Have different disciplines, different genders, ages, cultures, represented for the most successful results. Have some T shaped people. These are people who have more than one area of experience or training such as design and management. They will help your team collaborate productively.

MULTIDISCIPLINARY TEAM

A multidisciplinary team helps you to:
1. Build your service
2. Keep improving it based on user needs
3. Make decisions quickly

SOME TEAM SKILLS

1. Analyze user needs, including accessibility and assisted digital needs, and turn these into user stories
2. Create user stories and prioritize them
3. Manage and report to stakeholders and manage dependencies on other teams
4. Procure services from third parties, if needed
5. Test with real users
6. Find ways of accrediting and handling data

DEFINE YOUR TARGET

AUDIENCE

Creating a projected user models will keep the development team rooted to a realistic user requirements and minimizes user frustration with the real product. Having a deep understanding of users can help development team better understand the wants & needs of the targeted customers. This will help the development team relate better with the target user. Understanding user tasks helps in developing design solutions that will ensure that the user expectations are met & avoid design errors and customer frustration. Use research methods such as interviewing, observation, empathy maps and user experience maps to better understand your audience. Market segmentation is basically the division of market into smaller segments. It helps identify potential customers and target them.

TYPES OF SEGMENTATION

1. Behavior segmentation
2. Benefit segmentation
3. Psychographic segmentation
4. Geographic segmentation
5. Demographic segmentation

1. What is your target group's goals emotions, experiences, needs and desires?
2. Information collected from just a few people is unlikely to be representative of the whole range of users.
3. What are the user tasks and activities?
4. How will the user use the

product or service to perform a task?

5. What is the context of the user?
6. Where are they? What surrounds them physically and virtually or culturally?
7. How large is your user group?

When defining your target audience consider:
1. Age
2. Gender
3. Occupation
4. Industry
5. Travel
6. Citizenship status
7. Marital state
8. Income
9. Culture
10. Occupation
11. Language
12. Religion
13. Location
14. Education
15. Nationality
16. Mobility
17. Migration
18. Mental state
19. Abilities
20. Disabilities
21. Health

SHARE WHAT YOU KNOW
1. In the project kick off meeting ask every team member to introduce themselves and to describe in 3 minutes what experience they have that may be relevant to the project.
2. The moderator can list areas of knowledge on a white board.

IDENTIFY WHAT YOU NEED

TO KNOW
Arrange a project kick-off meeting. Invite your team and important stakeholders. On a white board or flip chart create two lists. Ask each person to introduce themselves and describe what they know or have experienced that may be useful for implementing the project. Brainstorm with your group the areas that are unknown and how that information may be obtained. Formulate a research plan and assign responsibilities, tasks and deliverables with dates.

UNCOVER NEEDS
1. "What causes the problem?"
2. "What are the impacts of the problem?"
3. ""What are possible solutions?"
4. Probe about workarounds How do people adapt their environment to solve problems that they have?
5. Ask what their single biggest obstacle is to achieve what they are trying to achieve How can you help them?
6. Ask what's changing in their world What are the trends?
7. Observe people
8. Can you see problems they have that they perhaps do not even recognize are problems?
9. Ask other stakeholders

DEFINE YOUR GOALS

A goal is the intent or intents of the design process.

1. Write a detailed description of the design problem.
2. Define a list of needs that are connected to the design problem.
3. Make a list of obstacles that need to be overcome to solve the design problem.
4. Make a list of constraints that apply to the problem.
5. Rewrite the problem statement to articulate the above requirements.

ETHNOGRAPHIC FRAMEWORKS

WHAT
If you are not sure where to start with research consider using a framework such as one of the following. This is a summary of some of the more common frameworks. Frameworks help give structure to your research. If you are not sure where to start with research consider using a framework.

A(X4) FRAMEWORK

1. **Atmosphere**
2. **Actors**
3. **Artifacts**
4. **Activities**

WHO INVENTED IT?
Rothstein, P. (2001).

4/ Bringing the Outside In Sotirin, P. (1999).

Territory including space and architecture
Stuff furniture, possession, private/public, visual signs, technology
People flows, dress, bodies, nonverbal behaviors, authority, affection
Talk conversation, vocabularies

Source: Jono Hey

AEIOU FRAMEWORK

WHAT
One of our principal analytic frameworks for looking at and understanding a situation is the AEIOU framework. AEIOU is a heuristic to help interpret observations gathered by ethnographic research. Its two primary functions are to code data, and to develop models to address the objectives and issues of a client.

Source Recording ethnographic observations: palojono

WHO INVENTED IT?
The AEIOU framework was originated in 1991 at Doblin by

Rick Robinson, Ilya Prokopoff, John Cain, and Julie Pokorny.

HOW DO YOU USE IT?

1. Materials are gathered via ethnographic methods: notes, photos, videos, interviews, field observation, etc.
2. During field observation, use the AEIOU framework as a lens to observe the surrounding environment.
3. Record observations under the appropriate headings.
4. Supplement direct observations with photos or video tape when appropriate.
5. Review and cluster observations to disseminate higher-level themes and patterns.

A - Activities are goal directed sets of actions-things which people want to accomplish
E - Environments include the entire arena where activities take place
I - Interactions are between a person and someone or something else, and are the building blocks of activities
O - Objects are building blocks of the environment, key elements sometimes put to complex or unintended uses, changing their function, meaning and context
U - Users are the consumers, the people providing the behaviors, preferences and needs (E-Lab 1997)

Source Christina Wasson's Ethnography in the field of design

LATCH FRAMEWORK

WHAT
"Information may be infinite, however...The organization of information is finite as it can only be organized by LATCH: Location, Alphabet, Time, Category, or Hierarchy."

Source Richard Saul Wurman, 1996

WHO INVENTED IT?
Richard Saul Wurman, 1996

Location
Compare information coming from various sources.
- Atlas
- Travel Guide
- Parts of the Body
- Parts of a System

Alphabet
Used for very large bodies of information. Not always the best organization method – forced organization rather than natural. dictionary
- List of states on a website
- List of student names in a class roster

Time
Used for events that occur over a fixed duration. Easy to understand, easy to draw comparisons and conclusions.
- a scenario

- a narrative

Category
Well reinforced by color & placement. Grouped by similar importance – a value judgment.
- Organization of goods.
- Types of activities
- Breeds of animals

Hierarchy
Assign value or weight to the information; usually on a scale
- largest to smallest
- High cost to low cost

Source Parsonsdesign4

SPOOL FRAMEWORK

WHAT
....
A list of focus questions, to keep top-of-mind as you observe people's context.

WHO INVENTED IT?
Jared Spool Jared Spool
February 22nd, 2007

Goals
1. What is the user trying to accomplish?
2. How will the user know when they are done? What will be different?
3. How does the user describe their goals?
4. How do the user's actions fit into the objectives of the organization?
5. Who established the goals for the user? Were they self anointed or were they assigned by someone else?
6. Are the user's immediate goals part of a larger scope? (For example, the new point-of-sale application is one piece of delivering an entire new line of business.)

Process
1. What are the steps the user will follow?
2. Who defined the steps?
3. How prepared is the user for each step? (Do they have it all laid out or
4. does it seem to be ad-hoc?)
5. How does information flow from one step to the next?
6. What are the various roles (such as creator, contributor, editor, or
7. approver) that are involved?
8. How long does the process take?
9. What artifacts (such as design documents, emails, or White-board drawings)
10. are used?
11. How do the various team members communicate with each other?
12. What other tools are used during the process?

Inputs & Outputs
1. What materials and information will the user need to successfully use the interface?
2. Who will they get that information from?
3. What do they do when the information isn't complete?
4. What will they need from the

interface to continue with their overarching goals?

5. Who do they give those results to?
6. What happens after they've turned them over? (Does the user move on to something else or do they have more interactions?)

Experience
1. What similar things has the user done in their past?
2. Is this something that repeats itself or is the use a first-time occasion?
3. What journals or magazines do they read?
4. What kind of "organizational memory" helps the user avoid mistakes of the past?
5. How has the organization survived without this design in the past?
6. What competitors systems have users taken advantage of?
7. How will the user learn how to use the tool?
8. What training has the user received?
9. What conferences has the user attended?

Constraints
1. What physical, temporal, or financial constraints are likely to impose themselves on the user's work?
2. What ideals are subverted by reality as the work progresses?
3. What constraints can the user predict in advance? What can't be predicted?

Physical Environment
1. How much room does the user have to work?
2. Do they have a place to store the documentation?
3. What materials on their desk?
4. What access do they have to necessary information (such as user manuals)?
5. What is taped to their monitor?

Tools In use
1. What hardware and software does the user currently use?
2. Do they participate in on-line forums?

Relationships
1. What are the interactions between the primary user and other people who are affected by the tool?
2. Does the user interact with other people who use the tool?

Source Jared M. Spool

NINE DIMENSIONS FRAMEWORK

WHAT

Spradley proposed that social situations generally may be described along nine dimensions for observational purposes.

Space: Layout of the physical setting, rooms outdoor spaces etc.

Actors: The names and details of the people involved

Activities: the various activities of the actors

Objects: Physical elements: furniture etc

Acts: Specific Individual actions

Events: Particular occasions Eg meetings

Time: The sequence of events

Goals: What actors are attempting to accomplish

Feelings: Emotions in particular contexts

Spradley, J. P. (1980) and Robson, C. (2002). in Recording Ethnographic Observations: Palojono

WHO INVENTED IT?
Spradley, J. P. 1980

WHY
1. To give structure to research
2. In order to collect most important information.
3. To provide some certainty in the uncertain environment of fieldwork

POSTA FRAMEWORK

WHAT
POSTA stands for:
1. People
2. Objects
3. Settings
4. Time
5. Activities

WHO INVENTED IT?
May have been invented by Pat Sachs Social Solutions and Gitte Jordan Institute for Research on Learning

WHY
1. To give structure to research
2. In order to collect most important information
3. To provide some certainty in the uncertain environment of fieldwork

HOW
Observe participant in the work setting around, observing what they do and how they interact with other people and tools in their environment. Or they may focus on key objects or artifacts in the environment, with special attention to the various roles that they play (functional, psychological and social). During another observation, the team may take notes and photo-graphs of the work setting and try to understand how the configuration of space mediates the work. Finally, they chart activities, including both formal

work flow and informal work practices.

SAM/ THINK FEEL DO FRAMEWORK

1. **Social context**
   - Who they do the 'action or activity' with?
   - What is their relationship, social interaction?
   - Why they behave the way they do?
2. **Action or behavior.**
   - What is the behavior?
   - What actions or activities they are involved?
   - Why?
3. **Motivations**
   - What do they think?
   - How do they feel?
   - What are the reason(s) for actions and/or behavior?
   - What are the beliefs?
   - What are the values?
   - What is the underlying thinking?
   - What are the aspirations?
   - What are the Emotions or Feelings?

Source: Adapted from Design Thinking Guidebook for Public Sector innovation in Bhutan

POEMS FRAMEWORK

WHO INVENTED IT?
Kumar and Whitney, 2003

WHAT

POEMS stands for:
P - People
O - Objects
E - Environments
M - Messages
S - Services

ACTIVITY MAP

WHAT

An activity map is a map that shows a company's strategic position in relation to company activities. A number of higher order strategic themes are implemented through linked activities.

"An activity map is a diagnostic tool to identify your organization's competitive advantage. It connects your organization's value proposition to the activities of your organization that enables you to deliver this value proposition better than any competitors."

Source: Activity Map | Business Strategy, https://strategicthinker. wordpress.com/activity-map/ (accessed July 06, 2016).

WHO INVENTED IT?

Walt Disney Corporation 1957

WHY

1. Activity maps are useful for understanding and strengthening organizational strategy.
2. The value of individual activities cannot be separated from the system of activities.
3. Helps develop a unique competitive position.
4. Helps align activities with strategy
5. Helps understand the trade-offs and choices.

WHEN

1. Make detailed decisions about whether a new opportunity or initiative complements existing activities
2. To communicate how each aspect of a business supports organizational strategy.
3. Identify activities that may undermine the organization's strategy.
4. Make decisions about outsourcing.
5. To make decisions for new activities or acquisitions.

HOW

1. Brainstorm the core activities that your company does. Core Activities are the most important actions a company must do to operate successfully. Discuss assets, resources, policies, culture and processes.
2. List your organizational strategic goals.
3. Connect activities to goals.
4. Identify the most important differentiated benefit from the value proposition.
5. Describe how well each of your competitors executes each of the core activities.
6. Brainstorm how you can improve your core activities
7. Iterate.
8. is there anything missing from your map?
9. Is each activity contributing positively to the overall strategy and customer needs?
10. How will you execute improvements

"

There is one very important future perspective he [Jonathan Ive] offers though around the increasing complexity and inter relatedness of products and how this requires more effective multidisciplinary working practice to create these products. He explains how they've designed Apple's new donut-like 'Ring' HQ to enable them to create more fully multi-disciplinary design teams, where industrial designers, sound engineers, hardware and software guys, UX people, electronics engineers etc, can all work together throughout the process.

2017 Soundcloud Interview
Sir Jonathan Ive
Apple VP of Design

https://www.realisedesign.co.uk

ANTHROPUMP

WHAT
....

This method involves the research videotaping one or more participant's activities. The videos are replayed to the participants, and they are asked to explain their behavior.

WHO INVENTED IT?
Rick Robinson, John Cain, E- Lab Inc.,

WHY
1. Used for collecting data before concept and for evaluating prototypes after concept phases of projects.

CHALLENGES
1. Best conducted by someone who has practice observing human interactions in a space.

HOW
1. People are first captured on video while interacting with products.
2. The participants are then asked to watch the tapes while researchers question them about what they see, how they felt, etc. Research subjects analyze their actions and experiences.
3. The company invites people who have been captured on video to watch their tapes as researchers pose questions about what's happening.

4. Create videotapes and examines these follow-up sessions, analyzing research subjects analyzing themselves.

BEHAVIORAL MAP

WHO INVENTED IT?
Ernest Becker 1962

WHY
1. This method helps develop an understanding of space layouts, interactions, experiences, and behaviors.
2. Helps understand way-finding.
3. Helps optimize the use of space.
4. A limitation of this method is that motivations remain unknown.
5. Use when you want to develop more efficient or effective use of space in retail environments, exhibits, architecture and interior design.

HOW
1. Identify the users.
2. Ask what is the purpose of the space?
3. Consider what behaviors are meaningful.
4. Consider different personas.
5. Participants can be asked to map their use of a space on a floor plan and can be asked to reveal their motivations.
6. Can use shadowing or video ethnographic techniques.
7. Create behavioral map.
8. Analyze behavioral map.
9. Reorganize space based on insights.

RESOURCES
A map of the space.
Video camera
Digital still camera
Notebook
Pens

BIAS

We all have unconscious biases. These biases can reduce the effectiveness of our decision making in design thinking. Understanding our own biases can help us overcome them. Understanding the biases of others can help us improve the user experience and help us better understand team dynamics and diversity.

COGNITIVE DISSONANCE

Cognitive dissonance is the stress experienced by a person who simultaneously holds contradictory beliefs, ideas, or values.

Leon Festinger proposed in 1957 that people strive for internal psychological consistency. A person is motivated to reduce the cognitive inconsistency by changing parts of the cognition to justify the behavior, by adding new parts, or by avoiding contradictory information that are likely to increase the cognitive dissonance.

FALSE CAUSALITY

A bias that involves concluding that since one event followed another in time, the first must have caused the second. False causality is jumping to a conclusion of a causal relationship without supporting evidence.

ACTION BIAS

When faced with an ambiguous problem we sometimes prefer to do something, if it is counterproductive, even when doing nothing is the best course of action.

AMBIGUITY BIAS

If an outcome is risky and unknown, there is a tendency to stick to what is already known and stay with what you've done previously.

STRATEGIC MISREPRESENTATION

This is understating the costs and overstating the likely benefits in order to get a project approved.

GROUPTHINK

Group-think is a type of bias that occurs within a group in which the desire for harmony in the group results in dysfunctional decision-making. Group members try to minimize conflict and reach a consensus decision without critical evaluation, and by isolating themselves from other points of view.

INNOVATION BIAS

Novelty and 'newness' are seen as good, regardless of potential negative impacts.

ANCHORING BIAS

This type of bias involves being influenced by information that is already known or that has just been shown.

STATUS-QUO BIAS

This bias involves favoring a current situation or status quo and maintaining it.. This bias makes us reduce risk and prefer what is familiar and can stand in the way of innovation.

FRAMING BIAS

Being influenced by the way in which information is presented rather than the information itself. People react to a particular choice in different ways depending on how it is presented. An audience tends to avoid risk when a positive frame is presented but seek risks when a negative frame is presented.

CONFLICTS OF INTEREST

A conflict of interest is when a person or organization has conflicting financial, personal or other interests which could corrupt and lead to improper actions.

FUNDING BIAS

Funding bias refers to the tendency of a study to support the interests of the financial sponsor.

Source: Jono Hey

RESEARCH PLAN

WHAT

The research plan gives a design team and stakeholders the opportunity to discuss proposed research, stating its importance, why and how it will be conducted and costs. It is best to keep it as short and concise as possible.

WHY

A well-structured research plan

1. A communication tool.
2. Provides a clear focus.
3. Creates team alignment
4. Provides a forum to ask questions.
5. Creates an expectation of knowledge gained.
6. Will improve your final design.

HOW

Sections to include

1. Executive Summary
2. Problem Statement
3. State concisely the goals of the proposed research.
4. Why is the work important
5. What has already been done
6. User Profile
7. Stakeholders and their Needs
8. Methodology
9. Research questions [5]
10. Number of Participants
11. Length Of Session
12. Where will the research take

place?

13. Roles and Responsibilities
14. Test Artifacts
15. Participant Incentive
16. Scenarios
17. Evaluation Methods
18. Test Environment and Equipment
19. Project Time-line
20. Deliverables
21. Where supporting information can be found

Sample research activities

1. Preparation for a single project: ten hours
2. Recruiting and scheduling: two to three hours per person
3. Contextual inquiry/task analysis: five hours per person
4. Focus groups: three hours per group
5. Usability tests: three hours per participant
6. Analyzing contextual inquiry/task analysis: five hours per person
7. Analyzing focus group results: four hours per group
8. Analyzing usability tests: two hours per person
9. Preparing a report for email delivery: twelve hours
10. Preparing a one-hour presentation: six hours

Sample time line

Pilot Testing date: November 25th, 2017 6PM-7PM Pilot User

Testing date: November 30th, 2017

8AM – 9AM Setup testing area
9AM – 10AM Participant 1
10:15AM – 11:15 Participant 2
11:15AM – 12:30 Lunch
12:30PM – 1:30 Participant 3
1:45PM – 2:45 Participant 4
3:00PM – 4:00PM Participant 5
4:15PM – 5:15
Debriefing and wrap-up
Presentation to Client: December 14th 6:00PM-8:00PM
Formal Report Submitted: April 28th

SAMPLE ONE-PAGE RESEARCH PLAN

Title

ABC Laptop Data-Entry Usability Test
By John Smith-Doe, Usability

Stakeholders

Wanda Answer (PM),
Sam Doe (Lead Engineer)

Background

Since January 2009, when the ABC laptop was introduced to the world, particularly after its market release, journalists, bloggers, industry experts, other stakeholders and customers have privately and publicly expressed negative opinions about the ABC laptop's keyboard. These views suggest that the keyboard is hard to use and that it imposes a poor experience on customers. Some have claimed this as the main reason why the ABC laptop will not succeed among business users. Over the years, several improvements have been made to keyboard design to no avail.

Goals

Identify the strengths and weaknesses of data entry on the ABC laptop, and provide opportunities for improvement.

Research Questions

1. How do people enter data on the ABC laptop?
2. What is the learning curve of new ABC laptop users when they enter data?
3. What are the most common errors users make when entering data?

Methodology

A usability study will be held in our lab with 20 participants. Each participant session will last 60 minutes and will include a short briefing, an interview, a task performance with an ABC laptop and a debriefing. Among the tasks: enter an email subject heading, compose a long email, check news updates on Washington Post's's website, create a calendar event and more.

Participants

These are the primary characteristics of the study participants:

- Business user
- Age 22 to 55,
- Never used an ABC Phone,
- Expressed interest in learning more about or purchasing an ABC laptop,
- Uses the Web at least 10 hours a week.
- [Link to a draft screener]

Schedule

Recruiting: begins October 12
Study day: October 22
Results delivery: November 2

Attachments

Script

Source: Adapted from smashingmagazine.com

BENCHMARKING

WHO INVENTED IT?
Robert Camp Xerox, 1989
Benchmarking: the search for industry best practices that lead to superior performance.

WHY
1. A tool to identify, and implement the best practices.
2. The practice of measuring your performance against best competitors.

CHALLENGES
1. Can be expensive
2. Organizations often think their companies were performing above the average for the industry when they are not.

HOW
1. Identify what your objective.
2. Identify potential partners
3. Identify similar industries and organizations.
4. Identify organizations that are leaders.
5. Identify data sources
6. Identify the products or organizations to be benchmarked
7. Select the benchmarking factors to measure.
8. Undertake benchmarking
9. Research the "best practice" organizations
10. Analyze the outcomes
11. Target future performance
12. Adjust goal
13. Modify your own product or service to conform with best practices identified in the benchmarking process.

RESOURCES
Post-it-notes
Pens
Dry-erase markers
White-board
Paper

BENEFITS MAP

WHY
1. Aids communication and discussion within the organization.
2. It is human nature to do tasks which are not most urgent first.
3. To gain competitive advantage,
4. Helps build competitive strategy
5. Helps build communication strategy
6. Helps manage time effectively

DESCRIPTIVE QUESTION MATRIX

Spradley, J. 1980. Participant observation. New York Holt, Rinehart & Winston

	SPACE	OBJECT	ACT	ACTIVITY
SPACE The physical place or places	Can you describe in detail all the places?	What are all the ways space is organized by objects?	What are all the ways that space are organized by actions?	What are all the ways space is organized by activities?
OBJECT The physical things that are present	Where are objects located?	Can you describe in detail all the objects?	What are all the ways objects are used in acts?	What are all the ways objects are used in activities?
ACT Single actions that people do	What are all the places acts occur?	What are all the ways acts incorporate objects?	Can you describe in detail all the acts?	What are all the ways that acts are involved in activities?
ACTIVITY A set of related acts people do	What are all the places activities occur?	What are all the ways activities incorporate objects?	What are all the ways activities incorporate acts?	Can you describe in detail all the activities?
EVENT A set of related activities that people carry out	What are all the places events occur?	What are all the ways events incorporate objects?	What are all the ways events incorporate acts?	What are all the ways events incorporate activities?
TIME The sequencing that takes place over time	Where do time periods occur?	What are all the ways time affects objects?	How do acts fall into time periods?	How do activities fall into time periods?
ACTOR The people involved	Where do actors place themselves?	What are all the ways actors use objects?	How are actors involved in acts?	How are actors involved in activities?
GOAL The things people are trying to accomplish	Where are goals sought and achieved?	What are all the ways goals involve use of objects?	What are all the ways goals involve acts?	What activities are goal seeking or linked to goals?
FEELINGS The emotions felt and expressed	Where do the various feeling states occur?	What feelings lead to the use of what objects?	What are all the ways feelings affect acts?	What are all the ways feelings affect activities?

EVENT	TIME	ACTOR	GOAL	FEELINGS
What are all the ways space is organized by events?	What spatial changes occur over time?	What are all the ways space is used by actors?	What are all the ways space is related to goals?	What places are associated with feelings?
What are all the ways objects are used in events?	What are all the ways objects are used in activities?	What are all the ways objects are used by actors?	How are objects used in seeking goals?	What are all the ways objects evoke feelings?
What are all the ways that acts are involved in events?	How do acts vary at different times?	What are all the ways acts incorporate actors?	What are all the ways acts involve goals?	How do acts involve feelings?
What are all the ways that activities are involved in events?	How do activities vary at different times?	What are all the ways activities incorporate actors?	What are all the ways activities involve goals?	How do activities involve feelings?
Can you describe in detail all the events?	How do events occur over time? Is there an order of events?	What are all the ways events incorporate actors?	What are all the ways events involve goals?	How do events involve feelings?
How do events fall into time periods?	Can you describe in detail all the time periods?	When are all the times actors are "on stage"?	How are goals related to time periods?	When are feelings evoked?
How are actors involved in events?	How do actors change over time or at different times?	Can you describe in detail all the actors?	Which actors are linked to which goals?	What are the feelings experienced by actors?
What are all the ways goals involve events?	Which goals are scheduled for which times?	How do the various goals affect the various actors?	Can you describe in detail all the goals?	What are all the ways goals evoke feelings?
What are all the ways feelings affect events?	How are feelings related to various time periods?	What are all the ways feelings involve actors?	What are the ways feelings influence goals?	Can you describe in detail all the feelings?

ACTIVITY MAP

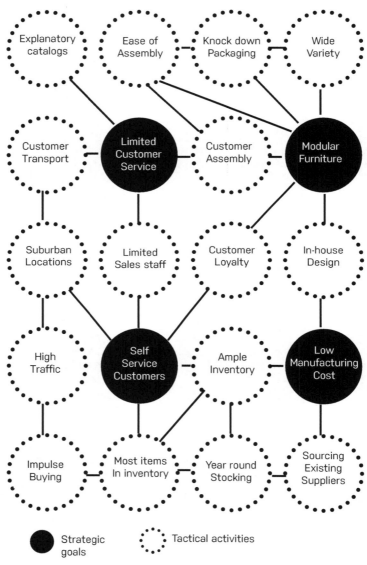

Source: Activity map for IKEA (after Porter)

CHALLENGES
Can be subjective

HOW
1. Moderator draws axes on white-board or flip chart.
2. Worthwhile activity at the start of a project.
3. Map individual tasks.
4. Interpret the map.
5. Create strategy.
6. Tasks which have high benefit with low investment may be given priority.

BOUNDARY SHIFTING

WHAT
Boundary shifting involves identifying features or ideas outside the boundary of the system related to the defined problem and applying to them to the problem being addressed.

WHY
It is fast and inexpensive.

HOW
1. Define the problem.
2. Research outside systems that may have related ideas or problems to the defined problem.
3. Identify ideas or solutions outside the problem system.
4. Apply the outside idea or solution to the problem being addressed.

RESOURCES
1. Pen
2. Paper
3. White-board
4. Dry-erase markers

CAMERA JOURNAL

WHAT
The research subjects record their activities with a camera and notes. The researcher reviews the images and discusses them with the participants.

WHY
1. Helps develop empathy for the participants.
2. Participants are involved in the research process.
3. Helps establish rapport with participants.
4. May reveal aspects of life that are seldom seen by outsiders.

CHALLENGES
1. Should obtain informed consent.
2. Be sensitive to vulnerable people.
3. May be a relatively expensive research method.
4. May be time consuming.
5. Best used with other methods.
6. Technology may be unreliable.
7. The method may be unpredictable'.
8. Has to be carefully analyzed

HOW

1. Define subject of study
2. Define participants
3. Gather data images and insight statements.
4. Analyze data.
5. Identify insights
6. Rank insights
7. Produce criteria for concept generation from insights.
8. Generate concepts to meet needs of users.

RESOURCES

Cameras
Voice recorder
Video camera
Notepad computer
Pens

OPEN CARD SORT

WHAT
This is a method for discovering the relationships of a list of items. Participants asked to arrange individual, unsorted items into groups. For an open card sort the user defines the groups rather than the researcher.

CARD SORTING IS APPLIED WHEN:

9. When there is a large number of items.
10. The items are similar and difficult to organize into categories.
11. Users may have different perceptions related to organizing the items.

WHO INVENTED IT?
Jastrow 1886
Nielsen & Sano 1995

WHY

1. It is a simple method using index cards,
2. Used to provide insights for interface design.

CHALLENGES

1. Ask participants to fill out a second card if they feel it belongs in two groups.
2. There are a number of on-line card sorting tools available.

HOW

1. Recruit between 5 and 15 participants representative of your user group.
2. Provide a small deck of cards.
3. Provide clear instructions. Ask your participants to arrange the cards in ways that make sense to them. One hundred cards take about 1 hour to sort.
4. The user sorts labeled cards into groups by that they define themselves.
5. The user can generate more card labels.
6. If users do not understand a card ask them to exclude it. Ask participants for their rationale for any dual placements of cards.
7. Analyze the piles of cards and create a list of insights derived from the card sort.
8. Analyze the data.

BENCHMARKING MATRIX
FOR PRODUCT DESIGN

Criteria	A	B	C	D	E	F	G	H	I
Usability	1	2	3	1	4	1	1	2	3
Speed to marke	2	1	1	2	2	4	2	1	4
Brand compatibility	2	4	0	2	2	4	0	4	4
Roi	2	3	1	1	4	1	1	3	3
Fits strategy	1	1	1	4	0	3	1	2	2
Aesthetic appeal	2	4	0	2	2	4	0	4	4
Differentiation	2	2	2	0	1	1	3	3	0
Tooling cost	2	2	1	1	1	2	0	4	3
Fits distribution	2	2	3	1	2	1	4	0	3
Uses our factory	3	3	5	3	0	3	2	1	3
Fits trends	1	3	2	2	1	3	4	3	2
Total	21	26	23	18	20	23	21	24	29

BENEFITS MAP

HIGH BENEFIT

Activity B

Activity A

Activity I

Activity C

Activity H

EASY TO IMPLEMENT

DIFFICULT TO IMPLEMENT

Activity F

Activity E

Activity D

Activity G

LOW BENEFIT

CLOSED CARD SORT

Card sorting is applied when:
1. When there is a large number of pieces of data.
2. The individual pieces of data are similar.
3. Participants have different perceptions of the data.

WHO INVENTED IT?
Jastrow 1886
Nielsen & Sano 1995

WHY
1. It is a simple method using index cards,
2. Used to provide insights for interface design.

HOW
1. Recruit 15 to 20 participants representative of your user group.
2. Provide a deck of cards using words and or images relevant to your concept.
3. Provide clear instructions. Ask your participants to arrange the cards in ways that make sense to them. 100 cards takes about 1 hour to sort.
4. The user sorts labeled cards into groups by under header cards defined by the researcher.
5. The user can generate more card labels.
6. If users do not understand a card ask them to exclude it. Ask participants for their rationale for any dual placements of cards.
7. Discuss why the cards are placed in a particular pile yields insight into user perceptions.
8. Analyze the data. Create a hierarchy for the information
9. Use post cards or post-it notes.

RESOURCES
Post cards
Pens
Post-it-notes
Laptop computer
A table

CONVERSATION CARDS

WHO INVENTED IT?
Originator unknown. Google Ngram indicates the term first appeared around 1801 in England for a collection of "Moral and Religious Anecdotes particularly

adapted for the entertainment and instruction of young persons, and to support instead of destroying serious conversation."

WHY
1. Questions are the springboard for conversations.
2. Can be used to initiate sensitive conversations.

CHALLENGES
1. How will data from the cards be used?
2. How will cards be evaluated?
3. How many cards are necessary to be representative?
4. What are potential problems relating card engagement
5. Use one unit of information per question.

HOW
1. Decide on goal for research.
2. Formulate about 10 questions related to topic
3. Create the cards.
4. Recruit the subjects.
5. Undertake pre -interview with sample subject to test.
6. Use release form if required.
7. Carry light equipment.
8. Record answers verbatim.
9. Communicate the purpose and length of the interview.
10. Select location. It should not be too noisy or have other distracting influences
11. Work through the cards.
12. Video or record the sessions for later review.
13. Analyze
14. Create Insights

RESOURCES
Conversation Cards.
Notebook
Video Camera
Pens
Interview plan or structure
Questions, tasks and discussion items
Interview cards

CULTURAL INVENTORY

WHAT
It is a survey focused on the cultural assets of a location or organization.

WHO INVENTED IT?
Julian Haynes Steward may have been the first to use the term in 1947.

WHY
1. Can be used in strategic planning
2. Can be used to solve problems.

CHALLENGES
Requires time and resources

HOW
1. Create your team
2. Collect existing research
3. Review existing research and identify gaps
4. Host a meeting of stakeholders
5. Promote the meeting
6. Ask open-ended questions

about the culture and heritage
7. Set a time limit of 2 hours for the meeting.
8. Plan the collection phase
9. Compile inventory. This can be in the form of a website
10. Distribute the inventory and obtain feedback.

RESOURCES
Diary
Notebooks
Pens
Post-it notes
Voice recorder
Postcards
Digital Camera

CULTURAL PROBES

WHAT
A cultural probe is a method of collecting information about people, their context, and their culture. The aim of this method is to record events, behaviors, and interactions in their context. This method involves the participants to record and collect the data themselves.

WHO INVENTED IT?
Bill Gaver Royal College of Art London 1969

WHY
1. This is a useful method when the participants that are being studied are hard to reach for example if they are traveling.
2. It is a useful technique if the activities being studied take place over an extended period or at irregular intervals.
3. The information collected can be used to build personas.

CHALLENGES
It is important with this method to select the participants carefully and give them support during the study.

HOW
1. Define the objective of your study.
2. Recruit your participants.
3. Brief the participants
4. Supply participants with kit. The items in the kit are selected to collect the type of information you want to gather and can include items such as notebooks, diary, camera, voice recorder or post cards.
5. You can use an affinity diagram to analyze the data collected

DAY EXPERIENCE METHOD

WHAT

The method requires participants to record answers to questions during a day. The person's mobile phone is used to prompt them The participants use a notebook, a camera or a voice recorder to answer your questions. The interviews are followed by a focus group.

WHO INVENTED IT?

Intille 2003

WHY

1. The participants are co-researchers.
2. Reduces the influence of the researcher on the participant when compared to methods such as interviews or direct observation.

CHALLENGES

1. Cost of devices.
2. This method should be used with other methods.

HOW

1. Conduct a preliminary survey to focus the method on preferred questions.
2. Recruit participants.
3. The experience sampling takes place over one day.
4. The participants are asked to provide answers to questions at irregular intervals when promoted by a SMS message via the participant's mobile phone.
5. The interval can be 60 to 90 minutes.
6. The participant can record the activity with a camera, notebook or voice recorder.
7. Soon after the day organize a focus group with the participants.
8. The participants describe their day using the recorded material.

RESOURCES

Mobile phone
Automated SMS messaging
Notebook
Camera
Software

Day Experience Resource Kit - Matthew Riddle, http://www.matthewriddle.com/papers/Day_Experience_Resource_Kit.pdf (accessed July 06, 2016).

DAY IN THE LIFE

WHAT

A study in which the designer observes the participant in the location and context of their usual activities, observing and recording events to understand the activities from the participant's point of view. Mapping a 'Day in the Life' as a storyboard can provide a focus for discussion.

WHO INVENTED IT?
Alex Bavelas 1944

WHY
1. This method informs the design process by observation of real activities and behaviors.
2. This method provides insights with relatively little cost and time.

CHALLENGES
1. Choose the participants carefully
2. Document everything. Something that seems insignificant may become significant later.

HOW
1. Define activities to study
2. Recruit participants
3. Prepare
4. Observe subjects in context.
5. Capture data,
6. Create storyboard with text and time line.
7. Analyze data
8. Create insights.
9. Identify issues
10. Identify needs
11. Add new/more requirements to concept development

RESOURCES
Camera
Notebook
Video camera
Voice recorder
Pens

DOT VOTING

WHAT
Dot voting is a way of efficiently selecting from a large number of ideas the preferred ideas to carry forward in the design process.

WHY
It is a method of selecting a favored idea by collective rather than individual judgment. It is a fast method that allows a design to progress. It leverages the strengths of diverse team member viewpoints and experiences.

CHALLENGES
1. The assessment is subjective.
2. Groupthink
3. Not enough good ideas
4. Inhibition
5. Lack of critical thinking

RESOURCES
Large wall
Adhesive dots

HOW
1. Gather your team of between four and twelve participants.
2. Brainstorm ideas, for example ask each team member to generate between ten and thirty ideas as sketches.
3. Each idea should be presented on one post-it-note or page.

4. Each designer should quickly explain each idea to the group before the group votes.
5. Spread the ideas over a wall or table.
6. Ask the team to vote on their two or three favorite ideas and total the votes. You can use sticky dots or colored pins to indicate a vote or a moderator can tally the scores.
7. Rearrange the ideas ranked from most dots to least.
8. Refine the preferred ideas.

DIARY STUDY

WHAT
This method involves participants recording particular events, feelings or interactions, in a diary supplied by the researcher. User Diaries help provide insight into behaviour. Participants record their behaviour and thoughts. Diaries can uncover behaviour that may not be articulated in an interview or readily visible to outsiders.

WHO INVENTED IT?
Gordon Allport, may have been the first to describe diary studies in 1942.

WHY
1. Can capture data that is difficult to capture using other methods.

2. Useful when you wish to gather information and minimize your influence on research subjects.
3. When the process or event you're exploring takes place over a long period.

CHALLENGES
1. Process can be expensive and time-consuming.
2. Needs participant monitoring.
3. It is difficult to get materials back.

HOW
1. A diary can be kept over a period of one week or longer.
2. Define focus for the study.
3. Recruit participants carefully.
4. Decide method: preprinted, diary notebook or on line.
5. Prepare diary packs. Can be preprinted sheets or blank twenty page notebooks with prepared questions or on line web based diary.
6. Brief participants.
7. Distribute diaries directly or by mail.
8. Conduct study. Keep in touch with participants.
9. Conduct debrief interview.
10. Look for insights.

RESOURCES
Diary
Preprinted diary sheets
On-line diary
Pens
Disposable cameras
Digital camera
Self-addressed envelopes

EMOTION CARDS

WHAT

Emotion cards are a field method of analyzing and quantifying people's emotional response to a design. The method classifies emotions into sets of emotions which each can be associated with a specific recognizable facial expression.

The emotion card tool consists of sixteen cartoon-like faces, half male, and half female, each representing distinct emotions. Each face describes a combination of two emotion dimensions, Pleasure and Arousal. Based on these dimensions, the emotion cards can be divided into four quadrants: Calm-Pleasant, Calm-Unpleasant, Excited-Pleasant, and Excited-Unpleasant.

WHO INVENTED IT?

Bradley 1994

WHY

1. It is an inexpensive method.
2. The results are easy to analyze.
3. Emotional responses are subtle and difficult to measure.
4. Emotion cards is a cross-cultural tool.

5. Facial emotions are typically universally recognized

CHALLENGES

1. Emotions of male and female faces are interpreted differently.
2. Sometimes users want to mark more than one picture to express a more complex emotional response.

HOW

1. Decide the goal of the study.
2. Recruit the participants.
3. Brief the participants.
4. When each interaction is complete the researcher asks the participant to select one of a number of cards that shows facial expressions that they associate with the interaction.

RESOURCES

Emotion cards
Notebook
Pens
Video camera
Release forms
Interview plan or structure
Questions, tasks and discussion items
Emotion cards

DAY IN THE LIFE

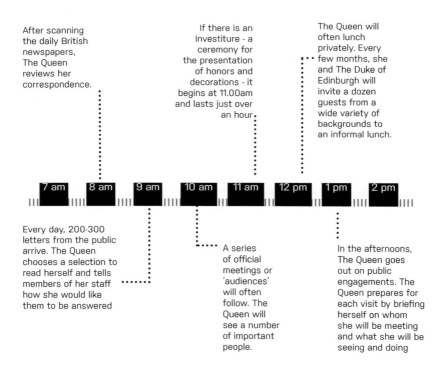

After scanning the daily British newspapers, The Queen reviews her correspondence.

If there is an Investiture - a ceremony for the presentation of honors and decorations - it begins at 11.00am and lasts just over an hour.

The Queen will often lunch privately. Every few months, she and The Duke of Edinburgh will invite a dozen guests from a wide variety of backgrounds to an informal lunch.

7 am   8 am   9 am   10 am   11 am   12 pm   1 pm   2 pm

Every day, 200-300 letters from the public arrive. The Queen chooses a selection to read herself and tells members of her staff how she would like them to be answered

A series of official meetings or 'audiences' will often follow. The Queen will see a number of important people.

In the afternoons, The Queen goes out on public engagements. The Queen prepares for each visit by briefing herself on whom she will be meeting and what she will be seeing and doing

DOT VOTING

CONCEPT 1

CONCEPT 2

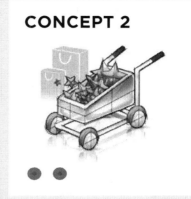

CONCEPT 3

CONCEPT 4

CONCEPT 5

CONCEPT 6

FIVE WHYS

WHAT
Five Whys is an iterative question method used to discover the underlying cause of a problem. For every effect there is a root cause. The primary goal of the technique is to determine the underlying cause of a problem by repeating the question "Why?"

WHO INVENTED IT
The technique was originally developed by Sachichi Toyoda Sakichi Toyoda was a Japanese inventor and industrialist. He was born in Kosai, Shizuoka. The son of a poor carpenter, Toyoda is referred to as the "King of Japanese Inventors". He was the founder of the Toyota Motor company. The method is still an important part of Toyota training, culture and success.

Sakichi Toyoda - Wikipedia, the free encyclopedia, https:// en.wikipedia.org/wiki/Sakichi_ Toyoda (accessed July 06, 2016).

WHY
When we fix the root cause the problem does not reoccur

HOW
1. Five whys could be taken further to a sixth, seventh, or higher level, but five is generally sufficient to get to a root cause.
2. Gather a team and develop the problem statement in agreement
3. Establish the time and place that the problem is occurring
4. Ask the first "why" of the team: why is this problem taking place?
5. Ask four more successive "whys," repeating the process
6. You will have identified the root cause when asking "why" yields no further useful information.
7. Discuss the last answers and settle on the most likely systemic cause.
8. Fix the root problem

FLY-ON-THE-WALL

WHAT
Observation method where the observer remains as unobtrusive as possible and observes and collects data relevant to a research study in context with no interaction with the participants being observed. The name derived from the documentary film technique of the same name.

WHO INVENTED IT?
Alex Bavelas 1944
Lucy Vernile, Robert A. Monteiro 1991

1. Low cost
2. No setup necessary
3. Can observe a large number of participants.
4. Objective observations
5. Compared to focus groups, setup, data collection, and processing are much faster.

CHALLENGES

1. No interaction by the observer.
2. Observer cannot delve deeper during a session.
3. No interruption allowed
4. Observer cannot obtain details on customer comments during a session

HOW

1. Define activity to study
2. Select participants thoughtfully
3. Choose a context for the observation
4. Carefully observe the interaction or experience. This is best done by members of your design team.
5. It is important to influence the participants as little as possible by your presence.
6. Observe but do not interact with participants while observing them in context.
7. Capture Data
8. Identify issues
9. Identify needs
10. Create design solutions based on observed and experienced human needs.

FOCUS GROUPS

WHAT

Focus groups are discussions usually with 6 to 12 participants led by a moderator. Focus groups are used during the the design of products, services and experiences to get feedback from people They are often conducted in the evening and take on average two hours. 8 to 12 questions are commonly explored in discussion.

"

The purpose of focus groups is not to infer, but to understand, not to generalize but to determine a range, not to make statements about the population but to provide insights about how people perceive a situation."

Richard A. Krueger

WHO INVENTED IT?

Robert K. Merton 1940 Bureau of Applied Social Research.

WHY

1. Low cost per participant compared to other research methods.
2. Easier than some other methods to manage

CHALLENGES

1. Removes participants from

9. List your goals.
10. How will the information be used?
11. How will you communicate the findings?
12. What is your primary question?
13. How many people should you interview?
14. How long will the interviews take and how long will it take to transcribe the interviews?
15. It takes 4 to 6 hours to transcribe one recorded hour of an interview.
16. Who is your audience and what method will you use to communicate with them?
17. What is the time line? Create a time line that addresses the following: preliminary research, locating interviewees, conducting interviews, transcribing the interviews, analyzing the transcripts, and formulating the finalized product of your project. Formulate rough deadlines to keep yourself on track.
18. Who will conduct the interviews?
19. Do the interviewers need to be trained?
20. Be aware of and minimize interviewer bias interviewees may respond differently to different interviewers based upon differences in interview style, age, race, class, gender, or culture.
21. What language will interviews be conducted in?
22. Is interpretation needed during the interview?

23. What tools or equipment will you need?
24. You will need tape, video, or digital recorders to record the interviews. A computer is needed transcribe the interview.
25. Who will transcribe the interviews?
26. What resources , people and money, will be needed?
27. How will you address confidentiality? Will you need a non disclosure agreement?
28. How will the data be analyzed?
29. Who will write the report or communicate the findings? materials?

CONDUCTING THE INTERVIEW

1. Create a list of people to interview.
2. Contact them and set up a time to meet.
3. Allow 2 hours face to face for each interview.
4. The best quality data is gathered face to face.

CREATE THE INTERVIEW GUIDE

1. An interview guide is a set of questions that you plan to ask during the interview.
2. Your interview guide is designed to guide you through process.
3. An interview guide directs the conversation to make sure that desired content is covered.
4. It creates uniformity when

you interview multiple interviewees or have multiple interviewers.

Adapted from Ash Maurya, Running Lean, 2012

PROBLEM DEFINITION INTERVIEW

WHAT
Identify your target audience. Test your assumptions about the audience and their needs. Interview at least ten people. Ask the participants to rank their top three needs. Ask the participant how each problem should be solved. How do the participants solve the problems today?

A SCRIPT FOR THE PROBLEM INTERVIEWS

WELCOME
Explain the interview process and the purpose of the interview.

COLLECT BACKGROUND INFORMATION
Ask introductory questions and collect necessary background information: "Before we go to the problems, I would like to know.... how often / with whom / do you...?"

TELL A STORY
Illustrate the top problems you want to explore. "Let me tell you about the problems we are tackling...do any of these resonate with you?"

PROBLEM RANKING
State the top 3 problems and ask the interviewee to rank them. Ask if the interviewee has any other problems related to the issue

EXPLORE CUSTOMER'S WORLDVIEW
Go through each problem and ask the interviewees how they address them today.

WRAP-UP
Ask for permission to follow-up.

DOCUMENT RESULTS.
Document thoughts that you did not have time to write down while interviewing.

Adapted from Ash Maurya, Running Lean, 2012

INTERVIEWING

WHAT
Interviewing is a method of ethnographic research that has been described as a conversation with a purpose.

WHY
1. Contextual interviews uncover tacit knowledge about people's context.
2. The information gathered can be detailed.
3. The information produced by contextual inquiry is

relatively reliable

CHALLENGES

1. End users may not have the answers
2. Contextual inquiry may be difficult to challenge even if it is misleading.
3. Keep control
4. Be prepared
5. Be aware of bias
6. Be neutral
7. Select location carefully

WHEN

1. Know Context
2. Know User
3. Frame insights

HOW

1. Contextual inquiry may be structured as 2 hour one on one interviews.
2. The researcher does not usually impose tasks on the user.
3. Go to the user's context. Talk, watch listen and observe.
4. Understand likes and dislikes.
5. Collect stories and insights.
6. See the world from the user's point of view.
7. Take permission to conduct interviews.
8. Do one-on-one interviews.
9. The researcher listens to the user.
10. 2 to 3 researchers conduct an interview.
11. Understand relationship between people, product and context.
12. Document with video, audio and notes.

RESOURCES

Computer
Notebook
Pens
Video camera
Release forms
Interview plan or structure
Questions, tasks and discussion items
Confidentiality agreement

WRITING AN INTERVIEW GUIDE

HOW

1. Plan in advance what you want to achieve
2. Research the topic
3. Select a person to interview.
4. Meet them in their location if possible.
5. Set a place, date, and time.
6. Be sure he or she understands how long the interview should take and that you plan to record the session.
7. Start with an open-ended question. It is a good way to put the candidate at ease,
8. Tape record the interview if possible.
9. Decide what information you need
10. Write down the information you'd like to collect through the interview. Now frame your interview questions around this information.
11. Prepare follow-up questions to ask.
12. Research the person that you are interviewing
13. Check your equipment and run through your questions.
14. Use neutral wording
15. Do not ask leading questions or questions that show bias.
16. Leave time for a General Question in the End
17. The last question should allow

SAMPLE INTERVIEW CONSENT FORM

Research should, be based on participants' freely volunteered informed consent. The researcher has a responsibility to explain what the research is about and who will see the data. Participants should be aware that they can refuse to participate; confidentiality, and how the research will be used.

The information contained within this book is strictly for educational purposes. If you wish to apply ideas contained in this book you are taking full responsibility for your actions. There are no representations or warranties, express or implied, about the completeness, accuracy, reliability, suitability or availability with respect to the information, products, services, or related graphics contained in this book for any purpose. Any use of this information is at your own risk.

Purpose of the research
The purpose of this project is [purpose]. *Provide a brief, usually one-paragraph, explanation of what the research is about and state why the subject is being asked to participate [e.g., inclusion/exclusion criteria]*

What we will ask you to do
If you agree to be in this study, you are asked to participate in a recorded interview. The interview will include questions about [topic] , The interview will take about [duration] minutes to complete. With your permission, we would also like to tape-record the interview.

Risks and benefits
There is the risk that you may find some of the questions about [topic] to be sensitive. *[Describe any possible benefit to the participants or others that may reasonably be expected from the research; then describe any reasonably foreseeable risks or discomforts to the participants, or state "there are no foreseeable risks," if none are identified.]*

Compensation:
There will be [amount of compensation] [type of compensation] compensation. *[Specify whether participants will be compensated and if so, the amount. If amount will be prorated for any reason, state this.]*

Taking part is voluntary
Taking part in this interview is completely voluntary. You may skip any questions that you do not want to answer. If you decide not to take part or to skip some of the questions, it will not affect your current or future relationship with Cornell University. If you decide to take part, you are free to withdraw at any time.

Your answers will be confidential

The records of this project will be kept private. In any sort of report we make public we will not include any information that will make it possible to identify you. Research records will be kept in a locked file; only [who] will have access to the records. [Regarding the storage of the tape, who will keep it, where will it be stored, after the transcription is done?] If we tape-record the interview, we will destroy the tape after it has been transcribed, which we anticipate will be within [duration] months of its taping.

If you have questions: [contact]

If you have questions

The researchers conducting this study are [researchers]. Please ask any questions you have now. If you have questions later, you may contact [name] at [email] or at [phone].

Statement of Consent

I have read the above information, and have received answers to any questions I asked. I consent to take part in the project. In addition to agreeing to participate, I also consent to having the interview tape-recorded. I understand the information presented above and that: My participation is voluntary, and I may withdraw my consent and discontinue participation in the project at any time. My refusal to participate will not result in any penalty.

You will be given a copy of this form to keep for your records.

Interviewee Signature ....Date ....
In addition to agreeing to participate, I also consent to having the interview tape-recorded.

Researcher's Signature ....Date ....
This consent form will be kept by the researcher for at least [duration] years beyond the end of the project and was approved by the [Organization] on [date].

This consent form will be kept by the researcher for at least [duration] years beyond the end of the project and was approved by the [Organization] on [date].

the interviewee to share any thoughts or opinions that they might want to share, such as "Thank you for all that valuable information, is there anything else you'd like to add before we end?"

18. Bring your questions to the interview
19. Explore the answers but return to your list of questions to follow your guide.
20. Record details such as the subject's name contact and details
21. Take detailed notes
22. Use empathy tools to encourage your participant to share information.
23. Final question: "Is there anything you think I should have asked that I didn't?"
24. Transcribe the interview
25. Write out both sides of the conversation, both question and answer.
26. Never change what the interviewee said or how they said it.
27. Outline the important points.
28. Edit the transcript for clarity, flow, and length.
29. Tell a story Now that you've gathered all of this great information and have accurately recorded it. It is important that you find a way to effectively document and share the story in a way that celebrates and accurately describes the story you were told.
30. Add details from your notes appearance and personality of your subject, ambient sounds, smells, visuals.
31. Check the facts.

Source: adapted from The Art of Interview" by Anne Williams

INTERVIEWING METHODS

CONTEXTUAL INQUIRY

WHAT

Contextual inquiry involves one-on-one observations and interviews of activities in the context. Contextual inquiry has four guiding principles:
1. Context
2. Partnership with users.
3. Interpretation
4. Focus on particular goals.

WHO INVENTED IT?

Whiteside, Bennet, and Holtzblatt 1988

WHY

1. Contextual interviews uncover tacit knowledge about people's context.
2. The information gathered can be detailed.
3. The information produced by contextual inquiry is relatively reliable

CHALLENGES

1. End users may not have the answers
2. Contextual inquiry may be difficult to challenge even if it is misleading.

HOW

1. Contextual inquiry may be structured as 2 hour one on one interviews.
2. The researcher does not usually impose tasks on the user.
3. Go to the user's context. Talk, watch listen and observe.
4. Understand likes and dislikes.
5. Collect stories and insights.
6. See the world from the user's point of view.
7. Take permission to conduct interviews.
8. Do one-on-one interviews.
9. The researcher listens to the user.
10. 2 to 3 researchers conduct an interview.
11. Understand relationship between people, product and context.
12. Document with video, audio and notes.

CONTEXTUAL LADDERING

WHAT
Contextual laddering is a one-on-one interviewing technique done in context. Answers are further explored by the researcher to uncover root causes or core values.

WHO INVENTED IT?
Gutman 1982, Olsen and Reynolds 2001.

WHY

1. Laddering can uncover underlying reasons for particular behaviors.
2. Laddering may uncover information not revealed by other methods.
3. Complement other methods
4. Link features and product attributes with user/customer values

CHALLENGES

1. Analysis of data is sometimes difficult.
2. Requires a skilled interviewer who can keep the participants engaged.
3. Laddering may be repetitive
4. Sometimes information may not be represented hierarchically.

HOW

1. Interviews typically take 60 to 90 minutes.
2. The introduction. The researcher gives information about the length of the interview, content, confidentiality and method of recording.
3. The body of the interview. The researcher investigates the user in context and documents the information gathered.
4. Ask participants to describe what kinds of features would be useful in or distinguish different products.
5. Ask why.
6. If this answer doesn't describe the root motivation ask why

again.
7. Repeat step 3. until you have reached the root motivation.
8. Wrap up. Verification and clarification

E-MAIL INTERVIEW

WHAT
With this method an interview is conducted via an e-mail exchange.

WHY
1. Extended access to people.
2. Background noises are not recorded.
3. Interviewee can answer the questions at his or her own convenience
4. It is not necessary to take notes
5. It is possible to use on-line translators.
6. Interviewees do not have to identify a convenient time to talk.

CHALLENGES
1. Interviewer may have to wait for answers.
2. Interviewer is disconnected from context.
3. Lack of communication of body language.

HOW
1. Choose a topic
2. Identify a subject.
3. Contact subject and obtain approval.
4. Prepare interview questions.
5. Conduct interview

6. Analyze data.

EXTREME USER INTERVIEW

WHAT
Interview experienced or inexperienced users of a product or service in order to discover useful insights that can be applied to the general users.

WHY
Extreme user's solutions to problems can inspire solutions for general users. Their behavior can be more exaggerated than general users so it is sometimes easier to develop useful insights from these groups.

CHALLENGES
1. Keep control
2. Be prepared
3. Be aware of bias
4. Be neutral
5. Select location carefully

HOW
1. Do a time line of your activity and break it into main activities
2. Identify very experienced or very inexperienced users of a product or service in an activity area.
3. Explore their experiences through interview.
4. Discover insights that can inspire design.
5. Refine design based on insights.

GROUP INTERVIEW

WHAT
This method involves interviewing a group of people.

WHY
People will often give different answers to questions if interviewed on=on=-one and in groups. If resources are available it is useful to interview people in both situations.

CHALLENGES
Group interview process is longer than an individual interview

HOW
1. Welcome everyone and introduce yourself
2. Describe the process.
3. Ask everyone to introduce themselves.
4. Conduct a group activity or warming-up exercise.
5. Break the larger group into smaller groups of 4 or 5 people and give them a question to answer. Ask each participant to present their response to the larger group.
6. Allow about 25 minutes.
7. Ask each interviewee to write a summary
8. Collect the summaries.
9. Ask if have any further comments.
10. Thank everyone and explain the next steps.
11. Give them your contact details.

GUIDED STORYTELLING

WHAT
Guided storytelling is interview technique, where the designer asks a participant to walk you through a scenario of use for a concept. Directed storytelling guides participants to describe their experiences and thoughts on a particular topic.

WHO INVENTED IT?
Whiteside, Bennet, and Holtzblatt 1988

WHY
Guided storytelling uncovers tacit knowledge.

CHALLENGES
1. Keep control
2. Be prepared
3. Be aware of bias
4. Be neutral
5. Select location carefully

HOW
1. Contextual inquiry may be structured as 2 hour one on one interviews.
2. The researcher does not usually impose tasks on the user.
3. Go to the user's context. Talk, watch listen and observe.
4. Understand likes and dislikes.

5. Collect stories and insights.
6. See the world from the user's point of view.
7. Take permission to conduct interviews.
8. Do one-on-one interviews.
9. The researcher listens to the user.
10. 2 to 3 researchers conduct an interview.
11. Understand relationship between people, product and context.

MAN IN THE STREET INTERVIEW

WHAT
Man in the street interviews are impromptu interviews recorded on video. They are usually conducted by two people, a researcher and a cameraman.

WHY
1. Contextual interviews uncover tacit knowledge.
2. The information gathered can be detailed.

CHALLENGES
1. Keep control
2. Be prepared
3. Be aware of bias
4. Be neutral
5. Ask appropriate questions
6. Select location carefully
7. Create a friendly atmosphere, interviewee to feel relaxed.
8. Clearly convey the purpose of the interview.
9. This method results in accidental sampling which may not be representative of larger groups.

HOW
1. Decide on goal for research.
2. Formulate about 10 questions related to topic
3. Use release form if required.
4. Conduct a preliminary interview.
5. Select location. It should not be too noisy or have other distracting influences
6. Approach people, be polite. Say, "Excuse me, I work for [your organization] and I was wondering if you could share your opinion about [your topic]."
7. If someone does not wish to respond, select another subject to interview.
8. Limit your time. Each interview should be no be longer than about 10 minutes.
9. Conduct 6 to 10 interviews

NATURALISTIC GROUP INTERVIEW

WHAT
Naturalistic group interview is an interview method where the participants know each other prior to the interview and so have conversations that are more natural than participants who do not know each other.

WHY

1. This method has been applied in research in Asia where beliefs are informed by group interaction.
2. Can help gain useful data in cultures where people are less willing to share their feelings.

CHALLENGES

Familiarity of participants can lead to Group-think.

HOW

1. The interview context should support natural conversation.
2. Select participants who have existing social relationships.
3. Group the participants in natural ways so that the conversation is as close as possible to the type of discussion they would have in their everyday life.
4. Groups should be no larger than four people for best results.

ONE-ON-ONE INTERVIEWS

WHAT

The one-on-one interview is an interview that is between a researcher and one participant in a face-to-face situation.

WHY

1. The best method for personal information
2. Works well with other methods in obtaining

information to inform design.
3. Can be used to exchange ideas or to gather information to inform design

CHALLENGES

1. Keep control
2. Be prepared
3. Be aware of bias
4. Be neutral
5. Select location carefully
6. Record everything
7. Combine one on one interviews with group interviews.

HOW

1. May be structured as 2 hour one on one interviews.
2. Select the questions and the subjects carefully.
3. Create interview guide,
4. Conduct a preinterview to refine the guide.
5. The researcher does not usually impose tasks on the user.
6. Go to the user's context. Talk, watch listen and observe.
7. Understand likes and dislikes.
8. Collect stories and insights.
9. See the world from the user's point of view.
10. Take permission to conduct interviews.
11. Understand relationship between person, product and context.
12. Document with video, audio and notes.

STRUCTURED INTERVIEW

WHAT

In a structured interview the researcher prepares a list of questions, script or an interview guide that they follow during the interview. Most interviews use a structured method.

INTERVIEW GUIDE

1. 4-5 distinct topics or questions
2. Distinct probes for each topic
3. Specific order
4. Order from general to specific
5. Begin with most important questions
6. Builds in transitions among topics

WHY

1. A structured interview is often used for phone interviews.
2. It is easy to analyze the results.
3. Structured interviews are often used by quantitative researchers.

TESTING THE INTERVIEW GUIDE

1. Are the questions phrased in a way that will elicit the information that you're seeking?
2. Are the questions clear?
3. Are the questions biased?
4. Are any of them closed ended?
5. Do any need expansion?
6. Did you use any double negatives?

CHALLENGES

1. Respondents may be less likely to discuss sensitive experiences.

HOW

1. The researcher should follow the script exactly.
2. The interviewer is required to show consistency in behavior across all interviews

ANALYSIS

1. Familiarization
2. Transcribing
3. Organizing
4. Coding
5. Reducing data
6. Displaying data
   - Helps organize data
   - See areas where analysis is complete
   - See patterns & themes
   - See how data "fits" theory
7. Drawing & Verifying Conclusions
8. Inductive: categories and themes emerge (grounded theory)
9. Deductive: processes of "fitting" the data into categories and themes (framework analysis)

PHOTO ELICITATION INTERVIEW

WHY
1. A method sometimes used to interview children.
2. Photos can make staring a conversation with a participant easier.
3. Photos can uncover meaning which is not uncovered in a face to face interview.

CHALLENGES
1. Photos can create ethical questions for the researcher.
2. A researcher may show bias in selecting subject of photos.

HOW
1. Define the context.
2. Select the participants
3. Either researcher or participant may take the photos.
4. Researcher analyses photos and plans the interview process
5. Researcher shows the photos to the participant and discusses their thoughts in relation to the photographs.
6. The interview is analyzed by the researcher.
7. Creeate a list of insights.

UNSTRUCTURED INTERVIEW

INTERVIEW GUIDE
1-2 broad topics

WHY
1. A useful technique for understanding how a subject may perform under pressure.
2. Unstructured interviews are used in ethnographic case studies
3. Respondents may be more likely to discuss sensitive experiences.

CHALLENGES
1. Interviewer bias is unavoidable.

HOW
Researchers need a list of topics to be covered during the interview.

The interviewer and respondents engage in a formal interview in that they have a scheduled time to sit and speak with each other and both parties recognize this to be an interview.
1. The interviewer has a clear plan of the focus and goal of the interview.
2. There is no interview guide.

3. The interviewer builds rapport with subject.
4. Questions are open-ended.
5. Unstructured interviews are used for developing an understanding of an as-of-yet not fully understood topic.

TELEPHONE INTERVIEW

WHAT

With this method an interview is conducted via telephone.

WHY

Wide geographical access
1. Allows researcher to reach hard to reach people.
2. Allows researcher to access closed locations.
3. Access to dangerous or politically sensitive sites

CHALLENGES
1. Lack of communication of body language.
2. Interviewer is disconnected from context.

HOW
1. Choose a topic
2. Identify a subject.
3. Contact subject and obtain approval.
4. Prepare interview questions.
5. Conduct interview
6. Analyze data.

MIXED METHOD RESEARCH

WHAT

Mixed methods research is a design for collecting, analyzing, and mixing both quantitative and qualitative data in a single study or series of studies to understand a research problem.

"

Mixed methods research is a systematic integration of quantitative and qualitative methods in a single study for purposes of obtaining a fuller picture and deeper understanding of a phenomenon."

Huey Chen

"

Mixed methods research is a set of procedures that should be used when integrating qualitative and quantitative procedures reflects the research question(s) better than each can independently. The combining of quantitative and qualitative methods should better inform the researcher and the effectiveness of mixed methods should be evaluated based upon how the approach enables the investigator to answer the research question(s) embedded in the purpose(s) (why the study is being conducted or is needed; the justification) of the study."

Newman, Ridenour, Newman & DeMarco, 2003

Qualitative and quantitative research provide a better understanding of users than either method can provide alone. Mixed methods research is becoming increasingly popular.

"

Combining qualitative and quantitative methods has gained broad appeal in public health research. The key question has become not whether it is acceptable or legitimate to combine methods, but rather how they will be combined to be mutually supportive and how findings achieved through different methods will be integrated."

NIH, Office of Behavioral and Social Science Research

QUALITATIVE:
1. Working with unfamiliar subjects.
2. When data is complex ambiguous or unclear
3. When you wish to understand meaning.
4. When you require flexibility.
5. For studying issues in detail

QUANTITATIVE
1. When the data is clearly defined
2. When metrics are known
3. When detailed numerical data is required
4. When repeatability is important
5. When generalizable across populations is needed

WHY USE MIXED METHODS?
Greene, Caracelli, and Graham (1989) identified the five purposes or rationales of mixed methodological studies:
1. Triangulation (i.e., seeking convergence and corroboration of results from different methods studying the same phenomenon),
2. Complementarity (i.e., seeking elaboration, enhancement, illustration, clarification of the results from one method with results from the other method),
3. Development (i.e., using the results from one method to other method),
4. Initiation (i.e., discovering paradoxes and contradictions

that lead to a reframing of the research question), and

5. Expansion (i.e., seeking to expand the breadth and range of inquiry by using different methods for different inquiry components).

WHEN TO USE IT

1. When you want to combine the advantages of quantitative (trends, large numbers, generalization) with qualitative (detail, small numbers, in-depth)
2. When you want to validate your findings
3. When you want to expand your quantitative findings
4. Both approaches have strengths and weaknesses

Some research methods such as interviews and observations can be either quantitative or qualitative. Quantitative data can be generalized to the larger population. In qualitative research subjects are selected because they have experienced the central phenomenon.

WHY USE MIXED METHODS"

1. Together quantitative and qualitative data provide both precise measurement and generalizability of quantitative research and the in-depth, complex picture of qualitative research
2. To validate quantitative results with qualitative data
3. Our quantitative data provide a general explanation and we need to follow-up with

participants and have them explain the quantitative results

4. When outcomes to be measured are not enough; and need to be complemented by understanding
5. Quantitative data may fail to provide specific reasons, explanations or examples
6. Qualitative research provides data about meaning and context
7. Findings are often not generalizable because of the small numbers & narrow range of participants
8. Qualitative research can provide specific examples of quantitative data.
9. Wit quantitative research it may be difficult to see the overall pattern
10. Selection of research methods should be made after the research questions are asked
11. Some methods work well in some contexts but not in other contexts
12. Mixed methods are used when one method only was is insufficient
13. If the results lead to divergent results, then more than one explanation is possible

SATURATION
Saturation occurs:
1. When no new information (redundancy) is obtained
   Source Lincoln & Guba, 1985; Patton, 1990
2. Through the constant comparison of data Recurrent

patterns and themes are seen

Source Glaser & Strauss, 1967, Cutcliffe & McKenna, 2002

MOBILE DIARY STUDY

WHAT
....

A mobile diary studies is a method that uses portable devices to capture a person's experiences in context when and where they happen such as their workplace or home. Participants can create diary entries from their location on mobile phones or tablets.

WHY

1. Most people carry a mobile phone.
2. It is a convenient method of recording diary entries.
3. It is easier to collect the data than collecting written diaries.
4. Collection of data happens in real time.
5. Mobile devices have camera, voice and written capability.

CHALLENGES

1. Can miss non verbal feedback.
2. Technology may be unreliable

HOW

1. Define intent
2. Define audience
3. Define context
4. Select the on-line diary study tool based.
5. Set up the diary study tool, create user accounts, and design study activities
6. Prepare introductory email or letter to participants, with study details and dates
7. Prepare the diary kit
   - User account on-line login details
   - Types of feedback
   - Contact details
   - Information about what to do regarding additional questions, user account issues,
8. Conduct on-line Meet & Brief sessions with participants
9. Create activity and assignment prompts can be written or video.
10. Monitor diary entries and maintain engagement with participants to keep them on task
11. Update and set next tasks
12. Respond to participant inquires, diary entries, or ensure technical support issues are being resolved
13. Pose additional questions or suggest alternative scenarios to gain deeper insights
14. Make notes and compile data to refer to for follow-up interviews and final data insights report
15. Conduct timely, final in-depth interviews to further probe and validate data revealed during the study
16. Thank participants and ensure compensation is given as applicable

BENEFITS

1. Participants record their experiences in their natural environment rather than an unrelated, unnatural environment such as a lab.
2. Participants more likely to capture influential external factors such as time, location, social or environmental triggers, etc.
3. Researchers can collect participant observations in longer durations
   + Diary studies offer participants more time for in-depth consideration and opportunities for creativity than traditional-type research sessions, allowing participants a few days per activity/question

DRAWBACKS

1. Researchers do not observe participants in their natural environment or collect their own real-time data
2. Participants may have a belief bias, adjust behaviors, or have difficulty recalling events
3. Researchers must trust participants on what they record or observe about their experiences and emotional behaviors
4. Finding the right respondents who can be creative is a MUST, which means recruiting might take longer to avoid selecting candidates that might plateau or withdraw before the study is complete

MYSTERY SHOPPER

WHAT

Mystery Shopping is a method used to anonymously evaluate products and services, operations, employee integrity, merchandising, and product quality. Mystery shoppers perform tasks such as purchasing a product, asking questions, registering complaints and then provide feedback about their experiences. Mystery shopping evaluation generates around $1.5 billion per annum and is growing.

MYSTERY SHOPPING IS ALSO KNOWN AS:

1. Secret Shopping
2. Experience Evaluation
3. Anonymous Audits
4. Mystery Customers
5. Digital Customers
6. Virtual Customers

WHO INVENTED IT?

Originally used in the 1940s as a way of evaluating employee integrity.n the 1940's, Wilmark coined the term "mystery shopping". In the 1970's and 80's, Shop 'n Chek popularized mystery shopping. Since 2010, mystery shopping has become a common form of evaluation in the medical tourism industry and in the UK in customer services provided by local authorities, and other non-profit organizations such as housing associations and churches. some fast-food restaurants are mystery-shopped three times a day and shoppers are rotated.

Source: Newhouse 2004: 2

WHO USES MYSTERY SHOPPING?
User include:
1. Banks
2. Gas stations
3. Retailers
4. Car dealers
5. Apartments
6. Manufacturers
7. Call Centers
8. E-Commerce services
9. Government agencies
10. Hospitals
11. Associations
12. Franchise operations
13. Promotions agencies Hotels
14. Restaurants
15. Movie Theaters
16. Recreation parks
17. Transportation systems
18. Fitness/health centers
19. Property management firms
20. Freight/courier services

WHO PROVIDES MYSTERY SHOPPING SERVICES?
1. Consultants
2. Marketing Firms
3. Private Investigators
4. Merchandising Companies
5. Advertising agencies

CHALLENGES
1. Time consuming
2. Employees may resist
3. Ethical management

BENEFITS OF MYSTERY SHOPPING
1. Metrics for service performance.
2. Improves customer retention.
3. Ensures service quality..
4. Competitive analyses.
5. Compliments marketing research data.
6. Identifies training needs and sales opportunities.
7. Educational tool.
8. Monitors employee integrity.

USE OF THE INTERNET
1. Many web sites use mystery shopping.
2. May be easier to implement on-line.

HOW
1. Define objectives.
2. Program & Questionnaire Design.
3. Create evaluation form for mystery shopper.
4. Recruit shoppers.
5. Train shoppers.
6. Conduct evaluation.
7. Analyze data.
8. Report conclusions and recommendations.
9. Review findings.
10. Implement actions.

OBJECTIVES & GOALS
Identify and define actionable goals.

QUESTIONNAIRE DESIGN
1. Design questionnaires to provide objective, observational feedback
2. Cover: greeting, customer

service, facility cleanliness and orderliness, speed of service, product quality and employee product knowledge
3. Ask only "yes" and "no" questions. Ask for clarification of no questions.
4. Include a "general comments" section
5. Use a scoring system. Give a weighting to the most important questions.

RECRUITING SHOPPERS
1. Mystery shoppers should match "real customer" profiles
2. Mystery shoppers are often employed as part time contractors.
3. Recruit through classified advertising,Internet or referrals.
4. There may be special requirements such as wearing glasses.
5. Shoppers may be asked to complete test shops during recruiting.

DATA COLLECTION
1. Provide shoppers with specific shopping tasks and clear written guidelines
2. Be consistent
3. Mystery shopper observations are limited to a choice of fixed alternatives

DATA PREPARATION
1. Check and validate each report.
2. Run quality control checks
3. Track data using relational database.

REPORTING
1. Process reports within 30 days.
2. The reports should be actionable.

REVIEW FINDINGS
1. Share the reports with training personnel
2. An ongoing program, is more effective than irregular audits.

HOW TO CHOOSE A MYSTERY SHOPPING PROVIDER
1. Experience
2. Reputation
3. Resources
4. Location

HOW TO MAKE THE MOST OF MYSTERY SHOPPING PROGRAMS
1. Inform employees of the program.
2. Promote the program.
3. Action the findings.
4. Take a positive approach.
5. Apply to employee training.
6. Share the findings
7. Evaluate only actionable issues.
8. Use yes/no questions
9. Limit use of open questions.
10. Benchmark and track trends.

Source: Adapted from Mark Michelson

OBSERVATION

WHAT
This method involves observing people in their natural activities and usual context such as work environment. With direct observation the researcher is present and indirect observation the activities may be recorded by means such as video or digital voice recording.

WHY
1. Allows the observer to view what users actually do in context.
2. Indirect observation uncovers activity that may have previously gone unnoticed

CHALLENGES
1. Observation does not explain the cause of behavior.
2. Obtrusive observation may cause participants to alter their behavior.
3. Analysis can be time consuming.
4. Observer bias can cause the researcher to look only where they think they will see useful information.

HOW
1. Define objectives
2. Define participants and obtain their cooperation.
3. Define The context of the observation: time and place.
4. In some countries the law requires that you obtain written consent to video people.
5. Define the method of observation and the method of recording information. Common methods are taking written notes, video or audio recording.
6. Run a test session.
7. Hypothesize an explanation for the phenomenon
8. Predict a logical consequence of the hypothesis
9. Test your hypothesis by observation
10. Analyze the data gathered and create a list of insights derived from the observations.

RESOURCES
Notepad computer
Pens
Camera
Video camera
Digital voice recorder

COVERT OBSERVATION

WHAT
Covert observation is to observe people without them knowing. The identity of the researcher and the purpose of the research are hidden from the people being observed.

1. This method may be used to reduce the effect of the observer's presence on the behavior of the subjects.
2. To capture behavior as it happens.
3. Researcher is more likely to observe natural behavior

CHALLENGES

1. The method raises serious ethical questions.
2. Observation does not explain the cause of behavior.
3. Can be difficult to gain access and maintain cover
4. Analysis can be time consuming.
5. Observer bias can cause the researcher to look only where they think they will see useful information.

HOW

1. Define objectives.
2. Define participants and obtain their cooperation.
3. Define The context of the observation: time and place.
4. In some countries the law requires that you obtain written consent to video people.
5. Define the method of observation and the method of recording information. Common methods are taking written notes, video or audio recording.
6. Run a test session.
7. Hypothesize an explanation for the phenomenon.
8. Predict a logical consequence of the hypothesis.
9. Test your hypothesis by observation
10. Analyze the data gathered and create a list of insights derived from the observations.

RESOURCES

Camera
Video Camera
Digital voice recorder

DIRECT OBSERVATION

WHAT
Direct Observation is a method in which a researcher observes and records behavior events, activities or tasks while something is happening recording observations as they are made.

WHO INVENTED IT?

Radcliff-Brown 1910
Bronisław Malinowski 1922
Margaret Mead 1928

WHY

To capture behavior as it happens.

CHALLENGES

1. Observation does not explain the cause of behavior.
2. Analysis can be time consuming.
3. Observer bias can cause the researcher to look only where they think they will see useful information.
4. Obtain a proper sample for

generalization.
5. Observe average workers during average conditions.
6. The participant may change their behavior because they are being watched.

HOW

1. Define objectives.
2. Make direct observation plan
3. Define participants and obtain their cooperation.
4. Define The context of the observation: time and place.
5. In some countries the law requires that you obtain written consent to video people.
6. Define the method of observation and the method of recording information. Common methods are taking written notes, video or audio recording.
7. Run a test session.
8. Hypothesize an explanation for the phenomenon.
9. Predict a logical consequence of the hypothesis.
10. Test your hypothesis by observation
11. Analyze the data gathered and create a list of insights derived from the observations.

RESOURCES

Notepad computer
Pens
Camera
Video Camera
Digital voice recorder

INDIRECT OBSERVATION

WHAT

Indirect Observation is an observational technique whereby some record of past behavior is used than observing behavior in real time. Humans cannot directly sense some things, we must rely on indirect observations with tools such as thermometers, microscopes, telescopes or X-rays.

WHY

1. To capture behavior or an event as it happens in it's natural setting.
2. Indirect observation uncovers activity that may have previously gone unnoticed
3. May be inexpensive
4. Can collect a wide range of data

CHALLENGES

1. Observation does not explain the cause of behavior.
2. Analysis can be time consuming.
3. Observer bias can cause the researcher to look only where they think they will see useful information.
4. Observe average workers during average conditions.
5. The participant may change their behavior because they are being watched.

HOW
1. Define objectives.
2. Make direct observation plan
3. Define participants and obtain their cooperation.
4. Define The context of the observation: time and place.
5. In some countries the law requires that you obtain written consent to video people.
6. Define the method of observation and the method of recording information.
7. Run a test session.
8. Hypothesize an explanation for the phenomenon.
9. Predict a logical consequence of the hypothesis.
10. Test your hypothesis by observation
11. Analyze the data gathered and create a list of insights derived from the observations.

NON-PARTICIPANT OBSERVATION

WHAT
The observer does not become part of the situation being observed or intervene in the behavior of the subjects. Used when a researcher wants the participants to behave normally. Usually this type of observation occurs in places where people normally work or live.

WHY
12. To capture behavior as it happens.

CHALLENGES
1. Observation does not explain the cause of behavior.
2. Analysis can be time consuming.
3. Observer bias can cause the researcher to look only where they think they will see useful information.
4. Obtain a proper sample for generalization.
5. Observe average workers during average conditions.
6. The participant may change their behavior because they are being watched.

HOW
1. Determine research goals.
2. Select a research context
3. The site should allow clear observation and be accessible.
4. Select participants
5. Seek permission.
6. Gain access
7. Gather research data.
8. Analyze data
9. Find common themes
10. Create insights

PARTICIPANT OBSERVATION

WHAT
Participant observation is an observation method where the researcher participates. The researcher becomes part of the situation being studied. The researcher may live or work in the context of the participant and may become an accepted member of the participant's community. This method was used extensively by the pioneers of field research.

WHO INVENTED IT?
Radcliff-Brown 1910
Bronisław Malinowski 1922
Margaret Mead 1928

WHY
1. The goal of this method is to become close and familiar with the behavior of the participants.
2. To capture behavior as it happens.

CHALLENGES?
1. My be time consuming
2. May be costly
3. The researcher may influence the behavior of the participants.
4. The participants may not show the same behavior if the observer was not present.
5. May be language barriers
6. May be cultural barriers

7. May be risks for the researcher.
8. Be sensitive to privacy, and confidentiality.

HOW
1. Determine research goals.
2. Select a research context
3. The site should allow clear observation and be accessible.
4. Select participants
5. Seek permission.
6. Gain access
7. Gather research data.
8. Analyze data
9. Find common themes
10. Create insights

OVERT OBSERVATION

WHAT
A method of observation where the subjects are aware that they are being observed.

WHO INVENTED IT?
Radcliff-Brown 1910
Bronisław Malinowski 1922
Margaret Mead 1928

WHY
To capture behavior as it happens.

CHALLENGES
1. Observation does not explain the cause of behavior.
2. Analysis can be time consuming.
3. Observer bias can cause the researcher to look only where they think they will see useful information.

HOW

1. Define objectives.
2. Define participants and obtain their cooperation.
3. Define The context of the observation: time and place.
4. In some countries the law requires that you obtain written consent to video people.
5. Define the method of observation and the method of recording information. Common methods are taking written notes, video or audio recording.
6. Run a test session.
7. Hypothesize an explanation for the phenomenon.
8. Predict a logical consequence of the hypothesis.
9. Test your hypothesis by observation
10. Analyze the data gathered and create a list of insights derived from the observations.

STRUCTURED OBSERVATION

WHAT

Particular types of behavior are observed and counted like a survey. The observer may create an event so that the behavior can be more easily studied. This approach is systematically planned and executed.

WHY

1. Allows stronger generalizations than unstructured observation.
2. May allow an observer to study behavior that may be difficult to study in unstructured observation.
3. To capture behavior as it happens.
4. A procedure is used which can be replicated.

CHALLENGES

1. Observation does not explain the cause of behavior.
2. Analysis can be time consuming.
3. Observer bias can cause the researcher to look only where they think they will see useful information.

HOW

1. Define objectives.
2. Define participants and obtain their cooperation.
3. Define The context of the observation: time and place.
4. In some countries the law requires that you obtain written consent to video people.
5. Define the method of observation and the method of recording information. Common methods are taking written notes, video or audio recording.
6. Run a test session.
7. Hypothesize an explanation for the phenomenon.
8. Predict a logical consequence of the hypothesis.
9. Test your hypothesis by

observation

10. Analyze the data gathered and create a list of insights derived from the observations.

UNSTRUCTURED OBSERVATION

WHAT
This method is used when a researcher wants to see what is naturally occurring without predetermined ideas. We use have an open-ended approach to observation and record all that we observe.

WHY
1. To capture behavior as it happens.
2. Observation is the most direct measure of behavior

CHALLENGES
1. Replication may be difficult.
2. Observation does not explain the cause of behavior.
3. Analysis can be time consuming.
4. Observer bias can cause the researcher to look only where they think they will see useful information.
5. Data cannot be quantified
6. In this form of observation there is a higher probability of observer's bias.

HOW
1. Select a context to explore
2. Take a camera, note pad and pen
3. Record things and questions that you find interesting
4. Record ideas as you form them
5. Do not reach conclusions.
6. Ask people questions and try to understand the meaning in their replies.

PERSONAL INVENTORY

WHAT
This method involves studying the contents of a research subject's purse, or wallet. Study the things that they carry every day.

WHO INVENTED IT?
Rachel Strickland and Doreen Nelson 1998

WHY
1. To provide insights into the user's lifestyle, activities, perceptions, and values.
2. To understand the needs priorities and interests.

HOW
1. Formulate aims of research
2. Recruit participants carefully.
3. Document the contents with photographs and notes
4. ask your research subject to talk about the objects and their meaning.

5. Analyze the data.

"

The participant is asked to bring their 'most often carried bag' and lay the objects they carry on a flat surface, talking through the purpose and last-use of each item. Things to look out for where the bag is kept in the home and what is clustered around it, what is packed/repacked on arrival/departure, and the use of different bags for different activities."

Jan Chipchase

RESOURCES
Camera
Notepad computer

PROBLEM DEFINITION INTERVIEW

WHAT
The problem interview is all about testing your assumptions about a problem and to whom it is a problem.

HOW
State the top 1-3 problems and ask the interviewee to rank them. Go through each problem and ask the interviewees how they

address them today. General rule of thumb: you are done with the problem interviews when.

6. You have a must-have problem.
7. You can identify the demographics.
8. Of an early adopter
9. You can describe how customers.
10. Solve this problem today
11. You should interview at least ten people.

A SCRIPT FOR THE PROBLEM INTERVIEWS

WELCOME: SET THE STAGE.
Shortly, explain how the interview works. "Thank you for taking the time...We are currently...."

COLLECT BACKGROUND INFORMATION
Ask introductory questions and collect necessary background information: "Before we go to the problems, I would like to know....how often / with whom / do you...?"

TELL A STORY TO SET THE CONTEXT
Illustrate the top problems you want to explore with your interviewee. "Let me tell you about the problems we are tackling...do any of these resonate with you?"

PROBLEM RANKING
State the top 1-3 problems and ask the interviewee to rank them.

Ask if the interviewee has any other problems related to the discussed issue that she would like to add.

EXPLORE CUSTOMER'S WORLD-VIEW

Go through each problem and ask the interviewees how they address them today. Let them go to as much detail as they wish. Consider (and ask if necessary) how they rate the problems: "must-have", "nice to have", or "don't need".

WRAP-UP

If you have a solution already in mind, give a conceptual description of what you have in mind in order to maintain interest. Then ask for permission to follow-up.

DOCUMENT RESULTS.

Take a few minutes to document your thoughts, that you did not have time to write down while interviewing.

Adapted from Ash Maurya, Running Lean, 2012

RECRUITMENT BRIEF

At the beginning of each phase, you must work as a team to:

1. Write your research questions
2. Decide what user research activities will help you answer your questions
3. Identify the target audience.

4. Decide recruitment method
5. Review your research.
6. Select your space and gather your materials.

A recruitment brief is the instructions that you will send to a recruiting company.
They will create a screener.

Always provide the agency with a written brief.

In your brief, you should cover:
1. Research dates.
2. Research location
3. The number of participants
4. A description of the people you would like to recruit.
5. Incentives

REVIEWING THE SCREENER

The agency will provide you with a screener. Check the screener to ensure that it aligns with your needs.

SERVICE SAFARI

WHAT

A service safari is a research method for understanding services. By using a service you will be able to understand how that service works and what the experience is like. A service safari could be used to find out information about a specific service.

When carrying out a service safari you should think about:

6. Different stages which make up the service
7. People involved in delivering the service and what they do
8. What objects you use or interact with
9. What spaces the service takes place in
10. What information is available to people
11. How people involved in delivering the
12. Service contribute to the experience.

Taking photos or video will help you to find out more about the service you are using

HOW
1. What is the service?
2. What information is there?
3. What makes this service work well?
4. What are users doing?
5. What products are used?
6. What makes this service not work well?
7. Who is involved?
8. What is the space like?

SHADOWING

WHAT
Shadowing is observing people in context. The researcher accompanies the user and observes user experiences and activities. It allows the researcher and designer to develop design insights through observation and shared experiences with users.

WHO INVENTED IT?
Alex Bavelas 1944
Lucy Vernile, Robert A. Monteiro 1991

WHY
1. This method can help determine the difference between what subjects say they do and what they really do.
2. It helps in understanding the point of view of people. Successful design results from knowing the users.
3. Define intent
4. Can be used to evaluate concepts.

CHALLENGES
1. Selecting the wrong people to shadow.
2. Hawthorne Effect, The observer can influence the daily activities under being studied.

HOW
1. Prepare
2. Select carefully who to shadow.
3. Observe people in context by members of your design team.
4. Capture behaviors that relate to product function.
5. Identify issues and user needs.
6. Create design solutions based on observed and experienced user needs.
7. Typical periods can be one day to one week.

RESOURCES
Video camera
Digital still camera
Notepad computer
Laptop Computer

MAPPING METHODS

CURRENT STATE MAPS
With a current-state journey map, you can:
1. Identify pain points and their causes.
2. Identify gaps in what you are offering customers.
3. Improve the efficiency and effectiveness of a current service or customer experience.
4. Craft a better customer experience for a product service or brand.
5. Plan systematically what your organization is delivering to customers.
6. Implement a more efficient system of touchpoints.
7. Understand how customers behave across multiple channels.
8. Identify where your current customer experience or service is most likely to fail.
9. Unite your team with the common goal of a better customer experience.
10. Identify opportunities for feedback or measurement.
11. Develop metrics for progress towards goals.
12. Align your organization with a better customer experience.

FUTURE STATE MAPS
1. With a future-state journey map, you can:
2. Plan a future service or customer experience.
3. Define a new service with better customer experience than your existing service.
4. Implement a new service or customer experience.
5. Develop a product or service road-map.
6. Envision the ideal customer experience or service.
7. Identify the infrastructure needed to create a new service or customer experience.
8. Plan for hiring new staff
9. Drive positive change in your organization.
10. Develop empathy for customers.

WHAT'S THE DIFFERENCE, BETWEEN A BLUEPRINT AND A JOURNEY OR EXPERIENCE MAP?
A customer journey map captures how your customer is feeling emotionally across touchpoints

over time.

A service blueprint captures the service or experience delivery process across touch points and the elements that make up the service including the things customers see and do not see.

The two types of maps complement each other. The order in which you create them depends on your goals.

SERVICE BLUEPRINT
1. Define employees roles about the customer experience.
2. Identify areas of service improvement.
3. Identify points where moments of truth will occur.
4. Capturing Dynamic Processes
5. Service blueprinting allows the capturing of dynamic processes in a visual manner.
6. A blueprint is one of few methods that allow you to visually convey events that change over time.
7. Relatively few methods allow for this type of dynamic, and at the same time visual, representation.
8. To identify where your customer experience is most likely to fail.
9. Opportunities for improvements
10. To plan and implement a new customer experience.
11. To implement metrics to measure your customer experience.
12. To audit and improve your service evidence or

touchpoints.

JOURNEY/EXPERIENCE MAP
1. To identify customer pain points and gaps in your touchpoints
2. To design a new service or experience with a focus on optimizing your customer's experience.
3. To audit the customer experience.
4. To develop new touch points to improve the customer experience.

USER STORIES

WHAT
User stories describe a user and the reason why they need to use the service you're building.

You must use user stories when building your service - they're essential to building and running a service that meets user needs.

WHAT TO INCLUDE
They should include:
1. The person using the service (the actor)
2. What the user needs the service for (the narrative)
3. Why the user needs it (the goal)

FORMAT
They have the following format:

As a... [who is the user?]

I needxxxx
So thatxxxx

FOCUS ON THE GOAL

The most important part of a user story is the goal. This helps you:

Make sure you're solving the need
Decide when the story is done and a user need is met
If you're struggling to write the goal then you should reconsider why you think you need that feature.

WHAT-HOW-WHY

WHAT

The What-How-Why method is a tool to help develop a deeper understanding of stakeholders.

You start with concrete observing what the behavior is then How the person is behaving then finally go to and then finally develop a model for Why. What is the underlying factors driving the behavior?

HOW

You should divide activities into What, How and Why.

1. Record concrete observations of what is happening. What is the person doing?

What is happening in the background? What is the person holding? Try to be as objective as possible.

2. How is the person doing what they are doing? Record how the person is doing their activity. Try to describe the emotional impact of performing the task.

3. Develop a theory for why the person is doing what they are doing? What are the underlying emotional drivers behind what you have observed? Make educated guesses regarding motivation and emotions.

4. Test your assumptions with stakeholders.

Source: adapted from Rikke Dam and Teo Siang, Interactive Design Foundation

WWWWWH

'Who, What, Where, When, Why, and How'? is a method for getting a thorough understanding of the problem, It is used to obtain basic information in police investigations. A well-known golden rule of journalism is that if you want to know the full story about something you have to answer all the five W's. Journalists argue your story isn't complete until you answer all six questions.

1. Who is involved?
2. What occurred?
3. When did it happen?
4. Where did it happen?
5. Why did it occur?

WHO INVENTED IT?

Hermagoras of Temnos, Greece 1st century BC.

WHY

This method helps create a story that communicates clearly the nature of an activity or event to stakeholders.

HOW

1. Ask the questions starting with the 5 w's and 1 h question words.
2. Identify the people involved
3. Identify the activities and make a list of them.
4. Identify all the places and make a list of them.
5. Identify all the time factors and make a list of them.
6. Identify causes for events of actions and make a list of them.
7. Identify the way events took place and make a list of them.
8. Study the relationships between the information.

"

I keep six honest serving men. They taught me all I knew. Their names are what and why and when and how and where and who."

Rudyard Kipling

SOME WWWWWH QUESTIONS

WHO

1. Is affected?
2. Who believes that the problem affects them?
3. Needs the problem solved?
4. Does not want the problem to be solved?
5. Could stand in the way of a solution?

WHEN

1. Does it happen
2. Doesn't it happen?
3. Did it start?
4. Will it end?
5. Is the solution needed?
6. Might it happen in the future?
7. Will it be a bigger problem?
8. Will it improve?

WHERE
1. Does it happen?
2. Doesn't it happen
3. Else does it happen?
4. Is the best place to solve the problem

WHY
1. Is this situation a problem?
2. Do you want to solve it?
3. Do you not want to solve it?
4. Does it not go away?
5. Would someone else want to solve it?
6. Can it be solved?
7. Is it difficult to solve?

WHAT
1. May be different in the future
2. Are its weaknesses?
3. Do you like?
4. Makes you unhappy about it?
5. Is flexible?
6. Is not flexible?
7. Do you know?
8. Do you not understand?
9. How have you solved similar problems?
10. Are the underlying ideas?
11. Are the values involved?
12. Are the elements of the problem and how are they related?
13. What can you assume to be correct
14. Is most important
15. Is least important
16. Are your goals?
17. Do you need to discover?

CHAPTER REVIEW

During this phase you will immerse yourself in the lives of your stakeholders and gain an understanding of what is important to them.

1. Develop empathy for your stakeholders.
2. Develop and implement a research plan.
3. Assume a beginner's mindset.
4. Carry out user research
5. Imagine yourself in that person's situation.
6. Adopt a beginner's way of thinking. Withhold judgement and preconceived bias.
7. Identify gaps in knowledge.
8. Set Aside Your Beliefs, concerns and personal agenda and try to see things from the stakeholders points point of view.
9. Question everything. Be curious.
10. Listen.
11. Talk to users to uncover underlying needs.
12. Immerse yourself in your customer's reality.
13. Walk in your user's shoes.
14. Look for your end user's workarounds for their problems.
15. Learn what the stakeholder would do.
16. Immerse yourself in the problem. Walk in your user's shoes, observe what's not being said.
17. Capture your learnings.

CHAPTER REVIEW

1. What is the purpose of the discovery phase?
2. What are four methods that can be used during the discovery phase?
3. What is the meaning of the word "empathy"?
4. What is the greatest single cause of failure of design developments?
5. What is a persona?
6. Who are the subjects of research during the discovery phase?
7. Why should an organization do customer research?
8. How many personas is a manageable number to cover an organizations different customer segments?
9. What are four possible outputs of the discovery phase?
10. What are four different types of customer segmentation?
11. What criteria should you consider when selecting a design team?
12. Name four types of ethnographic frameworks.
13. What does AEIOU stand for?
14. How many people are usually recruited for a focus group?
15. When and why should you use an interview consent form?
16. What are four things to consider when writing an interview guide?
17. What is contextual laddering?
18. Who are extreme users?
19. When should you use an unstructured interview?

EXERCISE ONE
INTERVIEW
QUESTION GUIDE

TASK
Develop an interview question guide related to service design with 10 to 15 questions. Answer the questions listed below under the heading "planning" to explain your thinking behind the questions that you have developed.

PROCESS
1. Select a topic for an interview related to a service design and develop ten to fifteen questions
2. Adjust the language of the interview according to the respondent.
3. Take care to word questions so that respondents are motivated to answer as completely and honestly as possible.
4. Develop probes that will elicit more detailed responses to key questions.
5. Begin the interview with a "warm-up" question— something that the respondent can answer easily. This initial rapport-building will put you more at ease with one another and thus will make the rest of the interview flow more smoothly.
6. Think about the logical flow of the interview. What topics should come first? What follows more or less

"naturally
7. More sensitive or difficult questions should be asked toward the end of the interview, when rapport has been established.
8. The last question should provide some closure for the interview.

PLANNING
In addition to creating the interview guide questions respond with at least a paragraph for each of the following:
1. Identify and summarize the purpose of your interview.
2. How will the information you gather be used?
3. Explain how you will structure the interview and your reasoning behind the structuring of the interview. Include a list of topics you plan to cover.
4. Compose the questions you will use. Develop a minimum of 5 open and 5 closed ended questions.
5. Identify the opening techniques you will utilize to build rapport with the interviewee.
6. Identify types/examples of questions you want to avoid during interview.
7. Identify your own beliefs (sympathetic, unsympathetic, or some mixture of both) and explain how these could affect your interview. Do you think that your beliefs are influenced by your own age, cultural, gender, sexual orientation, or ethnicity?

8. Identify steps you can take to limit the impact of your own beliefs on the interview. Be as specific as possible.

HOW

1. Biases: Avoid leading questions.
2. Language: Use terms that participants can understand, given their knowledge, language skills, cultural background, age, gender, etc. Be mindful of the social or cultural contexts of your questions.
3. Concise: Keep the questions as short and specific as possible. Avoid asking two-in-one questions, such as, "Do you travel by car and by bike?"
4. Frame: Avoid questions with a strong positive or negative association. Avoid phrasing questions as negatives (e.g., "How don't you like to get to work?").
5. Plan to interview people for 90 minutes to 2 hours.
6. Don't leave your most important questions until the very end in case your interview gets cut short.
7. Limit an interview to just three or four major topics and group three or four questions together under each topic.
8. Respondents should be able to choose their own terms when answering questions.
9. Questions should be as neutral as possible. .
10. Questions should be asked one at a time.

11. Questions should be worded clearly. This includes knowing any terms particular to the program or the respondents' culture.
12. Be careful asking "why" questions. This type of question infers a cause-effect relationship that may not truly exist. These questions may also cause respondents to feel defensive, e.g., that they have to justify their response, which may inhibit their responses to this and future questions.

ORDERING QUESTIONS

1. Start with earlier events and move on to more recent events;
2. Begin with simpler topics and move to those that are more complex;
3. Group questions on each domain/topic together;
4. Within domains, start with the most concrete issues and move to the more abstract
5. Start with the least-sensitive questions and move to most sensitive.

TYPES OF QUESTIONS

One can ask questions about:
1. Behaviors - about what a person has done or is doing
2. Opinions/values - about what a person thinks about a topic
3. Feelings - note that respondents sometimes respond with "I think ..." so be careful to note that you're looking for feelings
4. 4. Knowledge - to get facts

about a topic

5. Sensory - about what people have seen, touched, heard, tasted or smelled
6. Background/demographics - standard background questions, such as age, education, etc.
7. Direct questions: 'Do you find it easy to keep smiling when serving customers?'; 'Are you happy with the way you and your husband decide how money should be spent?' Such questions are perhaps best left until towards the end of the interview, in order not to influence the direction of the interview too much.
8. Indirect questions: 'What do most people round here think of the ways that management treats its staff?', perhaps followed up by 'Is that the way you feel too?', in order to get at the individual's own view.
   o Structuring questions: 'I would now like to move on to a different topic'.
9. Follow-up questions: getting the interviewee to elaborate his/her answer, such as 'Could you say some more about that?'; 'What do you mean by that . . .?'
10. Probing questions: following up what has been said through direct questioning.
11. Specifying questions: 'What did you do then?'; 'How did X react to what you said?'
12. Interpreting questions: 'Do you mean that your leadership role has had

to change from one of encouraging others to a more directive one?''

SEQUENCE OF QUESTIONS
1. Before asking about feelings and conclusions, first ask about some facts.
2. Intersperse fact-based questions throughout the interview to avoid leaving respondents disengaged.
3. Ask questions about the present before questions about the past or future.
4. The last questions might be to allow respondents to provide any other information they prefer to add and their impressions of the interview.

STRUCTURE
INTRODUCTIONS
10 minutes
Introduce yourself, introduce the project, tell them why you're interviewing people like them. You should think about how soon you will introduce the precise topic of your research area, or your client's name. We would usually introduce this at the beginning unless we feel that the client name might color the participant's responses. Let the participant know what to expect during the interview and give them a chance to ask questions. Most people won't have been interviewed before so take the time to put them at ease, make eye contact and smile!

GETTING TO KNOW YOUR PARTICIPANT
10 minutes
Start broad, ask them about their life, job, hobbies, family. Get them used to the process of being asked and answering questions. You don't need to move toward your design challenge too quickly — aim to build up a rapport. Listen out for interesting facts in this early stage as they may guide later questions. A great opening question is to ask your participant to describe a typical weekday and weekend day.

MORE FOCUSED QUESTIONS
20 minutes
Don't start with questions around your brief. You should move toward the detailed area gradually; ask more specific questions but still keep things open.

DETAILED QUESTIONS
40 minutes
Now it's time to get into the detailed questions around you brief. This time should be subdivided into smaller sections to keep the conversation varied and interesting. The individual nature of your brief will guide how best to use this time, a simple way to break it down would be to cover four main areas giving each 10 minutes.

WRAP UP
10 minutes
Tell the participant that the interview is over, give them a chance to ask any questions. Thank them for their time and explain what happens next. Leave your contact details with them in case they have questions once you've left. Source: Developed from:

Source: "Tips for writing a discussion Guide" Matt Cooper Wright IDEO 2015

EXERCISE TWO
IDENTIFY KEY STAKEHOLDERS

INSTRUCTIONS

Identify the stakeholders who may be affected by your design. Stakeholders are those who can have a positive or negative effect the success of your design. They can be recruited to give you useful feedback.

End-users
1.
2.
3.
4.

Vendors
1.
2.
3.
4.

Community
1.
2.
3.
4.

Organizations
1.
2.
3.
4.

Employees
1.
2.
3.
4.

Individuals
1.
2.
3.
4.

11
SYNTHESIS PHASE

SYNTHESIS

WHAT

Synthesis is the convergent part of the design process. In this stage we review the research, make connections, uncover insights, distill the data. We make sense of the information. What are the insights? What is connected? What are the unmet needs and desires of your audience? How can your design be unique, and better than what is already out there?

ACTIONABLE INSIGHTS

Design Thinking provides insights that are based on unrecognized or unmet needs. An insight is a fresh point of view based on a deep understanding of the way of thinking and behavior. An insight occurs by mentally connecting two or more things that have not been connected before. These things may be things that many people have seen or experienced but not connected before. A goal of Design Thinking is to build actionable insights

USER NEED STATEMENT

The user need statement or question is a statement of the desires or needs of end users expressed in their own words.

User Need Statement:
I am a doctor who has a hard time keeping babies warm because I do not have electricity.

POINT OF VIEW STATEMENT

A point-of-view (POV) is reframing of a design challenge into an actionable problem statement. The term Point of View Statement is often used in design thinking to describe a user need statement. The POV is used as the basis for design ideation. The POV defines the design intent. The POV helps reframe he design problem into an actionable focus for the generation of ideas.

Information Architecture and Design Strategy: The Importance of Synthesis during the Process of Design Jon Kolko, Savannah College of Art and Design

WHAT IS AN INSIGHT?

WHAT

1. An unrecognized fundamental human truth.
2. A new way of viewing the world that causes us to reexamine existing conventions and challenge the status quo.
3. A penetrating observation about human behavior that results in seeing consumers from a fresh perspective.
4. The act or result of understanding the inner nature of things or of seeing intuitively (called noesis in Greek)
5. A discovery about the underlying motivations that drive people's actions.
6. An understanding of cause and effect based on identification of relationships and behaviors within a model, context, or scenario
7. The power of acute observation and deduction, discernment, and perception

5. Simple in language and concept
6. Meaningful and memorable
7. Speaks to your audience
8. Inspires clear, direct action
9. Reinforces ownership and commitment
10.

Source: Michael Morgan Senior User Experience Researcher at ADP Innovation Labs New York

Groups typically perform better on insight problems than individuals. Insights that occur in the field are typically reported to be associated with a sudden "change in understanding" and with "seeing connections and contradictions" in the problem.

Source: Smith, C. M.; Bushouse, E.; Lord, J. "Individual and group performance on insight problems:

YOU HAVE A SIGNIFICANT INSIGHT WHEN

1. It reexamines existing conventions.
2. It solves a real problem.
3. It inspires action.
4. Grounded in real data

ACTIONABLE INSIGHTS

In order to be actionable, as the expression of a consumer truth, an insight should be stated as a sentence, containing:

1. An observation or a wish, e.g. "I would like to ...."
2. A motivation explaining the wish, e.g. " because ..."
3. A barrier preventing the consumer from being satisfied with the fulfillment of his/her

motivation, e.g. " but..."

INSIGHTS RECOGNIZE RELATIONSHIPS
1. Connections
2. Tensions
3. Contrasts.
4. Events
5. Failures
6. Cause & Effect
7. Gaps
8. Mismatches
9. Misaligned
10. Frustrations
11. Pain Points
12. Timeliness
13. Outcomes, planned and unintended.

ASK THOUGHTFUL QUESTIONS:
1. Put oneself in user situations, keep asking "why".
2. Capture the insights on post-its.

LOOK FOR EMERGING PATTERNS:
1. Recurring Points or themes; similar situations
2. Experiences
3. Intensity of the experience

UNDERSTAND THE ACTION AND BEHAVIOR:
1. Perceive the social context.
2. Sense the motivations.
3. Feel the Emotions.
4. Recognize the relationships.

INSIGHT TOOL SAM/ THINK FEEL DO FRAMEWORK

1. **Social context**
   - Who they do the 'action or activity' with?
   - What is their relationship, social interaction?
   - Why they behave the way they do?
2. **Action or behavior**
   - What is the behavior?
   - What actions or activities they are involved?
   - Why?
3. **Motivations**
   - What do they think?
   - How do they feel?
   - What are the reason(s) for actions and/or behavior?
   - What are the beliefs?
   - What are the values?
   - What is the underlying thinking?
   - What are the aspirations?
   - What are the Emotions or Feelings?

Source: Adapted from Design Thinking Guidebook for Public Sector innovation in Bhutan

ACTOR MAP

WHAT

An actor map is a visual depiction of the key actors within a system.

The Actors Map represents the system of stakeholders and their relationships. Some actors may not have a stake in the design outcome but may influence or be influenced by the project. It is a view of the service and its context. Stakeholders are organized by their function.

The goal of of an actor map is to produce a prioritized list of individuals or organizations to target as part of an action plan.

WHY

1. Understanding relationships is an important aspect of service design.
2. Inexpensive and fast.
3. Connects to existing research tools and methods
4. Makes implicit knowledge explicit
5. Structures complex reality
6. Flexible for use in different contexts.
7. Understand general landscape of key actors.
8. Determine who needs to be involved.
9. Explore various actors' roles in the system.
10. Diagnose the strength of connections among actors.
11. Consider how relationships, roles, or information flows are changing.
12. Patterns

13. Determine where tthere are gaps or blockages.
14. Understand how structures are changing.
15. Consider who is, has been, or should be involved.
16. Identify opportunities to build new relationships.

HOW

Estimated time 1.5 – 2 hours.
1. Identify an set of key actors.
2. Prepare a Draft Map
3. The desired geographic scale of the map local, regional, national.
4. Identify the core of the map
5. Label the core for example females aged 21 to 31 years.
6. Identify related subsystems that influence the core.
7. Identify relevant actors and roles
8. Brainstorm additional relevant actors and roles
9. What people or places do core stakeholders interact with on a regular basis?
10. What organizations support or influence those that interact with the core?
11. What types of local, regional, national, or international organizations influence the core's experiences related to the topic?
12. Who funds the people, places, or organizations?
13. Who conducts relevant research?
14. Who are the most influential actors based on perceived level of influence over the core.
15. Participants take a half hour to review the draft actor map before the session

16. What changes might you suggest?
17. What organizations, agencies, companies, or individuals would you suggest adding to the map? How do these actors connect to what's already depicted?

Adapted from sources including sources include: Systems Thinkinging Toolkit FSG

" "

We spend a lot time designing the bridge, but not enough time thinking about the people who are crossing it."

Dr. Prabhjot Singh
Director of Systems Design at the
Earth Institute

ACTOR MAP

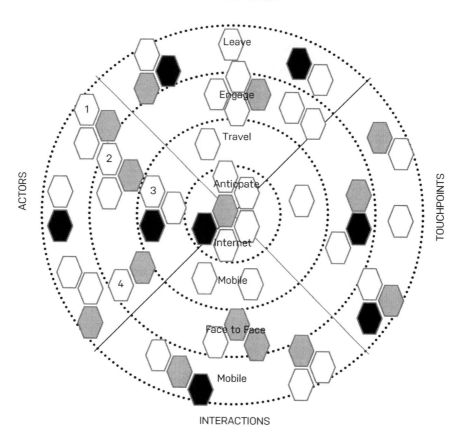

ACTIVITY STAGE

Leave

Engage

Travel

Anticipate

ACTORS

TOUCHPOINTS

1

2

3

4

Internet

Mobile

Face to Face

Mobile

INTERACTIONS

AFFINITY DIAGRAMS

An affinity diagram is a method used to organize many ideas into groups with common themes or relationships. Affinity diagrams are tools for analyzing large amounts of data and discovering relationships which allow a design direction to be established based on the associations. This method may uncover significant hidden relationships.

Traditional design methods struggle when dealing with complex or chaotic problems or with large amounts of data. The affinity diagram organizes a large quantity of information by natural relationships. This method taps a team's analytical thinking as well as creativity and intuition. It was invented in the 1960s by Japanese anthropologist Jiro Kawakita and is sometimes referred to as the KJ Method.

You can use an affinity diagram to:
1. Understand what is most important from ambiguous data.
2. Tame complexity.
3. Identify connections in data
4. Create hierarchies.
5. Identifying themes.

Identify what factors to focus on that will support the most successful design possible from a customer's perspective.

"Most groups that use this technique are amazed at how powerful and valuable a tool it is. Try it once with an open mind and you'll be another convert."

Nancy R. Tague

For around 50 years affinity diagrams have been an essential pillar of what is known as the Seven Management and Planning Tools, used in Japan.
The seven management and planning tools are used in leading global organizations for making and implementing better team decisions.

Jiro Kawakita developed the method, and so it was sometimes referred to as the K-J method.

The affinity diagram is a method that an individual or team can use for problem-solving. Affinity diagrams encourage creative input by everyone on the team.

The tool is used in project management to sort brainstorming ideas into groups, based on their natural relationships and for synthesis and analysis. It is also used in design research to synthesize insights from field research. Affinity diagrams are built through consensus of a design team on how the information should be grouped in logical ways.

WHY USE AFFINITY DIAGRAMS?

Traditional design methods do not work when dealing with complex or chaotic problems with large amounts of data. This tool helps to establish relationships or similarities between many pieces of information. From these relationships, insights can be determined which are the starting point of design solutions. It is possible using this method to reach consensus faster than many other methods.

You can use an affinity diagram to:
1. Understand what is most important from a large amount of complex or ambiguous data.
2. Tame complexity.
3. Understand connections between ideas.
4. Identify relationships in data.
5. Create hierarchies.
6. Exercise team decision making.
7. Make sense from brainstorming ideas.
8. Support design and data workshops.
9. Identifying themes from data
10. Identify patterns from data.
11. It helps to reduce "team paralysis," from too many options and lack of consensus.

HISTORY

Affinity diagrams were created in the 1950s by Japanese anthropologist Jiro Kawakita It is sometimes called the K-J Method. Jiro Kawakita worked in remote Nepalese villages researching problems, related to water supplies and transportation. He was awarded the Ramon Magsaysay Award in 1984.

Affinity diagrams were part of the Seven Management and Planning Tools, used in Total Quality Control in Japan. Jiro Kawakita named the method around 1967 and published a comprehensive description of the KJ method in 1986. Since 1969, Kawakita has presented KJ method workshops in Japan.

WHEN SHOULD WE USE AFFINITY DIAGRAMS?

An Affinity Diagram is useful when you want to:
1. Make sense out of large volumes of chaotic data.
2. Encourage new patterns of thinking. An affinity diagram can break through traditional or entrenched thinking.

STRENGTHS
1. It is a simple method.

2. Supports innovation.
3. Causes breakthroughs to emerge
4. Helps groups come to a consensus about most important issues
5. Multiple people can combine their ideas by on post-it notes and be organizing them.
6. Organizing generates useful discussions.
7. Builds critical thinking skills.
8. Allows for involvement of each team member
9. Helps your team to see the big picture and where the biggest problems are.
10. Post-it notes are a flexible method to organize ideas into various levels of groups and sub-groups.
11. It is both a creative and analytical method
12. Promotes the emergence of breakthrough thinking
13. Most effective when applied to a team with varied perspectives and open-mindedness.
14. Is useful to make sense of complex apparently unrelated ambiguous or chaotic data
15. It makes your analysis highly visible to others in the company.

WEAKNESSES

1. Good facilitation is required to when there is a lot of data.
2. Affinity diagrams are not portable or mobile.
3. Affinity diagrams occupy a large space for a period.
4. Can be time-consuming when there are a large number of pieces of data.
5. The small size of post-it notes and the effort of writing forces you to be brief,
6. It is an analog or physical activity
7. the rationale behind particular groupings can be lost.
8. Affinity diagrams are temporary and must be photographed to keep a permanent record.
9. It may be difficult find individual pieces of information.

USE AN AFFINITY DIAGRAM WHEN:

1. You have a large body of information in apparent chaos.
2. To uncover hidden connections between pieces of information or ideas
3. When issues seem too broad and complex to grasp.
4. There is no clear solution evident to your team.
5. When group consensus is necessary.
6. You wish to move beyond habitual thinking and preconceived categories.
7. When other solutions to a problem have failed.
8. To rethink how issues are connected.
9. To brainstorm root causes and solutions to problems, especially when little or no data is available
10. Organize qualitative data from stakeholders to uncover insights and themes

11. The solution requires consensus amongst the team members to work effectively
12. Extract requirements from user research
13. To organize ideas from brainstorming.
14. To brainstorm root causes of problems, especially when data is confusing or ambiguous.

DO NOT USE AN AFFINITY DIAGRAM WHEN:
if less than 15 items of data.

SELECT YOUR TEAM
Care should be taken in choosing your team. As many groups and diverse points of view involved in design delivery and use of the service as possible should be represented.
1. Keep groups to six people or less.
2. Break large groups into smaller groups of six or fewer people.
3. Have a diverse team with different genders, age, occupations and status represented.
4. Have at least two or three "T" shaped people. That is people with two or more areas of expertise such as technology and management or administration and design. T-shaped team members make the team more flexible and help group collaboration.
5. Involve external and internal stakeholders such as customers, suppliers, internal business management, engineering, design, and sales.
6. Have customer facing people where possible because they better see the client's perspective.

APPOINT YOUR MODERATOR
1. Create handouts with clear instructions
2. Provide copies of research summaries
3. Take breaks every 90 minutes
4. Photograph the map as it is being built.

MODERATOR SKILLS
1. Effective Listening Skills
2. Flexibility
3. Customer empathy
4. Sincerely Interested in People
5. Enthusiasm
6. People management skills
7. Able to establishing common direction and buy-in.
8. Understands Group Dynamics
9. Authority
10. Neutral and Objective
11. Patient and Persistent
12. Guide discussion promptly.

RESOURCES
White-board
Large wall spaces or tables
Dry-erase markers
Sharpies
Post-it notes

There are two ways to use affinity diagrams:

RESEARCH TOOL
To make sense of a large body of

GATHER YOUR DATA SPREAD IT OVER A WALL

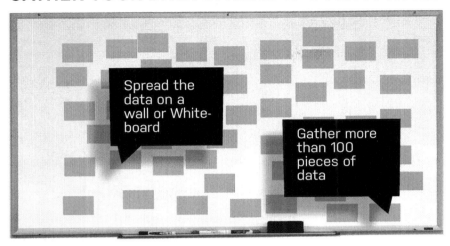

MOVE THE DATA INTO RELATED GROUPS

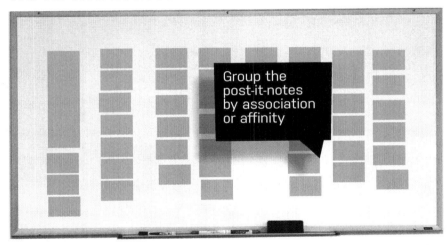

research data. This approach can be used to establish connections between different pieces of research, to uncover insights from the data that can then be used to develop design concepts. With this approach, the team can develop a hierarchy of significance of the connections or themes and the insights. This hierarchy helps to establish the levels of focus for different ideas and themes uncovered by the research for the ideation design phase.

BRAINSTORMING TOOL

Affinity diagrams can also be used during the ideation or idea generation phase of a design project. When the technique is used for ideation it helps synthesize a large number of design ideas. The design team can decide which ideas are the best ideas and then combine features of various ideas to develop themes and variations through iterative cycles of brainstorming, affinity diagrams and synthesis.

GATHER YOUR DATA

First gather your data. Break the data down into pieces. For example, if an interview subject has raised several interesting points during an interview transcribe the interview, highlight the interesting points then copy each point onto a separate post it note. Use only one color post-it notes at this stage. The most common color used at this phase for the raw data is yellow.

FIND YOUR SPACE

Once you have selected your team, your moderator, and space to work, spread the ideas randomly across a wall, a Whiteboard or large table. A floor in a little traffic area also can work for this stage of the process. You need plenty of space.

Affinity diagrams work best with more than 100 discreet pieces of information and work efficiently up to several thousand pieces of data.

CLUSTERING

Hand a block of blank 2" x 3" yellow post-it notes to each team member.

You can use the "Rule of 7 plus or minus 2". The summary should have no less than 5 and no more than 9 words in it, including a verb and a noun. Use also simple cartoon sketches and a combination of drawings and words. Gather your team around the place where you have placed the post-it notes. Look for ideas that seem to be related.

Go for volume, suspend judgment, build on each other's ideas and set a strict time limit. Allow 30 or 40 minutes for brainstorming ideas.

The moderator then asks the team to take two ideas that seem to belong together and place them together, at least, three feet away from the other post-it notes. Keep moving post-it notes into the groups until all the post-its have been placed into groups. It is OK to replace another person's group if it doesn't make sense to you. Some groups may have only a small number of items.

The type of relationship that you see will depend on your background, your profession your personality and your life experience.

Move related ideas into groups and continue moving the post-it notes until all notes are in groups. Some ideas may not seem to fit a group. Place those ideas into a group. If a note belongs in two groups, make a second note.

It is best that no one speaks at this stage, so different perspectives are represented.
Work silently. Ask the team to move the ideas into groups based on their gut instincts and without talking. This approach encourages unconventional thinking and discourages one person from steering the affinity. It is important to maintain silence at this stage, as it ensures that each member has an equal opportunity to apply their perspective without being influenced to conform to others' thinking.

Ask your team not to struggle over placing the data into groups, use gut instincts.
If consensus is not reached, make a duplicate of the idea and place one copy in two groups. The idea written on each post-it should be a phrase or sentence that clearly

conveys the meaning to people who are not on the team. Make the notes large enough to be readable from 10 feet distance.

HEADERS
Hand out a block of blank 2" x 3" blue post-it notes to each team member. Using the second color of post-it notes, ask each participant to assign a name to each group. Write a header above each cluster that describes what connects the data in the group. Use a different color post-it notes for the headers. Blue is a color that is often used for headers. You can use any color, but it should be the same color for all headers and a different color than the color utilized in the previous phase. The most efficient use of space is to position the post-it notes in a group vertically with the header above the group.

To create headers ask for each grouping: "What key words summarize the central idea that this grouping communicates?" Sometimes a post it from within the group can be used as a header.

Create a heading for each group that captures the theme of each group. Place it above the group. A header should capture the association or affinity among the ideas contained in a group.
The team develops headers by discussing and agreeing on the wording of the header post-it notes.

Review each group and write

MOVE THE DATA INTO RELATED GROUPS

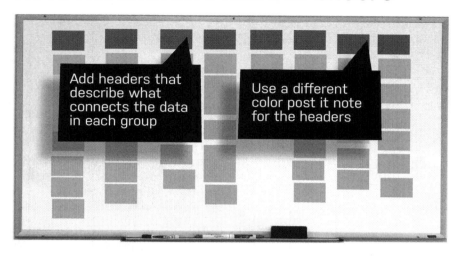

GROUP ASSOCIATED GROUPS
AND SUPERGROUPS WITH HEADERS

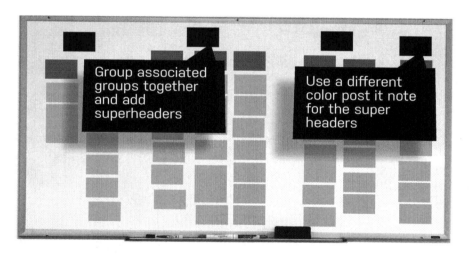

down a name that best represents each cluster on the new set of sticky notes. Do not use full sentences for headers but summarize the association with just one or two words.

If a group has two themes, then split the group into two groups. If two groups share the same theme combine the two groups into one or move the two groups near to each other and place a header above the headers of the two groups that defines the association of the two groups.

Making a simple title involves abductive thinking, which is the best form of problem solving for complex, changing and ambiguous problems. Some notes will not fit into any group. Put these in a separate group.

When people slow down it is time to break the silence, and start discussing the groups that have emerged. When consensus is reached, move on to the next step.

SUPERHEADERS
If two groups have the same theme then place an additional header in a third color above those two groups. Leave the previous headers in place. Pink is commonly used for a combined header of two groups. This type of header is sometimes called a super header. Repeat the process until the number of groupings is between 5 and 9 groups. Ask each participant to read through the post-it notes in each group.

The moderator should then say "We will now see if we can combine some groups. Please nominate two groups that you think we can combine. Only combine groups that have the same theme but not groups that are subsets of one another"

DOT VOTING
Give each participant 3 adhesive dots and ask them to place the dots next to the header of the three groups that they think are most important in relation to the design goals.
1. What are the user needs?
2. What are the needs of the business?
3. What technologies are most appropriate?

After each person has voted tally the number of votes for each group.

This gives you a hierarchy of importance for the themes in order to address these themes in the next phase of the design process, the ideation phase.

This is a way of efficiently selecting from a large number of ideas the preferred ideas to carry forward in the design process.

WHY USE DOT VOTING?
It is a method of selecting a favored idea by collective rather than individual judgment. It is a fast method that allows a design to progress. It leverages the

strengths of diverse team member viewpoints and experiences

CHALLENGES
1. The assessment is subjective.
2. Group-think
3. Not enough good ideas
4. Inhibition
5. Lack of critical thinking

HOW
1. Gather your team of 4 to 12 participants.
2. Brainstorm ideas, for example, ask each team member to generate ten ideas as sketches.
3. Each idea should be presented on one post-it-note or page.
4. Each designer should quickly explain each idea to the group before the group votes.
5. Spread the ideas over a wall or table.
6. Ask the team to vote on their two or three favorite ideas and total the votes. You can use sticky dots or colored pins to indicate a vote or a moderator can tally the scores.
7. Rearrange the ideas so that the ideas with the dots are ranked from most dots to least.
8. Refine the preferred ideas.

VOTE FOR GROUPS

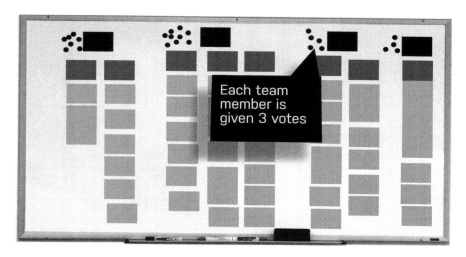

Each team member is given 3 votes

EMPATHY CANVASS

PERSONA

Name
Age
Job
Residence
Education
Goals
Needs
Frustrations

See

Hear

Think

Touch

Taste

Smell

Do

Feel

Say

Pain

Gain

Opportunities

PRIORITY OF CUSTOMER EXPERIENCE IMPROVEMENTS

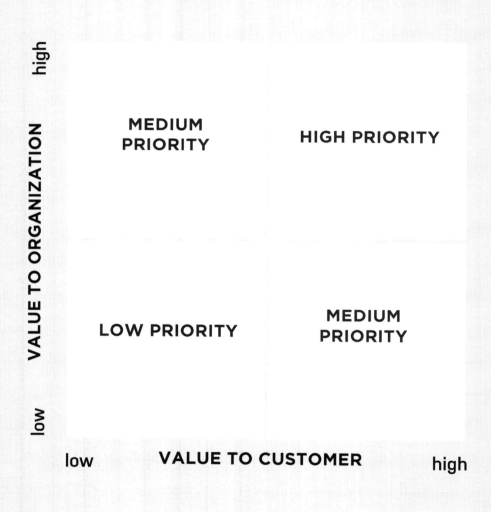

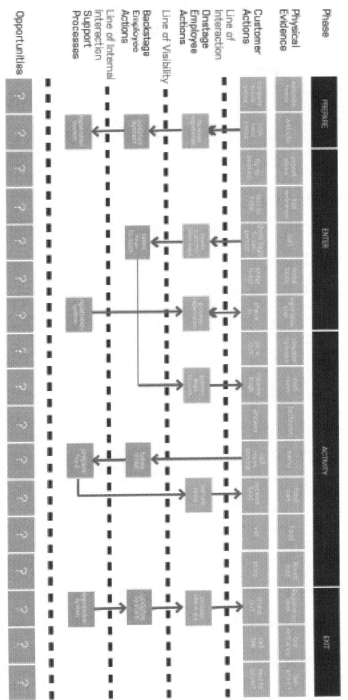

HOTEL SERVICE BLUEPRINT

ASSUMPTION SURFACING

WHO INVENTED IT?

Richard O. Mason, Ian Mitroff 1981

WHY

1. The purpose of this method is to analyze assumptions to understand which are most plausible and may have the highest impact.
2. A method for approaching ill-structured or "wicked"problems
3. To compare and to evaluate systematically the assumptions of different people.
4. To examine the relationship between underlying assumption

RESOURCES

Pen
Paper
White-board
Dry Erase markers

HOW

1. List the decisions that you have made.
2. For each decision list the assumptions that you made
3. Under each assumption list an alternative counter assumption.
4. Delete from your list choices where it makes little difference whether the original assumption or the counter assumption are correct.
5. Analyze the remaining assumptions on a 2x2 matrix high low impact on one axis and high low plausibility on the other axis.
6. High impact and plausibility assumptions should be given high priority.

BACKCASTING

WHO INVENTED IT?

AT&T 1950s, Shel 1970s

WHY
1. It is inexpensive and fast
2. Backcasting is a tool for identifying, planning and reaching future goals.
3. Backcasting provides a strategy to reach future goals.

CHALLENGES
1. Need a good moderator
2. Needs good preparation

HOW
an example of a backcasting question is"How would you define success for yourself in 2015?

1. Define a framework
2. Analyze the present situation in relation to the framework
3. Prepare a vision and a number of desirable future scenarios.
4. Back-casting: Identify the steps to achieve this goal.
5. Further elaboration, detailing
6. Step by step strategies towards achieving the outcomes desired.
7. Ask do the strategies move us in the right direction? Are they flexible strategies?. Do the strategies represent a good return on investment?
8. Implementation, policy, organization embedding, follow-up

ALTERNATIVE APPROACH
1. Participants form break-out groups, each of which chooses one of the scenarios generated in previous brainstorming session.
2. Participants draw a time-line on a white-board with "now" at the left and the future date of the chosen scenario at the right.
3. Participants are asked to contribute ideas about what events and decisions could lead from the present situation to a future in which the scenario is true.
4. Each participant is encouraged to write one or two key events or decisions on post-it notes. The events may contribute to a common narrative, or it may be that person's own opinion.
5. Each participant places their note on the time-line.
6. A final discussion phase converges on common themes among the narrative strands represented by the notes.
7. Participants choose a small set of near-term and mid-term goals or decisions, or signals to watch for, based on the narratives that have emerged from the process. These are written up as the process deliverable.

Source: Adapted from Dee Balkissoon and Christine Keene

RESOURCES
Post-it-notes
White-board
Pens
Dry-erase markers

BENEFITS MAP

WHAT
The benefits map is a simple tool that helps your team decide what will give you the best return on investment for time invested.

WHY
1. Aids communication and discussion within the organization.
2. It is human nature to do tasks which are not most urgent first.
3. To gain competitive advantage,
4. Helps build competitive strategy
5. Helps build communication strategy
6. Helps manage time effectively

CHALLENGES
1. Can be subjective

HOW
1. Moderator draws axes on White-board or flip chart.
2. Worthwhile activity at the start of a project.
3. Map individual tasks.
4. Interpret the map.
5. Create strategy.
6. Tasks which have high benefit with low investment may be given priority.

BENJAMIN FRANKLIN

WHAT
A method developed by Benjamin Franklin for making difficult decisions.

WHO INVENTED IT?
Benjamin Franklin 1772

WHY
1. It is simple
2. It is an effective way to make decisions related to complex ambiguous or ill defined problems.

RESOURCES
1. Pen
2. Paper
3. White-board
4. Dry erase markers
5. Post-it-notes

HOW
Quote from a letter from Benjamin Franklin to Joseph Priestley London, September 19, 1772

To get over this, my way is, to divide half a sheet of paper by a line into two Columns, writing over the one pro, and over the other con. Then during three or four days consideration I put down under the different heads short hints of the different motives that at different times occur to me for or against the measure. When I have thus got them

all together in one view, I endeavor to estimate their respective weights; and where I find two, one on each side, that seem equal, I strike them both out: If I find a reason pro equal to some two reasons con, I strike out the three. If I judge some two reasons con equal to some three reasons pro, I strike out the five; and thus proceeding I find at length where the balance lies; and if after a day or two of farther Consideration nothing new that is of Importance occurs on either side, I come to a determination accordingly.

And tho' the weight of reasons cannot be taken with the precision of algebraic quantities, yet when each is thus considered separately and comparatively, and the whole lies before me, I think I can judge better, and am less likely to take a rash step; and in fact I have found great advantage from this kind of equation, in what may be called moral or prudential algebra"

CONTEXT MAP

WHAT
A context map is a tool for representing complex factors affecting an organization or design visually. Context maps are sometimes used by directors or organizations as a tool to enable discussion of the effects of change and related interacting business, cultural and environmental factors in order to create a strategic vision for an organization. A context map can be used to analyze trends.

WHO INVENTED IT?
Joseph D. Novak Cornell University 1970s.

WHY
Uses include:
1. New knowledge creation
2. Documenting the knowledge existing informally within an organization.
3. Creating a shared strategic vision

HOW
1. Put together a team of between 4 and 20 participants with diverse backgrounds and outlooks.
2. Appoint a good moderator
3. Prepare a space. Use a private room with a White-board or large wall.
4. Distribute post-it notes to

each participant.

5. Brainstorm the list of factors one at a time.
6. These can include Trends, technology, trends, political factors, economic climate customer needs, uncertainties.
7. Each participant can contribute.
8. All contributions are recorded on the White-board or on the wall with the post-it-notes.
9. When all factors have been discussed prioritize each group of contributions to identify the most critical.
10. This can be done by rearranging the post-it-notes or White-board notes.
11. Video the session and photograph the notes after the session.
12. Analyze the map and create strategy.

RESOURCES

Template
White-board
Paper flip chart
Pens
Dry-erase markers
Post-it-notes

EMPATHY MAPS

...WHAT

A mapping method that analyzes each part of a user experience. An Empathy Map gives a high-level view of where an experience is good or bad. Used to improve a customer experience.

The biggest single cause of failure of new products and services in the marketplace is that the organization creating the product or service did not thoroughly understand the customer's perspective. This method helps draw out the main components of the client's experience so that problems can be identified and fixed.

Empathy Map is a tool that helps the design team empathize with the end users. You can create an empathy map for a group of customers or a persona.

WHAT IS EMPATHY?

The identification with the feelings, thoughts, or attitudes of another. Keep in mind, empathy and sympathy are different things

WHO INVENTED THEM?

Scott Matthews and Dave Gray at XPLANE now Dachis Group.

HOW LONG DOES IT TAKE?
One to three hours per persona.

WHY
This tool helps a design team understand the customers and their context. It is an outside-in technique.

CHALLENGES
1. Emotions must be inferred by observing clues.
2. This method is not as rigorous as traditional personas but requires less investment.

RESOURCES
Empathy map template
White-board
or chalkboard
or video projector
or Large sheet of paper
Dry-erase markers
Post-it-notes
Pens
Video Camera

HOW
1. A team of 4 to 12 people is a good number for this method.
2. The best people to involve are individuals who have direct interaction with customers.
3. The team should represent various functions in your organization such as management, design, marketing, sales, and engineering. It is helpful also to include some stakeholders such as customers and others affected by the end design. The process will help draw out useful information from them.
4. This method can be used with personas.
5. The map should be based on real information from customers. Research can be gathered from sources such as interviews, observation, web analytics, customer service departments and focus groups.
6. Segment your market then create a persona representing an average customer in each segment. Create four to six personas.
7. Draw a circle. The circle will represent your target persona.
8. Create some radial boxes around the circle to represent aspects of that person's sensory experience. It is common to have boxes for seeing and hearing. Some experiences such as drinking coffee could include boxes for other senses such as taste and smell.
9. Place two boxes at the bottom of the map and label them "Pain" and "Gain".
10. Ask your team to describe from the persona's point of view their experience.
11. Populate the map by using the research gathers through your fieldwork: What are they thinking, feeling, saying, doing, hearing, seeing?
12. Once you have filled all of the top boxes move the post-it notes for negative

ON A WHITE-BOARD DRAW A CIRCLE
THEN 4 RADIATING BOXES

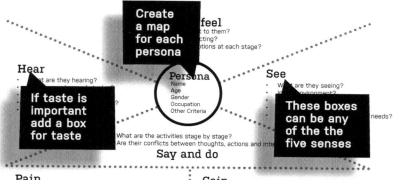

Create a map for each persona

feel
t to them?
cting?
tions at each stage?

Hear
· t are they hearing?

If taste is important add a box for taste

Persona
Name
Age
Gender
Occupation
Other Criteria

See
· W t are they seeing?
· I vironment?

These boxes can be any of the the five senses

needs?

What are the activities stage by stage?
Are their conflicts between thoughts, actions and inte

Say and do

Pain
· What are the pain points?
· What are the frustrations?
· What are the obstacles?
· What are the fears?
· What are the risks?

Gain
· What are their goals?
· What are they trying to achieve?
· What are their needs?
· What are their desires?
· How do they measure success?

Think and feel
· What is important to them?
· How are they reacting?
· What are the emotions at each stage?

Hear
· What are they hearing?
· Which sounds are obstacles?
· In the environment?
· From interactions with people?
· What are pleasant sounds?

Persona
Name
Age
Gender
Occupation
Other Criteria

See
· What are they seeing?
· In the environment?
· Which sights are obstacles?
· What are pleasant sounds?
· Are sights conflicting with their needs?

· What are the activities stage by stage?
· Are their conflicts between thoughts, actions and intentions?

Say and do

Pain
· What are the pain points?
· What are the frustrations?
· What are the obstacles?
· What are the fears?
· What are the risks?

Gain
· What are their goals?
· What are they trying to achieve?
· What are their needs?
· What are their desires?
· How do they measure success?

components of the experience into the lower pain box and positive into the gain box.

13. The pain box can serve as a start for identifying the problems to fix in the ideation phase.

On a large White-board draw a circle about 6 inches to one foot in diameter near the center of the board.

Inside this circle describe the persona that you are about to map. This persona represents a significant segment of your customers.

Fill in the persona's name, age, gender, occupation, income, location and any other important information.

Write down the answers to the following questions:
• What's their role i.e. how do they spend their day?
• What are their goals?
How do they measure success?
• What are their top hopes and hurdles?
• What's their age, marital status, income and location.
Select an appropriate name for your persona.

For your product or service, what are the most important sensory inputs? For example, sight sound smell and taste may be essential for a coffee shop. Now divide the top three quarters of the board space into a number of boxes

radiating from your persona circle. Name these boxes "Think and Feel", "Say and Do" and the appropriate senses selected from the five senses

1. See
2. Hear
3. Touch
4. Taste
5. Smell

With your team seated around the board populate the boxes one box at a time.

What is the perspective of your customer? Take a walk in her shoes?
What are your customer segments?
1. List all customer segments
2. Pick one to work on
3. Give the customer a name
4. Develop some demographic characteristics
5. Income, marital status, etc.
6. Create Story

SEE
1. What does he see in his Environment that influences him?
2. What is the persona seeing in their surroundings?
3. Who surrounds them?
4. Who are their friends?
5. What visual problems do they encounter?

HEAR
1. What does your customer hear in the context of the experience?

START BY LISTING WHAT YOUR PERSONA SEES

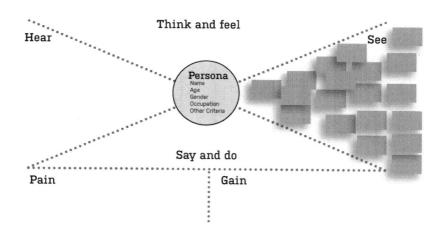

THEN WHAT YOUR PERSONA SAYS AND DOES

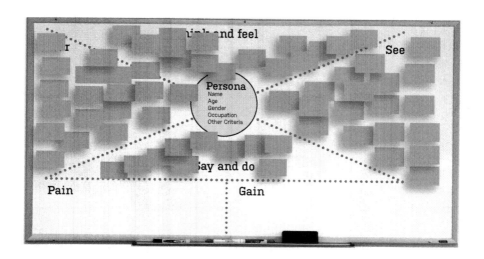

2. What do their friends say?
3. What does their partner say?
4. Which media channels do they access?
5. What friends say
6. What work colleagues say?
7. What news says
8. What influences say

THINK AND FEEL
1. What matters most to your customers?
2. What is your client thinking?
3. Talk to them and ask them what they are thinking.
4. What concerns them most?
5. What are their dreams, desires and aspirations?
6. What doesn't your customer articulate?
7. What things move her?

SAY AND DO
Some questions:
1. What do they say when experiencing your product or service?
2. What do they say when experiencing competitor's goods or services?
3. What do they say to their friends or colleagues?
4. What do they do? What are the activities?
5. How do they behave?
6. Are there differences between what they say and do?
7. What is common for her to say?
8. How does she behave?
9. What are her hobbies?
10. What does he like to say?
11. How is the world in which he lives?

12. What do people around him / her do?
13. Who are her friends?
14. What is popular in his daily life?
15. What people and ideas influence her?
16. What do the important people in his life say?
17. What are her favorite brands?
18. Who are his role models?
19. What does he want to achieve?
20. How does she measure success?
21. What would make it a better experience?
22. What are his aspirations?
23. Imagine what the customer might say, or how they might behave in public
24. What is her attitude?
25. What could she be telling others?
26. Pay particular attention to potential conflicts between what a customer might say and what the customer truly thinks and feels.
27. What is his attitude?
28. What could he be telling others?
29. What does he say that normally contradicts to what he thinks and feels?

PAIN
What are the fears, frustrations, and the obstacles that concern your customer most? What obstacles stand in the way of your customer reaching their goals?
1. What are the pain points?
2. What does the persona fear?
3. What is the persona

frustrated by in relation to the experience?

4. Why doesn't the customer come back?
5. What is standing in the way of your client reaching their goals?
6. What does your customer need?
7. What does your customer desire?
8. What do competitors do better?
9. When is your customer most unhappy?
10. Where is your customer most unhappy?
11. Here are some questions:
12. What are their fears? What do they worry about?
13. What are their aspirations? What do they dream about?
14. What else do they think about during the day?
15. Do they love or hate what they do?
16. What are the differences between what they say/do and think/feel?
17. • How do they feel about using your product or alternative solution?
18. What are the customer's biggest frustrations?
19. What obstacles stand between the customer and what they want or need to achieve?
20. Which risk might she fear taking?
21. What are his biggest frustrations?

GAIN

What are their goals, desires, and needs; how do they work towards these goals?

1. How does your customer measure success?
2. Is the customer satisfied?
3. What short term goals does your customer have?
4. What long term goals does your customer have?
5. When is your customer happy?
6. What do you do better than your competitors?
7. When is your customer happy
8. Where is your customer happy?
9. What is ultimate dream? What are they desperately hoping to achieve?
10. Why is getting that outcome so important? What would that mean for them?
11. What have you learned by building the empathy map? What are the themes and insights? How can you improve your customer's holistic experience?
12. What does the customer want or need to achieve?
13. How does your customer measure success?
14. What are the strategies the customer might use
15. to achieve their goals.

MOVE ALL THE NEGATIVE EXPERIENCES TO THE PAIN BOX

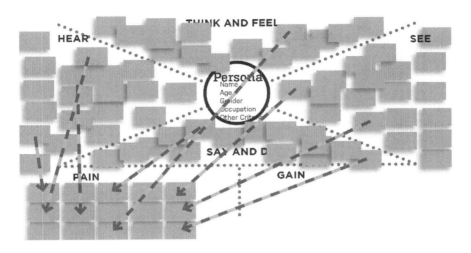

MOVE ALL THE POSITIVE EXPERIENCES TO THE GAIN BOX

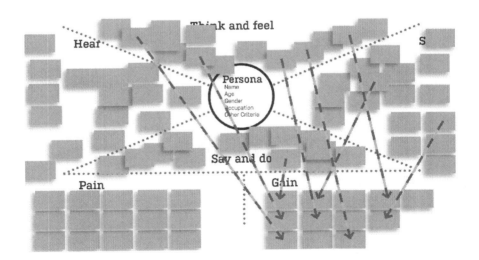

EXPERIENCE & JOURNEY MAPS

Experience maps are diagrams that allow a designer or manager to describe the elements of a customer experience in concise terms.

A journey map focuses on identifying touch points, An experience map focuses on the emotions your customer experiences. In practice many people use these terms interchangeably. The particular lanes included can be mixed and matched to your goals.

Customer journeys depict what customers really want. These methods help us to understand interactions from users' point of view. They must be developed from your customers' perspective. They are a framework to craft a better customer experience.. With these tools you can identify problem areas and opportunities for improvement.

Maps are usually created to help understand a particular segment or persona. The more complex your service or customer experience, the more value there is in mapping the customer journey and experience.

HISTORY

The origin of journey and experience mapping is less apparent than Service Blueprints, but they have been used at least since 1991 (Whittle & Foster, 1991).
Several sources mention these methods from 2006 (Parker & Heapy, 2006; Voss & Zomerdijk, 2007). The detailed application is still evolving (Følstad et al., 2013). Følstad defines a customer journey as the process a customer goes through to reach a particular goal. The value of these techniques is greatest when the complexity of the route is higher. Customer journey maps describe not only what a customer experiences but also the customer's response to those experiences.

Wechsler (2012) describes internal workshops for creating customer journey maps. The analysis of customer journeys may also concern quantitative measurement of the customer's experience. In the scientific literature, such analysis is

EXAMPLE OF AN EXPERIENCE MAP

STAGES	EVALUATE	ENTER	USE/ENGAGE			EXIT		
TOUCH POINTS	Home Interior	Car	Counter Coffee cup	Coffee shop Interior Chair Table	Laptop Power socket Internet	Laptop Internet Chair Table Cup	Cup Trash can Coffee shop Interior	Car Bar Car	Car
DOING	Checks location of coffee shop on Internet	Drives car to coffee shop	Pays and picks up coffee	Selects drink and waits in line to order	Drinks coffee and makes small on laptop	Writes and sends emails, Tops up coffee	Finishes coffee and puts cup in trashcan	Returns to car	Drives own to supermarket
THINKING	Should I call a friend? Will I have a long wait to be served?	Will I be able to park close to this coffee shop?	Should I have a latte or a drip coffee?	Is there a seat available at the window?	The coffee is very hot, is there a plug for my laptop?	Not a plug available, How long will my battery last?	Where is the trashcan?	Will the traffic be heavy?	There was a long queue. I will go to another coffee shop next time.
FEELING	Should I call a friend? Will I have a long wait to be served?	Will be able to park closest to the coffee shop?	Should I have a latte or a drip coffee?	Is there a seat available at the window?	The coffee is very hot, let there a plug for my laptop?	No plug available for laptop. Music too loud.	Where is the trashcan?	Will the traffic be heavy?	I will go to another coffee shop next time.
PAIN POINTS	Hard to find coffee shop	No parking place available.	Too many choices on menu	Needs to wait for an available chair. Chairs uncomfortable	Coffee too hot to drink. Coffee shop cold.	No plug available for laptop. Music too loud.	No visible trashcan	Long walk back to car. Traffic heavy	
OPPORTUNITIES	Improve website	Make more parking available.	Reduce number of options	Replace chairs. Open up second room	Coffee at coffee temperature. Re-lay out seats.	Add power points	Relocate trash cans. Increase number of trashcans.	Make more parking available.	

typically conducted as part of the mapping process to quantify changes in experiential quality during the customer journey (Trischler & Zehrer, 2012). Kankainen et al. (2012) describe the use of customer journeys for co-design, where customers formulate "dream journeys". In 2007 the British Government published guidelines on customer journey mapping (HM Government, 2007).

WHY

Journey and experience mapping can be used for the following purposes:

1. Understand the collective experiences of customer segments
2. To create a more streamlined, consistent, and efficient customer experience.
3. Create a more seamless customer experience across business departments, and channels.
4. Design a new service or product customer experience
5. Allocate people and resources more effectively.
6. Develop alignment across departments of an organization.
7. Craft a better customer experience.
8. Expose places where your service or customer experience may fail.
9. Craft a better customer experience
10. Strategic and tactical innovation
11. Building and sharing knowledge
12. Designing the moments of truth
13. Understand competitive positioning
14. Understanding the ideal experience
15. Reveal the truth from your customer's perspective
16. Identify opportunities
17. Empathize with your custom
18. Designing and improving Systems
19. Develop a better product road map
20. Take cost & complexity out of the system
21. Prioritize competing deliverables
22. Plan for hiring
23. Bring different parts of your business together to work to improve the customer experience
24. Build knowledge of customer behaviors and needs across channels
25. Identify specific areas of opportunity to drive ideation and innovation
26. Make intangible services tangible.
27. Develop customer insights
28. Understand where friction exists between the needs of different market segments
29. Introduce metrics for what matters most for your customers.
30. Align your offerings to brand promise.
31. Identify failure points.
32. Improve efficiency.
33. Imagine future product and

service experiences.

34. More Holistic thinking.
35. Making better decisions.
36. A living document that can evolve with your business.
37. Is a holistic view of key touch points and interactions personas have with the brand.
38. Communicate the experience visually.
39. Promotes better coordination of across channels.

A MAP HELPS YOU

1. Plan your product or service offering most efficiently for various customer segments.
2. Evaluate customer experience gaps or fail points before they occur.
3. Identify opportunities to improve you customer experience.
4. identify ways to improve your touchpoints and remove duplication.
5. You can create a map as a concept for a customer's ideal future experience.
6. Put all stakeholders on the same page so that you can reach a common understanding and agreement on how to move forward towards your organizational goals.
7. Helps make measures of success clear.
8. From analyzing your map recommendations and a plan to reach your objectives can be put into place.

HOW

Here is a list of stages that you can complete creating a Service Blueprint. Consider the blueprint to be a living document that will develop and improve, so it doesn't have to be perfect first time. Concentrate on your customers and their point of view.

SELECT YOUR TEAM

Care should be taken in choosing your team. As many groups and diverse points of view involved in design delivery and use of the service as possible should be represented.

1. Keep groups to six people or less.
2. If your total group size is larger than six break the large group into smaller groups of six or less.
3. Have a diverse team with different genders, age, occupations and seniority represented.
4. Have at least two or three "T" shaped people. That is, people with two or more areas of expertise such as technology and management or management and design. This makes the team more flexible and helps group collaboration. This experience can be gained through education or work. Look for people with at least 10,000 hours of experience in each of two areas. That corresponds to three or four years of work experience in each area.
5. Involve external and internal stakeholders such as

EXPERIENCE & JOURNEY MAP PROCESS

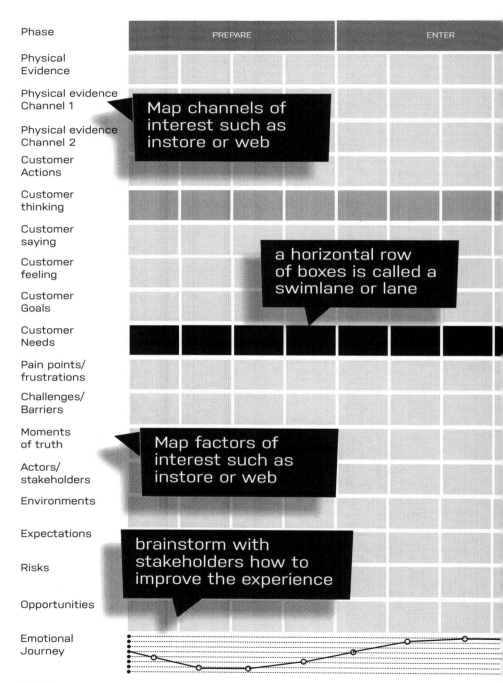

Phase	PREPARE	ENTER

Physical Evidence

Physical evidence Channel 1

Physical evidence Channel 2

Customer Actions

Customer thinking

Customer saying

Customer feeling

Customer Goals

Customer Needs

Pain points/ frustrations

Challenges/ Barriers

Moments of truth

Actors/ stakeholders

Environments

Expectations

Risks

Opportunities

Emotional Journey

Map channels of interest such as instore or web

a horizontal row of boxes is called a swimlane or lane

Map factors of interest such as instore or web

brainstorm with stakeholders how to improve the experience

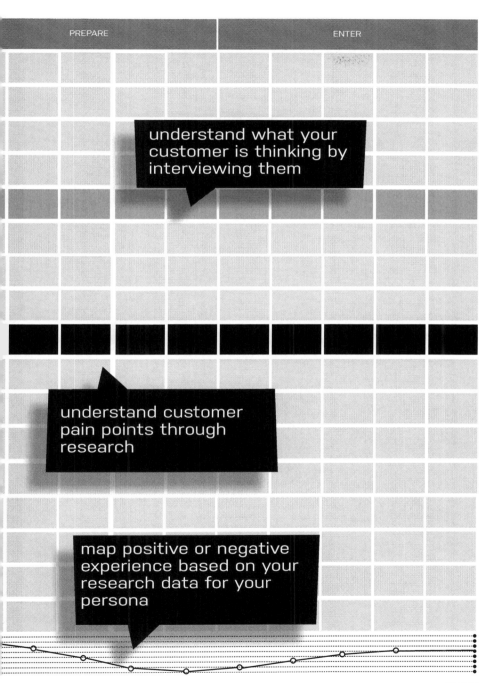

understand what your
customer is thinking by
interviewing them

understand customer
pain points through
research

map positive or negative
experience based on your
research data for your
persona

customers, suppliers, internal business management, engineering, design, marketing, distribution, IT and sales. Have customer facing people where possible because they better understand the customer's perspective.

CREATE YOUR GOAL STATEMENT

1. What is the problem, unmet needs or opportunities that you wish to analyze?
2. Create a clear outline of customer goals and needs that is compatible with your goals and with an outcome that satisfies them.
3. Who are the stakeholders?
4. Where is the service or experience delivered?
5. When is the service or experience provided?
6. What are the channels?
7. Why is there a need for a new design solution?
8. Do you want to enhance the customer experience?
9. Do you wish to engage your customers more effectively?
10. Do you wish to create a more efficient process?
11. Define your goals in a statement.

DEFINE YOUR TARGET AUDIENCE SEGMENT AND THEIR NEEDS

The most successful products services and experiences target precise customer segments.

GATHER YOUR EXISTING RESEARCH

Start by auditing internal customer experience data that has been previously gathered. Do you have existing research? Where are the gaps in your knowledge?

Interviews are one of the most usual methods used to gather data. Ask them to walk you through their experience and talk about their problems, needs desires and feelings at each stage. Start by talking to between five and twenty people as a minimum sample size. Ask them what touch points they are engaging at each phase. Ask them where they are experiencing problems or frustrations in achieving their goals. Document your interviews or observations by using video or a digital recorder.

To be useful, your map needs to be based on real and truthful information.

REVIEW YOUR EXISTING RESEARCH

Review existing research Identify gaps in data and create a list of recurring customer experience problems.

CREATE A RESEARCH PLAN TO FILL THE GAPS

1. What do you still need to know?
2. What questions do you need to ask?
3. How many people will you study?

4. What type of people will you research?
5. What will be the context of the research?
6. What methods will you use?
7. When will you select and screen the subjects, conduct the research and report on findings?

SYNTHESIZE YOUR RESEARCH

Put each potentially useful piece of information on a separate post-it note. Put the post-it notes on a wall and ask your team to organize the customer's comments into related groups or themes. Which issues are most significant to more customers? Build a hierarchy of issues.

APPOINT YOUR MODERATOR

SELECT AND PREPARE YOUR WORKSPACE

A safe space is a large room with plenty of natural light with a large table and sufficient chairs for your team.
Some useful materials
1. A large wall
2. Butcher paper
3. Masking tape
4. Mobile dry erase boards
5. Dry erase markers
6. Sharpies
7. Adhesive notes in 5 colors
8. Digital camera
9. Tripod

IDENTIFY YOUR TARGET SEGMENT/S TO MAP

Identifying customer segments.

CREATE A PERSONA FOR EACH TARGET SEGMENT

Create 3 to 6 personas to cover all your customers.

IDENTIFY STAKEHOLDERS

A stakeholder is someone who may be in some way influenced by your design when it is complete and marketed.

HOLD STAKEHOLDER WORKSHOPS

Organize a workshop, and guide internal and external stakeholders through the process of creating the first draft. Go over the user experience in detail and discuss the experience from the perspective of customers and diverse stakeholders,

SELECT THE SERVICE TO BE MAPPED

Select your journey or experience to map. We suggest starting small with part of an experience that is important or problematic. For example rather than mapping an entire customer journey for air travel from New York to London, map a part of it that is important such as selecting the airline and booking the travel on-line. Then explore several challenging sub-journeys before tackling the whole journey.

DECIDE PRESENT OR

FUTURE SERVICE TO MAP

It is most usual to first map your existing customer experience. A current state map can help identify ways to make your existing customer experience better or more efficient.
After mapping your existing service you may be interested in creating a map as a scenario for a future service or customer experience.

SELECT START AND END POINTS OF THE CUSTOMER EXPERIENCE

Define the scope in terms of time and customer activities.

SELECT CHANNELS TO MAP

Some examples of channels include
1. In-store experience
2. Face to face
3. Print
4. Web
5. Call center
6. Tablet app
7. TV
8. Mobile phone

The channel defines the opportunities and constraints of a touchpoint. You can map all channels on one map in parallel lanes. This type of map is called a multichannel map. You can map just one channel per map and create as m,any separate maps as you have channels.

START SMALL

Consider picking a specific scenario or sub -activity of your entire customer experience.

DRAFT THE MAP

Use a large wall or table. Create your first rough draft using post-it notes. When it is complete photograph and share it with as many internal and external stakeholders as possible and ask for their feedback. If insights don't fit on a single map, keep maps simple by creating one map for each persona.

CREATE THE STORY

What are the main elements of the customer experience from a customer perspective? What parts of their experience leave a lasting impression on them either positive or negative.

MAP USER ACTIONS & ACTIVITIES STEP-BY-STEP

Start at the beginning of the service or experience and list each thing a customer commonly does step by step. Put each sub- activity on a separate post-it note. For example, if the activity is visiting a coffee shop the activities may include.
1. At work decide to get a coffee on the way home
2. Check the location of coffee shops on the Internet.
3. Select coffee shop
4. Go to car
5. Drive to coffee shop
6. Park
7. Enter coffee shop

8. Stand in line
9. Order
10. Pick up coffee
11. Find table
12. Sit down
13. Drink coffee
14. Read news on tablet
15. Pack up
16. Return to car
17. Drive home
18. Reflect on the experience.

Describe each activity on a separate post-it note and place them in a line on your wall or table. Continue till your team is happy that all important activities have been included.

MAP TIME

How long does each customer activity usually take? Does a stage usually last ten seconds or ten minutes. Place the time taken on a post-it note above each stage of customer activity.

Time to consider:

1. Critical periods service actions, such as response to a proposal.
2. Duration of each service step, such as airline check-in
3. Time between service steps such as walking to a hotel room after check-in.
4. End to end service experience.

BUILD THE MAP

Now you are ready to create the map.

MAP USER ACTION PHASES

Break the list of customer activities into four or six phases of sub-activities. Some examples of phases of activities are:

1. Explore
2. Evaluate
3. Engage
4. Experience

1. Aware
2. Join
3. Use
4. Develop
5. Leave

1. Research
2. Evaluate and compare
3. Commit
4. Use and Monitor
5. Refine and review

MAP THE PHYSICAL EVIDENCE STEP-BY-STEP

Physical evidence is usually the lane shown at the top of a blueprint. Services consist of the interactions with people, the processes, and the physical proof of the experience. Designed objects in the service environment are sometimes referred to as "physical evidence" because they are physical proof of service that has taken place. Physical evidence is the tangible things that help to communicate and perform the service and influence a customer's perception of a service.

Physical evidence is the visible manifestation of service. It conveys to customers whether the service provider cares about their customers and whether they trust their customers. Physical facilities and staff appearance; and uniforms. Physical evidence should be considered important by the customer and the promise implied by these tangible objects should be delivered. A bank card is an example of physical evidence of a service. It helps a bank differentiate their service from another bank. It separates the service from the seller.

Other examples of physical evidence are
1. The building
2. The interior
3. The car park
4. Internal signs.
5. Packaging.
6. Promotional materials
7. Web pages.
8. Paperwork
9. Brochures.
10. Stationery
11. Billing statement
12. Furnishings.
13. Signs
14. Uniforms and employee dress.
15. Business cards.
16. Mailboxes.

MAP THE PAIN POINTS

A pain point is any part of the customer experience that they find people disturbing, frustrating, urgent or uncomfortable. Many customer needs are for things the end users don't clearly understand or can articulate. A pain point is a problem for you customer and a problem and an opportunity for you. Solving pain points create value for you and your customer. "customer pain" is a synonym

evidence cues are what customers use to evaluate service quality.

Physical evidence can convey intended and unintended messages to customers. Physical evidence is the interface between a service provider and a customer. Key to delivering a successful service is to clearly identify a simple, consistent message, and then manage the evidence to support that message.

" Well-prepared small details represent sincerity in serving guests which reflects the hotel's good service spirit. For example, welcome fruit, an electric kettle and fresh flowers in hotel rooms are service evidence that often evoked delight as they show the hotel's thoughtfulness"

"For example, a research participant talked about disappointment caused by "fake" hangers in a hotel room's closet. She complained: They're not real hangers, because they're attached to the railing. So if you want to take out a hanger and then hang it on a chair or hang it on a door, you can't, because there's no hook... That's kind of a fake hanger. It shows that they think I'm going to steal the hangers. So it makes me feel not trusted."

Source: Kathy Pui Ying Lo Loughborough University

Physical evidence includes the service providers building/

LIST THE PHASES OF CUSTOMER ACTIONS

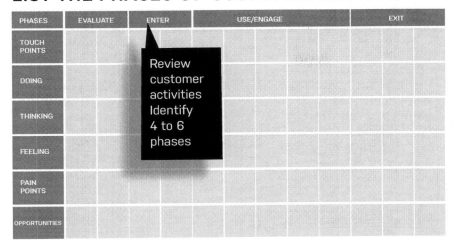

PHASES	EVALUATE	ENTER	USE/ENGAGE			EXIT
TOUCH POINTS						
DOING						
THINKING						
FEELING						
PAIN POINTS						
OPPORTUNITIES						

> Review customer activities Identify 4 to 6 phases

LIST THE STAGE-BY-STAGE TOUCHPOINTS FOR EACH CHANNEL

STAGES	EVALUATE		ENTER		USE/ENGAGE						EXIT	
TOUCH POINTS	Home Interior	Internet Laptop	Car	Car park Coffee shop exterior	Coffee shop interior Menu board	Counter Coffee cup	Coffee shop interior Chair table	Laptop Power socket Internet	Laptop Internet chair table Cup	Cup Trashcan coffee shop interior	Car Par Car	Car
DOING												
THINKING												
FEELING												
PAIN POINTS												
OPPORTUNITIES												

for "customer needs". Customers spend money to combat pain or to pursue pleasure. Examples of service pain points are airport security lines, hospital directions, or the cost of travel. A pain point is the why customers choose you if you offer a solution to their need. If you engage your customers and listen, they'll tell you their pain points

To identify customer 'pain-points':
1. In-depth interviews with customer facing internal employees
2. Requests from your most valuable customers.
3. Customer interviews.
4. Customer focus groups.
5. Review of customer support or warranty claims to identify persistent problems.
6. Review of competitor offerings.
7. You can list the root causes of pain for your customers at each stage.

CUSTOMER OR STAKEHOLDER COMMENTS
List significant or representative comments in a lane. What do customers think?

MAP BRAND IMPACT
List brand impact of touchpoints and customer comments in a lane.

KEY PEOPLE
Identify internal owners of experiences that support

customer's needs.

CUSTOMER NEEDS
Do customers have unrecognized needs that could be addressed? What do customers want to accomplish at each stage of interaction?

MAP CONNECTIONS
Use arrows to illustrate the flow of responsibility who is driving the service at any moment and should be initiating service action:

1. Model expectations of "proactive" provider activity.
2. Model the customer responsibility for next steps.
3. Model partner expectations.
4. Define points of hand off between roles, such as from backstage to onstage.

MAP MOMENTS OF TRUTH
Map those interactions that have the most impact on the customer. A moment of truth is an interaction between a customer and a service provider that allows the end user to form an impression about the organization. For example waiting in line in a coffee shop. A moment of truth is a point in time when a customer can make a judgment about the value of a service delivery and a business relationship. Identifying moments of truth and improving their outcomes is a focus of service blueprinting.

LIST THE STAGE-BY-STAGE CUSTOMER ACTIONS

STAGES	EVALUATE		ENTER		USE/ENGAGE						EXIT	
TOUCH POINTS	Home interior	Internet Laptop	Car	Car park Coffee shop exterior	Coffee shop interior Menu board	Counter Coffee cup	Coffee shop interior Chair table	Laptop Power socket Internet	Laptop Internet chair table Cup	Cup Trashcan coffee shop interior	Car Par Car	Car
DOING	Customer At home decides to go out to have a coffee	Checks location of coffee shop on internet	Drives car to coffee shop	Parks and enters coffee shop	Selects drink and waits in line to order	Pays and picks up coffee	Finds a table and sits down	Drinks coffee and reviews emails on laptop	Writes and sends some emails. Tops up coffee	Finishes coffee and puts cup in trashcan	Returns to car	Drives on to supermarket
THINKING												
FEELING												
PAIN POINTS												
OPPORTUNITIES												

LIST CUSTOMER THOUGHTS STAGE-BY-STAGE

STAGES	EVALUATE		ENTER		USE/ENGAGE						EXIT	
TOUCH POINTS	Home interior	Internet Laptop	Car	Car park Coffee shop exterior	Coffee shop interior Menu board	Counter Coffee cup	Coffee shop interior Chair table	Laptop Power socket Internet	Laptop Internet chair table Cup	Cup Trashcan coffee shop interior	Car Par Car	Car
DOING	Customer At home decides to go out to have a coffee	Checks location of coffee shop on internet	Drives car to coffee shop	Parks and enters coffee shop	Selects drink and waits in line to order	Pays and picks up coffee	Finds a table and sits down	Drinks coffee and reviews emails on laptop	Writes and sends some emails. Tops up coffee	Finishes coffee and puts cup in trashcan	Returns to car	Drives on to supermarket
THINKING	Should I call a friend? Will I have a long wait to be served?	Which coffee shop should I go to?	Will be able to park close to the coffee shop?	Will there be a long queue?	Should I have a latte or a drip coffee?	The coffee is more expensive than last time	Is there a seat available at the window?	The coffee is very hot. Is there a plug for my laptop?	Not a plug available. How long will my battery last?	Where is the trashcan?	Will the traffic be heavy?	There was a long queue. I will go to another coffee shop next time.
FEELING												
PAIN POINTS												
OPPORTUNITIES												

ROOT CAUSE OF PAIN POINT

Ask why the experience is painful for the customer. If necessary, ask why several times to understand the cause of the pain.

MAP BARRIERS

What are the obstacles to the optimal experience for the customer at each stage of their interaction?

ADD PHOTOS OR PICTURES WHERE POSSIBLE

Maps sometimes have a lane of photographs that show pain points or other aspects of customer activities. Use pictures if they are the best way of communicating something. For example lack of cleanliness on a train platform.

IDENTIFY POINTS OF FAILURE

Where is the experience failing or likely to fail?

OPPORTUNITIES

Brainstorm ways to change to better meet customer needs.

1. Brainstorm ways to change to meet better customer needs.
2. Bullet these ideas in a separate lane stage by stage.
3. What is the ideal customer experience
4. Analyze every touch point
5. Identify physical evidence at each phase - moment of truth
6. Simplify and refine the process
7. Remove pain points and surprises.
8. Add touchpoints that are missing
9. Build scenarios.
10. Think about extreme users, new users, average users.

PHOTOGRAPH THE DRAFT

Photograph the whole blueprint and photograph the blueprint in sections with sufficient resolution to enable you to transfer the map into a graphics program such as Adobe Illustrator or InDesign.

CREATE A PRESENTATION COPY

Photograph the whole map and photograph the map in sections with sufficient resolution to enable you to transfer the map into a graphics program such as Adobe Illustrator or InDesign. Templates can be used for future maps.

DISTRIBUTE TO STAKEHOLDERS FOR FEEDBACK

Distribute draft to internal and external stakeholders for feedback. Circulate you map as widely as possible to get feedback from internal departments, executives, external customers and stakeholders.

REFINE THE MAP BASED ON THE FEEDBACK

Does it tell the story of your customer's experience that is complete, from beginning to end? Is it understandable to

LIST HOW THE CUSTOMER IS FEELING STAGE-BY-STAGE

STAGES	EVALUATE		ENTER		USE/ENGAGE					EXIT		
TOUCH POINTS	Home interior	Internet Laptop	Car	Car park Coffee shop exterior	Coffee shop interior Menu board	Counter Coffee cup	Coffee shop interior Chair table	Laptop Power socket Internet	Laptop Internet chair table Cup	Cup Trashcan coffee shop interior	Car Par Car	Car
DOING	Customer At home decides to go out to have a coffee	Checks location of coffee shop on internet	Drives car to coffee shop	Parks and enters coffee shop	Selects drink and waits in line to order	Pays and picks up coffee	Finds a table and sits down	Drinks coffee and reviews emails on laptop	Writes and sends some emails. Tops up coffee	Finishes coffee and puts cup in trashcan	Returns to car	Drives on to supermarket
THINKING	Should I call a friend? Will I have a long wait to be served?	Which coffee shop should I go to?	Will be able to park close to the coffee shop?	Will there be a long queue?	Should I have a latte or a drip coffee?	The coffee is more expensive than last time	Is there a seat available at the window?	The coffee is very hot. Is there a plug for my laptop?	Not a plug available. How long will my battery last?	Where is the trashcan?	Will the traffic be heavy?	There was a long queue. I will go to another coffee shop next time.
FEELING	Should I call a friend? Will I have a long wait to be served?	Which coffee shop should I go to?	Will be able to park close to the coffee shop?	Will there be a long queue?	Should I have a latte or a drip coffee?	The coffee is more expensive than last time	Is there a seat available at the window?	The coffee is very hot. Is there a plug for my laptop?	Not a plug available. How long will my battery last?	Where is the trashcan?	Will the traffic be heavy?	I will go to another coffee shop next time.
PAIN POINTS												
OPPORTUNITIES												

LIST PAIN POINTS STAGE-BY-STAGE

STAGES	EVALUATE		ENTER		USE/ENGAGE					EXIT		
TOUCH POINTS	Home interior	Internet Laptop	Car	Car park Coffee shop exterior	Coffee shop interior Menu board	Counter Coffee cup	Coffee shop interior Chair table	Laptop Power socket Internet	Laptop Internet chair table Cup	Cup Trashcan coffee shop interior	Car Par Car	Car
DOING	Customer At home decides to go out to have a coffee	Checks location of coffee shop on internet	Drives car to coffee shop	Parks and enters coffee shop	Selects drink and waits in line to order	Pays and picks up coffee	Finds a table and sits down	Drinks coffee and reviews emails on laptop	Writes and sends some emails. Tops up coffee	Finishes coffee and puts cup in trashcan	Returns to car	Drives on to supermarket
THINKING	Should I call a friend? Will I have a long wait to be served?	Which coffee shop should I go to?	Will be able to park close to the coffee shop?	Will there be a long queue?	Should I have a latte or a drip coffee?	The coffee is more expensive than last time	Is there a seat available at the window?	The coffee is very hot. Is there a plug for my laptop?	Not a plug available. How long will my battery last?	Where is the trashcan?	Will the traffic be heavy?	There was a long queue. I will go to another coffee shop next time.
FEELING	Should I call a friend? Will I have a long wait to be served?	Which coffee shop should I go to?	Will be able to park close to the coffee shop?	Will there be a long queue?	Should I have a latte or a drip coffee?	The coffee is more expensive than last time	Is there a seat available at the window?	The coffee is very hot. Is there a plug for my laptop?	Not a plug available. How long will my battery last?	Where is the trashcan?	Will the traffic be heavy?	I will go to another coffee shop next time.
PAIN POINTS	Should I call a friend? Will I have a long wait to be served?	Hard to park at best coffee shop	No parking place available close to coffee shop	Queue takes 20 minutes	Too many choices on menu	Price has increased	Needs to wait for an available table. Chairs uncomfortable.	Coffee too hot to drink. Coffee shop cold.	No plug available for laptop. Music too loud.	No visible trashcan	Long walk back to car. Traffic heavy	
OPPORTUNITIES												

people outside the team? Are the insights actionable? Does it inspire and support a change in strategy? Does it communicate the necessary information, without further explanation? Simplify the map. Identify gaps and do further research to fill the gaps. Gaps in touchpoints may suggest opportunities to add new touchpoints.

ITERATE
Distribute the refined map to other stakeholders and refine the map again.

BRAINSTORM THE IDEAL EXPERIENCE
Put together what you have learned to generate a better experience for your customers that you can implement. Develop step-by-step corrective actions for fail points.

RAPID PROTOTYPING
Experience prototyping is the most efficient way to implement an improved service. The goal is to observe customers interacting with the new experience and obtain their feedback about the experience. Use methods such as:
1. Video prototyping,
2. Role playing,
3. Desktop walkthroughs
4. Bodystorming
5. Paper prototyping
6. Empathy tools
7. Wireframing
8. Service staging
9. Wizard of Oz
10. Start with low-fidelity

methods and move to higher fidelity prototyping methods as you find clarity with the best design direction.

SERVICE STAGING
Test the refinements in a staged setting. Sets up space that imitates the real environment, but with simple props to represent physical objects.

CONDUCT USER STUDIES IN THE TARGET CONTEXT
Test with target users iteratively and refine the service until the pain points have become points of pleasure for customers.
1. Do people understand the service
2. Do people see the value of the service?
3. Do people understand how to use it?
4. Is the experience positive?
5. What ideas do the customers have that could improve the service?

IMPLEMENT THE SERVICE
The end purpose of a blueprint is to take action and improve the journey and drive the ROI to justify the investment.
After the new service design is tested, the design team documents the new experience and creates implementation guidelines to roll out of the new service across the organization. The service blueprint is now a tool to communicate the new design.

1. Use your map for employee training.
2. Map upcoming product launches or your desired future state

MEASURE YOUR PROGRESS TOWARDS YOUR GOALS

Define ways of tracking your progress towards measurable goals. Metrics will help you measure the quality of your customer experience, now and in the future.

1. Net Promoter Score and customer loyalty measures
2. Customer satisfaction measures
3. Quantitative assessments of the customer emotions.
4. Metrics of customer effort
5. The measure of the performance of each touchpoint.
6. New sales.
7. Increased loyalty and retention of customers
8. The increase in revenue per customer.
9. More sales.
10. Reduced costs
11. Better delivery processes.
12. Better quality
13. Increased competitiveness

BRAINSTORM OPPORTUNITIES TO IMPROVE THE EXPERIENCE

STAGES	EVALUATE		ENTER		USE/ENGAGE					EXIT		
TOUCH POINTS	Home Interior	Internet Laptop	Car	Car park Coffee shop exterior	Coffee shop interior Menu board	Counter Coffee cup	Coffee shop interior Chair table	Laptop Power socket Internet	Laptop Internet chair table Cup	Cup Trashcan coffee shop interior	Car Par Car	Car
DOING	Customer At home decides to go out to have a coffee	Checks location of coffee shop on Internet	Drives car to coffee shop	Parks and enters coffee shop	Selects drink and waits in line to order	Pays and picks up coffee	Finds a table and sits down	Drinks coffee and reviews emails on laptop	Writes and sends some emails. Tops up coffee	Finishes coffee and puts cup in trashcan	Returns to car	Drives on to supermarket
THINKING	Should I call a friend? Will I have a long wait to be served?	Which coffee shop should I go to?	Will be able to park close to the coffee shop?	Will there be a long queue?	Should I have a latte or a drip coffee?	The coffee is more expensive than last time	Is there a seat available at the window?	The coffee is very hot. Is there a plug for my laptop?	Not a plug available. How long will my battery last?	Where is the trashcan?	Will the traffic be heavy?	There was a long queue. I will go to another coffee shop next time.
FEELING	Should I call a friend? Will I have a long wait to be served?	Which coffee shop should I go to?	Will be able to park close to the coffee shop?	Will there be a long queue?	Should I have a latte or a drip coffee?	The coffee is more expensive than last time	Is there a seat available at the window?	The coffee is very hot. Is there a plug for my laptop?	Not a plug available. How long will my battery last?	Where is the trashcan?	Will the traffic be heavy?	I will go to another coffee shop next time.
PAIN POINTS	Should I call a friend? Will I have a long wait to be served?	Hard to park at best coffee shop	No parking place available close to coffee shop	Queue takes 20 minutes	Too many choices on menu	Price has increased	Needs to wait for an available table. Chairs uncomfortable.	Coffee too hot to drink Coffee shop cold.	No plug available for laptop. Music too loud.	No visible trashcan	Long walk back to car Traffic heavy	
OPPORTUNITIES	Improve web site	Differentiate coffee shop from other coffee shops	Make more parking available.	Order coffee On-line. Add second cash register.	Reduce number of options	Offer some lower priced menu items	Replace chairs. Open up second room	Adjust coffee temperature. Fix leaky windows.	Add power points	Relocate trash cans. Increase number of trashcans.	Make more parking available.	

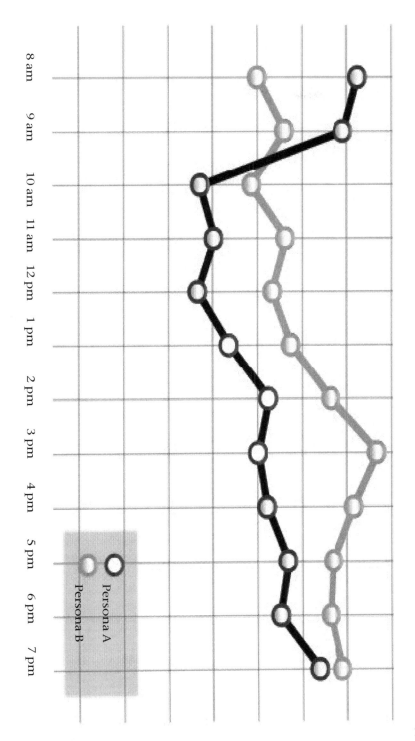

EMOTIONAL JOURNEY MAP

8 am
9 am
10 am
11 am
12 pm
1 pm
2 pm
3 pm
4 pm
5 pm
6 pm
7 pm

Persona A
Persona B

313

EMOTIONAL JOURNEY MAP

WHAT

An emotional journey map is a map that visually illustrates people's emotional experience throughout an interaction with an organization or brand.

WHY

1. It provides a focus for discussion.
2. It focuses on what may make your customers unhappy
3. Provides a visually Compelling story of customer experience.
4. Customer experience is more than interaction with a product.
5. By understanding the journey that your customers are making, you will be in a position to make informed improvements.

CHALLENGES

1. Customers often do not take the route in an interaction that the designer expects.
2. Failure to manage experiences can lead to lost customers.

HOW

1. Define the activity of your map. For example it could be a ride on the underground train.
2. Collect internal insights.
3. Research customer perceptions.
4. Analyze research.
5. Map journey.
6. Across the top of the page do a time line Break the journey into stages using your customer's point of view
7. Capture each persona's unique experience.
8. Use a scale from 0 to 10. The higher the number, the better the experience.
9. Plot the emotional journey.
10. Analyze the lease pleasant emotional periods and create ideas for improving the experience during those periods.
11. Create a map for each persona.

MULTI-CHANNEL MAP

Interactions can cross channels, touchpoints or physical evidence and take place in multiple contexts. More than 50% of companies according to one study have little understanding of the complex nature of their customers typical purchase routes. Customers desire seamless interactions across channels and touchpoints. A multichannel map can help uncover opportunities for your business to improve the customer experience.

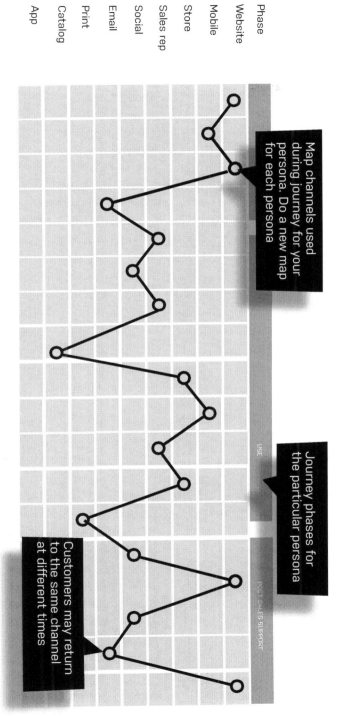

Phase

Website

Mobile

Store

Sales rep

Social

Email

Print

Catalog

App

Map channels used during journey for your persona. Do a new map for each persona

Journey phases for the particular persona

Customers may return to the same channel at different times

USE

POST SALES SUPPORT

FISHBONE DIAGRAM

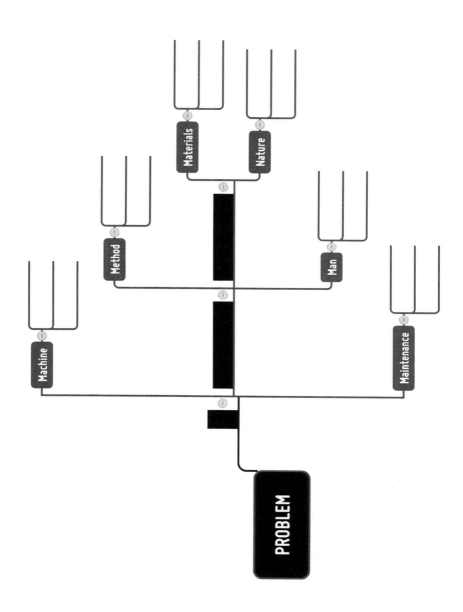

FISHBONE DIAGRAMS

Fishbone diagrams also called Ishikawa diagrams, are diagrams that show the causes of a specific event. Mazda Motors used an Ishikawa diagram to design the Miata sports car, The goal was was "Jinba Ittai" Horse and Rider as One. Every factor identified in the diagram was included in the final design. Ishikawa described the process as fishboning your problem and letting it cook overnight.

WHO INVENTED IT?
Kaoru Ishikawa University of Tokyo 1968

WHY
1. People tend to fix a problem by responding to an immediately visible cause while ignoring the deeper issues. This approach may lead to a problem reoccurring.
2. Use in the synthesis phase to understand the root causes of a problem to serve as the basis for design.
3. Identifies the relationship between cause and effect.

HOW
1. Prepare the six arms of the Ishikawa Diagram on a White-board.
2. Define the problem clearly as a short statement in the head of the diagram.
3. Describe the causes of each bone and write them at the end of each branch. Use the 4 M's as categories; Machine, Man Methods, Materials.
4. Conduct the brainstorming session using brainstorming guidelines Ask each team member to define the cause of the problem. You may list as many causes as necessary. Typically 3 to 6 are listed.
5. Minor causes are then listed around the major causes.
6. Interpret the Ishikawa Diagram once it's finished.

RESOURCES
White-board
Dry-erase markers
Room with privacy
Paper
Pens

FORCE FIELD DIAGRAM

Force field analysis is a method of mapping and analyzing factors which assist or work against desired goals.

WHO INVENTED IT?
Kurt Lewin 1940s
John R. P. French 1947

WHY
1. Allows visual comparison of factors affecting the success of a project for discussion of

FORCE FIELD DIAGRAM

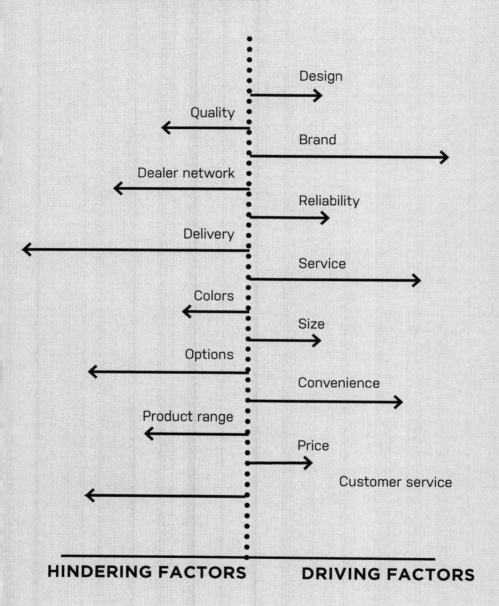

Design

Quality

Brand

Dealer network

Reliability

Delivery

Service

Colors

Size

Options

Convenience

Product range

Price

Customer service

HINDERING FACTORS   DRIVING FACTORS

SYNTHESIS PHASE

solutions.

CHALLENGES
1. It is best to focus on barriers.
2. Assign a strategy to each barrier

HOW
1. Select a moderator and a team of stakeholders.
2. The moderator describes the problem being focused on to the team
3. The moderator draws the letter T on a White-board
4. The moderator writes the problem above the cross stroke on the T
5. The team brainstorms a list of forces working against the goal and the moderator lists them on the right hand of the upstroke on the letter T.
6. The team brainstorms a list or forces working towards the goal and the moderator writes them on the right hand of the upstroke on the letter T.
7. Forces listed can be internal and external.
8. They can be associated with the environment, the organization, people strategy, culture, values, competitors, conflicts or other factors.
9. Prioritize and quantify both lists of forces
10. The moderator draws a horizontal letter T and above the horizontal line draws arrows for each factor indicating their relative significance in the opinion of the team.
11. The moderator draws arrows for each negative factor below the line showing their relative significance.

RESOURCES
Pen
Paper
White-board
Dry erase markers
Post-it notes.

FUTURE WHEEL

WHAT
The future wheel is a method to graphically represent and analyze the direct and indirect outcomes of a proposed change.

WHO INVENTED IT?
Jerome Glenn 1972

WHY
1. A method of envisioning outcomes of decisions.
2. Can be used to study possible outcomes of trends.
3. Helps create a consciousness of the future.

CHALLENGES
1. Can be subjective

HOW
1. Define the proposed change
2. Identify and graph the first level of outcomes
3. Identify and graph the subsequent level of outcomes
4. Link the dependencies
5. Identify insights
6. Identify the actions

FUTURE WHEEL

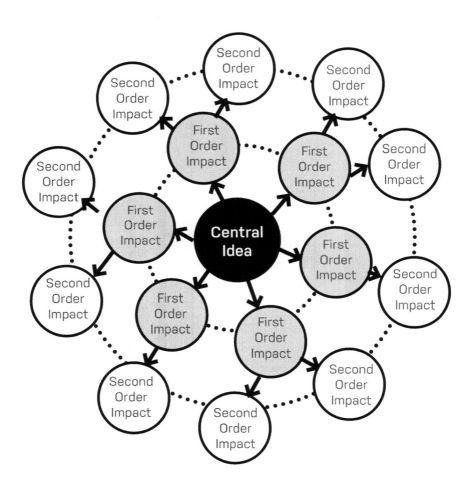

7. Implement the actions

RESOURCES
Pen
Paper
White-board
Dry erase markers

MIND MAPS

WHAT
A mind map is a diagram used to represent the affinities or connections between a number of ideas or things. Understanding connections is the starting point for design. Mind maps are a method of analyzing information and relationships.

WHO INVENTED IT?
Porphry of Tyros 3rd century BC.
Allan Collins, Northwestern University 1960, USA

WHY
1. The method helps identify relationships.
2. There is no right or wrong with mind maps. They help with they help with memory and organization.
3. Problem solving and brainstorming
4. Relationship discovery
5. Summarizing information
6. Memorizing information

CHALLENGES
Print words clearly, use color and images for visual impact.

HOW
1. Start in the center with a key word or idea. Put box around this node.
2. Use images, symbols, or words for nodes.
3. Select key words.
4. Keep the key word names of nodes s simple and short as possible.
5. Associated nodes should be connected with lines to show affinities.
6. Make the lines the same length as the word/image they support.
7. Use emphasis such as thicker lines to show the strength of associations in your mind map.
8. Use radial arrangement of nodes.

RESOURCES
Paper
Pens
White-board
Dry-erase markers

MAKING MEANING FROM RESEARCH

CODING
Coding is a method of processing information into categories so that the meaning of the information can be understood.

Codes identify interesting

DESIGN THINKING MIND MAP

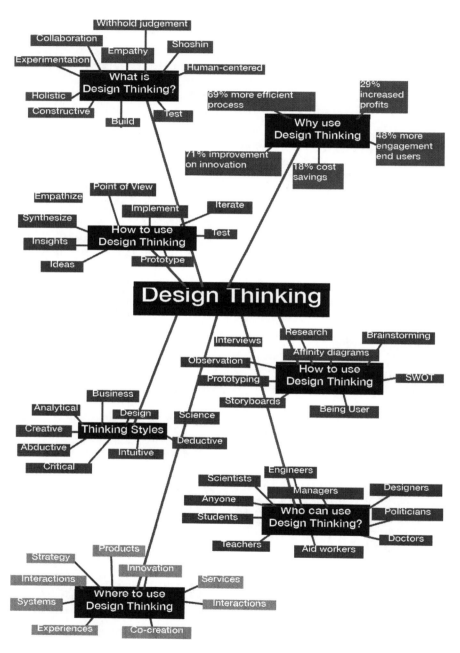

content. Codes usually are applied to "chunks" of data

INDUCTIVE CODING
As data is reviewed, the codes are developed and refined to fit the data. The researcher refines the dimensions of existing codes and identifies new codes.

DEDUCTIVE OR A PRIORI CODING
Using this approach you create a list of codes before you start based on established questions of theories. The start list may have between 10 and 40 codes.

HOW TO CODE
1. Gather data.
2. Read through the data.
3. Divide the Data into segments of information.
4. Identify and code interesting data,
5. Label the segments with codes

CLUSTERING
1. Make a list of all code words.
2. Start with 10 to 40 codes
3. Cluster together similar codes to a smaller number of codes 15 to 20

THEMES
1. Create themes, sub-themes,
2. Reduce the number of clusters to 5 to 9 themes
3. Name the themes.
4. Themes should reflect your research goals.

DISPLAY THE DATA VISUALLY

1. Matrices
2. Tree diagrams
3. Connection diagrams
4. Spider diagrams
5. Personas

VALIDATE YOUR FINDINGS
1. Triangulation
2. Fresh eyes
3. Consider researcher bias

TRIANGULATION
Use of two or more independent sources to support findings within a study.

REPORT
Write a report with conclusions and recommendations.

NETWORK MAP

WHAT
This is a method which maps and helps the researcher understand systems or services that involve many stakeholders. The map identifies the stakeholders, their links, influence and goals.

WHO INVENTED IT?
Eva Schiffer 2004 to 2008

WHY
1. Inexpensive and fast.
2. Connects to existing research tools and methods
3. Makes implicit knowledge explicit
4. Structures complex reality
5. Flexible for use in different

contexts.

RESOURCES
Large sheets of paper for network map
Felt pens for drawing links
Adhesive paper as actor cards
Flat discs for building Influence-towers
Actor figurines

HOW
1. Define problems and goals.
2. Recruit participants
3. Define interview questions
4. Define network links to study
5. Ask participant to go through the process in detail.
6. Make a card with the name and description of each stakeholder. Place the cards on your map.
7. Show links between the stakeholders as lines on the map.
8. Number the links.
9. Create a legend describing each link.
10. Setting up influence towers:
11. Describe the influence of each stakeholder.?
12. Quantify the strength of influence of each stakeholder.
13. Stack discs next to each stakeholder card showing the relative level of influence.
14. Write descriptions of perceived problems next to each stakeholder.

INTERVIEW PROCESS
Question 1: Who is involved? Ask: "Who is involved in this process?"Write names on actor cards (with different colors of cards for different groups of actors) and distribute on empty Net-Map sheet.

Question 2: How are they linked? Ask: "Who is linked to whom?" Go through the different kinds of links one by one Draw arrows between actor cards according to interviewee directions. If two actors exchange something draw double headed arrows. If actors exchange more than one thing, add differently colored arrow heads to existing links.

Question 3: How influential are they? Ask: "How strongly can actors influence (our complex issue)?" Explain / agree on a definition of influence with your interviewee, clarify that this is about influence only and not influence in the world at large. Ask interviewee to assign influence towers to actors: The higher the influence on the issue at stake, the higher the tower. Towers of different actors can be of the same height. Actors with no influence can be put on ground level. Towers can be as high as participants want. Place influence towers next to actor cards. Verbalize set-up and give interviewee the chance to adjust towers before noting height of tower on the Net-Map.

Question 4: What are their goals? Ask according to predefined goals, actor by actor, e.g. "Does this actor support environmental, developmental goals or both?"

Note abbreviations for goals next to actor cards, allow for multiple goals where appropriate, by noting more than one goal next to the actor.

Discussion
Discuss the result with your interview partners. Depending on the goal of this specific mapping process, you might ask your participants to think strategically about the network and develop ideas to improve the situation in the future.

Source: Eva Schiffer http://netmap. wordpress.com/process-net-map

SEGMENTATION

WHAT
Market segmentation involves subdividing a market into a number of groups where the people in each group have some commonality, or similarity. Members of a market segment share something in common. Segmentation is done to provide deign solutions that work for a group of people without the expense of developing a different solution for each person. There are many ways to segment a market. The best way to segment customers depends on your goals. For example if you are entering a new global market one way is to segment your customers by where they live.

GEOGRAPHIC SEGMENTATION
This is one of the more common methods of market segmentation. For example, a company selling products in Europe may segment their customers by the country that they live in. In Europe regional differences in customer preferences exist. You may decide to segment you customers by those who live in a city and those who live in a rural location.

DISTRIBUTION SEGMENTATION
Experience maps and Service blueprints help designers understand a market where most people access multiple channels when purchasing or using a product or service

PRICE SEGMENTATION
Another common way of segmenting a market is by income. Different price-points for a product or service may appeal to people with different incomes. Mass market car companies like ford have models that appeal to people with lower incomes and luxury models that appeal to customers with higher incomes.

DEMOGRAPHIC SEGMENTATION
Demographic segmentation is possibly the most commonly used type of segmentation. There are large number of demographic factors such as gender, age, type of employment and education that are often used for segmentation. Some products

and brands are targeted mainly at men. Most people over the age of 40 require glasses to read.

TIME SEGMENTATION
Some products are sold at a particular time of day or year. For example surfboards are sold in summer.

PSYCHOGRAPHIC OR LIFESTYLE SEGMENTATION
Psychographic or lifestyle segmentation, is based on, values, behaviors, emotions, perceptions, beliefs, and interests. For example some customers prefer luxury products. Some customers may follow a particular sporting team.

Markets segments should be large enough to justify creating targeted products and services. Four to six market segments is often a manageable number. Targeting too many segments is sometimes unsuccessful. Products usually do not appeal to everyone.

Consider the income potential of each segment carefully when defining segments.
When defining segments consider:
1. Can you measure the segment?.
2. Is the segment big enough to make a profit?
3. Is the segment changing or evolving?
4. Can you reach the segment?
5. Is there one factor that unites everyone in the segment?
6. Do you have enough data to understand the segment?

PERSONAS

WHAT
· ·
"A persona is a archetypal character that is meant to represent a group of users in a role who share common goals, attitudes and behaviors when interacting with a particular product or service personas are user models that are presented as specific individual humans. They are not actual people, but are synthesized directly from observations of real people."*(Cooper)*

WHO INVENTED IT?
Alan Cooper 1998

WHY
1. Helps create empathy for users and reduces self reference.
2. Use as tool to analyze and gain insight into users.
3. Help in gaining buy-in from stakeholders.
4. Personas are user models, characters with a purpose who will represent your target users throughout the design process from brainstorming ideas to designing ideal user experience journey.
5. Personas support storytelling, foster user understanding and evolve design. Stories help communicate information

in a compelling manner and
evoke emotions and action.

HOW

1. Inaccurate personas can lead
   to a false understandings of
   the end users. Personas need
   to be created using data from
   real users.
2. Collect data through
   observation, interviews,
   ethnography.
3. Segment the users or
   customers
4. Create the Personas
5. Avoid Stereotypes
6. Each persona should be
   different. Avoid fringe
   characteristics. Personas
   should each have three to
   four life goals which are
   personal aspirations,
7. Personas are given a name,
   and photograph.
8. Design personas can be
   followed by building
   customer journeys.

RESOURCES

Raw data on users from
interviews or other research
Images of people similar to
segmented customers.
Computer
Graphics software

HISTORY OF PERSONAS

The Inmates Are Running the
Asylum, written by Alan Cooper
published in 1998, introduced
the use of personas as a design
tool. Alan Cooper describes his
first application of the persona
technique:

"In 1995 I was working with
the three founders of Sagent
Technologies, pioneers in the
field of what is now called
"Business Intelligence" software.
It was almost impossible
for those brilliant, logical
programmers to conceive of
a single use of their product
when it was obviously capable
of so many uses. In frustration I
demanded to be introduced to
their customers.

The users fell into three distinct
groups, clearly differentiated by
their goals, tasks, and skill levels.
Had I been creating the software
myself, I would have role-played
those users as I had with Ruby
and Super Project, but in this
case I had to describe those user
models to the Sagent team. So
I created Chuck, Cynthia, and
Rob. These three were the first
true, Goal-Directed, personas.
At the next group meeting,
I presented my designs from
the points of view of Chuck,
Cynthia, and Rob instead of
from my own. The results were
dramatic. While there was still
resistance to this unfamiliar
method, the programmers
could clearly see the sense in
my designs because they could
identify with these hypothetical
archetypes. The product was so
successful that it defined a new
product segment. The company
was a success, too, going public
four years later.

Susan Margolis

Demographic

Age

Marital status

Occupation

Location

Income

Archytype

Personality

Introvert/extravert

Driven

Social

Active

Competitive

Technology

IT & internet

Software

Mobile apps

Social networks

Frustrations

Fears

Pain points

Unmet needs

Goals

Motivations

Brands

Bio/ background

Quote:

You can obtain a pdf copy of this template from our site www.dcc-edu.org

EXAMPLE OF A PERSONA TEMPLATE

PHOTO OF PERSONA

PERSONA NAME

image of persona

GRAPHICS

upation
ation

Income
Gender
Education

RACTERISTIC

GOALS

What does this person want to achieve

demograhic factors

MOTIVATIONS
Incentives
Fear
Growth

Achievement
Power
Social

FRUSTRATIONS

What experiences does this person
wish to avoid?

QUOTE

Characteristic quote

BRANDS

What brands doe

sliders show relevant factors

CHARACTERIST
····X·······

EXTROVERT
···········X·······

TRAVEL
····X···········

LUXURY GOODS
···X················

TECHNICAL SAVVY
··············X·······

SPORTS
·············X·······

SOCIAL NETWORKING

MOBILE APPS

Over the next few years, we developed and perfected the technique.

Many of my predecessors have employed ethnographic user research and created persona-like constructs to aid their designing. Product marketing professionals have also been using persona-like entities for many years to define demographic segments. But personas are unique and uniquely effective."

TYPES OF PERSONAS

PRIMARY
The users who are the main focus of the product or service.

SECONDARY
Secondary users may use the product but are not the primary focus.

STAKEHOLDERS
Stakeholders are people who may be affected by the products or services. A patient may be the primary persona but stakeholders may be doctors, nurses, hospital workers, medical insurance company employees, or relatives of the patient.

Usually persona are not created for each stakeholder. There may be conflicts between the needs of different stakeholders that should be considered.

EXCLUSIONARY
Someone we're not designing for. It is useful to consider non users when defining personas.

BIOGRAPHICAL INFORMATION

NAME
Give each persona a name that may be representative of the user group.

PHOTO
Choose a photograph which represents someone like the persona that you have constructed.

COUNTRY/ REGION
Where within the country does the persona live?

CITY/METROPOLITAN SIZE
9.   Under 5,000,
10. 5,000-10,000,
11. 10,000 -20.000
12. 20,000-50,000,
13. 50,000- 250,000,
14. 250,000-500,000,
15. 500,000-1 million,
16. 1 million-4 million,
17. More than 4 million

URBAN OR RURAL?
Do they live in the city or in the country?

DEMOGRAPHIC

AGE
Give the persona a precise age. Segments often give age as a

range:
1. Under 6
2. 6-11
3. 12-20
4. 20-35
5. 35-50
6. 50-65
7. Over 65

GENDER
Male or female?

FAMILY SIZE
1. 1-2
2. 3-4
3. More than 5

SINGLE OR MARRIED?
Single married or divorced?

LIFE STAGE
1. Child
2. Teenager
3. Young
4. Middle aged
5. Elderly

INCOME
1. Under $10,000;
2. $10,000-20,000,
3. $20,000-30,000,
4. $30,000-50,000,
5. $50,000-100,000,
6. $100,000-150,000
7. Over 150.000

HOUSING
Renter or owner?
Type of dwelling?

OCCUPATION
1. Sales
2. Office worker
3. Nurse
4. Waiter
5. Administration
6. Building
7. Professional
8. Other

EDUCATION
1. Grade school
2. High school
3. College
4. Post Graduate

ETHNICITY
Consider with nationality

NATIONALITY
Many different groups are represented with nationality.

PSYCHOGRAPHIC

SELF-IMAGE
Outgoing, leader, shy

BELIEFS
Focus on those beliefs that may be most relevant to your product or service.

ATTITUDES
Favorable and unfavorable attitudes relevant to the product or service.

TECH STATUS
1. Innovator
2. Early adopter
3. Fast followers
4. Early mainstream
5. Late mainstream
6. Lagger

INTERESTS
1. Music

2. Sport
3. Food
4. Others

MEDIA
1. Web sites
2. TV shows
3. Magazines
4. Other

WEB

TENURE
How long has the persona been using the web?

TIME ON-LINE
Hours per week or month

TYPE OF USAGE
1. Email
2. Social networking
3. News
4. Other

BANDWIDTH
How fast is their connection?

INTERNET DEVICE
1. Desk
2. Tablet
3. Phone
4. Other

BROWSER
Type of browser

Sources:"Principles of Marketing" 8th Edition, Phillip Kotler and Gary Armstrong, "The People Who Make Organization Go – Or Stop," Rob Cross and Laurence Prusak, Havard Business Review, June Persona Creation and Usage Toolkit, George Olsen 2004

PROBLEM STATEMENT

CREATING A PROBLEM STATEMENT
A problem statement includes three elements:
1. user
2. need
3. insight

User xxxx needs xxxx because xxxx

1. What is the need?
2. Who has the need?
3. Why is there a needs?

1. Create a number of problem statements based on different user groups and different needs.
2. Compare the problem statements.
3. Use the problem statement during the ideation phase. Don't try to solve all problems.

SERVICE BLUEPRINTS

WHAT
A service blueprint is a map showing how a service will be provided, what physical and virtual things that customers will interact with, employee actions, and support systems to deliver the service across channels.

INTERACTION PLANES

PHYSICAL
EVIDENCE

CUSTOMER
ACTIONS

Line of interaction

Frontstage

FACE TO FACE
EMPLOYEE
ACTIONS

Line of visibility

Backstage

EMPLOYEE
ACTIONS
NOT VISIBLE TO
CUSTOMER

Line of internal interaction

SUPPORT
PROCESSES

EXAMPLE OF A SERVICE BLUEPRINT

Phase	PREPARE			ENTER			ACTIVITY					EXIT	REFLECT
Physical Evidence	work building	Internet computer	car	car park	building	chalkboard menu	cash register	coffee machine	table chair	computer	table chair	car park	car
Customer Actions	Decide to have a coffee	Locate coffee shop	Drive to coffee shop	Park	Enter coffee shop	Stand in line	Order	Picks up coffee	Sit down	Drink & Work	Pack up	Finish & return to car	Drive home
Line of Interaction													
Onstage Employee Actions					Greet customer		Take order	Make order	Escort to table		Ask if they need refill	Pick up empty cup	
Line of Visibility													
Backstage Employee Actions						Accounting	Order supplies					Cleans room	
Line of Internal Interaction													
Support Processes													
Opportunities													

The idea behind services blueprinting is fairly simple: companies put themselves in their customers' shoes to find out what's working, what's not, and what needs to be changed." It's a very versatile technique that can be used for both innovation and services improvement."

Mary Jo Bitner

"A service blueprint allows a company to explore all the issues inherent in creating or managing a service."

Lyn Shostack

WHY
Service blueprints can be used for the following purposes

4. Understand the structure of a service or experience system.
5. Understand the collective experiences of customer segments
6. To create an improved customer service or experience.
7. Create a more seamless customer experience across business departments, and channels.
8. Design a new service or product customer experience
9. Allocate people and resources efficiently.
10. Develop alignment across departments of an organization.
11. Craft a better customer experience.
12. Expose places where your service or customer experience may fail.
13. Craft a better customer experience
14. Strategic and tactical innovation
15. Building and sharing knowledge
16. Understand competitive positioning
17. Understanding the ideal experience
18. Identify opportunities
19. Empathize with your end users
20. Designing and improving Systems
21. Develop a better product road map
22. Take cost & complexity out of the system
23. Prioritize competing deliverables
24. Plan for hiring
25. Bring different parts of your business together to work to improve the customer experience
26. Identify specific areas of opportunity to drive ideation and innovation
27. Make intangible services tangible
28. Develop customer insights
29. Introduce metrics for what

matters most to your customers
30. Align your offerings to brand promise
31. Improve efficiency
32. Imagine future product and service experiences
33. Making better decisions
34. A living document that can evolve with your business

HOW

Here is a list of stages that you can complete creating a service blueprint. Consider the blueprint to be a living document that will develop and improve, so it doesn't have to be perfect first time. Concentrate on your customers and their point of view.

CREATE YOUR GOAL STATEMENT

1. What is the problem, unmet needs or opportunities that the blueprint is to realize?
2. A clear map of customer needs should be compatible with your goals and with an outcome that satisfies them.
3. Who are the stakeholders?
4. Where is the service delivered?
5. When is the service delivered?
6. What are the channels?
7. Why is there a need for a new design solution?
8. Are you looking to address issues already identified?
9. Do you want to enhance the customer experience?
10. Do you want to engage your customers more effectively? Do you want to create a more efficient process? Define your goals in a statement and return to that statement as you build your map to ensure that your efforts contribute to reaching the goal.

DEFINE YOUR TARGET AUDIENCE SEGMENT AND THEIR NEEDS

The most successful products and services target precise customer segments. Designs that try to please everyone do not satisfy anyone.

GATHER YOUR EXISTING RESEARCH

Start by auditing internal customer experience data that was gathered. Review existing user data, including call center logs, customer satisfaction surveys, existing personas, mystery shopping data, web analytics and customer satisfaction data. Review the data and determine what new research is necessary to fill in the knowledge gaps. To be useful data should be current. The most significant insights will come directly from engaging the stakeholders located in their natural context with the service. Engage stakeholders through a variety of possible research techniques in the physical location of the service such as contextual observation and interviews.

Quantitative data is less useful than qualitative research when trying to understand the feelings and emotions of your customers.

Interviews are a common method used to gather data. Ask them to walk you through their experience and talk about their problems, needs desires and feelings at each stage. Start by talking to between five and twenty people as a minimum sample size. Focus your questions on the areas relevant to the lanes of the service blueprint. If you are creating a journey map, ask what are they doing, thinking, and feeling at each stage of the activity. Ask them what touch points they are engaging at each stage. Ask them where they are experiencing problems or frustrations in achieving their goals. Document your interviews or observations by using video or a digital recorder. Quantitative data with a larger sample size is also useful. Create a survey for existing or prospective customers.

To be useful, your service blueprint needs to be based on real and truthful information. Use prototype maps in focus group discussions to validate findings directly with customers..

REVIEW YOUR EXISTING RESEARCH

Review existing research. Identify gaps in data and create a list of recurring customer experience problems.

CREATE A RESEARCH PLAN TO FILL THE GAPS.

1. Create a research plan to fill the gaps.
2. What do you still need to know?
3. What questions do you need to ask?
4. How many people will you involve?
5. What type of people will you research?
6. What will be the context of the customer?
7. What methods will you use?
8. When will you select and screen the subjects, conduct the research and report on findings?

SYNTHESIZE YOUR RESEARCH

Put each potentially useful piece of information on separate post-it notes. Put the post-it notes on a wall and ask your team to organize the customer's comments into related groups or themes. Which issues are most significant to more customers? Build a hierarchy of problems. Identify themes and patterns from the interviews.
What are your customers' needs and goals at each stage of their activity? What touchpoints are they engaging at each step?

SELECT YOUR TEAM

Care should be taken in selecting your team. As many groups and diverse points of view involved in design delivery and use of the service as possible should be represented.

1. Keep groups to six people or less.
2. If your total group size is larger than twelve people, break the large group into smaller groups of six or fewer people.
3. Have a diverse team with different genders, age, occupations and status represented.
4. Have at least two or three "T" shaped people. "T" shaped people are individuals with two or more areas of expertise such as technology and management or design. This makes the team more flexible and helps group collaboration.
5. Involve external and internal stakeholders such as customers, suppliers, internal business management, engineering, design, and sales.
6. Have customer facing people where possible because they better understand the customer's perspective.

APPOINT YOUR MODERATOR

Create handouts with clear instructions. Provide copies of research summaries. Take breaks every 90 minutes. Photograph the map as it is being built.

MODERATOR SKILLS

1. Effective Listening Skills
2. Flexibility
3. Customer empathy
4. Sincerely Interested in People
5. Enthusiasm
6. People management skills
7. Able to establishing common direction and buy-in.
8. Understands Group Dynamics
9. Authority
10. Neutral and Objective
11. Patient and Persistent
12. Curious
13. Guide discussion promptly.
14. Able to draw our quieter group members.
15. Able to read between the lines and understand what is not said.
16. Beginner's mind
17. Get Panelists to talk to each other.
18. Get the audience involved early.
19. Able to read body language
20. Able to create an atmosphere where divergent views can be explored
21. Encourage all participants to share their views openly.
22. Keep the conversation focused and relevant
23. Track and record the key themes and ideas expressed by the group.
24. Make sure the best and needed people are in the room.
25. Make sure all roles are clearly defined.
26. State the meeting purpose

before or at the start of the meeting
27. Set objectives for the meeting.
28. Define next steps and action items at the conclusion of the meeting.

SELECT AND PREPARE YOUR WORKSPACE

A good space is a large room with plenty of natural light with a large table and sufficient chairs for your team.
Useful materials
1. A large wall
2. Butcher paper
3. Masking tape
4. Mobile White-boards
5. Dry erase markers
6. Sharpies
7. Adhesive notes in 5 colors
8. Digital camera
9. Tripod

IDENTIFY YOUR TARGET SEGMENT TO MAP

Identifying customer segments.

CREATE PERSONAS

Create your customer personas. Personas are archetypal characters created to represent the different user types that might use a product or service in a similar way. Create 3 to 6 personas to cover all your customers.

IDENTIFY STAKEHOLDERS

A stakeholder is someone who may be in some way influenced by your design. For example in a hospital stakeholders may be patients, relatives of patients, hospital workers, doctors, nurses, health insurance workers. Stakeholders are also people who represent various areas within your organization such as technology, design, business management, sales, customer experience.

HOLD STAKEHOLDER WORKSHOPS

Organize a workshop, and guide internal and external stakeholders through the process of creating the first draft. Go over the user experience and discuss the the perspective of customers and diverse interested parties,

SELECT THE SERVICE TO BE BLUEPRINTED

Choose your experience to map. We suggest starting small with part of an experience that is important or problematic. For example rather than mapping an entire customer journey for air travel from New York to London, map a part of it that is important su8ch as selecting the airline and booking on-line. Explore several challenging sub-journeys before tackling the whole journey.

DECIDE PRESENT OR FUTURE SERVICE TO MAP

It is most usual first to map your existing customer experience. A current state map can help identify ways to make your existing customer experience better or more efficient.

After mapping your current service you may be interested

in creating a map as a concept for a future service or customer experience. You may not have a current service in which case go straight to a map of a future service or experience.

SELECT START AND END POINTS OF THE CUSTOMER EXPERIENCE

Define the scope in terms of time ad customer activities.

SELECT CHANNELS TO MAP

Typical examples of channels include
1. In-store experience
2. Print,
3. Web,
4. Mobile

The channel defines the opportunities and constraints of a touchpoint.

START SMALL

Consider picking a particular scenario or sub-activity of your entire customer experience.

DRAFT THE MAP

Use a large wall or table. Create your first rough draft using post-it notes. Share the first blueprint with as many internal and external stakeholders as possible and ask for their feedback. If insights don't fit on a single map, keep maps simple by creating building one map for each persona.

CREATE THE STORY

What are the main elements of the customer experience from their perspective? What parts of their experience leave a lasting impression on them either positive or negative.

MAP USER ACTIONS & ACTIVITIES STEP-BY-STEP

Start at the beginning of the service or experience and list each thing a customer commonly does step by step. Put each sub-activity on a separate post-it note. For example, if the activity is visiting a coffee shop the activities may include.
1. At work decide to get a coffee on the way home
2. Check the location of coffee shops on the Internet.
3. Select coffee shop
4. Go to car
5. Drive to coffee shop
6. Park
7. Enter coffee shop
8. Stand in line
9. Order
10. Pick up coffee
11. Find table
12. Sit down
13. Drink coffee
14. Read news on tablet
15. Pack up
16. Return to car
17. Drive home
18. Reflect on the experience.

Describe each activity on a separate post-it note and place them in a line on your wall or table. Continue till your team is happy that all important events are included

MAP TIME

How long does each customer activity usually take? Does a stage usually last ten seconds or ten minutes. Place the time required on a post-it note above each stage of customer activity.

Time to consider:

1. Critical periods service actions, such as response to a proposal.
2. Duration of each service steps, such as airline check-in
3. The time between service steps such as walking to a hotel room after check-in.
4. End to end service experience.

BUILD THE BLUEPRINT

Now you are ready to create the map.

MAP USER ACTION PHASES

Break the list of customer activities into four or six phases of sub-activities. Some examples of sets of phases of activities are:

Example One

1. Explore
2. Evaluate
3. Engage
4. Experience

Example two

1. Aware
2. Join
3. Use
4. Develop
5. Leave

Example Three

1. Research
2. Evaluate and compare
3. Commit

4. Use and Monitor
5. Refine and review

MAP THE PHYSICAL EVIDENCE STEP-BY-STEP

Physical evidence is usually the lane shown at the top of a blueprint. Services consist of the interactions with people, the processes, and the physical evidence of the experience. Objects in the service environment that customers engage are sometimes referred to as "physical evidence" because they are proof of the service that has taken place. Physical evidence is the tangible things that help to communicate and perform the service and influence a customer's perception of a service.

Physical evidence is the tangible manifestation of service. It conveys to customers whether the service provider cares about their customers and whether they trust their customers. Physical evidence cues are what customers use to evaluate service quality.

Physical evidence can convey intended and unintended messages to customers. Physical evidence is the interface between a service provider and a customer.

The key to delivering a successful service is to identify clearly a simple, consistent message, and then manage the evidence to support that message.

> **Well-prepared small details represent sincerity in serving guests which reflect the hotel's good service spirit. For example, welcome fruit, an electric kettle and fresh flowers in hotel rooms are service evidence that often evoked delight as they show the hotel's thoughtfulness."**

For example, a research participant talked about disappointment caused by "fake" hangers in a hotel room's closet. She complained: They're not real hangers, because they're attached to the railing. So if you want to take out a hanger and then hang it on a chair or hang it on a door, you can't, because there's no hook... That's kind of a fake hanger. It shows that they think I'm going to steal the hangers. So it makes me feel not trusted."

Source: Kathy Pui Ying Lo Designing Service Evidence for Positive Relational Messages, http:// www.ijdesign.org/ojs/index.php/ IJDesign/article/viewFile/898/333 (accessed March 23, 2016).

The physical evidence lane on the blueprint appears above the "line of visibility" in a service blueprint. Physical evidence includes the service providers building/facilities and staff appearance; and uniforms. Physical evidence should be considered important by the customer and the promise implied by these tangible objects should be delivered. A bank card is an example of physical evidence of a service. It helps a bank differentiate their service from another bank. It separates the service from the seller.

Other examples of physical evidence are
1. The building
2. The interior
3. The car park
4. Internal signage,
5. Packaging.
6. Promotional materials
7. Web pages.
8. Paperwork (such as invoices, tickets and dispatch notes).
9. Brochures.
10. Stationery
11. Billing statement
12. Furnishings.
13. Signage
14. Uniforms and employee dress.
15. Business cards.
16. Mailboxes.

Blueprint the physical evidence of service. Physical evidence should be refined developed and improved over time. Work cross-functionally.

DRAW THE LINE OF INTERACTION
Separates customer activities from face-to-face onstage and unseen backstage actions.

MAP FRONT STAGE OR ONSTAGE EMPLOYEE ACTIONS

Onstage employee actions are separated from the customer by the line of interaction. Onstage or front stage employee actions are the things that your employees do during a face-to-face encounter with the customer. Examples are a waiter in a restaurant taking your order or a hotel front desk employee checking you into a hotel.

DRAW THE LINE OF VISIBILITY

The line of visibility separates actions that are face-to-face from those that are not visible to the end user. Divides actions of onstage employees from backstage actions. Below the line of visibility, actions that involve non-visible interaction with customers such as contact by telephone is described

MAP BACK STAGE OR OFFSTAGE EMPLOYEE ACTIONS

Back stage actions are the activities by your employees to provide the service that the end user doesn't see.

DRAW THE LINE OF INTERNAL INTERACTION

This line separates contact employees activities from non-contact support actions.

SUPPORT PROCESSES

Support functions needed to support the employees. These are internal services, which help the contact employees in delivering the service.
An example is the registration computer system in a hotel.

Support processes are other actions, systems, and resources that the service provider relies upon that must be provided to deliver the service to the customer.

MAP THE PAIN POINTS

A pain pint is any part of the customer experience that they find people disturbing, frustrating, urgent or uncomfortable. Some customer needs are needs which the customers themselves are not aware of and cannot articulate. A pain point is a problem for you customer and a problem and an opportunity for you. Solving pain points create value for you and your customer. "customer pain" is a synonym for "customer needs". Customers spend money to combat pain or to pursue pleasure.

Examples of service pain points are airport security lines, hospital directions, or the cost of travel.

A pain point is the why customers choose you if you offer a solution to their need. If you engage your customers and listen they'll tell you their pain points.

To identify customer 'pain-points':

17. In-depth interviews with customer facing internal employees
18. Requests from your most valuable customers.
19. Customer interviews.
20. Customer focus groups.
21. Analysis of customer calls and warranty claims to identify problems.
22. Review of competitor offerings.

You can list the root causes of pain for your customers at each stage.

CUSTOMER OR STAKEHOLDER COMMENTS

List significant or representative comments in a lane. What do customers think?

MAP BRAND IMPACT

List brand impact of touchpoints and customer comments in a lane.

KEY PEOPLE

Identify internal owners of experiences that support customer's needs.

CUSTOMER NEEDS

Do customers have unrecognized needs that could be addressed? What do customers want to accomplish at each stage of interaction?

MAP CONNECTIONS

Use arrows to illustrate the flow of responsibility—who is "driving" the service at any moment and should be initiating service action:

1. Model expectations of ''proactive'' provider activity.
2. Model the customer responsibility for next steps.
3. Model partner expectations.
4. Define points of hand off between roles, such as from backstage to onstage.

MAP MOMENTS OF TRUTH

Map those interactions that have the most impact on the customer. A moment of truth is a contact or interaction between a customer and a service provider that gives the customer an opportunity to form or change an impression about the organization.

For example waiting in line in a coffee shop. A moment of truth is a point in time when a customer has the opportunity to make a judgment about the value of a service delivery and a business relationship. Identifying moments of truth and improving their outcomes is a focus of service blueprinting.

ROOT CAUSE OF PAIN

Ask why the experience is painful for the customer. If necessary ask why several times to understand the underlying cause of the pain.

Phase: RESEARCH/RESERVATION · STAY · CHECK OUT · DEPART

	RESEARCH/RESERVATION			STAY									CHECK OUT		DEPART
Physical Evidence	hotel website	banking website					bag cart	elevator hallway	room	TV fridge bathroom	shower watch movie	menu	food tray	lobby desk		car park
Customer activity	compare prices	make reservation	park				give bags to bell person	go to room	Picks up coffee	shower watch movie		order meal	receive meal	check out		return to car
Pain points		best hotel full	car park full	long line	no one at desk			get lost	coffee stale	shower cold		argument next room	food cold	charged additional fees		
Line of interaction																
Onstage employee actions		reserve room	greet	clean lobby	update system	take bags		deliver bags to room	refill coffee			take order prepare food	deliver food to room	process check out		clean room
Line of visibility																
Backstage employee actions	maintain website					process registration										
Line of internal interaction																
Support processes	registration system				registration system					video system		food system		registration system		

pain points

MAP BARRIERS

What obstacles are standing in the way of the optimal experience for the customer at each stage of their interaction?

PRIORITIZE TOUCHPOINTS TO IMPROVE OR DEVELOP

ADD PHOTOS OR PICTURES WHERE POSSIBLE

Add photos or pictures where possible

Blueprints sometimes have a lane of photographs that show pain points of customer activities. Use pictures if they are the best way of communicating something. For example lack of cleanliness on a train platform.

Identify points of failure
Where is the service failing or likely to fail?

IDENTIFY POINTS OF FAILURE

Where is the service failing or likely to fail?

OPPORTUNITIES

Brainstorm ways to change to better meet customer needs.

1. Bullet point these ideas in a separate lane stage by stage.
2. Bullet points these ideas in a separate lane stage by stage.
3. What is the ideal customer experience
4. Analyze every touch point
5. Identify physical evidence at each stage - moment of truth
6. Simplify and refine the process

7. Remove pain points and surprises.
8. Add touchpoints that are missing
9. Build scenarios Think about extreme users, new users, average users.

PHOTOGRAPH THE DRAFT

Photograph the whole blueprint and photograph the blueprint in sections with sufficient resolution to enable you to transfer the map into a graphics program such as Adobe Illustrator or InDesign.

CREATE A PRESENTATION COPY

Transfer the map into a graphics program such as Adobe Illustrator or InDesign.

DISTRIBUTE TO STAKEHOLDERS FOR FEEDBACK

Distribute draft to internal and external stakeholders for feedback. Circulate you map as widely as possible to get feedback from internal departments, executives, external customers, and stakeholders.

REFINE THE MAP BASED ON THE FEEDBACK

Does it tell the story of your customer's experience that is complete, from beginning to end? Is it understandable to people outside the team? Are the insights actionable? Does it inspire and support a change in strategy? Does it communicate the necessary information, without further explanation? Simplify the map. Identify gaps and do further research to fill the gaps. Gaps in touchpoints may suggest opportunities to add new touchpoints.

BRAINSTORM THE IDEAL EXPERIENCE

Put together what you have learned to generate a better experience for your customers that you can implement. Develop step-by-step corrective actions for fail points.

RAPID PROTOTYPING

Experience prototyping is the most efficient way to implement an improved service. The goal is to observe customers interacting with the new experience and obtain their feedback about the experience. Use methods such as:

1. Video prototyping,
2. Role playing,
3. desktop walkthroughs
4. Bodystorming
5. Paper prototyping
6. Empathy tools
7. Wireframing
8. Service staging
9. Wizard of Oz

Start with low fidelity methods and move to higher fidelity prototyping methods as you find clarity with the best design direction.

SERVICE STAGING

Test the service refinements in a staged setting. Sets up a space that imitates the real environment, but with simple props to represent physical objects. For example cardboard boxes could be used to describe a counter. The design team can work through the experience "on stage" and adapt it based on feedback from customers.

CONDUCT USER STUDIES IN THE TARGET CONTEXT

Test with target users iteratively and refine the service until the pain points have become become points of pleasure for customers.

1. Do people understand the service
2. Do people see the value of the service?
3. Do people understand how to use it?
4. Is the experience positive?
5. What ideas do the customers have that could improve the service?

IMPLEMENT THE EXPERIENCE

The end purpose of a blueprint is to take action and improve the journey and drive the ROI to justify the investment.

After the new service design is tested, the design team documents the new experience and creates implementation guidelines to roll out of the new service across the organization. The service blueprint is now a tool to communicate the new design.

1. Use your map for employee training/
2. Map upcoming product launches or your desired

CONNECTING THE BOXES
Arrows show value exchanges through touchpoints

SINGLE ARROW
A single arrow shows
a single direction
value exchange

> **CUSTOMER
> EATS MEAL**

> **WAITER BRINGS
> FOOD TO TABLE**

DOUBLE ARROW
A double arrow
indicates that
two parties
must agree

> **REGISTRATION
> EMPLOYEE GIVES
> CUSTOMER
> PRICE OF ROOM**

> **CUSTOMER
> PAYS FOR ROOM**

Service Blueprint example: Visit...

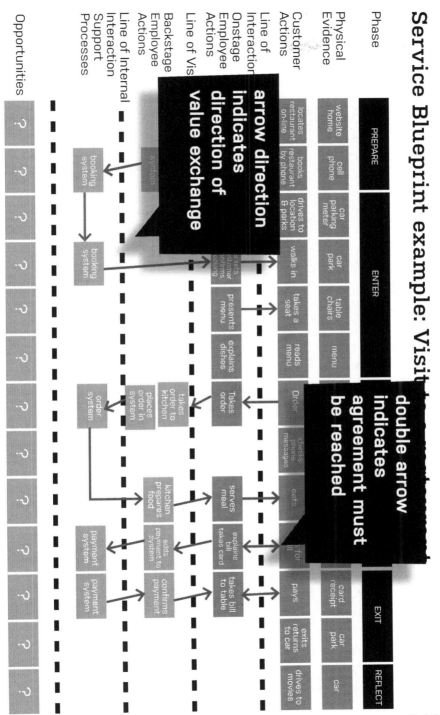

Phase		PREPARE		ENTER			Order					EXIT	REFLECT
Physical Evidence	website home	cell phone	car parking meter	car park	table chairs	menu		checks phone messages		card receipt	car park	car
Customer Actions	locates restaurant on-line	books restaurant by phone	drives to location & parks	walks in	takes a seat	reads menu	Takes order	eats	pays	exits returns to car	drives to movies
Line of Interaction												
Onstage Employee Actions		system	booking system	greets confirms booking	presents menu	explains dishes	takes order to kitchen	serves meal	explains bill takes card	confirms payment	takes bill to table
Line of Visibility												
Backstage Employee Actions		booking system					places order in system	kitchen prepares food	adds payment to system	payment system
Line of Internal Interaction												
Support Processes							order system		payment system	payment system
Opportunities	?	?	?	?	?	?	?	?	?	?	?	?	?	?

arrow direction indicates direction of value exchange

double arrow indicates agreement must be reached

SYNTHESIS PHASE 349

Service Blueprint example: Hotel

Phase	PREPARE			ENTER				ACTIVITY							EXIT		
Physical Evidence	website home	website	airport plane	taxi entrance	cart	access bags to bell person	hotel lobby	registration desk	elevator hallways	cart room	bathroom	menu	food cart	food	Room Bed	registration desk	taxi entrance	taxi support
Customer Actions	compare hotels online	book hotel online	fly to location	taxi to hotel	access bags to bell person	enter hotel	check in	go to room	receive bags	shower	call room service	receive food	eat	sleep	check out	call taxi	taxi to airport

Line of Interaction

| Onstage Employee Actions | | renews reservation | | | greets customer takes bags | | process registration | | delivers bags to room | | takes order | carry on food | | | process check out | | |

Line of Visibility

| Backstage Employee Actions | | updates system | | | takes bags to room | | | | | | | | | | updates system | | |

Line of Internal Interaction

| Support Processes | | registration system | | | | | registration system | | | | prepare food | | | | registration system | | |

| Opportunities | ? | ? | ? | ? | ? | ? | ? | ? | ? | ? | ? | ? | ? | ? | ? | ? | ? | ? |

PATIENT STAKEHOLDER MAP

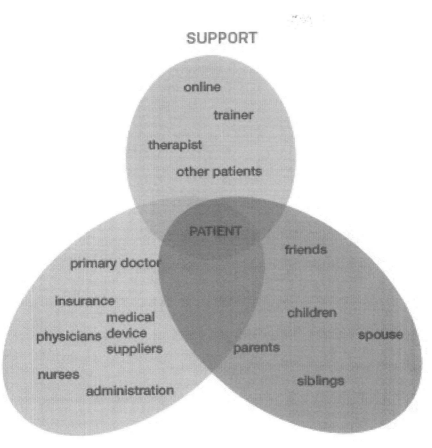

SUPPORT

online

trainer

therapist

other patients

PATIENT

friends

primary doctor

insurance

medical

physicians device

suppliers

children

spouse

parents

nurses

siblings

administration

HEALTH CARE

FAMILY & FRIENDS

future state

MEASURE YOUR PROGRESS TOWARDS YOUR GOALS

Define ways of tracking your progress towards measurable goals. Metrics will help you measure the quality of your customer experience, now and in the future.

1. Net Promoter Score and customer loyalty measures
2. Customer satisfaction measures
3. Quantitative assessments of the customer emotions.
4. Metrics of customer effort
5. Measure of performance of each touchpoint.
6. New sales.
7. Increased loyalty and retention of customers
8. Increase in revenue per customer.
9. More sales.
10. Reduced costs
11. Better delivery processes.
12. Better quality: i
13. Increased competitiveness

STAKEHOLDER MAPS

WHAT
Stakeholders maps are used to document the key stakeholders and their relationship. At the beginning of a design project it is important to identify the key stakeholders and their relationships. The map serves as a reference for the design team.

WHO INVENTED IT
Mitchell 1997

WHY
14. Stakeholder mapping helps discover ways to influence other stakeholders.
15. Stakeholder mapping helps discover risks.
16. Stakeholder mapping helps discover positive stakeholders to involve in the design process.

CHALLENGES?
Stakeholder mapping helps discover negative stakeholders and their associated risks.

HOW
1. Invite six known stakeholders to a meeting.
2. Give each stakeholder a block of post-it notes.
3. Brainstorm with the group additional stakeholders
4. Cluster stockholders into relevant groups
5. Assign priorities for individ-

ual stakeholders based on the value of their potential feedback during the design process,
6. Map the stakeholders.
7. Can initially be documented on a White-board, cards, post-it-notes and consolidated as a diagram through several iterations showing hierarchy and relationships.

CHAPTER SUMMARY

1. Synthesis is the convergent part of the design process. In this stage we review the research, make connections, uncover insights, distill the data. We make sense of the information.

2. An insight is A new way of viewing the world that causes us to reexamine existing conventions.

3. A service blueprint is a graphic representation of the structure of a service or of an experience.

4. An experience map is a graphic representation of the customer experience from the point of view of the customer. It focuses on the emotional experience.

5. Affinity diagrams are tools for analyzing large amounts of data and discovering relationships which allow a design direction to be established based on the associations.

6. Empathy is the identification with the feelings, thoughts, or attitudes of another. m

7. Market segmentation involves subdividing a market into a number of groups where the people in each group have some commonality, or similarity.

8. An actor map is a visual depiction of the key actors within a system.

9. An Empathy Map gives a high-level view of where an experience is good or bad.

10. Used to improve a customer experience.

11. "A persona is a archetypal character that is meant to represent a group of users in a role who share common goals, attitudes and behaviors when interacting with a particular product or service personas are user models that are presented as specific individual humans. They are not actual people, but are synthesized directly from observations of real people."(Cooper)

12. Stakeholders maps are used to document the key stakeholders and their relationship. At the beginning of a design project it is important to identify the key stakeholders and their relationships. The map serves as a reference for the design team.

CHAPTER REVIEW

1. What are the activities of the synthesis phase?
2. What is an insight?
3. What is a user need statement?
4. What is an actionable insight?
5. How do you know when you have a significant insight?
6. What is an affinity diagram?
7. Who invented affinity diagrams?
8. When should you use an affinity diagram?
9. Why should you use an affinity diagram?
10. What is an actor map?
11. Why would you use an actor map?
12. What is an empathy map?
13. Why should you use an empathy map?
14. What is an experience map?
15. Why should you use an experience map?
16. What is an emotional journey map?
17. What is a persona?
18. Why should you use personas?
19. Name four different types of customer segmentation.
20. What is a service blueprint?
21. What are the typical lanes of a service blueprint?
22. Why should you use a service blueprint?
23. What is a stakeholder?
24. What is a stakeholder map?
25. Why should you use a stakeholder map?

EXERCISE ONE
PERSONAS

PERSONAS
What are personas?
Personas are archetypal users of a product or service that represent the needs of larger groups of users, in terms of their goals and personal characteristics. They act as place markers for real users and help guide decisions about functionality and design.

TASKS
Create three one-page personas for primary user groups of a service.

PROCESS
1. Identify a service
2. Brainstorm three substantial groups of users for the service.
3. Create three personas.
4. Add personal details but don't go overboard.

DEFINE FOR EACH OF THREE PERSONAS
1. Persona Name
2. Persona image
3. Brief description up to 7 words
4. Age
5. Income
6. Education
7. Where persona lives
8. Where persona works
9. Family description
10. Household income
11. Behaviors
12. Unmet needs
13. Goals
14. Main problems
15. Frustrations
16. 12. Places this persona spends time.
17. Things standing in the way of what they are trying to achieve.

DELIVERABLES
One page pdf persona for each of three personas

A GOOD PERSONA
1. Reflects patterns observed in research.
2. Focuses on the current state, not the future
3. Is realistic, not idealized
4. Describes a challenging but achievable design target.
5. Helps understand users'
• Context
• Behaviors
• Attitudes
• Needs
6. Challenges pain points
7. Identifies goals and motivations.
8. Represents a major user group
9. Expresses and focus on the major needs and expectations of the important user groups
10. Describes realistic people with backgrounds, goals, and values.

EXERCISE TWO
EMPATHY MAP

BACKGROUND
The Empathy Map is a tool intended to help you to systematically consider the perspectives of those who a service may affect. Empathy maps can be created to help understand and improve the customer experience. Empathy maps can be completed by individuals or as a team. Invite real stakeholders to complete first-person empathy maps.

INSTRUCTIONS
Select a service experience to map. A period of around 30 minutes of customer experience is a good length of time to study. Draw the empathy map framework or use a template.
3. Identify the group of people your design will serve. Choose a Persona that represents a market segment, Define the gender and age for this persona. What culture do they come from? Where
do they live? How are they employed? What is their income? What are their interests?
Add observations on post-it notes to the empathy map in the appropriate sections.

Think about their experience in relation to a particular service:
1. What does she see?
2. Describe what the customer sees in her environment:
3. What does it look like?
4. Who surrounds her?
5. Who are her friends?
6. What problems does she encounter?
7. What does she hear?
8. Describe how the environment influences the customer.
9. What do her friends say? Her family?
10. Who really influences her, and how?
11. Which media Channels are influential?
12. 3- What does she really think and feel?
13. What is really important to her (which she might not say publicly)?
14. Imagine her emotions. What moves her?
15. What might keep her up at night?
16. What are her dreams and aspirations.
17. What does she say and do?
18. Imagine what the customer might say, or how she might behave in public:
19. What is her attitude?
20. What could she be telling others?
21. Pay particular attention to potential conflicts between what a customer might say and what she may truly think or feel.
22. What is the customer's pain?
23. What are her biggest frustrations?
24. What obstacles stand between her and what she wants or needs to achieve?
25. Which risks might she fear

taking?

26. 6- What does the customer gain?
27. What does she truly want or need to achieve?
28. How does she measure success?
29. Think of some strategies she might use to achieve her goals.
30. Populate each area in the template with 6 or more observations.
31. Analyze the completed map. What have you learned about this stakeholder group?
32. What patterns do you see?
33. How can you best serve their needs?
34. Move the appropriate post it notes into the pain and gain boxes.

PAIN:
1. What are their frustrations?
2. What obstacles and challenges stand in their way?
3. What keeps the customer up at night?
4. Where are they unhappy?

GAIN:
1. What do they want to achieve?
2. What are their hopes and dreams?
3. How do they measure success?
4. What strategies could help them reach their goals?

DELIVERABLES
One Empathy Map

EXERCISE THREE
EXPERIENCE MAP

Experience mapping is a strategic process of capturing and communicating complex interactions and experiences. The activity of mapping builds knowledge and consensus across your organization, and the map helps build seamless customer, user or employee experiences.

INSTRUCTIONS
1. 1. Choose a service, customer, user, or employee experience you find interesting, that you will be able to find people to interview about, and that you believe can be improved by some intervention. It should involve at least 12 steps and take at least 30 minutes on average.
2. Interview at least 4 Users: Discover user's emotional state throughout the experience. Try to understand what they feel, what they care about, and what that implies.
3. Create an experience map to describe the customer or employee journey.
4. What is the customer or employee doing? Break the experience down into at least one dozen activities that take place over at least 30 minutes
5. List the touchpoints that the employee or customer engages through the activities at each stage of their activity.

12
POINT OF VIEW

POINT OF VIEW STATEMENT

....

WHAT

A Point of View (POV) is an opportunity statement. It condenses the need you have uncovered, description of the user who has this need, the underlying reason for the need and the angle from which you are looking at the problem.

What is a Point of View?
[USER] needs to [USER'S NEED] because [SUPRISING INSIGHT]

WHY

A strong POV will help you in many ways:

1. Stay focused on the problem.
2. Inspire your team.
3. Keep your user in mind
4. Communicate to and get buy-in from others.
5. Keeps the team grounded.
6. Captures the hearts and minds of the stakeholders
7. Fuels brainstorming.
8. Allows team members to determine the relevance of competing ideas.
9. Saves teams from the impossible task of developing concepts trying to be all things to all people.
10. helps to ensure that you are working on something that was actionable, largely applicable, and resonates with potential user base.

HOW

To write a helpful POV, you need a solid description of the user, a clear need, and an insight (something remarkable you have uncovered about why the need is there.

1. Define your audience
2. Define the problem that you will solve
3. Define the need that you will address.
4. Keep in mind that POVs often evolve over time...
5. It is important to keep in mind the perspectives of all key stakeholders.

THE POV SHOULD:

1. Provide focus
2. Frame the problem
3. Provide a reference for evaluating competing ideas
4. Empower and inspire team members
5. Fuel brainstorms and "how might we" statements
6. Be captivating
7. Allow you to revisit and reformulate the POV as you learn by doing.
8. Support innovation

MAKE YOUR OWN POV STATEMENT

END USER [OR STAKEHOLDER]:

....

NEEDS TO:

....

BECAUSE [YOUR INSIGHT]:

....

REFRAMING THE PROBLEM

WHAT
Reframing is to look at, present, or think of (beliefs, ideas, relationships, etc) in a new or different way or from this new perspective. Innovative solutions usually involve reframing a problem.

WHO INVENTED IT?
Tudor Rickards 1974 Manchester Business School

WHY
1. To create different perspectives and new ideas.

RESOURCES
1. Pen
2. Paper
3. White board
4. Dry Erase markers

HOW
Define the problem that you would like to address.

Complete these sentences while considering your problem.
1. There is more than one way of looking at a problem. You could also define this problem in another way as."
2. "The underlying reason for the problem is."
3. "I think that the best solution is."
4. "If I could break all laws of reality I would try to solve it by."
5. "You could compare this problem to the problem of."
6. "Another, different way of thinking about it is"

REFRAMING MATRIX

WHAT
The reframing matrix is a method of approaching a problem by imagining the perspectives of a number of different people and exploring the possible solutions that they might suggest.

WHO INVENTED IT?
Michael Morgan 1993

WHY
1. This is a method for assisting in empathy which is an important factor in gaining acceptance and creating successful design.

CHALLENGES
The reframing is not done with stakeholders present or in context so may be subjective

HOW
1. Define a problem.
2. On a white board or paper draw a large square and divide it into four quadrants.
3. Select 4 different perspectives to approach the problem. They could be four professions or four people

REFRAMING MATRIX

PRODUCT	PLANNING
1. Is there something wrong with the product or service? 2. Is it priced correctly? 3. How well does it serve the market? 4. Is it reliable?	1. Are our business plans, marketing plans, or strategy at fault? 2. Could we improve these?
POTENTIAL	**PEOPLE**
1. How would we increase sales? 2. If we were to seriously increase our targets or our production volumes, what would happen with this problem?	1. What are the people impacts and people implications of the problem? 2. What do people involved with the problem think? 3. Why are customers not buying the product?

DESIGN PROBLEM ....

....

....

....

....

....

....

....

....

or four other perspectives that are important for your problem.

4. With your team brainstorm a number of questions that you believe are important from the perspectives that you have selected.
5. The moderator writes the questions in the relevant quadrants of the matrix.
6. The group discusses each of these questions.
7. The answers are recorded and the perspectives are incorporated into the considerations for design solutions.

"WHAT IF" AND "HOW MIGHT WE" QUESTIONS

WHAT

When you've defined your design challenge in a problem statement or Point Of View, you can ask some "How Might We". questions. The "How Might We" question maintains a level of ambiguity, and opens up the exploration space to a range of possibilities.

"How Might We" questions are the best way to open up Brainstorm sessions.

HOW

1. Define your point of view statement before asking how might we questions.
2. Your Point Of View should neither be too narrow so as to make it overly restrictive, nor too broad so as to leave you wandering forever in infinite possibilities.
3. Break that larger POV challenge up into smaller actionable questions.
4. Six to twelve "How Might We" questions for one POV is good.
5. Brainstorm the "How might we" questions before the ideation brainstorm.
6. Do your " How Might We" questions allow for a variety of solutions? If not, then broaden them.
7. Aim for a narrow enough frame to let you know where to start your ideation Brainstorm

CHAPTER SUMMARY

A Point of View (POV) is an opportunity statement. It condenses the need you have uncovered, description of the user who has this need, the underlying reason for the need and the angle from which you are looking at the problem.

What is a Point of View?
[USER] needs to [USER NEED] because [INSIGHT].

When you've defined your design challenge in a problem statement or Point Of View, you can ask some "How Might We". questions. The "How Might We" question maintains a level of ambiguity, and opens up the exploration space to a range of possibilities.

CHAPTER REVIEW

1. What is a point of view statement?
2. Why is a Point of View Statement useful?
3. Why are "How might we" questions useful?
4. How many "How might we" questions should you ask?
5. What is reframing?
6. Why should we try to reframe problems?
7. Who invented reframing?
8. What is a reframing matrix?
9. Who invented reframing matrices?

EXERCISE ONE
POINT OF VIEW

BACKGROUND

Developing a Point of View requires you and your team to extract relevant insights from the research that you have collected. You should start by reframing your insights in different ways. The POV should be a meaningful and actionable problem statement. A point-of-view (POV) is your reframing of a design challenge into an actionable problem statement that will launch you into generative ideation. It defines the right challenge to address based on your new empathy with your target audience.

The POV statement is created by making sense of who the users are, what their needs are, and the insights that come from the observations made. 'Needs' should be verbs, and the insight should reflect your clear synthesis of the research material.

A good Point of view is one that:
1. Provides focus and frames the problem.
2. Inspires your team.
3. Takes you somewhere that you haven't been before
4. Helps you see things from the end user's perspective.
5. Focuses on implicit needs rather than explicit problems.
6. Offers criteria for evaluating competing ideas.

7. Empowers your team to make decisions independently, in parallel.
8. Captures the hearts and minds of the people you meet
9. Keeps you awake at night.
10. Saves you from the impossible task of developing concepts that are all things to all people.
11. Is actionable with your available team, time and resources.

STRUCTURE OF A POINT OF VIEW STATEMENT

[End user] needs to [user need] because [insight]

TASK

Create a point of view statement for an end user.

DELIVERABLES

One Point Of View Statement.

EXERCISE TWO
GOALS

INSTRUCTIONS

What are your goals?
Answer the following questions

Specific
What will you design?

Measurable
How will you know when you have the best solution.
How will you measure progress toward your goal?

Attainable
Is your goal a possible to achieve with your time and resources?

Realistic
Is your goal realistic and within your reach? Are you willing to commit to your goal?

Relevant
Is your goal relevant to your long term needs?

Time
What is your target time-frame to reach the gaols?

13

IDEATION PHASE

THE IDEATION PHASE

Populate the solution space.
Use the diverse perspectives of
the team members to create 75
to 120 good design solutions.
that effectively balance the
needs of people, appropriate
use of technology and business
goals. Keep an open mind until
the ideas have been tested and
compared. Once you have
identified your target audience
unmet needs, the starting
point of ideation phase is the
problem statement.

[CUSTOMER] XXXX [NEEDS]
XXXX Because XXXX[INSIGHT]

*To have a great idea,
you have to have lots of
ideas."*

Davis Kelley IDEO

Now you can start generating ideas.
Find a good space with natural
lighting a large table and some white
boards.

Your most productive creative team
is a diverse group of people. Have
different genders, cultures, ages and

professions represented. Between four
and eight people is the ideal team size
for ideation. A larger team becomes
harder to manage. Before you start,
review the insights and themes from
the previous synthesis stage.

Try to generate as many ideas as
possible. At first it is good to explore
wild blue sky directions. You can
always pull the ideas back to reality
and budgets as they are refined.
We like to generate around 100 to
120 ideas as a starting point. Then
narrow them down to around seven
preferred directions by combining
and developing the ideas through
several stages of iteration.

Physical prototypes and acting out
activities will allow you to make
intangible ideas tangible so that
you can get feedback and discuss
alternative concept directions.

Designers use a range of techniques
which include sketches, scenarios,
video, body storming, paper
prototypes, wireframes and
PICTIVES to explore and create low
fidelity prototypes of ideas. In this
chapter we will look at some of the
commonly used techniques.

Make sure that you have ample
display space. Sheets of foam core
board make low cost pin boards. Put
a box of post its and markers in the

center of a large table to be shared by the group.

WHY

In this phase your team moves from identifying unmet needs to exploring possible solutions. You to harness the collective perspectives and strengths of your team to go bravely where no one else has gone before you. This is innovation.

WHY IS INNOVATION NECESSARY?

Innovation is the key element in providing growth, and for increasing bottom-line results.

> **"**
> *Innovation is: production or adoption, assimilation, and exploitation of a value-added novelty in economic and social spheres; renewal and enlargement of products, services, and markets; development of new methods of production; and establishment of new management systems. It is both a process and an outcome.*

Crossan and Apaydin

HOW

1. Generate ten "what are ways of " questions base on your POV statement. For example "what are ways of giving each train traveler a personal experience?"
2. Defer judgment
3. Encourage wild ideas
4. Build on ideas of others (and not but)
5. Stay focused
6. Be visual
7. One conversation
8. Go for quantity!
9. We need fluency-lots of ideas and flexibility-lots of different ideas.

Use different techniques to generate ideas, not just one. Go through iterative cycles of generating ideas and then voting with you team on the best of the ideas. Then develop more ideas based on the selected ideas. The goal is to select a small set of possible solutions to take into prototyping.

> **"**
> *Inspiration is for amateurs. The rest just show up and get to work."*
>
> Chuck Close, artist

WHAT IS GOOD DESIGN?

Source: www.ncsu.edu/ncsu/design/cud/about_ud/udprinciplestext.htm

WHAT IS UNIVERSAL DESIGN?

Universal design (UD) is a set of guidelines that aims to produce environments that work well for everyone. The Center for Universal Design at North Carolina State University identified seven principles of universal design

UNIVERSAL DESIGN GUIDELINES

1. The design is equitable in use to people with diverse abilities.
2. The design is flexible enough to allow a wide range of individual preferences and abilities.
3. The use of the design is simple and intuitive, easy to understand regardless of previous experience or skill.
4. The design is perceptible, such that it communicates information effectively to the user.
5. The design is tolerant of error, such that it minimizes adverse consequences
6. if used incorrectly. The design requires low physical effort, allowing use with minimal effort.
7. The design accommodates the size, space, and approach necessary for use.

DIETER RAMS TEN PRINCIPLES OF "GOOD DESIGN"

1. Good design is innovative
2. Good design is useful
3. Good design is aesthetic
4. Good design is understandable
5. Good design is unobtrusive
6. Good design is honest
7. Good design is long-lasting
8. Good design is thorough down to the last detail
9. Good design is environmentally friendly
10. Good design is as little design as possible

Source: http://www.archdaily.com/198583/dieter-rams-10-principles-of-good-design

50 PHRASES THAT WILL PREVENT YOU FROM BEATING YOUR COMPETITORS

1. Our place is different.
2. We tried that before.
3. It costs too much.
4. That is not my job.
5. They're too busy to do that.
6. We don't have the time.
7. Not enough help.
8. It is too radical a change.
9. The staff will never buy it.
10. It is against the company policy.
11. The union will scream.
12. That will run up our overhead.

13. We don't have the authority.
14. Let's get back to reality.
15. That's not our problem.
16. I don't like the idea.
17. I am not saying you are wrong but..
18. You're two years ahead of your time.
19. Now is not the right time.
20. It isn't in the budget.
21. Can't teach an old dog new tricks.
22. Good thought but impractical.
23. Let's give it more thought.
24. We'll be the laughing stock of the industry.
25. Not that again.
26. Where did you dig that one up?
27. We did alright without it before.
28. It's never been tried.
29. Let's put that one on the back burner for now.
30. Let's form a committee.
31. It won't work in our place.
32. The executive committee will never go for it.
33. I don't see the connection.
34. Let's all sleep on it.
35. It can't be done.
36. It's too much trouble to change.
37. It won't pay for itself.
38. It's impossible.
39. I know a person who tried it and got fired.
40. We've always done it this way.
41. We'd lose money in the long run.
42. Don't rock the boat.
43. That's what we can expect from the staff.
44. Has anyone else tried it?
45. Let's look into it further.
46. We'll have to answer to the stock holders.
47. Quit dreaming.
48. If it ain't broke don't fix it.
49. That's too much ivory tower.
50. It's too much work.

Source: Daniel DuFour

BRAINSTORMING

WHAT
Process for generating creative ideas and solutions through intensive group discussion. each participant suggests as many ideas as possible. Criticism of the ideas is allowed only when the brainstorming session is evaluation begins after the session.

WHO INVENTED BRAINSTORMING?

Brainstorming was taught at UCLA in the 1920s. Advertising executive Alex F. Osborn is credited with popularizing brainstorming in the United States. He began developing methods for creative problem-solving in 1939. He was frustrated by employees' inability to develop creative ideas individually for ad campaigns. In response, he began hosting group-thinking sessions and discovered a significant improvement in the quality and quantity of ideas produced by employees.

Osborn outlined his method in the 1948 book "Your Creative Power" in chapter 33, "How to organize a squad to create ideas."

Source: Adapted from Wikipedia.

PREPARING FOR BRAINSTORMING

Come to the brainstorm session prepared.
1. Bring a lot of paper and markers.
2. Pens
3. Post-it-notes
4. Index cards
5. A flip chart
6. White-board or wall
7. Video camera
8. Camera
9. One clear goal per brainstorming session.
10. Determine who will write things down and document the proceedings?
11. Allow one to two hours for a brainstorming session.
12. Recruit good people.
13. 8 to 12 people is a good number
14. Prepare brainstorm questions that you think will help guide the group.

CREATE A STRATEGY
1. What do you want to achieve?
2. What problem do you want solved?
3. Define the goal
4. How will you define the problem to the participants?
5. How long will the session be?
6. How many people will be involved?
7. What will be the mix of people?
8. Will there be a follow up session?
9. Will you send out information before the session?
10. Do the participants have the information that they need?
11. Who should you invite?
12. Assemble a diverse team.
13. Do the participants have the right skills and knowledge for the task?
14. Where will the brainstorm be held?
15. Who owns the intellectual property?
16. Will the session be free of interruptions?
17. How will you record the ideas?
18. What will you do with the information?
19. What brainstorming technique will be used and is it best for your purpose?
20. Be mindful of the scope brainstorm questions. Neither too broad nor too narrow.
21. 45-60 minutes for brainstorm time. Warm up 15-30 minutes.
22. Wrap up 15-30 minutes.

CHOOSING A TECHNIQUE
1. There are many different brainstorming methods.
2. Choose a method that suites your task and participants
3. Try different methods over time to find which ones work best for you.

REFRESHMENTS
1. An army marches on it's stomach
2. Offer tea, coffee water, soda.

FACILITATING
1. The basic brainstorming

procedure seems simple enough that anyone could facilitate a session, but the social dynamics of product groups are both complex and subtle

2. Motivate participants.
3. Understand the issues that affect small group interaction.
4. Keep the focus on the topic.
5. Encourage everyone to contribute.
6. A facilitator also needs to understand how to organize and analyze the data from brainstorming sessions.
7. Review the rules and ask group to enforce them.
8. Encourage an attitude of shoshin.
9. Ask participants to turn phones off or onto vibrate mode.
10. A facilitator isn't a leader.
11. Do not steer the discussion
12. Do not let particular people dominate the conversation.
13. Keep the conversations on topic.
14. Set realistic time limits for each stage and be sure that you keep on time.
15. 5. Have a brainstorm plan and stick to it.
16. The facilitator should create an environment where it is safe to suggest wild ideas.
17. Provide clear directions at the beginning of the meeting.
18. Clearly define the problem to be discussed.
19. Write the problem on the White-board where everyone can see it.
20. Provide next steps at the end of the meeting.
21. Select final ideas by voting.
22. Use your camera or phone to take digital pictures of the idea output at the end of your meeting.
23. Facilitators should avoid inviting someone that is generally feared by the group since this is likely to reduce the quantity of ideas.
24. Facilitators must not let participants belabor their points or start telling long stories. This can reduce the quantity of items and act as an inhibitor since the stories often include some subtle guidance or implied criticism.
25. Good facilitation requires good listening skills
26. The facilitator should run the White-board, writing down ideas as people come up with them,
27. Prevent people from interrupting others
28. Invite quieter people to contribute.
29. Hire a facilitator if necessary.
30. Start on time.
31. End on time.
32. Keep things moving
33. You can filter the best ideas after the session or get the team to vote on their preferred ideas during the session.
34. Listen
35. Write fast & be visual
36. Use humor and be playful
37. Thank the group after the session.
38. Provide next steps to the group after the meeting.
39. Keep participants engaged
40. Encourage inter activity
41. 100 ideas per hour.
42. Avoid social hierarchy
43. Organize small break-out sessions that cut across traditional office boundaries to establish teams.
44. Encourage passion.

45. Use questioning words such as "What, What if, Where, Why, When, and How", to develop quality questions.

RULES FOR BRAINSTORMING

1. "Defer judgment Separating idea generation from idea selection strengthens both activities. For now, suspend critique. Know that you'll have plenty of time to evaluate the ideas after the brainstorm.
2. Encourage wild ideas
3. One conversation at a time Maintain momentum as a group. Save the side conversations for later.
4. Headline Capture the essence quickly "
5. Focus on quantity not on quality."

POST-IT VOTING

1. Give every participant 4 stickers and have everyone put stickers next to their favorite ideas.
2. Each person tags 3 favorite ideas
3. Cluster favorite ideas
4. Clustering of stickers indicate possible strong design directions.

GROUP REVIEW

Ask everyone to review the boards of ideas, and discuss the specific ideas or directions they like and why.

Source adapted from Hasso Plattner Institute of Design

THE ENVIRONMENT

1. Select a space not usually used by your team.
2. Refreshments
3. Find a comfortable quiet room
4. Comfortable chairs
5. No interruptions
6. Turn phones off
7. Go off-site. A new environment might spur creativity and innovation by providing new stimuli. Helps participants mentally distance themselves from ordinary perceptions and ways of thinking.
8. Location matters:
9. Use big visible materials for writing on
10. Keep the temperature comfortable Adequate lighting
11. Suitable external noise levels
12. A circular arrangement of seats allows participants to read body language and with no "head of the table."
13. Seats should be not too far apart
14. Have a space with a lot of vertical writing space.

METHODS OF ARRANGING IDEAS

1. 2X2 matrix
2. Clustering
3. Continuum
4. Concentric circles
5. Time-line
6. Pyramid
7. Prioritization
8. Adoption curve

TYPES OF BRAINSTORMING

1. Warm up with wild ideas brainstorm
2. Ideal brainstorm. Imagine your ideal solution if you had the resources.
3. Analogous brainstorm. How do other industries or situations

solve this problem? Where else do we see this problem or need?

4. Hurdles brainstorm. What is standing in the way of solving this problem?

5. Bodystorm. Go to the place your stakeholders are in and act out your users journey with your team members and stakeholders giving feedback to generate ideas.

FOCUS YOUR IDEAS

1. Look for ways to combine ideas.
2. Dot voting. Each team member selects their three favourite ideas.
3. Category voting. choose two ideas from the following.
- The most rational solutions
- The most innovative ideas
- The idea that the stakeholder would prefer.
4. Decision Matrix. Choose criteria to decide what is important.
5. Ask your stakeholders and end users which ideas they prefer.

SOME USEFUL MATERIALS FOR BRAINSTORMING

POST-IT NOTES
I allow at least one block per participant per session.

SHARPIES
A range of different sizes

WHITE-BOARD
A White-board is a good tool as it allows connections to be drawn between groups of post-it notes

DRY ERASE MARKERS
3 or 4 colors

TAPE
One inch masking tape

CAMERA
A camera with still and video capability. This can be used to record the groups of post-it notes or to create a video of the session for sharing.

FOAM CORE BOARDS
These can be used as an alternative display surface to White-boards and are portable if you are working with a number of groups.

LARGE TABLE
Large enough to seat all the participants.

CHAIRS
For all the participants.

COFFEE AND REFRESHMENTS
People work better with coffee and snacks.

TYPES OF SKETCHES

IDEA SKETCH
Idea sketches are 2D visual design representations used at a personal level for externalizing thoughts quickly and to show how the design looks as a physical object.

STUDY SKETCH
Study sketches are 2D visual design representations used for investigating the appearance and visual impact of ideas such as aspects of geometric

proportion, configuration , scale, layout and mechanism .

REFERENTIAL SKETCH
Referential sketches are 2D visual design representations
used as a diary to record observations for future reference or
as a metaphor.

MEMORY SKETCH
Memory sketches are 2D visual design representations that help users recall thoughts and elements from previous work with notes and text annotations.

CODED SKETCH
Coded sketches are 2D visual design representations that categorize information to show an underlying principle or a scheme.

INFORMATION SKETCH
Information sketches are 2D visual design representations that allow stakeholders to understand the designer's intentions by explaining information clearly and to provide a common graphical setting.

RENDERINGS
Renderings are 2D visual design representations showing formal proposals of design concepts that involve the application of color, tone and detail for realism.

INSPIRATION SKETCH
Inspiration sketches are form-

orientated 2D visual design representations used to communicate the look or feel of a product by setting the tone of a design. brand or a product range.

PRESCRIPTIVE SKETCH
Prescriptive sketches are informal 2D visual design representations that communicate design decisions and general technical information such as dimensions, material and finish.

Source: 4 into 35 Does Go: Dr. Mark Evans, Eujin Pei and Dr. R. Ian Campbell Department of Design & Technology, Loughborough University, United Kingdom

Sketch Prototype
Evocative –Didactic
Suggest –Explore
Question –Answer
Propose –Test
Provoke –Resolve
Tentative – Specific
Noncommittal –Depiction

The sketch to prototype continuum. The difference between the two lies in the intent, or purpose they serve. The arrows represent the continuum of sketches developing into prototypes.

Bill Buxton

INNOVATION IS A NUMBERS GAME

Source: Adapted from Why Creativity Is a Numbers Game - Scientific American

True innovators follow a type of Darwinian process in which they try out many possibilities. Trial and error is essential for innovation.

To develop one successful idea professional designers often ideate more than one hundred and sometimes thousands of concepts.

"

Good ideas come from bad ideas but only if there are enough of them."

Seth Godin
American author and business executive.

Like everyone else creative geniuses don't really know what they're doing when they embark on a new project. They immerse themselves in many diverse ideas and projects. They are extraordinarily productive.

The quality of creative ideas is a function of quantity: The more ideas creators generate the greater the chance of a successful outcome.

Innovators fail early and often. Indeed, the creative act is often. Creative people learn to see failure as a steppingstone to success.

"

I have not failed; I have just found 10,000 ways that will not work."

"Genius is one percent inspiration and ninety percent perspiration."

"Opportunity is missed by most people because it is dressed in overalls and looks like work."

"The most certain way to succeed is always to try just one more time."

Thomas A Edison

"

Out of a hundred ideas, the first sixty ideas produced five that were actually new or different, the next twenty produced nothing but laughter, and ideas eighty to a hundred produced another ten that were amazing. Thankfully, we didn't give up when the well ran dry around idea number sixty."

Dev Patnaik,

EVALUATING AN IDEA
PHYSICAL PRODUCT

GENERAL CRITERIA
1. Is your idea legal
2. What is its environmental impact?
3. Is it safe?
4. Is it high quality?
5. Will it have wide social acceptance?
6. Will it have any negative impact?

INDUSTRY CRITERIA
1. Who is your competition?
2. Does your product require the assistance   of existing products?
3. Is there just one product or a line of products?
4. Will pricing be competitive?

MARKETING CRITERIA
1. Does your idea fit into a trend?
2. Is there a need for it?
3. Is it seasonal?
4. Is it a fad, or does it have long-term value?
5. Who will buy it?
6. Does it need instructions?

PRODUCT CRITERIA
1. How much will it cost to get your idea to market?
2. Does it require service or maintenance?
3. Is there a warranty?
4. Does it need packaging?
5. Is it the simplest and most attractive it can be?

Source: Prof. dr. Miroslav Rebernik Barbara Bradač. Idea evaluation methods and techniques.

CHECKLIST FOR
ENVIRONMENTALLY RESPONSIBLE DESIGN

1. Use environmentally responsible strategies appropriate to the product;
2. Reduce overall material content and increase the percentage of recycled material in products;
3. Reduce energy consumption of products that use energy;
4. Specify sustainability grown materials when using wood or agricultural materials;
5. Design disposable products or products that wear out to be more durable and precious;
6. Eliminate unused or unnecessary product features;
7. Design continuously transported products for minimal weight;
8. Design for fast, economical disassembly of major components prior to recycling;
9. Design products so that toxic components are easily removed prior to recycling;
10. Perform comprehensive environmental assessment;
11. Consider all of the ecological impacts from all of the components in the products over its entire life cycle, including extraction of materials from nature, conversion of materials

into products, product use, disposal or recycling and transport between these phases;

12. Consider all ecological impacts including global warming, acid rain, smog, habitat damage, human toxicity, water pollution, cancer causing potential, ozone layer depletion and resource depletion;
13. Strive to reduce the largest ecological impacts,
14. Conduct life cycle impact assessment to comprehensively identify opportunities for improving ecological performance
15. Encourage new business models and effective communication
16. Support product 'take back' systems that enable product up-grading and material recycling;
17. Lease the product or sell the service of the product to improve long-term performance and end-of-life product collection;
18. Communicate the sound business value of being ecologically responsible to clients and commissioners
19. Discuss market opportunities for meeting basic needs and reducing consumption.

Source: adapted from design-sustainability.com

EVALUATING AN IDEA
COST-BENEFIT ANALYSIS

WHAT
Cost-benefit analysis is widely used and relatively simple tool for deciding whether to make a change or not. The quality of decision depends on depth of analysis of benefits and costs connected with idea.

HOW
Cost-benefit analysis finds, quantifies, and adds all the positive and negative factors. First ones are the benefits. Then it identifies, quantifies, and subtracts all the negatives, the costs. The difference between the two indicates whether the planned action is advisable.

1. Define costs of idea implementation. (includes direct, indirect, financial and social costs).
2. Define benefits of idea implementation (includes if possible direct, indirect, financial and social benefits).
3. Compare of sum of all costs with the sum of all benefits.

EXAMPLE OF AN EVALUATION MATRIX

| | | ALTERNATIVES | | | | | |
| | | Option A | | Option B | | Option C | |
Criteria	Weight	Rating	Score	Rating	Score	Rating	Score
1							
2							
3							
Total							

KEPTNER TREGOE MATRIX

WEIGHTED SCORE MATRIX

OBJECTIVE	WEIGHT	ALTERNATIVE 1 SATISFACTION SCORE	WEIGHTED SCORE (WEIGHT X SCORE)

ADVERSITY RATING MATRIX

ADVERSE EFFECT	PROBABILITY	SIGNIFICANCE	WEIGHTED SCORE (PROBAB. X SIGN.)

WEIGHTED SCORE MATRIX

IDEA	INNOVATION	NEED	FEASIBILITY	TOTAL
Idea 1				
Idea 2				
Idea 3				
Idea 4				

EVALUATION MATRIX

WHAT
The main aim of evaluation matrix is to evaluate an idea in accordance to several factors or criteria. It is applicable when considering more characteristics or criteria of an idea. Evaluation matrix has many application possibilities in different areas. However, to use it efficiently must the scoring criteria must be carefully selected. It is individual or group technique which enables more detailed analysis of vital factors.

HOW
4. Specify and prioritizing needs in accordance with a listed criteria,
5. Evaluate, rate, and compare different solutions, selecting the best matching solution.
6. Select the best solution.

Source: Adapted from Prof. dr. Miroslav Rebernik Barbara Bradač. Idea evaluation methods and techniques.

KEPTNER TREGOE MATRIX

WHAT
Kepner Tregoe matrix is meant for decision making and is a structured methodology for gathering information and prioritizing and evaluating it. It is called also a root cause analysis and decision-making method. It is a step-by-step approach for systematically solving problems, making decisions, and analyzing potential risks.

HOW
The Kepner Tregoe analysis is performed in following steps:

7. Prepare a decision statement with desired result and required action.
8. Define strategic requirements, operational objectives and limits rank objectives from the most to the least important and weigh them from 1 to 10 in a table.
9. Generate a list of alternative courses of action and keep only those that are suitable for the desired result.
10. Eliminate other ideas.
11. Score alternatives against each objective on a scale of 1 to 10.
12. Multiply the weight of the objective by the satisfaction

score to come up with the weighted score.

13. Repeat for each alternative
14. Choose the top three alternatives and consider potential problems with each.
15. Consider each alternative idea against all of the negative effects.
16. Rate chosen alternatives against adverse effects, and score them for probability and significance.

EVALUATING AN IDEA
INNOVATION, NEED & FEASIBILITY

WHAT
This is a quick way of assessing ideas before further development based on the three criteria.

HOW
1. Score each idea based on the following criteria.
2. How innovative is the idea?
3. Does the idea meet an umet need? How well does it meet the need?
4. Feasibility - How feasibly is it to put this into practice?

Source: Adapted from Prof. dr. Miroslav Rebernik Barbara Bradač. Idea evaluation methods and techniques.

EVALUATING NEW IDEA
PARETO ANALYSIS THE 20:80 RULE

WHAT
80% of problems have 20% of root causes. Pareto Analysis is the 20:80 rule. It is a simple method that helps to identify the most important problems to solve. Pareto analysis is a formal technique for finding the actions that will give the greatest benefits. It is a good technique where there are many possible competing courses of action.

HOW
Score each idea based on the following criteria.
1. How innovative is the idea?
2. Does the idea meet an unmet need? How well does it meet the need?
3. Feasibility - How feasibly is it to put this into practice?
4. Listing all relevant problems and available options.
5. Group options that are solving the same problem.
6. Apply a score to each group
7. Continue developing the group with the highest score

EVALUATING NEW IDEA
ANALOGIES

2. Half-day to two-day sessions

WHAT
An analogy is a comparison between two things. Solutions are often found by looking to other contexts that have relevance to the problem that you are trying to solve. One can reason by inference similarities between entities, based on observed similarities.

"

Analogies constitute an uncommon juxtaposition of the familiar and the unusual."

Source: H.P. Casakin. 2007. Metaphors in Design Problem Solving: Implications for Creativity. International Journal of Design, 1(2): 21-33

HOW
1. Define the problem.
2. Consider similar situations in nature.
3. Consider other industries.
4. Consider people who you could interview.
5. Brainstorm connections.

STRUCTURED DESIGN THINKING IDEATION SESSIONS

1. Stakeholders and cross functional teams

FORMAT:
1. Background briefing: users, context, goals, constraints
2. Break into small groups (6-10) with facilitators
3. Ideas on Post-its; Posti-ts on board
4. 40-60 minutes facilitated brainstorm
5. Cluster Post-its on poster boards
6. Participants pick promising ideas & form teams
7. Each team develops a concept and story
8. Stories presented to entire group

Source: Gayle Curtis Structured Ideation and Design Thinking

"

If you always do what you always did, you will always get what you always got."

Albert Einstein,
Theoretical physicist

OSBORN'S CHECKLIST FOR TRANSFORMING IDEAS

PUT TO OTHER USES?
1. New ways to use as is?
2. Other uses if modified?

ADAPT?
1. What else is like this?
2. What other idea does this suggest?
3. Does the past offer parallel?
4. What could I copy?
5. Whom could I emulate?

MODIFY?
1. New twist?
2. Change meaning, color,
3. motion, sound, odor, form, shape?
4. Other shapes?

MAGNIFY?
1. What to add?
2. More time?
3. Greater frequency?
4. Stronger?
5. Higher?
6. Longer?
7. Extra Value?
8. Plus ingredient?
9. Duplicate?
10. Multiply?
11. Exaggerate?

COMBINE?
1. How about a blend, an
2. alloy, an assortment,
3. an ensemble?
4. Combine units?
5. Combine purposes?
6. Combine appeals?
7. Combine ideas?

MINIFY?
1. What to subtract?
2. Smaller?
3. Condensed?
4. Miniature?
5. Lower?
6. Shorter?
7. Lighter?
8. Omit?
9. Streamline?
10. Split up?
11. Understate?

SUBSTITUTE?
1. Who else instead?
2. What else instead?
3. Other ingredient?
4. Other process?
5. Other place?
6. Other approach?
7. Other tone of voice?

REVERSE?
1. Transpose positive
2. and negative?
3. How about opposites?
4. Turn it backward?
5. Turn it upside
6. down?
7. Reverse roles?
8. Change shoes?
9. Turn tables?
10. Turn other cheek?

REARRANGE?
1. Interchange components?
2. Other pattern?
3. Other layout?
4. Other sequence?
5. Transpose cause and effect?
6. Change pace?

Source: Alex Osborn, Applied Imagination.

10 X 10 SKETCH METHOD

10 X 10 SKETCH METHOD

WHAT

This method is an approach to making early concept generation sketching more efficient in use of time than the method that stresses finished sketches early in the design process. It allows more time to explore ideas and so stresses the quality of thinking and the final solution. The 10 x 10 method involves creating ten rows with ten thumbnail sketches per row on each page.

This method is an approach to making early concept generation sketching more efficient in use of time than the method that stresses finished sketches early in the design process. It allows more time to explore ideas and so stresses the quality of thinking and the final solution. The 10 x 10 method involves creating ten rows with ten thumbnail sketches per row on each page.

WHY

1. It allows more exploration of alternative ideas in a shorter time
2. May lead to a final concept which is a better design than traditional approaches.
3. Prevents sketches from becoming jewelry in the mind of the designer and more important than the quality of the final design solution.

CHALLENGES

This method takes discipline

HOW

1. Traditional design concept exploration involves a designer producing six to 12 alternative design concepts presented as attractive renderings
2. This method involves a designer making ten rows of ten simple fast cartoon like sketches per page.
3. Each sketch should be no larger than one inch by one inch.
4. The designer produces 5 to 20 pages of very fast sketches during first phase of concept exploration
5. Designs are reviewed and ranked by the design team following a discussion and presentation by the designer and a relatively small number are selected for iteration, recombination and further development.
6. At the next stage more finished and larger concept sketches are produced

BRAINSTORMING

WHAT

Brainstorming is a group creativity technique involving the exploration of a problem by the group where each member proposes possible solutions to the problem.

WHO INVENTED IT?

Popularized by Alex Osborn. The method was first presented in 1948 by Osborn in the book called "Your creative power". He was frustrated by employees' inability to develop creative ideas individually for ad campaigns. It is now used by an estimated 75% of US corporations

WHY

This method can generate a lot of good ideas.
This method draws upon the expertise of a group of people. It is democratic. Have a team of 4 to 12 people.
This is a relatively efficient and fast way to generate idea.

HOW

1. Define problem statement.
2. Select a room and moderate
3. The facilitator defines the brainstorming challenge.
4. Generated as many ideas as possible We recommend aiming to generate 75 to 120 ideas in a session.
5. Stay focused on the topic.
6. Encourage adventurous ideas.
7. One conversation at a time.
8. Build on ideas of others. Defer judgment. No negative criticism. Consider all ideas.
9. Be visual.
10. Make each explanation short and sweet.
11. Ideas can be recorded on post-it notes and placed by the moderator on a wall or they can be called out and written on a White-board or black board by the moderator or an assistant.
12. Allow 30 to 45 minutes.
13. Cluster the ideas into similar groups.
14. Photograph the post-it notes.

RESOURCES

Paper
Pens
White-board
Dry-erase markers
Post-it-notes.

PREPARING FOR BRAIN-STORMING

Come to the brainstorm session prepared.
1. Bring a lot of paper and markers.
2. Pens
3. Post-it-notes
4. Index cards
5. A flip chart
6. White-board or wall
7. Video camera
8. Camera
9. One clear goal per brainstorming session.
10. Determine who will write things down and document the proceedings?

11. Allow one to two hours for a brainstorming session.
12. Recruit good people.
13. 8 to 12 people is a good number
14. Prepare brainstorm questions that you think will help guide the group.

CREATE A STRATEGY
1. What do you want to achieve?
2. What problem do you want to be solved?
3. Define the goal
4. How will you define the problem to the participants?
5. How long will the session be?
6. How many people will be involved?
7. What will be the mix of people?
8. Will there be a follow-up session?
9. Will you send out information before the session?
10. Do the participants have the information that they need?
11. Who should you invite?
12. Assemble a diverse team.
13. Do the participants have the right skills and knowledge for the task?
14. Where will the brainstorm be held?
15. Who owns the intellectual property?
16. Will the session be free of interruptions?
17. How will you record the ideas?
18. What will you do with the information?
19. Be mindful of the scope brainstorm questions. Neither too broad nor too narrow.
20. 45-60 minutes for brainstorm time. Warm up 15-30 minutes.
21. Wrap up 15-30 minutes.

CHOOSING A TECHNIQUE
1. There are many different brainstorming methods.
2. Choose a method that suits your task and participants
3. Try different methods over time to find which ones work best for you.

REFRESHMENTS
1. An army marches on its stomach
2. Offer tea, coffee water, soda.

FACILITATING
1. Encourage everyone to contribute.
2. Review the rules and ask the group to enforce them.
3. Ask participants to turn phones off or onto vibrate mode.
4. A facilitator isn't a leader.
5. Do not steer the discussion
6. Do not let particular people dominate the conversation.
7. Keep the conversations on topic.
8. Set realistic time limits for each stage and be sure that you keep on time.
9. Have a brainstorm plan and stick to it.
10. The facilitator should create an environment where it is safe to suggest wild ideas.
11. Provide clear directions at the beginning of the meeting.
12. Clearly define the problem to be discussed.
13. Write the problem on the White-board where everyone can see it.
14. Provide next steps at the end of the meeting.
15. Select final ideas by voting.
16. Use your camera or phone to take digital pictures of the idea output

at the end of your meeting.
17. Good facilitation requires good listening skills
18. The facilitator should run the White-board, writing down ideas as people come up with them,
19. Prevent people from interrupting others
20. Invite quieter people to contribute.
21. Hire a facilitator if necessary.
22. Start on time.
23. End on time.
24. Keep things moving
25. You can filter the best ideas after the session or get the team to vote on their preferred ideas during the session.
26. Listen
27. Write fast & be visual
28. Use humor and be playful
29. Thank the group after the session.
30. Provide next steps to the group after the meeting.
31. Keep participants engaged
32. Encourage interactivity
33. 100 ideas per hour.
34. Avoid social hierarchy
35. Organize small break-out sessions.
36. Encourage passion.

RULES FOR BRAINSTORMING

1. "Defer judgment Separating idea generation from idea selection strengthens both activities. For now, suspend critique. Know that you'll have plenty of time to evaluate the ideas after the brainstorm.
2. Encourage wild ideas
3. One conversation at a time Maintain momentum as a group.

Save the side conversations for later.
4. Headline Capture the essence quickly "
5. Focus on quantity not on quality."

POST-IT VOTING

1. Give every participant three adhesive dots and ask them to place the dots next to their favorite ideas.
2. Each person tags three favorite ideas
3. Cluster favorite ideas
4. Develop the design directions with the most dots.

GROUP REVIEW

Ask everyone to review the boards of ideas, and discuss the specific ideas or directions they like and why.

Source adapted from Hasso Plattner Institute of Design

THE ENVIRONMENT

1. Select a space not usually used by your team.
2. Refreshments
3. Find a quiet comfortable room
4. Comfortable chairs
5. No interruptions
6. Turn phones off
7. Disney believe that using different spaces helps the creative process. Go off-site.
8. Use big visible materials for writing on
9. Keep the temperature comfortable
10. Adequate lighting
11. Suitable external noise levels
12. Seats should be not too far apart.

635 BRAINSTORMING PROCESS

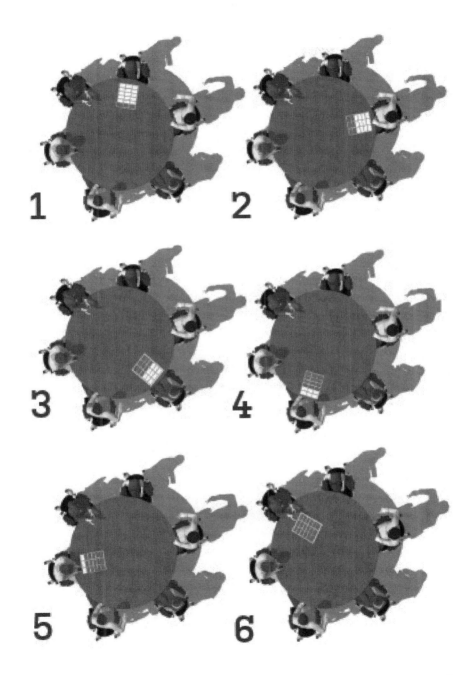

7. Have a space with a lot of vertical writing space.

METHODS OF SYNTHESIZING IDEAS
1. 2X2 matrix
2. Clustering
3. Continuum
4. Concentric circles
5. Time-line
6. Prioritization
7. Adoption curve

101 BRAINSTORMING METHOD

WHAT

This is a brainstorming method focuses on creating volumes of ideas.

WHY
1. Leverages the diverse experiences of a team.
2. A large volume of ideas helps overcome people's inhibitions to innovating.
3. Makes group problem solving fun.
4. Helps build team cohesion.
5. Everyone can participate.

CHALLENGES
1. Because the focus is on volume some ideas will not be useful.
2. Best used with other creativity methods

HOW
1. Define a problem

2. Select a moderator
3. Select a diverse design team of 4 to 12 people and a moderator.
4. The moderator asks the team to each generate 101 solutions to the design problem in a defined time. Allow 30 to 60 minutes.
5. Analyze results and prioritize.
6. Develop actionable ideas.

RESOURCES
Pens
Post-it-notes
A flip chart
White-board or wall
Refreshments

6 THINKING HATS

WHAT

Six thinking hats is a tool for thinking described in a book by the same name by Edward de Bono. It can help a design team understand the effects of decisions from different viewpoints.
7.

WHO INVENTED IT?
Edward de Bono 1985

CHALLENGES
1. When describing your concept, be specific about your goal.
2. Utilize your thinking for practical solutions.
3. Always think in the style of the hat you're wearing.
4. Stick to the rules.

EXAMPLE OF 635 BRAINSTORM

PROBLEM STATEMENT: HOW CAN WE IMPROVE THE KNOWLEDGE OF ENGLISH IN THE SERVICE DEPARTMENT?			
Nikos	Evening classes	Motivation for holiday abroad	"English Speaking Day" each week in the department
Pierre	Evening class paid by company	Motivation for summer university in English	Project meetings in English
Alan	Evening classes with 2 hours off	Contribution by the company for Summer-university in GB, Ireland or US	Conversation circle once per month after work.
Sue	2 hours per week with a teacher in the company	Higher remuneration for a certificated instructor	English version of professional literature
Lelia	E-learning with a tutor and classes in the company	English "library" at the company Going to the Irish pub as often as possible	Conversation circle with foreign colleagues from the company
Caryn	Intensive course twice a year on the weekend		Inter-cultural evening with foreign colleagues from the company

Source: Adapted from http://www.becreate.ch

WHY

The key theoretical reasons to use the Six Thinking Hats are to:

1. Encourage Parallel Thinking
2. Encourage full-spectrum thinking
3. Separate ego from performance
4. Encourage critical thinking.

HOW

1. Optimum number of participants is 4 to 8.
2. Present the facts White Hat.
3. Generate ideas on how the issue should be handled Green Hat.
4. Evaluate the ideas. Yellow Hat.
5. List the drawbacks Black Hat.
6. Get the feelings about alternatives Red Hat.
7. Summarize and finish the meeting. Blue Hat.
8. White Hat thinking is information, numbers, data needs and gaps.
9. Red Hat thinking is intuition, desires and emotion.
10. Black Hat thinking is the hat of judgment and care.
11. Yellow Hat thinking is the logical positive.
12. Green Hat thinking is the hat of creativity, alternatives, proposals, provocations and change.
13. Blue Hat thinking is the overview or process control.
14. Time required 90 minutes.

RESOURCES

Paper and
Pens,

Descriptions of different hats
Symbols of hats
Space to sit in the circle

Most executives, many scientists, almost all business school graduates believe that if you analyze data, this will give you new ideas. Unfortunately this belief is totally wrong.

There is no doubt that creativity is the most important resource of all. Without creativity, there would be no progress, and we would be forever repeating the same patterns."

Edward de Bono

635 BRAINSTORMING

WHAT

Method 635 is a structured form of brainstorming. The outcome of each session is 108 ideas in 18 minutes.

WHO INVENTED IT?

Professor Bernd Rohrbach 1968

WHY

15. Can generate a lot of ideas quickly
16. Participants can build on

each others ideas
17. The participants record ideas
18. Democratic process.
19. Ideas are contributed privately.
20. Ideas are iteratively refined five times.
21. Does not need a moderator

HOW
1. Your team should sit around a table.
2. Each team member is given a sheet of paper with the design objective written at the top.
3. The sheet can be divided into six rows of three boxes.
4. Each team member is given three minutes to generate three ideas.
5. Your participants then pass the sheet of paper to the person sitting on their left.
6. Each participant must come up with three new ideas.
7. The process can stop when sheets come around the table.
8. Repeat until ideas are exhausted. No discussion during the idea generating period.
9. Ideas can be sketches or written or a combination.
10. You can use an egg timer
11. You can also use post-it notes. One per box. This makes it easier to process the ideas after the session.
12. Analyze ideas as a group,
13. Put the ideas on a Whiteboard or wall cluster and vote for the preferred ideas.

RESOURCES
Large room
Large table
Paper
Pens
Post-it notes.

AOKI BRAINSTORMING

WHAT
The Aoki or MBS method is a structured brainstorming method that stresses input by all team members.

WHO INVENTED IT?
Sadami Aoki. Used by Mitsubishi

WHY
1. There is a hierarchy of ideas
2. This method requires that a quantity of ideas is generated.
Shifts you from reacting to a static snapshot of the problem and broadens your perspective toward the problem and the relationships and connections between its components

CHALLENGES
1. Group-think
2. Not enough good ideas
3. Taking turns
4. Freeloading
5. Inhibition
6. Lack of critical thinking
7. A group that is too large competes for attention.

HOW
1. Warm Up: Participants generate ideas for 15 minutes.

2. Participants present their ideas verbally to the larger group.
3. The larger group continues to generate ideas during the individual presentations.
4. For one hour the individual team members further explain their ideas to the group
5. Idea maps are created by the moderator.

RESOURCES
Paper
Pens
White-board
Dry-erase markers
Post-it-notes.

BRAINSTORMING ALONE

WHAT
Recent research has suggested that some individuals are more creative working alone for brainstorming sessions rather than in groups. In this case the divergent idea generation is done by an individual and the convergent phase is done by the team.

WHO INVENTED IT?
Alex Faickney Osborn 1953 is often credited with inventing brainstorming.

WHY
1. Leverages the diverse experiences of a team.
2. Uses the creativity of the individual free from distractions.
3. Helps build empathy.

CHALLENGES
1. Some ideas that you generate using the tool may be impractical.
2. Best used with other creativity methods

HOW
1. Define a problem
2. Find a quiet place
3. Generate as many ideas as possible in 30 minutes.
4. Get the team together and present the ideas to them.
5. Get the team to vote on which ideas they like the most. Two votes per person.
6. Analyze results and prioritize.
7. Develop actionable ideas.

RESOURCES
Pens
Post-it-notes
A flip chart
White-board or wall
Refreshments

BRAINSTORMING CHALLENGES

COLLABORATIVE FIXATION
members may conform their ideas to other members reducing the range of exploration.

EVALUATION APPREHENSION
Participants may be less creative

because of fear of criticism by others.

FREE-RIDING
Members may sit at the back and not contribute.

PERSONALITY CHARACTERISTICS
Strong personalities may dominate the conversations.

SOCIAL MATCHING
Members may become less productive to match others in the group.

BRAINSTORMING FOR THE 5 SENSES

WHAT
Design in northern Europe and the United States focuses on the visual sense which is only a component of the design experience. A design such as an Italian sports car gives greater consideration to other senses such as hearing, smell touch to give a consistent experience of through all senses to a product user.

WHY
1. It gives a design a greater experience of quality than a design that focuses on the visual sense.
2. It gives a consistent experience.
3. It provides a more stimulating experience than a design that focuses on the visual experience.

CHALLENGES
1. Group-think
2. Not enough good ideas
3. Taking turns
4. Freeloading
5. Inhibition
6. A group that is too large competes for attention.

HOW
1. The moderator frames the design challenge.
2. Team members generate ideas on post-it notes.
3. The team works through 20 minute brainstorming sessions in each sense, Vision, smell, touch hearing, taste.
4. Ask team members to generate 6 to 10 ideas each under each category.
5. Use up to 25 words for non visual senses and simple sketches for the visual ideas.
6. Organize post-it notes into groups through discussion with five concepts in each group, one idea from each sense group or five different senses in each group.
7. Ask team to vote on which groups have the most potential for further development.

RESOURCES
Paper
Pens
White-board
Dry-erase markers

Post-it-notes.

DISNEY METHOD

WHAT

The Disney Method is a parallel thinking technique. It was invented before Design Thinking evolved to it's current state but has many of the elements of the Design Thinking approach. It allows a team to discuss an issue from four perspectives. It involves parallel thinking to analyze a problem, generate ideas, evaluate ideas, and to create a strategy. It is a method used in workshops. The four thinking perspectives are Spectators, Dreamers, Realists and Critics.

WHO INVENTED IT?
Dilts, 1991

WHY
Allows the group to discuss a problem from four different perspectives

CHALLENGES
1. An alternative to De Bono Six Hat Method.
2. Can deliver a workable solution quickly.

HOW
1. Have Four different brainstorming sessions in four different rooms.
2. At the end of each of the four sessions the participants leave the room and then at a later time reenter the next room then assuming the personas and perspectives of the next group. Time taken is often 60 to 90 minutes per session. The sessions adopt the following themes.
3. The spectator's view. Puts the problem in an external context. How would a consultant, a customer or an outside observer view the problem?
4. The Dreamers view. Looking for an ideal solution. What would our dream solution for this be? What if? Unconstrained brainstorm.
5. Realists view. The realists are convergent thinkers. How can we turn the dreamer's views into reality? Looking for ideas that are feasible, profitable, customer focused and can be implemented within 18 months.
6. The Critics view. What are the risks and obstacles? Who would oppose this plan? What could go wrong? Refine, improve or reject. Be constructive.

"

Around here, we do not look backwards for very long. We keep moving forward, opening up new doors and doing new things, because we're curious and curiosity keeps leading us down new paths."

Walt Disney
American entrepreneur,
cartoonist, animator, voice actor,
film producer and Design Thinker

HEURISTIC IDEATION

WHAT
Heuristic ideation method is used to create new concepts, ideas, products or solutions.

WHY
1. To create new connections and insights for products, services and experiences

WHO INVENTED IT?
Couger 1995, McFadzean 1998, McFadzean, Somersall, and Coker 1998, VanGundy 1988

RESOURCES
Pens
Markers
White-board or flip chart
Dry erase markers

HOW
1. The group will first make two lists of words
2. Each team member selects three words from the first list and connects each word to a different word in the second list.
3. Each team members develops these ideas into concepts and illustrates or describes each concept on an index card.
4. The index cards are places on a pin board and each concept is briefly described by the team member who generated the idea.
5. The team votes to prioritize the ideas

IDEA ADVOCATE

WHAT
This method involves appointing advocates for ideas that were previously created during a brainstorming session.

WHO INVENTED IT?
Battelle Institute in Frankfurt, Germany

WHY
1. Idea advocate is a simplified form of the dialectical approach
2. To ensure fair examination of all ideas.
3. To give every presented idea equal chance of being selected.
4. To uncover the positive aspects of ideas

CHALLENGES
1. Consideration should be given to also assigning a devil 's advocate for a more balanced assessment of certain proposed ideas.
2. There should be little difference in status amongst the idea advocates.

LOTUS TEMPLATE

A1	A2	A3	B1	B2	B3	C1	C2	C3
A4	A	A5	B4	B	B5	C4	C	C5
A6	A7	A8	B6	B7	B8	C6	C7	C8
D1	D2	D3	A	B	C	E1	E2	E3
D4	D	D5	D	■	E	E4	E	E5
D6	D7	D8	F	G	H	E6	E7	E8
F1	F2	F3	G1	G2	G3	H1	H2	H3
F4	F	F5	G4	G	G5	H4	H	H5
F6	F7	F8	G6	G7	G8	H6	H7	H8

HOW

1. The team reviews a list of previously generated ideas.
2. Assign idea advocate roles to:
3. A team member who proposed an idea, will implement an idea, or argues for the selection of a design direction.
4. The idea advocates present arguments to the design team on why the idea is the best direction.
5. After the advocates have presented the team votes on their preferred idea.

RESOURCES

Pens
Markers
White-board or flip chart
Dry erase markers

LOTUS METHOD

WHAT

The lotus blossom is a creativity technique that consists a framework for idea generation that starts by generating eight concept themes based on a central theme. Each concept then serves as the basis for eight further theme explorations or variations.

WHO INVENTED IT?

Yasuo Matsumura, Director of the Clover Management Research

WHY

6. This method requires that a quantity of 81 ideas is generated. To generate one good idea it is necessary to generate many ideas.
7. You can explore a spectrum of ideas from low risk to high risk or other spectrum.
8. Each idea can be developed in the outer boxes.

CHALLENGES

It is a somewhat rigid model. Not every problem will require the same number of concepts to be developed.

HOW

1. Draw up a lotus blossom template of 9 x 9 empty boxes.
2. Write the design problem in the center box of the diagram.
3. Write eight related ideas around the center.
4. Each idea then becomes the central idea of a new theme or blossom.
5. Follow step 3 with all central ideas.

RESOURCES

Paper
Pens
White board
or large sheet of paper
Dry-erase markers
Post-it-notes.

NHK BRAINSTORMING

WHAT
The NHK method is a rigorous iterative process of brainstorming of ideas following a predetermined structure.

WHO INVENTED IT?
Hiroshi Takahashi

WHY
This method requires that a quantity of ideas is generated.

CHALLENGES
1. Group-think.
2. Not enough good ideas.
3. Taking turns.
4. Freeloading.
5. Inhibition.
6. Lack of critical thinking.
7. A group that is too large competes for attention.

HOW
1. Define problem statement.
2. Each participant writes down five ideas on five separate cards.
3. Create groups of five participants
4. While each person explains their ideas, the others continue to record new ideas.
5. Collect, and create groups of related concepts.
6. Form new groups of two or three people Brainstorm for half an hour.
7. Groups organize ideas and present them to the larger group.
8. Record all ideas on the White-board.
9. Form larger groups of ten people and work further brainstorm each of the ideas on the White-board.

NOMINAL GROUP BRAINSTORMING

WHAT
The nominal group method is a brainstorming method that is designed to encourage participation of all members of the team and minimizes the possibility of more vocal members from dominating the discussion.

WHO INVENTED IT?
This technique was originally developed by Andre Delbecq and Andrew H. Van de Ven,and has been applied to adult education program planning by Vedros,and has also been employed as a useful technique in curriculum design and evaluation in educational institutions

HOW
1. Distribute information about the process to participants before the meeting.
2. Introduction and explanation: The facilitator welcomes the participants and explains to them the purpose and procedure of the meeting.
3. Silent generation of ideas:

The facilitator provides each participant with a sheet of paper with the question to be addressed and asks the participants to write down all ideas that come to mind when considering the question. During this period, the facilitator asks participants not to consult or discuss their ideas with others. This stage lasts approximately thirty minutes.

4. Participants drop anonymous suggestions into a box.
5. In the meeting the moderator writes the suggestions on to a White-board
6. Each participant has the opportunity to speak in support or against any of the suggestions.
7. Sharing ideas: The Facilitator invites participants to share the ideas they have generated. There is no discussion at this stage and group list 5 to 10 ideas that the like the most, in order of importance, and to pass them to the moderator.
8. Group discussion: The moderator leads the team in to clarify each idea, Participants explain their top ideas. Allow one minute per idea. This stage lasts 30–45 minutes.
9. The participants vote for and rank the ideas.
10. It may be necessary to have more than one meeting.
11. The moderator tallies the votes
12. Participants record their votes on blank postcards.

WHEN
The nominal group technique is particularly useful:

1. When some group members dominate the conversation
2. When some group members are quiet
3. When some group members do not participate
4. When the group does not easily generate many ideas
5. When there are new group members
6. When the issue is conflict
7. When there is a power-imbalance

ADVANTAGES AND DISADVANTAGES
1. Avoids the problem of group members not participating.
2. Ensures relatively equal participation.
3. Can only deal with one problem at a time.
4. Requires preparation.
5. There is no spontaneity involved with this method.
6. The process may appear to be too mechanical.

RESOURCES
White-board
Paper
Pens
Dry erase markers
Blank postcards

NYAKA

WHAT
....
The Nyaka method is a form of brainstorming. The Nyaka method places emphasis on exploring problems and solutions to problems.

WHY
1. There is a hierarchy of ideas
2. This method generates many ideas.

CHALLENGES
1. Group-think
2. Not enough good ideas
3. Taking turns
4. Freeloading
5. Inhibition
6. Lack of critical thinking
7. A group that is too large competes for attention.

RESOURCES
Paper
Pens
White-board
Dry-erase markers
Post-it-notes. **HOW**
1. Define a moderator
2. The moderator draws a vertical line on a White-board.
3. Time limit of 30 minutes
4. The moderator asks the team to define as many things that are wrong with a design or service or experience as possible.
5. The moderator asks the team to define solutions for as many of the problems defined as possible.

6. Create a hierarchy of problems and a hierarchy of solutions for each problem.
7. A group size of 4 to 20 people is optimum.
8. For larger groups the moderator can break the group into groups of 4 or 5 people.

OBJECTSTORMING

WHAT
....
A brainstorming technique that uses found objects for inspiration.

WHO INVENTED IT?
Alex Faickney Osborn 1953 is often credited with inventing brainstorming.

WHY
1. Leverages the diverse experiences of a team.
2. Makes group problem solving fun.
3. Helps build team cohesion.
4. Everyone can participate.

CHALLENGES
1. Group-think
2. Not enough good ideas
3. Taking turns
4. Freeloading
5. Inhibition
6. Lack of critical thinking
7. A group that is too large competes for attention.

HOW
1. The moderator introduces the method to the group.
2. The problem is defined by the

moderator.

3. The larger group is broken down into groups of 4 or 5 participants. The moderator collects a diverse collection of objects before the brainstorming session.
4. Each participant is given two objects and asked to use them as inspiration to generate 10 ideas
5. Allow 20 minutes
6. The participants are asked to vote for their three preferred solutions.
7. Select the top ideas for further development.

RESOURCES
Pens
Post-it-notes
A flip chart
White-board or wall
Refreshments

PERSONA BRAINSTORMING

WHAT
This is a brainstorming method that uses the imagined perspectives of an identified persona or group identified as one of your client's customer groups such as students look at a design problem.

WHO INVENTED IT?
Alex Faickney Osborn 1953 is often credited with inventing brainstorming.

WHY
1. Leverages the diverse experiences of a team.
2. Helps build empathy.
3. Makes group problem solving fun.
4. Helps build team cohesion.
5. Everyone can participate.

CHALLENGES
1. Some ideas that you generate using the tool may be impractical.
2. Best used with other creativity methods

HOW
1. Define a problem
2. Select a diverse design team of 4 to 12 people and a moderator.
3. Identify a persona to focus on. See personas.
4. Ask the team how they would deal with the problem if they were the persona
5. Analyze results and prioritize.
6. Develop actionable ideas.

PREMORTEM BRAINSTORMING

WHAT
The premortem is a risk-mitigation planning tool that attempts to identify project threats at the outset.

WHO INVENTED IT?
Gary Klein, 1998

WHY
The premortem technique is low cost and high value

RESOURCES
Evaluation forms can be printed or on-line.

HOW
1. Determine a period after completion of the project when it should be known whether the project was successful, for example, one or five years.
2. Imagine the project was a complete failure.
3. What could have been the cause?
4. Ask each team member to suggest ten reasons for the failure.
5. Think about the internal and external context and the stakeholders relationships.
6. Ask each team member to select one of the reasons for failure they have listed and describe it to the group.
7. Each person should present one reason.
8. Collect and review the full list of reasons from each participant.
9. Review the session and strengthen the strategy based on the premortem.

QUESTSTORMING

WHAT
This brainstorming method is brainstorming the questions to ask. The participants do no need to provide solutions. The questions form the framework for strategy plans. After brainstorming a list of questions, prioritize them.

Innovators ask a lot of questions.

WHO INVENTED IT?
Jon Roland 1985.

Discovering problems actually requires just as much creativity as discovering solutions. There are many ways to look at any problem, and realizing a problem is often the first step toward a creative solution. To paraphrase John Dewey, the inventor of the Dewey Decimal System, a properly defined problem is partially solved."

Scott Berkun
The Myths of Innovation

HOW

1. Have a group of people start asking questions and write them down one-by-one.
2. As in brainstorming, refrain from judging, censoring, or discussing the questions as you collect them.
3. The goal is to go for volume.
4. Develop 50 questions. Group the questions by type.
   - What is? – These questions focus on facts and as-is situation
   - What caused? – These questions get at the root of a problem
   - Why? Why Not? – This type reflects the rationale behind a given problem space.
   - What if? – These are the questions that point to a different future and lead to real innovation.
5. Prioritize the questions and pick the most relevant ones to discuss and develop further.

RESOURCE BRAINSTORMING

WHAT
This is a brainstorming method that uses the availability of resources to look at a design problem.

WHO INVENTED IT?
Alex Faickney Osborn 1953

is credited with inventing brainstorming.

WHY
6. Leverages the diverse experiences of a team.
7. Helps build empathy.
8. Makes group problem solving fun.
9. Helps build team cohesion.
10. Everyone can participate.

CHALLENGES
1. Some ideas that you generate using the tool may be impractical.
2. Best used with other creativity methods

HOW
1. Define a problem
2. Select a diverse design team of 4 to 12 people and a moderator.
3. Identify a resource to limit or make more available such as finance, time, people, materials or process.
4. Ask the team how they would deal with the problem if the resource was changed as proposed
5. Analyze results and prioritize.
6. Develop actionable ideas.

RESOURCES
Pens
Post-it-notes
A flip chart
White-board or wall
Refreshments

NOMINAL GROUP METHOD

WHAT

The nominal group method is a brainstorming method that is designed to encourage participation of all members of the team and minimizes the possibility of more vocal members from dominating the discussion.

WHO INVENTED IT?

William Fox

WHY

1. To define and prioritize problems or opportunities
2. To understand the best solution to a problem
3. To create a plan to implement an opportunity

HOW

1. Distribute information about the process to participants before the meeting.
2. Participants drop anonymous suggestions into an unmonitored suggestion box written on blank postcards.
3. The suggestions are distributed to participants before the meeting so that they can think about them.
4. In the meeting the moderator writes the suggestions on to a Whiteboard
5. Each participant has the opportunity to speak in support or against any of the suggestions.

6. The moderator leads the team in to clarify each idea,
7. The moderator instructs each person to work silently and independently for five minutes, recording as many ideas, thoughts, or answers as possible on paper.
8. The moderator asks the group to list 5 to 10 ideas that the like the most, in order of importance, and to pass them to the moderator.
9. The moderator counts up the number of votes for each idea.
10. Each participant is given a number of votes that they record on blank postcards which are collected face down and tallied.

SCAMPER

WHAT

SCAMPER is a brainstorming technique and creativity method that uses seven words as prompts.
1. Substitute.
2. Combine.
3. Adapt.
4. Modify.
5. Put to another use.
6. Eliminate.
7. Reverse.

WHO INVENTED IT?

Alex Osborne

WHY

1. Scamper is a method that can help generate innovative

solutions to a problem.
2. Leverages the diverse experiences of a team.
3. Makes group problem solving fun.
4. Helps get buy in from all team members for solution chosen.
5. Helps build team cohesion.
6. Everyone can participate.

CHALLENGES
1. Some ideas that you generate using the tool may be impractical.
2. Best used with other creativity methods

HOW
1. Select a product or service to apply the method.
2. Select a diverse design team of 4 to 12 people and a moderator.
3. Ask questions about the product you identified, using the SCAMPER mnemonic to guide you.
4. Create as many ideas as you can.
5. Analyze
6. Prioritize.
7. Select the best single or several ideas to further brainstorm.

SCAMPER QUESTIONS

SUBSTITUTE
1. What materials or resources can you substitute or swap to improve the product?
2. What other product or process could you substitute?
3. What rules could you use?
4. Can you use this product in another situation?

COMBINE
1. Could you combine this product with another product?
2. Could you combine several goals?
3. Could you combine the use of the product with another use?
4. Could you join resources with someone else?

ADAPT
1. How could you adapt or readjust this product to serve another purpose or use?
2. What else is the product like?
3. What could you imitate to adapt this product?
4. What exists that is like the product?
5. Could the product adapt to another context?

MODIFY
1. How could you change the appearance of the product?
2. What could you change?
3. What could you focus on to create more return on investment?
4. Could you change part of the product?

PUT TO ANOTHER USE
1. Can you use this product in another situation?
2. Who would find this product useful?
3. How would this product function in a new context?
4. Could you recycle parts of this product to create a new

product?

ELIMINATE
1. How could you make the product simpler?
2. What features, parts, could you eliminate?
3. What could you understate or tone down?
4. Could you make the product smaller or more efficient?
5. What components could you substitute to change the order of this product?

SCENARIOS

WHAT

A scenario is a narrative or story about how people may experience a design in a particular future context of use. They can be used to predict or explore future interactions with concept products or services. Scenarios can be presented by media such as storyboards or video or be written. They can feature single or multiple actors participating in product or service interactions.

WHO INVENTED IT?
Herman Kahn, Rand Corporation 1950, USA

WHY
1. Scenarios become a focus for discussion which helps evaluate and refine concepts.
2. Usability issues can be explored at a very early stage in the design process.
3. The are useful tool to align a team vision.
4. Scenarios help us create an end to end experience.
5. Interactive experiences involve the dimension of time.
6. Personas give us a framework to evaluate possible solutions.

CHALLENGES
1. Generate scenarios for a range of situations.
2. Include problem situations
3. Hard to envision misuse scenarios.

HOW
1. Identify the question to investigate.
2. Decide time and scope for the scenario process.
3. Identify stakeholders and uncertainties.
4. Define the scenarios.
5. Create storyboards of users goals, activities, motivations and tasks.
6. Act out the scenarios.
7. The session can be videotaped.
8. Analyze the scenarios through discussion.
9. Summarize insights

RESOURCES
Storyboard templates
Pens
Video cameras
Props
White-board
Dry-erase markers

SCENARIO GENERATION

Scenarios describe what the future may be. Scenarios are not predictions of the future.

They should be engaging and credible and have internal logic and consistency. However, they should also be challenging and stretch thinking about the range of possible futures. If a robust set of scenarios has been developed, it is likely that the actual future will contain elements of each of them. What cannot be predicted is the combination of outcomes from each of the scenarios."

Scenarios – that can be a powerful tool for thinking about the future and the potential opportunities and challenges. . They provide a 'safe environment' for discussion. They can also be used to explore the different future possibilities, time frames. and risks.

Before developing a set of scenarios first review the past, going back twice as far as the time horizon of the scenarios.

HOW

1. Define the scope
It is important to have a 'focal question' for the scenarios that is not too broad.
2. Identify the drivers of change
3. Identify predictable elements and critical uncertainties
Some drivers will result in a range of different outcomes.

SELECTING THE SCENARIOS

1. Does it allow both negative and positive aspects to emerge?
2. Is there a plausible path to the scenario?
3. Does it stretch current thinking?

COMMUNICATING THE SCENARIOS

Does the communication convey the facts as well as the emotions?

Consider:
1. The relevance.
2. The practicality. Is it deliverable?
3. The implementation.

THE SEVEN QUESTIONS

Start with an invitation to the stakeholder to talk about the key factors shaping the future of your topic. When your subject has provided initial thoughts use these questions as a set of "triggers" for drawing further response. Thinking over a time horizon of XX years:

CLAIRVOYANT.

If you could spend some time with someone who knew the future of it, a clairvoyant or oracle if such existed, what would you want to know? (i.e. what are the critical issues?)

AN OPTIMISTIC OUTCOME

Optimistic but realistic. If things went well, how would you expect the it to develop and what would be the signs of success?

A PESSIMISTIC OUTCOME

How could the environment change to threaten it? How could it deteriorate?

THE INTERNAL SITUATION

From your knowledge of the culture, organization, systems and resources (including people), which impact on it, how would these have to be changed to achieve the optimistic outcome?

LOOKING BACK 10/20 YEARS

What factors shaped it as it is today?

LOOKING FORWARD

What decisions need to be made in the near term to achieve the desired long-term outcome for it?

THE EPITAPH

If you had a mandate, free of all constraints, what more would you do to ensure a successful future for it?

IT IS IMPORTANT TO

1. Gathering information beyond the usual timescales;
2. Consult people with different perspective and expertise.
3. Look beyond the usual cultures and technologies."

Sources Shell, University of St Andrews. SAMI Guidelines, UK Government office for Science.

"

Science has, to date, succeeded in solving a bewildering number of relatively easy problems, whereas the hard problems, and the ones which perhaps promise most for man's future, lie ahead"

Warren Weaver
American scientist and mathematician
1948

SEMANTIC IDEATION

WHAT

Semantic intuition is a method of generating ideas based on word associations.

SEMANTIC IDEATION

Verb list	Adjective list	Adverb list	Product list
walk	adaptable	accidentally	GPS
stand	adventurous	anxiously	marine
reach	affable	beautifully	printer
sit	affectionate	blindly	copy
jump	agreeable	boldly	chair
fly	ambitious	bravely	sofa
accept	amiable	brightly	video
allow	amicable	calmly	game
advise	amusing	carefully	camera
answer	brave	carelessly	desk
arrive	bright	cautiously	tv
ask	broad-minded	clearly	music
avoid	calm	correctly	floor
stop	careful	courageously	bookcase
agree	charming	cruelly	tools
deliver	communicative	daringly	fence
depend	compassionate	deliberately	cart
describe	conscientious	doubtfully	car
deserve	considerate	eagerly	house
destroy	convivial	easily	bean bag
disappear	courageous	elegantly	audio

WHO INVENTED IT?
Warfield, Geschka, & Hamilton, 1975. Battelle Institute

WHY
1. To find new solutions to a problem.

RESOURCES
Pens
Paper
Post-it -notes
White-board
Dry erase markers.

HOW
1. Define the problem to be explored.
2. The team brainstorms two to four word lists that are related to the problem. They could be for example a list of nouns, a list of verbs and a list of adjectives.
3. The team makes a forth lists of associations of two or three words from the lists that can form the basis of new ideas.
4. Combine one word from one set with another word from the other set.
5. The team visualizes new products services or experiences based on the word associations.
6. Each team member produces five to ten ideas based on the word associations over a 30 minute period.
7. The ideas are prioritized by the group by voting.

STP METHOD

WHAT
STP is a brainstorming method designed to help define ways of reaching a goal.

WHO INVENTED IT?
Ava S Butler 1996

WHY
1. To generate new ideas

CHALLENGES
1. Group-think
2. Not enough good ideas
3. Taking turns
4. Freeloading
5. Inhibition
6. Lack of critical thinking
7. A group that is too large competes for attention.

HOW
1. The moderator writes three headings on a White-board. Situation, target and proposal.
2. The moderator reviews the rules of brainstorming. Go for quantity.
3. The moderator asks the question "What do you see as the current situation?"
4. When all ideas have been recorded the moderator asks "Which comments need clarification?"
5. After team members provide clarification the moderator asks " What is our ideal goal?"
6. After all ideas have been

recorded and clarifies the moderator asks" What is our preferred target?"

7. After the team votes and a preferred target is selected the moderator asks "How can we get from our current situation to our preferred target?"

8. After all ideas have been recorded and clarified the team selects a preferred way to get to the target by voting.

SYNECTICS

WHAT

Synectics is a structured creativity method that is based on analogy. Synectics is based on observations collected during thousands of hours of group process and group problem solving and decision making activities (Nolan 1989)The word synectics combines derives from Greek "the bringing together of diverse elements."

WHO INVENTED IT?
George Prince and William Gordon 1976

WHY
1. Use to stimulate creative thinking and generate new problem solving approaches.
2. Synectics provides an environment in which risk taking is validated.
3. Synectics can be fun and productive.

CHALLENGES
1. Synectics is more demanding than brainstorming,
2. If the analogy is too obvious, then it may not promote innovative thinking.
3. Synectics works best as a group process.

HOW
1. Problem definition.
2. Create an analogy. Use ideas from the natural or man-made world, connections with historical events, your location, etc.
3. Use this Sentence Stem: An is a lot like a y because...
4. Use a syntectic trigger Mechanism like a picture, poem, song, drawing etc. to start your analogical reasoning.
5. The group generates as many solution approaches, called springboards, as possible.
6. Idea selection.
7. Excursions - Structured side trips.
8. Develop the selected ideas into concepts.
9. Analyze the connections in the analogy you have created.

SKETCHES
TYPES OF SKETCHES

Idea sketch
Idea sketches are 2D visual design representations used at a personal level for externalizing thoughts quickly and to show how the design looks as a physical object.

Study Sketch
Study sketches are 2D visual design representations used for investigating the appearance and visual impact of ideas such as aspects of geometric proportion, configuration , scale, layout and mechanism .

Referential Sketch
Referential sketches are 2D visual design representations used as a diary to record observations for future reference or as a metaphor.

Memory Sketch
Memory sketches are 2D visual design representations that help users recall thoughts and elements from previous work with notes and text annotations.

Coded Sketch
Coded sketches are 2D visual design representations that categorize information to show an underlying principle or a scheme.

Information Sketch
Information sketches are 2D visual design representations that allow stakeholders to understand the designer's intentions by explaining information clearly and to provide a common graphical setting.

Renderings
Renderings are 2D visual design representations showing formal proposals of design concepts that involve the application of color, tone and detail for realism.

Inspiration Sketch
Inspiration sketches are form-orientated 2D visual design representations used to communicate the look or feel of a product by setting the tone of a design. brand or a product range.

Prescriptive Sketch
Prescriptive sketches are informal 2D visual design representations that communicate design decisions and general technical information such as dimensions, material and finish.

TYPES OF DRAWINGS

Concept Drawing
Concept drawings are 2D visual design representations that show the design proposal in color with orthographic views and precise lines.

Presentation Drawing
Presentation drawings are 2D

visual design representations drawn in perspective that act as final drawings for clients and other stakeholders.

Scenario and Storyboard

Scenarios and storyboards are 2D visual design representations to suggest user and product interaction, and to portray its use in the context of artifacts, people and relationships.

Diagram

Diagrams are 2d visual design representations that show the underlying principle of an idea or represent relationships between objects with simple geometric elements.

Single View Drawing

Single view drawings are 2d visual design representations drawn in axonometric projection made up of either isometric, trimetric, diametric, oblique or perspective views drawn with little aesthetic detail.

Multi View Drawing

Multi view drawings are 2d visual design representations employed through first or third angle projects.

General Arrangement Drawing

General arrangement drawings are 2d visual design representations that embody the refined design but omit the internal details. They are used for the production of appearance models with limited details

Technical Drawing

Technical drawings are 2d visual design representations used to define, specify and graphically represent the built object and to cover every detail for manufacture.

Technical Illustration

Technical illustrations are 2d visual design representations that simplify the engineering details and highlight key features without omitting important information form the product.

Source: 4 into 35 Does Go: Dr. Mark Evans, Eujin Pei and Dr. R. Ian Campbell Department of Design & Technology, Loughborough University, United Kingdom

CHAPTER SUMMARY

Dieter rams ten principles of "good design"
1. Good design is innovative
2. Good design is useful
3. Good design is aesthetic
4. Good design is understandable
5. Good design is unobtrusive
6. Good design is honest
7. Good design is long-lasting
8. Good design is thorough down to the last detail
9. Good design is environmentally friendly
10. Good design is as little design as possible

Advertising executive Alex F. Osborn is credited with popularizing brainstorming in the United States.

Rules for brainstorming
1. "Defer judgment Separating idea generation from idea selection strengthens both activities. For now, suspend critique. Know that you'll have plenty of time to evaluate the ideas after the brainstorm.
2. Encourage wild ideas
3. One conversation at a time Maintain momentum as a group. Save the side conversations for later.
4. Headline Capture the essence quickly "
5. Focus on quantity not on quality."

CHAPTER REVIEW

1. Name five of Dieter Ram's rules of good design.
2. What is universal design?
3. What is brainstorming?
4. Who popularized brainstorming?
5. Describe five rules of brainstorming.
6. Describe five characteristics of a good environment for team ideation and brainstorming..
7. What does the 635 stand for in 635 brainstorming method?
8. Describe the 10 x 10 method.
9. Describe the stages of the Disney Method.
10. What do the letters in SCAMPER stand for?

EXERCISE ONE IDEATION

BACKGROUND

The ideation phase in Design Thinking is the part of the process where you generate ideas. The ideation process involves divergent thinking. In this stage you move from identifying needs that your end users have to generating possible solutions. By exploring as widely as possible initially followed by testing and feedback an innovative solution will be developed.

PROCESS

1. Interpreting needs. Interview five people for 15 minutes each. Identify at one unmet need they each have for a new service or product. Explore how things makes them feel, what they wish could be different,

what they enjoy, what gets in their way. Listen and learn, so don't be afraid to ask "Why?"

2. Brainstorm. This is best done in a group of 4 to 12 people but can also be done individually. Select one of the unmet needs that you have identified. Imagine some new solutions that might address your subject's needs. First originate ten possible solutions. Then develop six variations of each of the four solutions to create a total of at least sixty possible solutions. Try thinking of the problem in relation to the questions who, what, when, where, why, and how.

3. Consider human needs, business needs and optimum applications of technology.

4. Develop possible solutions that go beyond anything that currently exists in solving the problems or needs that you have identified.

DELIVERABLES

Describe each of your sixty ideas on a post-it note with a simple cartoon sketch and/or no more than seven words.

EXERCISE TWO 10 X 10 SKETCH METHOD

BACKGROUND

The ideation phase in Design Thinking is the part of the process where you generate ideas. The ideation process involves divergent thinking. In this stage you move from identifying needs that your end users have to generating possible solutions. By exploring as widely as possible initially followed by testing and feedback an innovative solution will be developed.

PROCESS

1. Interpreting needs. Interview five people for 15 minutes each. Identify at one unmet need they each have for a new service or product. Explore how things makes them feel, what they wish could be different, what they enjoy, what gets in their way. Listen and learn, so don't be afraid to ask "Why?"

2. Brainstorm. Select one of the unmet needs that you have identified. Imagine some new solutions that might address your subject's needs. First originate ten possible solutions. Then develop ten variations of each of the four solutions to create a total of at least one hundred possible solutions. Try thinking of the problem in relation to the questions who, what, when, where, why, and how.

3. Consider human needs, business needs and optimum applications of technology.

4. On a piece of paper sketch in a one hour period sketch 100 thumbnail sketches of different ideas in ten rows of ten sketches.

DELIVERABLES

One page with one hundred thumbnail sketches of ideas.

14

PROTOTYPING

THE PROTOTYPING PHASE

Make your ideas tangible with a series of fast, inexpensive prototypes starting as early as possible in the design process.

1. Detect and fix problems early
2. Build fast and cheap.
3. Build, observe, and learn quickly.
4. Get feedback from users.
5. Iterate easily

Design thinking stresses the development of fast low fidelity prototypes and testing them iteratively with stakeholders. Low-fidelity prototypes, are rough representations of concepts that help us to validate those concepts early on in the design process. Low- fidelity prototyping. Unlike high-fidelity prototyping, requires less time, specialized skills and resources. Its purpose is to learn not to sell ideas. Ask diverse stakeholders to give you feedback and use their feedback to improve the designs.

What do you want to learn about? Every prototype should answer a question.

Build prototypes that encourage dialogue about improvements. Give your prototype an unfinished appearance. Prototypes can also be an effective tool if you are rethinking or creating new, complex solutions.

A storyboard or a video can help you convey the basic aspects of more complex and intangible experiences.

You can use the prototype to engage the most important actors in co-creating a new solution, developing, modifying and refining it iteratively in close cooperation.

A prototype is worth a thousand meetings"

IDEO

WHEN TO PROTOTYPE

SERVICE LABORATORY
1. The location doesn't exist
2. The location is not available
3. The location may be inconvenient for users
4. Use of space is under exploration

ON-SITE WHEN
1. The real context is important
2. You can modify the space

NOT REAL END USERS
1. A novel service
2. Everyone is a potential user
3. Cannot recruit real users
4. The hypothesis is unclear.

REAL END USERS WHEN
1. A novel service
2. The value proposition is clear.
3. The target audience has specific needs.
4. Real users are available
5. Failure will not affect the users trust.

USE MOCK-UPS WHEN
1. The object doesn't yet exist.
2. The real thing is too expensive
3. You need to produce something quickly.
4. The object is not a crucial touchpoint.

REAL PROPS WHEN
1. Props exist
2. Props are available
3. They can be change or modified

4. The service experience should be tested with real props.
5. The look and feel of the service will have a strong effect on users.

REAL EMPLOYEES WHEN
1. Their expertise is needed
2. Their skills cannot be imitated
3. The staff are co-creators
4. The goal is to communicate to the employees.

ARTIFICIAL EMPLOYEES WHEN
1. The employees do not exist
2. The prototyping process will hinder the employees
3. The role of the employees is unclear.

LOW-FIDELITY PROTOTYPING

WHAT
Low-fidelity prototyping is a quick and cheap way of gaining insight and informing decision-making without the need for costly investment. Simulates function but not aesthetics of proposed design. Prototypes help compare alternatives and help answer questions about interactions or experiences.

WHY
1. May provide the proof of concept
2. It is physical and visible

3. Inexpensive and fast.
4. Useful for refining functional and perceptual interactions.
5. Assists to identify any problems with the design.
6. Helps to reduce the risks
7. Helps members of team to be in alignment on an idea.
8. Helps make abstract ideas concrete.
9. Feedback can be gained from the user

CHALLENGES

A beautiful prototype completed too early can stand in the way of finding the best design solution.

HOW

1. Construct models, not illustrations
2. Select the important tasks, interactions or experiences to be prototyped.
3. Build to understand problems.
4. If it is beautiful you have invested too much.
5. Make it simple
6. Assemble a kit of inexpensive materials
7. Preparing for a test
8. Select users
9. Conduct test
10. Record notes on the 8x5 cards.
11. Evaluate the results
12. Iterate

SOME LOW FIDELITY PROTOTYPING RESOURCES

WHAT

Here are some suggestions for a kit of materials to help you construct low fidelity prototypes.

1. Copy paper
2. Magnets
3. Masking tape
4. Duct tape
5. Tape
6. Post-it notes
7. Glue sticks
8. Paper clips, (asst colors ideal)
9. Hole punch
10. Scissors
11. Stapler (with staples)
12. Hot glue
13. Glue guns
14. Rulers
15. Pipe Cleaners
16. Colored card
17. Zip ties
18. Foam core sheets
19. Velcro
20. Rubber bands, multicolored
21. Assorted foam shapes
22. Markers
23. Scissors
24. Glue sticks
25. Tape
26. Glue guns
27. Straws
28. Paper Clips
29. Construction Paper
30. ABS sheets
31. Felt
32. Foam sheets
33. String
34. Foil
35. Butcher paper
36. Stickers
37. Pipe cleaners
38. Popsicle sticks
39. Multicolored card

Evelyn Huang. Director of Design
Thinking at Capital One Labs

"

Prototype. Build to think. A simple, cheap and fast way to shape ideas so you can experience and interact with them. Start building: Create an artifact in low resolution. This can be a physical object or a digital clickable sketch. Do it quick and dirty. Storyboard: create a scenario you can role play in a physical environment and let people experience your solution."

Pieter Baert
Strategic Consultant

"

This human-centered methodology, coupled with a 'fail fast' attitude, allows us to quickly identify, build, and test our way to success. We spend less time planning, more time doing, and, above all else, challenge ourselves to see the world through the eyes of our customers every step of the way."

HIGH FIDELITY APPEARANCE PROTOTYPES

WHAT
Appearance prototypes look like but do not work like the final product. The are often fabricated using a variety of rapid prototyping techniques from digital 3d models or by hand in materials such as hard foam, wood or plastics. Usually, appearance prototypes are "for show" and short term use and are not designed to be handled.

CHALLENGES
1. Designers can become too attached to their prototypes and allow them to become jewelry that stands in the way of further refinement.
2. Clients may believe that the design is finalized when more refinement is required.
3. They are expensive to produce,

WHY
May be used to get approval for a final design from a client or to create images for literature or a web site prior to the availability of manufactured products.

HOW

Prototypes give non-designers a good idea of what the production object will look like and feel like.

SERVICE PROTOTYPING

WHAT

Make your ideas tangible with a series of fast, inexpensive prototypes. Ask people to give you feedback and use it to improve the design of the service. In this stage we validate an improve our designs through prototyping, testing and feedback.

There are many different service prototyping tools from acting out scenarios to creating a fully operating beta prototype of the service. A service prototype simulates a service experience over time. Service prototypes are best tested in the real world operating environment or context of the service.

SERVICE STAGING & ROLE PLAY

This techniques involve acting out the service in the real life surroundings. Stakeholders review possible scenarios for the service. Each scenario represents a possible service solution. The stakeholders and design team review and discuss the alternative

SERVICE BLUEPRINTS & EXPERIENCE MAPS

These tools are detailed rwo dimensional representations of the components that make up a working service. They also describe the emotional response of a user of a service.

These tools are also often used in the synthesis stage. Read a detailed description of mapping methods in that chapter.

STORYBOARDS

This is a technique which has been adopted from cinema by service designers. It is a four dimensional techniques that can effectively describe a customer experience from their point of view.

OTHER TECHNIQUES

There are many specialized service design prototyping techniques. In this chapter we describe some techniques that are widely used across different service industries as well as some specialized methods used in particular industries such as web service design.

BODYSTORMING

WHAT
Bodystorming is method of prototyping experiences. It requires setting up an experience - complete with necessary artifacts and people - and physically "testing" it. A design team play out scenarios based on design concepts that they are developing. The method provides clues about the impact of the context on the user experience.

WHO INVENTED IT?
Buchenau, Fulton 2000

WHY
1. You are likely to find new possibilities and problems.
2. Generates empathy for users.
3. This method is an experiential design tool.
4. Bodystorming helps design by exploring context.
5. It is fast and inexpensive.
6. It is a form of physical prototyping
7. It is difficult to imagine misuse scenarios

WHEN
1. Understand-"Where to look"
2. Issue Discovery and identification
3. Observation- "Re-creations"
4. Share Observations from the field
5. Visualization- Bodystorming"

6. Doing generative work: exploring contexts to develop new ideas and uses
7. Evaluation and Refinement- "Debugging"
8. Building scenarios for use; discovering hidden nuances
9. Implementation – Informance"
10. Creating physical performances to communicate developed ideas.

Source: Christine Keene

CHALLENGES
1. Some team members may find acting a difficult task.

HOW
1. Select team.
2. Give everyone a role
3. Define the locations or context where a design will be used.
4. Go to those locations and observe how people interact. the artifacts in their environment.
5. Develop the prototypes and props that you need to explore an idea. Identify the people, personas and scenarios that may help you with insight into the design directions.,
6. Create props, including large cards that identify roles. Create thought-bubble cards to show thoughts vs. saying or doing. Your props can have feelings and thoughts, and they can talk.
7. Have a narrator, or color commentator explain things

to observers.
8. Bodystorm the scenarios.
9. When your group is working through its presentation, try to approach it with the spirit of improv's "Yes, and . . . " rather than "No, but . . . "
10. Perform at least two skits showing a before and after service scenario.
11. Record the scenarios with video and analyze them for insights.

Drucker, P. F. (2007). The Essential Drucker. Oxford: Elsevier Ltd.

Oulasvirta, A., Kurvinen, E., & Kanjaunen, T. (2003). Understanding Contexts by Being There: Case Studies in Bodystorming . Personal Ubiquitous Computing, 7, 125-134.

RESOURCES
Empathy tools
A large room
White-board
Video camera

DARK HORSE PROTOTYPE

WHAT
A dark horse prototype is your most creative idea built as a fast prototype. The innovative approach serves as a focus for finding the optimum real solution to the design problem.

WHO INVENTED IT?
One of the methods taught at Stanford University.

WHY
1. This method is a way of breaking free of average solutions and exploring unknown territory
2. A way of challenging assumptions.

CHALLENGES
1. Fear of unexplored directions
2. Fear of change
1. Designers can become too attached to their prototypes and allow them to become jewelry that stands in the way of further refinement.
2. Client may believe that system is real.

HOW
1. After initial brainstorming sessions select with your team the most challenging, interestingly or thought provoking idea.
2. Build also a prototype of your idea that best balances business, human needs with appropriate use of technology
3. Create a low resolution prototype of the two selected ideas
4. Test with end users
5. With your team analyze and discuss the prototype.
6. Brainstorm ways of bringing back the dark horse concept into a realizable solution.
7. Refine and implement.

EMPATHY TOOLS

WHAT

Empathy tools are aids or tools that help designers empathize with the people they are designing for. With empathic modeling the designer/developer tries to put themselves in the position of the user. They can be used to test a prototype design or in activities such as role playing or body storming.

WHO INVENTED IT?

Brandt, E. and Grunnet, C 2000

WHY

1. To help a designer understand the experiences of people that they are designing for.

CHALLENGES

1. Empathy tools are imperfect approximations of user experiences.

HOW

1. Wear heavy gloves to experience less sensitivity in your hands
2. Wear fogged glasses to experience less acute vision
3. Wear black glasses to eat to experience issues locating food and utensils.
4. Spend a day in a wheelchair.
5. Wear earplugs to experience diminished hearing

SIMULATING IMPAIRMENT

VISUAL IMPAIRMENT

Smearing the lenses of an old pair of glasses with Vaseline can simulate visual impairment due to cataracts. A more permanent pair of glasses can be made by taking an old pair of plastic lensed sunglasses and rubbing them with fine emery or sand paper. This has the added advantage of simulating the greater need for light the elderly eye needs. A scarf or bandage tied over the eyes can simulate blindness.

HEARING IMPAIRMENT

Hearing impairment can be simulated with wax or plastic earplugs Tinnitus can be simulated by recording white noise on an audio tape

MOBILITY IMPAIRMENT

Some of the effects of arthritis can be simulated by taping buttons from clothing to the backs of the joints on the fingers and knuckles and then wear gloves. The buttons make joint movement difficult and painful whilst the gloves reduce tactile sensitivity and make the hands larger. through the use of a wheelchair some of the aspects of mobility restrictions can also be simulated.

LACK OF MOTOR CONTROL

One technique that can be tried is to use the product in an environment where there is vibration or movement.

The effects of dyslexia and other reading problems can be simulated by giving a subject text which has been constructed to emulate the sorts of reading problems such people have e.g. transposition of letters and words.

Source: http://www.idemployee. id.tue.nl/

MAGIC THING

WHAT
• •

A Magic Thing is a prop that is a focus for ideas in the context where an proposed design will be used. It can be a material such as wood or hard foam without surface detail. Participants carry a "magic thing" with them as they undertake their activities in context to imagine how a portable device could function.

WHO INVENTED IT?

Jeff Hawkins. Howard 2002. Jeff Hawkins, one of the inventors of the Palm Pilot PDA, carried a small block of wood to help him brainstorm interaction in various environments.

WHY

It is a form of physical prototype that simulates interaction when little information is available.

CHALLENGES

The researcher can put some imaginary constraints on the device so that it's technological capabilities are not too far from reality.

HOW

1. The researcher briefs the participants on a design scenario.
2. The participants are given a prop, their magic thing.
3. The participants are briefed on the technological capabilities of the magic thing.
4. The participants and design team then act out scenarios in context.
5. The role playing is recorded by video or user diaries.
6. The material is analyzed and insights identified.

RESOURCES

A magic thing such as a block of wood about the size of a proposed device.
Video camera

PICTIVE

PICTIVE (Plastic Interface for Collaborative Technology Initiative through Video Exploration) is a low fidelity participatory design method used to develop graphical user interfaces. It allows users to participate in the development process. A PICTIVE prototype gives a user a sense of what a system or a piece of software will look like and how it will behave when completed.

WHO INVENTED IT?

Developed by Michael J. Muller and others at Bell Communications Research around 1990

WHY

7. Less development time.
8. Less development costs.
9. Involves users.
10. Gives quantifiable user feedback.
11. Facilitates system implementation since users know what to expect.
12. Results user oriented solutions.
13. Gets users with diverse experience involved.

HOW

1. A PICTIVE is usually made from simple available tools and materials like pens, paper, Post-It stickers, paper clips and icons on cards.
2. Allow thirty minutes for initial design.
3. Allow ten minutes for user testing.
4. Ten minutes for modification.
5. Five minutes for user testing.
6. Create task scenario.
7. Anything that moves or changes should be a separate element.
8. The designer uses these materials to represent elements such as drop-down boxes, menu bars, and special icons. During a design session, users modify the mock up based on their own experience.
9. Take notes for later review.
10. Record the session with a video camera
11. The team then reviews the ideas and develops a strategy to apply them.
12. A PICTIVE enables non technical people to participate in the design process.

ROLE PLAYING

WHAT
Role playing is a research method where the researcher physically acts out the interaction or experience of the user of a product, service or experience. It is a type of prototyping, a narrative or story about how people may experience a design in a particular future context. Role playing can be used to predict or explore future interactions with concept products or services.

WHY
1. Role playing helps a designer gain empathy and insights into the experience of the user.
2. Useful for unfamiliar situations.
3. It is a physical activity so may uncover insights not apparent when using storyboarding
4. It helps designers empathize with the intended users and their context.
5. Is an inexpensive method requiring few resources.

CHALLENGES
1. It is difficult to envision all the ways a product or service could be misused.
2. Some people feel self conscious when asked to role play

HOW
1. Identify the situation.
2. Identify scenarios and tasks users undertake.
3. Create storyboards.
4. Assign roles.
5. Isolate moments where the users interact with the product or service.
6. Use your own intuitive responses to iterate and refine the design.
7. This method can be used to test physical prototypes.
8. You can act out the tasks in the environments or context of use.
9. You can use empathy tools such as glasses to simulate the effects of age or a wheelchair.
10. Consider typical misuse cases.
11. Discuss insights.

RESOURCES
Notepad computer
Pens
Video camera
Empathy tools

STORYBOARDS

WHAT
The storyboard is a narrative tool derived from cinema. A storyboard is a form of prototyping which communicates each step of an activity, experience or interaction. Used in films and multimedia as well as product and UX design. Storyboards consists of a number of 'frames' that communicate a sequence of events in context.

WHO INVENTED IT?
Invented by Walt Disney in 1927. Disney credited animator

Webb Smith with creating the first storyboard. By 1937-38 all studios were using storyboards.

WHY

1. Can help gain insightful user feedback.
2. Conveys an experience.
3. Can use a storyboard to communicate a complex task as a series of steps.
4. Allows the proposed activities to be discussed and refined.
5. Storyboards can be used to help designers identify opportunities or use problems.

HOW

1. Decide what story you want to describe.
2. Choose a story and a message: what do you want the storyboard to express?
3. Create your characters
4. Think about the whole story first rather than one panel at a time.
5. Create the drafts and refine them through an iterative process. Refine.
6. Illustrations can be sketches or photographs.
7. Consider: Visual elements, level of detail, text, experiences and emotions, number of frames, and flow of time.
8. Keep text short and informative.
9. 6 to 12 frames.
10. Tell your story efficiently and effectively.
11. Brainstorm your ideas.

THINK OUT LOUD PROTOCOL

WHAT

Think aloud or thinking out loud protocols involve participants verbalizing their thoughts while performing a set of tasks. Users are asked to say whatever they are looking at, thinking, doing, and feeling. A related but method is the talk-aloud protocol where participants describe their activities but do not give explanations. This method is thought to be more objective

WHO INVENTED IT?

Clayton Lewis IBM 1993

WHY

1. Helps a researcher understand interaction with a product or service,.
2. Enables observers to see first-hand the process of task completion
3. The terminology the user uses to express an idea or function the design or and documentation.
4. Allows testers to understand how the user approaches the system.

CHALLENGES

1. The design team needs to be composed of persons with a variety of skills.
2. Pick a diverse, cross

STORYBOARD TEMPLATE

PROJECT

NAME

DATE

DIALOGUE

DIALOGUE

DIALOGUE

ACTION

ACTION

ACTION

PROJECT

NAME

DATE

DIALOGUE

DIALOGUE

DIALOGUE

ACTION

ACTION

ACTION

PROJECT

NAME

DATE

DIALOGUE

DIALOGUE

DIALOGUE

ACTION

ACTION

ACTION

TYPES OF STORIES

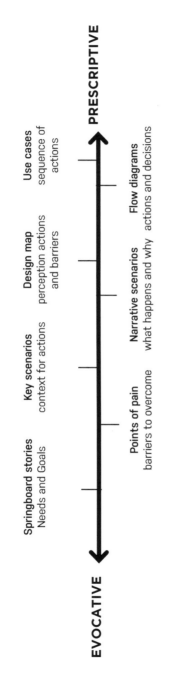

PRESCRIPTIVE

Use cases
sequence of actions

Design map
perception actions and barriers

Key scenarios
context for actions

Springboard stories
Needs and Goals

Flow diagrams
actions and decisions

Narrative scenarios
what happens and why

Points of pain
barriers to overcome

EVOCATIVE

Adapted from The Personas Lifecycle Pruitt, J., Adlin, T.

❝

And then in the whole project, which can sometimes be multiple years long, the most significant change happens when you bring into a room, a model. A lot of people can't understand drawings, completely. So, with a model you go through this dramatic shift where you go from something exclusive, to suddenly you have something which is inclusive, which suddenly can galvanize people; and at last everyone is looking at the same thing; rather than just looking around and wondering when they're going to be done!"

Sir Jonathan Ive
Apple VP of Design
2017 Soundcloud Interview

disciplinary team.

WHEN
1. Know Context
2. Know User
3. Frame insights
4. Explore Concepts

HOW
1. Identify users.
2. Choose Representative Tasks.
3. Create a Mock-Up or Prototype.
4. Select Participants.
5. Provide the test users with the system or prototype to be tested and tasks.
6. Brief participants.
7. Take notes of everything that users say, without attempting to interpret their actions and words.
8. Iterate
9. Videotape the tests, then analyze the videotapes.

RESOURCES
Computer
Video camera
Notepad computer
Pens

TYPES OF MODELS

3D Sketch Model
3D sketch models are 3D visual design representations that represent an idea.

Design development model
Design development models are 3D visual design representations used to understand the relationships between

Appearance Model
Appearance models are 3d visual design representations used to understand the relationships between components, cavities, interfaces, structure and form.

Functional concept model
Functional concept models are 3D visual design representations that show functionality and highlight important functional parameters including yield and performance factors.

Concept of operation model
Concept of operation models are 3D visual design representations that help communicate an understanding of the operational strategies and usage procedures relating to the product.

Production concept model
Production concept models are 3D visual design representations used to help assist the evaluation of production processes or manufacturing technologies for final

Assembly concept model
Assembly concept models are 30 visual design representations that provide confidence regarding the component relationships in terms of assembly, cost and investment.

Service concept model
Service concept models are 30

visual design representations that illustrate how the product may be serviced or maintained.

TYPES OF PROTOTYPES

Appearance prototype
Appearance prototypes are highly detailed, full-scale 30 visual design representations that combine function and aesthetics.

Alpha prototype
Alpha prototypes are 3D visual design representations used to verify the outlook and construction of sub-systems thai have been individually proven and accepted with the materials aesthetics and layout for the product

Beta prototype
beta prototypes are full-scale and fully-functional 30 visual design representations constructed from the actual materials and used to examine how the product would be used in its intended environment and to work out regulatory issues .

Pre-production prototype
pre-production prototypes are final 30 visual design representations used to check the product and its finishing as a whole and to perform production and assembly assessment
in small batches.

Experimental prototype
Experimental prototypes are 30 visual design representations that parameterizes the layout or shape of a product, usually to replicate the actual product's physics.

System prototype
System prototypes are 3D visual design representations that combines the numerous components specified for the final product to test and assess functional aspects such as mechanism and performance

Final hardware Prototype
Final hardware prototypes are 30 visual design representations used to assist in the design and evaluation of product fabrication and other assembly issues.

Text-based scenarios

Flowchart

Paper prototypes

Storyboard

Foam model

Dramatization

Concept prototype

Explainer video
Create a catchy and concise video explaining your idea.

Talking sketch
Use graphics to make complex

ideas quickly understandable.

Roleplay
Act out your idea in front
of an audience or camera.

Storyboard
Describe how the user
interacts with your idea

Scale model
Show form, arrangement and
working at a smaller scale.

Virtual/augmented reality
Use projections or VR goggles
for an immersive experience.

Product hack
Make adjustments to an
existing product.

Foam model
Express a general form using
foam, clay or other materials.

Feasibility prototype
Determine feasibility of various
solutions Proof of concept for
specific

Operational model
Performs desired functionalities
for usability testing.

Appearance model
Accurate physical representation
of product appearance.

Wizard of Oz

Interact with a prototype
operated by a hidden person.

3D-printed model
Computer generated design
with a realistic touch.

Wireframes
A wireframe is a bare bones
description of a web page

Role playing
Physically act out scenarios, by
vocalizing sounds, moving body
parts etc in order to determine
physical and temporal properties
of the desired experience.

*Source: 4 into 35 Does Go:
Extending Sketches, Drawings,
Models and Prototypes to Define a
Taxonomy of 35 Design
Representations for Improved
Communication during New
Product Development
Dr. Mark Evans, Eujin Pei and Dr.
R. Ian Campbell Department of
Design & Technology, Loughborough
University, United Kingdom.*

VIDEO PROTOTYPING

....

Video prototypes use video to illustrate how users will interact with a new system. Video prototypes can be thought of as sketches that illustrate what the interaction with the new system will be like.

WHY

1. Capturing an experience over time requires a linear medium like video

2. Video prototypes are a good way of communicating a complex system of interactions in an easy to access way that can be shared with a large number of people.

RESOURCES

1. Video camera
2. Smartphone camera
3. Card for titles
4. Simple props
5. Actors
6. Lights
7. Post-it-notes

HOW

1. Choose a director and a camera person.
2. Decide who the actors are and who will create the storyboard and props.
3. Decide how you will communicate the story: title-cards only, an off-camera voice-over or through dialog.

4. Storyboard the sequence of shots.

5. Begin by shooting the initial title card 4 seconds with the name of the project, group, date, time and version number.

6. Shoot a title card 6 seconds that identifies the personas and the context.

7. Shoot an establishing shot that shows the user(s) in context.

8. Shoot the series of interaction points that tell the story and communicate the interaction.

9. Use mid shots to show conversation and close-ups to show devices.

10. "editing-in-the-camera" involves shooting each sequence of the video prototype in the order that it will be viewed,so that it does not need to be edited afterward.

11. Some video prototypes use a narrator or voice over, others use only title cards others rely on the actors to explain interactions.

WIREFRAMING

WHAT
Website wireframes are a simplified outline of the elements of a web page. They are useful for communicating the functionality of a website in order to get feedback on the design. The wireframe depicts the page layout, interface and navigation, and how these elements interact in use.

WHO INVENTED IT?
Matthew Van Horn claims to have invented the term around 1994 in New York.

WHY
1. Wireframes are useful for getting feedback on a design.
2. Wireframes can speed up the iteration process of a website design.
3. Enable on-line collaboration
4. Helps Identify needed changes early on in the development.
5. Wireframes are low cost

CHALLENGES
1. Notes to explain behavior are useful
2. Wireframes do not explain interactive details involving movement.

HOW
1. There are a several ways to create wireframes. These include drawing by hand. Using Adobe Photoshop or Illustrator and using wireframe software.
2. Start by listing all of the elements that you want on your website.
3. Use simple boxes or outlines of the shape of elements, and name them. These elements can include: navigation: buttons, Company logo: can just be represented by a box, content areas and search box.
4. Review your design and adjust as necessary.
5. Make wireframe for each page in your site.

RESOURCES
Paper
Pens
Wireframe software
Computer

CHAPTER SUMMARY

1. The word "prototype" comes from the Greek prototypos4 , a compound of protos ("first") and typos ("mold," "pattern," "impression").
2. During this phase we will start to make our ideas real so we can get feedback from stakeholders.
3. Make your ideas tangible with a series of fast, inexpensive prototypes starting as early as possible in the design process.
4. Detect and fix problems early
5. Build fast and cheap.
6. Build, observe, and learn quickly.
7. Get feedback from users Iteratively then refine and retest.
8. Design thinking stresses the development of fast low fidelity prototypes and testing them iteratively with stakeholders.
9. A storyboard or a video can help you convey the basic aspects of more complex and intangible experiences.
10. Every prototype should answer a question.

CHAPTER REVIEW

1. 'Why do we build prototypes?
2. What is a low fidelity prototype?
3. What are some materials we can use to build a low fidelity prototype?
4. Who do we test prototypes with?
5. What is iterative prototyping?
6. What are three ways that we can prototype intangible services and experiences?
7. What is bodystorming?
8. Why do we use bodystorming?
9. What is Dark horse prototyping.
10. Why do we use dark horse prototyping?
11. What is role playing?
12. What is the think out loud protocol.
13. Why do we use the think out loud protocol?
14. What is wireframing?
15. Why do we use wireframing?

EXERCISE ONE
LOW-FIDELITY PROTOTYPE

TASK

Create a low fidelity prototype of your favored design

Here are some suggestions for a kit of materials to help you construct low fidelity prototypes

1. Copy paper
2. Magnets
3. Snaps
4. Masking tape
5. Duct tape
6. Tape
7. Post-it notes
8. Glue sticks
9. Paper clips
10. Decorative brads (square, crystal)
11. Hole punch
12. Scissors
13. Stapler (with staples)
14. Hot glue
15. Glue guns
16. Pipe Cleaners
17. Colored card
18. Zip ties
19. Rubber bands, multicolored
20. Assorted foam shapes
21. Markers
22. Paper Clips
23. Construction Paper
24. ABS sheets
25. Felt
26. Foam sheets
27. String
28. Foil
29. Butcher paper
30. Popsicle sticks

OBTAIN FEEDBACK

Use some of the materials on the facing page to make a fast prototype of your design. Show the prototype to five people and ask them to answer the following questions.

What works in the design?
1.
2.
3.
4.

What doesn't work in the design?
1.
2.
3.
4.

What refinements should be made?
1.
2.
3.
4.

EXERCISE ONE USABILITY TEST PLAN

BACKGROUND

The purpose of the test plan is to document what you are going to do, how you are going to conduct the test, what metrics you are going to capture, number of participants you are going to test, and what scenarios you will use.

The researcher meets with the team and stakeholders to decide on the major elements of the plan. The researcher then drafts the plan, and circulates it to the team and stakeholders for comments. The researcher revises the written plan to reflect the final decisions.

TASKS

1. Elements of a test plan
2. You will need to include these elements in the usability test plan.
3. Scope: indicate what you are testing.
4. Purpose: identify the concerns, questions, and goals for this test.
5. Schedule & location: indicate when and where you will do the test. I
6. Sessions: you will want to describe the sessions, the length of the sessions (typically one hour to 90 minutes). When scheduling participants, remember to leave time, usually 30 minutes, between session to reset the environment,
7. Equipment: indicate the type of equipment you will be using in the test;
8. Participants: Indicate the number and types of participants to be tested you will be recruiting. Describe how these participants will be recruited a
9. Scenarios: Indicate the number and types of tasks included in testing. Typically, for a 60 min. test, you should end up with approximately 10 (+/-2) scenarios for desktop or laptop testing and 8 (+/-2) scenarios for a mobile/smartphone test.
10. Metrics: Include the questions you are going to ask the participants prior to the sessions, after each task scenario is completed and overall ease, satisfaction and likelihood to use/recommend questions when the sessions is completed.
11. Quantitative metrics: Indicate the quantitative data you will be measuring in your test (e.g., successful completion rates, error rates, time on task).
12. Roles: Include a list of the staff who will participate in the usability testing and what role each will play.

DELIVERABLES

One usability test plan of 2 to pages.

Sources include www.usability.gov user testing

15
TESTING & ITERATION

USABILITY TESTING

WHAT

Usability testing helps improve a design to make it more usable. Real users undertake particular tasks. Researchers and other stakeholders observe and collect data.

GOALS
Meet with stakeholders, to define your goals.
1. Who uses the product or service?
2. What are their needs and goals?
3. What tasks does the user need to perform?
4. Where are the problems?

PROCESS
1. Develop a test plan
2. Choose a testing space
3. Recruit participants
4. Prepare test materials
5. Conduct the tests
6. Debrief participants
7. Analyze data
8. Conclusions and recommendations

WHAT TO TEST
1. Low-fidelity prototype or paper prototype
2. Wireframes
3. High-fidelity prototype and experience system.
4. Alpha and Beta prototypes.
5. Test competitor's designs

6. Test in the real context of use.
7. Test iteratively
8. Use heuristics and usability guidelines.
9. Test the final design

HOW MANY TO TEST
Test at least four people from each user group.

DIAGNOSTIC EVALUATION
1. Test 4-6 users
2. Find and fix problems
3. When? During design development
4. Test iteratively

SUMMATIVE TESTING
1. How many? 6-12 users
2. Metrics based on usability goals
3. Test to measure the success of a design.
4. When? At end of process
5. Test once

Source: Ginny Redish

DESIGN THE TEST
Document your test plan checklist Test participants tasks under controlled conditions.

WHERE
Usability tests can take place in a lab, conference room, quiet office space, or a quiet public space.

SCENARIOS AND TASKS
Tasks are the activities that

your participants undertake. Scenarios frame tasks and provide motivation.

TIPS FOR WRITING SCENARIOS
Start with a scenario. Scenarios should be a story that provides motivation to your participants. The scenario is a narrative that explains the background of the task in a real world situation. Create believable scenarios. Keep them simple.

WRITING TASKS
Categories:
1. Prescribed tasks. You determine what the participant will do.
2. Participant defined Have them do the task they describe.
3. Open ended Participants organically explore the activity based on a scenario you provide.

The order of tasks should follow a natural flow of product use. Don't use jargon. Provide information as needed. Avoid leading the participant.

SELECT DATA TO CAPTURE
Log:
1. Task start and end points
2. Milestones
3. Errors
4. Failures
5. Problems
6. Requests for help

QUALITATIVE DATA
Record behavior, reactions, cody

language.

SUCCESS PATHS
Is there only one or several success paths?

RECRUIT PARTICIPANTS
Select participants who represent typical novice average and experienced users.

RECRUITMENT IDEAS
1. Contact databases
2. Recruitment agencies
3. Craig's List
4. Your web site
5. Media ads
6. Identify the target criteria for your participants.

SCREENER.
Filter the participants with a screener.

COMPENSATION
Motivate participants with cash, a gift certificate or products.

SETTING
Pick a large room with good natural lighting and low background noise.

SCHEDULE PARTICIPANTS
Allow time for contingencies between sessions.

STAKEHOLDERS
Brief stakeholders that their task is to observe. The facilitator may interact with participants or not interact.

OBSERVERS
Enlist one person to log

observations. Create a list of stakeholders. Observing testing helps make the team make improvements to the design. Do not change the design until you understand the meaning of your observations.

SCRIPT
Create a facilitator script .

QUESTIONNAIRES AND SURVEYS
A typically usability study usually has at least two surveys (questionnaires), one administered before the participant starts tasks and one administered at the end of the test,

PRE-TEST SURVEY
Collects demographic and product usage data about participants s

POST-TASK SURVEY
Questions about the usability and satisfaction related to test tasks. Collect only data that you can legally collect. Use age ranges rather than specific ages when asking participants for their age. Include comment fields

RUN-THROUGH
Run through your test yourself to make sure the tasks make sense Conduct a pilot test with a participant. Allow time before the test session to make changes.

TEST SESSION
1. Welcome participant
2. Use the script

3. Ask participants to fill out the consent form with a non-disclosure agreement.
4. Allow enough time

FACILITATION
Keep the participant focused. Participants may be asked to keep a running commentary or "think-aloud" protocol
Ask open ended questions
What are you thinking?
What are you trying to do?
What did you expect to happen?
Keep neutral and do not show emotion, approval or disapproval.

TASK FAILURES
If a participant fails a task ask them to do the task again.

AFTER THE SESSION
Debrief with observers.
Clean the space.

ANALYSIS
1. Review observations
2. Identify problems
3. Identify solutions.

RECOMMENDATIONS
Make sure your recommendations should address the underlying cause of the problem. Keep recommendations short and concise. Use video, wireframes and other visual means to illustrate your conclusions. Recommendations should be objective and evidence based.

RECRUITMENT SCRIPT
Hello, may I speak with X We are looking for participants to take part in a research study

evaluating the usability of the X Product. There will be $xx payment for the hour long session, which will take the X Building located downtown. The session would involve one-on-one meeting with a researcher where you would sit down in front of a computer and try to use a product while being observed and answering
questions about the product. Would you be interested in participating? If not: Thank you for taking the time to speak with me. If you know of anyone else who might be interested in participating please have them call me, at xxx-xxx-xxxx

SCREENING SCRIPT

I need to ask you a couple of questions to determine whether you meet the eligibility criteria— Do you have a couple of minutes? If not: When is a good time to call back? Keep in mind that your answers to these questions to not automatically allow or disallow you take part in the study—we just need accurate information about your background, so please answer as well as you can.
Have you ever used X product? If yes:
How long have you used it for? [criteria: at least 1 yr.] And how often do you use it? [criteria: at least 3 times a month] If no:
Have you ever used any data processing products, such as [list competitor or similar products]? [criteria: Yes]

If yes: How long have you used it for? [criteria: at least 1 yr.] And how often do you use it? [criteria: at least 3 times a month] Self-identify participant gender via voice and name and other cues.

SCHEDULING

If participant meets criteria: Will you be able to come to the X Building located downtown for one hour between May 15 and 19? Free parking is available next to the building. How is [name available times and dates]? You will be participating in a one-on-one usability test session on [date and time]. Do you require any special accommodations? I need to have an e-mail address to send specific directions and confirmation information to. Thanks again! If participant does not meet criteria: Unfortunately, you do not fit the criteria for this particular evaluation and will not be able to participate. Thank you for taking the time to speak with me.

PARTICIPANT RECRUITMENT SCREENER

The usability test of the X Product requires 12 participants from 2 user groups.

User type experienced Product users Number 6 Characteristics current product users/customers who have used x product For at least 1 year and use it at least 3 times a month

3 males, 3 females

User type New product
users
Number 6
Characteristics People who
have no prior experience with
X Product, but do have at least 1
year's experience using similar
products
(e.g. data processing tools).
3 males, 3 females

THINK OUT LOAD SCRIPT

When you are doing the testing
there may be times that you
become frustrated or confused,
but you do not say anything,
We want you to say it out loud
so we can see the problem and
improve the design. We only can
recognize what you tell us is a
problem. Let us know what you
are thinking. There here are no
wrong answers. We're looking for
your genuine impressions. Your
comments will help us improve
the design.

Source: Usability Testing Basics.

ALPHA TESTING

WHAT
The alpha is a low fidelity
prototype with enough
resolution to give your
intended audience an
understanding of how the
service will work. An alpha
prototype has some of the
required features integrated
into the prototype for
testing.

An alpha prototype allows us to:
4. Explore the major risks
5. Discover whether the project
   is viable
6. Cost of the project
7. Identify risks

This document covers how to
go about executing an alpha
project. With an alpha prototype
we begin the testing process. The
alpha prototype gives you the
opportunity to test your proposed
design with your intended
audience. The alpha is used to
resolve important technical
challenges.

The alpha prototype will give you
a clear idea of what is required for
the beta prototype.

Some questions:
1. Is the concept the best
   solution?
2. Will the concept work?
3. Do you have a clear
   understanding of your

customer's needs?

4. Do you need a second prototype to refine the direction?

WHY CREATE A BETA?

A beta prototype has most of the required features integrated into the prototype.

1. Do people want the design solution?
2. Is the investment warranted?
3. Does it meet the user's expectations?
4. What are the risks?
5. Does the design respond correctly in situations unforeseen during the development?

Involve a wide range of stakeholders both internally and externally. Present workshops with stakeholders to get feedback and refine your design. Sometimes an alpha prototype may lead you to reject your design direction but more commonly it will help you refine the design through a second or beta prototype.

DURATION

The duration will vary but for software development testing may require a 6 to 8 week period.

TEAM REQUIREMENTS

Keep the team small and multidisciplinary so the development is agile including a variety of stakeholders.

OUTPUT

The outputs for the alpha phase are:

1. Story cards
2. Functioning system that provides that can be shown to a number of stakeholders
3. Decision whether a beta prototype is necessary.
4. Analysis of user needs

GOALS

Define your goals clearly before testing.

IDENTIFYING RISKS

One of the purposes of the alpha prototype is to define the greatest risks and to explore those risks.

Risks may include:

1. Risks associated with usability
2. Business risks
3. Technical risks

It make take several iterations to solve the user problems.

1. Is it easy to use and understand?
2. What are the user errors?
3. What is the meaning of the user research?
4. How can I build a prototype most efficiently?

how to operate the service
The technical risks tend to be about integrating into the existing systems. For example:

THE TEAM

The well-rounded team will need to have skills, including:

1. Design

2. User research
3. User journey
4. Prototyping skills
5. Service integration
6. Implementation management
7. Business skills

Try to complete testing and iterations in one week cycles.

The team must have the core skills to:

PROCESS
Alphas consist of:
1. Inception
2. Iterations design, development and test
3. Alpha termination or
4. Alpha to Beta transition
5. Execution

During the inception the team shares information about hopes and hurdles.
The inception phase should take no longer than 7 days.
and should will look at a variety of business, technical and user aspects of the project.
1. Shared understanding of the service
2. Personas
3. a clarified current business process (where applicable)
4. Goals
5. Understanding of technology

The facilitator will of course give up time to various specialists to run individual sessions. The aims include:

You can run a warming up exercise to help the team get to know each other.

ITERATIONS
Alphas are help clarify alternative design directions Expect to produce several prototypes
If the prototype is uncovering faults in your design then it is doing its job. To iterate faster create lower fidelity prototypes such as paper prototypes.
Rework the experience map at the end of each user testing cycle.

ENDING THE ALPHA
The alpha process helps identify the risks to the Beta program. At the end of the alpha testing the team should be able to show what the alpha has achieved and the feasibility of the beta program.

BETA TESTING

WHAT
The Beta prototype is the prototype that you will test in public and prepare to go live.

OBJECTIVE
The objective of this phase is to build a fully working service which you test with real customers.

You should be rapidly releasing updates and improvements and testing the impact of your changes.

A beta should involve testing a full, end-to-end version of the service.

PRIVATE BETA
This is a beta testing by invitation only. You might want to do private testing if:

1. gives more control over the audience demographic that gets to use the beta
2. allows you to restrict the volume of transactions
3. lets you start small and faster

PUBLIC BETA
A public beta is available to everyone.

You may make further refinements before going live.

TEAM
Include designers, developers, web operations specialists and performance analysts as appropriate.

OUTPUT
At the end of the beta phase, you'll have:
1. Delivered an end-to-end service
2. A user testing plan
3. Metrics
4. A working system that can be used, by real end users

DATA ANALYSIS

CODING
1. Read through the text data. Divide the text into segments of information.
2. Label the segments with codes

CLUSTERING
1. After open coding an entire text, make a list of all code words.
2. Assign a code word or phrase that accurately describes the meaning of the text segment (30 to 40 codes)
3. Objective: reduce the long list of codes to a smaller, more manageable number (25 or 30)
4. Reduce the overlap and redundancy of codes(reduce to 20 codes) Cluster together similar codes and look for redundant codes

THEMES
Themes are similar codes aggregated together to form a major idea. Themes can also be referred to as categories.
The process of looking for categories that cut across all data sets. You can't classify something as a theme unless it cuts across the preponderance of the data.(5 to 7 themes)
This core is a theoretical

framework that further guides the research and design process.

Name the themes. The names can come from at least three sources:

The researcher

The participants

Most common: when the researcher comes up with terms, concepts, and categories that reflect what he or she sees in the data

Themes should Reflect the purpose of the research

Be exhaustive--you must place all data in a category

TYPES OF THEMES

1. Ordinary: themes a researcher expects
2. Unexpected: themes that are surprises and not expected to surface
3. Hard-to-classify: themes that contain ideas that do not easily fit into one theme or that overlap with several themes
4. Major & minor themes: Themes that represent the major ideas, or minor, secondary ideas in a database.
5. Codes such as "seating arrangements," "teaching approach," or "physical layout of the room," might all be used to describe a classroom where instruction takes place

DISPLAY THE DATA VISUALLY

1. Comparison table or matrix
2. Hierarchical tree diagram that represents themes and their connections
3. Boxes that show connections between themes
4. Physical layout of the setting
5. Personal or demographic information for each person or site

VALIDATE YOUR FINDINGS

1. Prolonged engagement & persistent observation in the field
2. Triangulation
3. Peer Review
4. Clarifying researcher bias
5. Member Checking
6. Rich, thick description
7. External Audit

"In qualitative research, a single case or small nonrandom sample is selected precisely because the researcher wishes to understand the particular in depth, not to find out what is generally true of the many" (Merriam, 1998, p. 208).

TRIANGULATION

Use of two or more independent sources of data or data collection methods to corroborate research findings within a study. The researcher looks for patterns of convergence to develop or corroborate an overall interpretation

REPORT

Write a qualitative report providing detailed information about a few themes rather than general information about many themes. Written account should include sufficient data to allow the reader to judge whether the interpretation offered is adequately supported by the data.

TEST PLAN

WHAT

A usability test plan is a type of research plan that explains what testing will be done, the reasons for the testing, who will be tested, the timeline and other factors. It helps ensure that team, client and stakeholders are in alignment on what needs to be tested and why.

SCOPE

Indicate what you are testing Specify how much of the service the test will cover.

PURPOSE

Identify the concerns, questions, and goals for this test. These can be quite broad or specific Identify your focus. Base your test scenarios on your gaols and focus.

SCHEDULE & LOCATION

Indicate when and where you will do the test. How many sessions and when will they be held?

SESSIONS

Describe the sessions, sessions are often 60 to 90 minutes. Allow 30 minutes contingency between sessions.

EQUIPMENT

Computer, phone,. Are you planning on recording the session?

PARTICIPANTS

1. Number and types of participants to be tested you will be recruiting.
2. How will they be recruited?
3. Screener.

SCENARIOS

Number and types of tasks included in testing.

For a 60 min. test, you should have 10 (+/-2) scenarios for desktop or laptop testing and 8 (+/- 2) scenarios for a mobile/smart phone test. Include more in the test plan so the team can choose the appropriate tasks.

METRICS

Subjective metrics Include the questions you are going to ask the participants prior to the sessions

QUANTITATIVE METRICS

Successful completion rates, error rates, time on task.

ROLES

A list of the staff involved in the usability testing and what role each will play.

Few ideas work on the first try. Iteration is key to innovation."

Sebastian Thrun
Director of the Artificial Intelligence Laboratory at Stanford University

APPRECIATIVE INQUIRY

WHAT

Appreciative Inquiry is an evaluation method which focuses on strengths rather than on weaknesses.

"

Appreciative Inquiry (AI) is a group process that inquires into, identifies and further develops the best of "what is" in organizations in order to create a better future. Often used in the organization development field as an approach to large-scale change, it is a means for addressing issues, challenges, changes and concerns of an organization in ways that builds on the successful, effective and energizing experiences of its members. Underlying AI is a belief that the questions we ask are critical to the world we create."

Preskill & Catsambas 2006

HOW

1. Discover
- What gives life?
- What is the best?
- Appreciating and identifying processes that work well.

2. Dream
- What might be?

- What is the world calling for? Envisioning results, and how things might work well in the future.

3. Design
- What should be--the ideal? Co-constructing - planning and prioritizing processes that would work well.

4. Deliver
- How to empower, learn and adjust/improvise?
- Sustaining the change

Source: The 4-D Model was developed by Suresh Srivastva, Ron Fry, and David Cooperrider

USER ASSESSMENT

WHAT

An approach that assesses the value of ideas as perceived by the intended end users, allowing them to voice to their priorities and concerns.

HOW

1. Prototyping
2. User Interviews
3. User observation

Source: Toward a Listening Bank: A review of best practices and the efficacy of Beneficiary Assessment, World Bank, 1998

USER WORKSHOPS

WHAT

Horizontal evaluation is an

EVALUATION OF USABILITY TESTING

NAME	WHAT'S MEASURED	WHEN TO USE
TASK SUCCESS	Whether or not the participant was successful, and to what degree. (For example, completed with ease, completed with difficulty, failed to complete.)	Critical when effectiveness of the product is a primary goal.
TIME ON TASK	The length of time it takes the participant to complete a task. May be averaged for all participants, and can be compared between tests.	Critical when efficiency is a primary usability goal, and when efficiency is a primary influence on satisfaction.
ERRORS	A count of the errors each participant makes in each task. Errors may be categorized or predefined.	Critical to both efficiency and effectiveness, use this measure when you want to minimize the problems a user may encounter in the product.
LEARNABILITY	A task is repeated at least once to determine whether the time on task is shorter, fewer errors are made, or the task is more successful.	Important to measure whether the interface will be easier to use over time.
SATISFACTION	Enumerates participants' overall feelings about a product before, during and/or after a test.	Allows the participants to quantify and describe their emotional reaction to a product before, during or after a study.
MOUSE CLICKS	Measures the number of clicks that a participant makes.	Measures the effectiveness and efficiency of a product, suggests that a participant was able to accomplish a task with less effort.
MOUSE MOVEMENT	Measures the distance the mouse travels.	Measures efficiency, suggests that a participant was able to accomplish a task with less effort.
PROBLEM/ ISSUE COUNTS	Records, counts, ranks and/or categorizes problems observed.	Provides an overview of the issues that may be causing other measures to be less ideal. Allows comparison across studies to determine improvement. These are often weighted by how severe an issue may be.
OPTIMAL PATH	Observes the path a participant takes to accomplish a task, and compares it to a predefined optimal path.	Measures the variance from the ideal path.

Source: Techsmith

approach that combines self-assessment by end users and external review by peers through a three-day workshop.

The facilitator first .
1. Identifies the appropriate process.
2. Selects participants .

HOW
Day 1
3. At the start of the event, the facilitator introduces the objectives and the process.
4. S/he encourages the visitors to be critical but constructive by identifying the strengths and positive aspects of the methodology as well as its weaknesses.
5. S/he also encourages the local participants to be open and receptive to comments and suggestions.

Day 2
Field visits: Field visits provide the opportunity for visitors to see first hand the methodology under development and to talk with users.
Visitors conduct semi-structured interviews and observe what they see.

Day 3
Comparative analysis.
separately identify strengths,

weaknesses and suggestions for improvement. Each group is asked to limit itself to identifying no more than six strengths, six weaknesses and six suggestions for each evaluation criterion.

Participants present their findings in separate sessions. The facilitator then helps all participants to identify convergent and divergent ideas.

WHY

1. Overcomes some of the failings of 'external expert-led' evaluations.
2. Facilitates the sharing of information, experiences and knowledge, interactive learning.
3. Facilitates the building of trust and sense of community
4. Promotes ownership of results.
5. Creates the conditions for the adaptation.

Horizontal Evaluation: Stimulating social learning among peers. - Thiele, G. et al. (2006). ILAC Brief 13. ILAC, Bioveristy

EYE TRACKING

.... WHAT ....
Eye tracking is a group of methods of studying and recording a person's eye movements over time. The most widely used current designs are video-based eye trackers. One of the most prominent fields of commercial eye tracking research is web usability but this method is also used widely for evaluating retail interiors and products.

WHO INVENTED IT?
Louis Émile Javal 1879
Alfred L. Yarbus 1950s

WHY
1. Examine which details attract attention.
2. To record where a participant's attention is focused . For example on a supermarket shelf eye tracking can reveal which products colors and graphics attract the most attention from shoppers.

CHALLENGES
1. Each method of eye tracking has advantages and disadvantages, and the choice of an eye tracking system depends on considerations of cost and application.
2. A poorly adjusted system can produce unreliable information.

TYPES OF SYSTEMS
1. Measures eye movement with a device attached to the eye. For example a contact lens with a magnetic field sensor.
2. Non contact measurement of eye movement. For example infrared, is reflected from the eye and sensed by a video camera.
3. Measures eye movement with electrodes placed around the eyes.

TYPES OF OUTPUTS
1. Heat maps
2. Gaze plots
3. Gaze replays

EYE TRACKING BEST PRACTICES
1. Choose an office with good, but not overly bright lighting. Too much light could impact the eye tracker.
2. Seat the participant in a stationary chair without wheels, leaning or swivel capability.
3. Implement a pilot test to make sure you are comfortable with setting up, calibrating and testing well in advance of your participants' arrival.
4. You will in all likelihood need to adjust the chair, monitor, and equipment to properly calibrate the eye tracker. Let the participant know this at the outset. Allowing time to do this properly is imperative to assure that you get good data out of the

session.

5. This will have to be done each session so be sure to build this into your schedule.
6. You will need to do this right before testing – so make sure to have any consent forms or pre-session questions completed before you begin calibrating the equipment
7. Conduct a practice activity to get your participant comfortable with the equipment before you begin the actual tasks.
8. Remove distracting elements from the test area. They should not have to read or make note of anything during testing.
9. The moderator should sit next to and slightly behind the user so as not to encourage conversation
10. The moderator should watch the participant's eye movement on a separate monitor out of the participant's line of sight so as not to distract him/her.
11. To generate pure heat maps or Saccade paths, do not ask the participant to "think-aloud"
12. Be aware that when you initially present a task the participant may scan the screen to get familiar with the elements before they pursue the actual task, so take that into account when you begin your analysis.

Image: SMI Eye Tracking https:// creativecommons.org/licenses/ by/2.0/

USABILITY HEURISTICS

1. Visibility of System Status-Let users know where they are and what is going on.
2. Match to the real world-Use familiar working methods, language and terms.
3. User control and freedom-Let users control what they do and how they do it.
4. Consistency and standards-Be consistent, adopt appropriate standards.
5. Error Prevention-Prevent errors with maintenance, monitoring, design.
6. Recognition not Recall-easy to learn -don't rely on user memory –don't make me think.
7. Flexibility and efficiency of use-Make it quick and easy to use –efficient for all types of users (e.g. experts v novices)
8. Aesthetic and minimalist. Design should be as aesthetic and minimalist, and clear as possible.
9. Assist users to recognize, diagnose & recover from errors-clear notification, no blame, support fix.
10. Help and documentation-contextual, supportive, directive.

Source: Nielsen & Molich (1993)

NORMAN'S DESIGN PRINCIPLES

Visibility
Controls or information easy to locate & see

Affordance
Physical form dictates or directs function

Signifiers
Visual form directs function

Mapping
Logical and clear correspondence of control to effect

Constraints
Minimise options to direct action / remove error

Feedback
Action confirmed clearly and immediately

Consistency
Aesthetically & functionally, internally and externally

Don Norman,' The design of everyday things' 1988

WIZARD OF OZ TESTING

WHAT
Wizard of Oz method is a research method in which research participants interact with a computer interface that subjects believe to be responding to their input, but which is being operated by an unseen person. The unseen operator is sometimes called the "wizard"

WHO INVENTED IT?
John F. Kelley
Johns Hopkins University. 1980
USA Nigel Cross

WHY
1. Wizard of Oz is good for the testing of preliminary interface prototypes.
2. A relatively inexpensive type of simulation
3. Identify problems with an interface concept
4. Investigate visual of an interface.

CHALLENGES
1. Requires training for the wizard.
2. It is difficult for wizards to provide consistent responses across sessions.
3. Computers respond differently than humans

HOW
1. The wizard sits in a place not visible to the research participant.
2. The wizard observes the user's actions, and initiates the system's responses.
3. The "wizard" watches live video from a camera focused on the participant's hands and simulate the effects of the participant's actions.
4. Users are unaware that the actions of the system are being produced by the wizard.

HOW MANY USERS SHOULD YOU TEST?

Nielsen found that testing 5 users uncovered 85% of problems

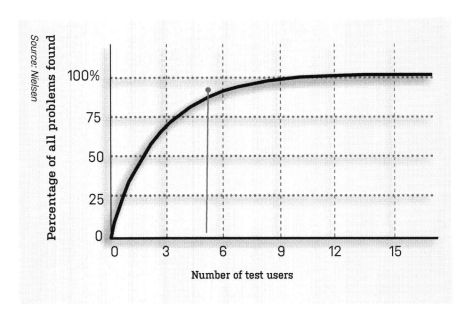

Source: Nielsen

Percentage of all problems found

Number of test users

USER TESTING VS HEURISTIC EVALUATION

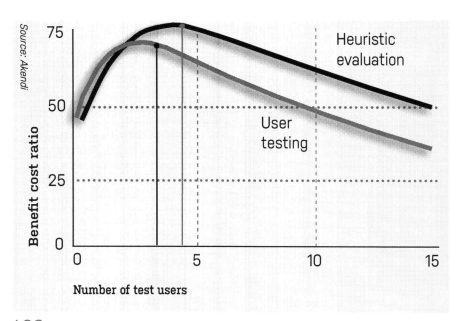

Source: Akendi

Benefit cost ratio

Heuristic evaluation

User testing

Number of test users

SAMPLE USABILITY TEST TIME-LINE

TEST-2 WEEKS	Determine test audience, start recruiting
TEST-2 WEEKS	Determine feature set to be tested
TEST-1 WEEK	Write first version of guide, discuss with team, check on recruiting
TEST-3 DAYS	Write second version of guide, recruiting should be completed
TEST-2 DAYS	Complete guide, schedule practice test, set up and check equipment
TEST-1 DAY	Do practice test in the morning, adjust guide/tasks as appropriate
TEST	Test (usually 1-2 days, depending on scheduling)
TEST+1 DAY	Discuss with observers, collect copies of all notes
TEST+3 DAYS	Watch all tapes, take notes
TEST+1 WEEK	Combine notes, write analysis
TEST+1 WEEK	Present to team, discuss and note directions for further research

Source: Adaptive Path

ITERATE

Modify the design prototype and test with real people and refine until it works

Steps of iterative design process are as follows:
1. Complete an initial design
2. Create a low fidelity prototype.
3. Present the design to a minimum of 5 test users
4. Identify any problems experienced by the test user
5. Refine the design to fix the problems
6. Repeat steps 2-5 until all design problems are resolved

DO A REALITY CHECK

At each milestone in a design development, the design team and important stakeholders such as customers, clients, manufacturers representatives can meet and review the design to see how real the solution is and refine the direction as necessary.

IDENTIFY STAKEHOLDERS

OBTAIN FEEDBACK

Usability testing is a technique used in user-centered interaction design to evaluate a product by testing it on users. Usability testing focuses on measuring a designs fitness for an intended purpose. Usability testing involves observation under controlled conditions to determine how well people can use the design

1. Methods include:
2. Hallway testing five to six people are brought in to test the product, or service. The name of the technique refers to the fact that the testers should be random people who pass by in the hallway.
3. Remote usability Usability evaluators, developers and end users are located in different countries and time zones, .
4. Expert review. Involves bringing in experts with experience in the field to evaluate the usability of a product system or service.
5. Automated expert review Though an automated review might not provide as much detail and insight as reviews from people, they can be finished more quickly and consistently.
6. A/B Testing. Two versions (A and B) are compared, which are identical except for one variation that might impact a user's behaviour.

CHAPTER SUMMARY

Usability testing helps improve a design to make it more usable. Real users undertake particular tasks. Researchers and other stakeholders observe and collect data.

Process
1. Develop a test plan
2. Choose a testing space
3. Recruit participants
4. Prepare test materials
5. Conduct the tests
6. Debrief participants
7. Analyze data
8. Conclusions and recommendations

What to test
1. Low-fidelity prototype or paper prototype
2. Wireframes
3. High-fidelity prototype and experience system.
4. Alpha and Beta prototypes•
5. Test competitor's designs
6. Test in the real context of use.
7. Test iteratively
8. Use heuristics and usability guidelines.
9. Test the final design

How many to test
Test at least four people from each user group.

CHAPTER REVIEW

1. What is the process of usability testing?
2. Who do we test prototypes with?
3. What do we test with usability testing?
4. How many people should we test as a minimum?
5. What is the difference between scenarios and tasks?
6. What is a screener?
7. What is the difference between alpha and beta testing?
8. What is coding in data analysis?
9. What is usually in a test plan?
10. What is eye tracking?
11. What are heuristics?
12. What is Wizard of Oz testing?

EXERCISE ONE
USABILITY TEST PLAN

COFFEE ORDERING APP

BACKGROUND
A usability test plan is a type of research plan that explains what testing will be done, the reasons for the testing, who will be tested, the timeline and other factors. It helps ensure that team, client and stakeholders are in alignment on what needs to be tested and why.

TASKS
Complete a usability test plan dash based on the coffee ordering app paper prototype that you prepared
in the last exercise.
Include the following in your plan
1. 1. Description of app
2. 2. Business case
3. 3. Test objectives
4. 4. Participants
5. 5. Equipment required
6. 6. Test tasks
7. 7. Responsibilities
8. 8. Location and dates
9. 9. Procedure

DELIVERABLES
One 1 to 2 page test plan.

EXERCISE TWO
ITERATION QUESTIONS

INSTRUCTIONS
Modify and improve your prototype based on your previous feedback. Show it to five people and answer the following questions.

What works in the design?

1.

2.

3

4.

What doesn't work in the design?

1.

2.

3.

4.

What refinements need to be made?

1.

2.

3.

4.

16

IMPLEMENTATION

IMPLEMENTATION

WHAT

During implementation phase small scale, iteratively tested, working solutions are brought to market. The design is prepared for low quantity manufacturing or minimum viable product distribution and market testing.. Gather feedback from stakeholders, and determine if your solutions are meeting their needs and fine tune the design. Launch of a new product or process is communicated to stakeholders. Manufacturers, distributors, and retailers or service providers are educated about new product or service, and trained.

WHY

Design thinking has value only when combined with design doing. The implementation stage is where you take your idea into people's homes, workplaces and lives.

HOW

Finalize your design

The details of this phase will depend on the type of design area that you are working in.

Pitch & commit

Create a short, compelling case for your project. Include:
1. User unmet need
2. Insights
3. Design solution
4. Summary of work
5. Challenges
6. Investment
7. Value to stakeholders.

This pitch will help
1. Secure support,
2. Partnerships,
3. Funding
4. Organizational commitment

The pitch should be short. Identify the possible "deal breakers". Prototype and test these. Run the solution by as many stakeholders as possible.

Build external partnerships

Collaboration with other organizations and individuals is an integral part of the design process. Organizations benefit from their partners' insights and expertise.

Sign off from stakeholders

When you believe that you have a design that can be successfully distributed and sold, show it to all your stakeholders one last time before documenting the design for final distribution.

Authorize vendors

Review design with vendors.

Deliver

Do final testing obtain sign off from stakeholders and launch. The design should successfully address the problem identified in the user research phase of the process.

THE PITCH

WHAT
....
A simple statement of what change you and your product are making in the world. A memorable one-sentence explanation of what you do for customers.

HOW
Pain (+ Gain)
1. What problem is out there in the world?
2. What are you solving for your customers?
3. What opportunities do you provide for people to be faster, more cost-effective, more efficient, happier, safer,..?

Product
1. As simple as possible: what does your product do for customers?
2. How does it work?
3. How have you tested it with customers?
4. (Be sure not to let the product dominate the pitch.)

Product Demo
1. Live demo? (always risky, but powerful if it works...)
2. Or screenshots? Physical product?
3. Can you show a real customer using it?
4. And do you really need to do a demo?

What's Unique
1. Technology/Relationships/ Partnerships

2. How do you help your customers get
3. results differently to your competition, or
4. alternatives?

Customer Traction
1. Success so far?
2. Pilot customers? Major brands?
3. Customer reference quotes/ movies?
4. PR coverage?
5. Use data and facts to strengthen.

Business Model
1. How do you get paid?
2. What's the opportunity for growth?
3. How can you scale beyond your current scope:
4. new industries, territories, applications of
5. partnerships and technology?

Investment
1. Amount of investment?
2. In how many rounds? How many investors?
3. What type of investor are you looking for?
4. What expectations do you have of your
5. investors; network, expertise?

Team
1. What relevant experience does your
2. team have that supports your story?
3. Brands worked for?
4. Achievements? Sales success?

End statement with call to action

TIPS

Intrigue/Surprise

1. Don't give the whole game away:
2. leave them wanting to know more.
3. Surprising facts or insights about the industry and its trends?
4. New information about a known subject?

Why You?

1. Why do you care about solving this problem for your customers?
2. How has your life been affected by this industry and business?
3. Why should your audience get involved with you?

Interaction

1. Challenge the audience with questions and something to take action on.
2. How can you re-set their attention?
3. What media can you use to give energy to your story?

Portable Story

What story can the audience go away and tell on your behalf?
What key things do you want them to remember about you and your company?

Source: The Pitch Canvas
Best3Minutes.com

A SIMPLER PITCHING STATEMENT

FOR	Target Customers/Users
WHO	Pain, Need, Opportunity or Problem
WHAT	Product/Service Name
IS A	Product/service Category
THAT	Key User Benefits & business opportunity
UNLIKE	Competitors & Their Competing Product/Service
WE (OUR SOLUTION)	Solution and Primary Differentiation

Key activities and objectives during the deliver stage are:

1. Final testing, approval and launch
2. Targets, evaluation and feedback loops.

Pre-launch
3-4 Weeks before launch:
1. Create the campaign.
2. Evoke emotion.
3. Create desire.
4. Prepare marketing materials.
5. Be original.
6. Review what's working.
7. Create urgency.

Mid-launch
1. Post on blogs, social media and other various communication channels.
2. Listen and adapt.

Go live
Now you are ready to go live.

Launch
Liaise with internal teams in areas such as marketing, communications, and brand.

1. How can you reduce the risk of failure?
2. Have you met your goals.
3. Is it compelling?
4. Set a launch date.

Post-launch stages
The design should now be improved continuously, based on user feedback, analysis, and further research.

Post-launch
1. Ask for feedback from first buyers
2. Make it memorable.
3. Review and improve.
4. Plan ahead.

Did the design meet it's goals?
Ideas that have emerged during the design process or in post-launch feedback may be put to one side but developed later, and will then go through the design process again on its own.

Measure success
1. Determine metrics to measure level of success.
2. 2 To 3 months after release measure the success
3. Measure the success and objectively evaluate.
4. Implement metrics and measurements

Some ways to measure success:
1. Customer satisfaction
2. ROI is A common business measure of project profitability, over the market life of the design expressed as a percentage of initial investment.
3. Increased usage
4. Increased revenue from existing customers
5. Did your design solve the user problem?
6. How many new customers have you gained?
7. What is your real product margin?
8. Cash flow
9. Is your design team satisfied?
10. Improved customer retention rate
11. Increased market share

What could be improved?
Invite customers to co-create, and integrate feedback.

Define next vision
Time to start planning the next design so that you can stay ahead of the many competitors.

Source: Adapted from Jonathan Mead
"The 40 Step Checklist for a Highly
Successful Launch"

"There's no such thing
as a creative type. As
if creativity is a verb,
a very time-consuming
verb. It's about taking an
idea in your head, and
transforming that idea
into something real. And
that's always going to
be a long and difficult
process. If you're doing
it right, it's going to feel
like work."

Milton Glaser
American graphic designer

"If an idea can't reach
consumers, improve
their lives, and create
commercial value, it's
not a great idea."

"Design Thinking
taught forward looking
businesses the value
of bringing creative
inventiveness (aka,
abductive thinking) to
the center of modern
innovation practice."

"Design Thinking taught
modern institutions that
human life should be the
primary springboard of
21st century innovation."

Farenheit 212
Rethinking design thinking

CHAPTER SUMMARY

During implementation phase small scale, iteratively tested, working solutions are brought to market. The design is prepared for low quantity manufacturing or minimum viable product distribution and market testing. Gather feedback from stakeholders, and determine if your solutions are meeting their needs and fine tune the design. Launch of a new product or process is communicated to stakeholders. Manufacturers, distributors, and retailers or service providers are educated about new product or service, and trained.

Some common activities during this phase are:
1. Finalize your design
2. Pitch & commit
3. Build external partnerships
4. Sign off from stakeholders
5. Authorize vendors
6. Deliver
7. Pre-launch
8. Mid-launch
9. Go live
10. Launch
11. Post-launch stages
12. Post-launch
13. Did the design meet it's goals?
14. Measure success
15. What could be improved?
16. Define next vision

CHAPTER REVIEW

1. Name four activities undertaken by the design team during the implementation phase.
2. What is a pitch?
3. Why do you need to do a pitch?
4. Who might you pitch to?
5. What is in a pitch?
6. What types of external partnerships may be developed during the implementation phase?
7. What activities may be part of a per-launch?
8. When should a pre-launch be undertaken?
9. What activities may be part of a post launch?
10. Name four ways of measuring success.

17
DESIGN THINKING
FOR YOUR LIFE

DESIGN THINKING FOR YOUR LIFE

Can design thinking also be applied to your personal life? If design isn't just "how it looks, but how it works," then we should be able to apply it to the problems that come up in our everyday lives. Life Design, like all design, is a team sport.

You don't have to choose between doing what you love and making a living."

One of the most popular courses at Standford University is ME104B "Designing Your Life". The course is taught by professors Dave Evans and Bill Burnett. The course uses design thinking to help students from any discipline to address the "wicked problem" of designing your life and career. Topics include the integration of work and worldview, the realities of engaging the workplace, and practices that support vocation formation throughout your life. The capstone assignment is the creation of an "Odyssey Plan" for the 3-5 years following Stanford graduation.

Evans and Burnett recently released a book, "Designing Your Life: How to Build a Well-Lived, Joyful Life", which has been on the NY Times best seller list since its release in September of last year.

Because of DYL, I not only got my dream job after college, but was super intentional about my life-friendships, health, hobbies, relationships, etc, in a way that I wouldn't have been otherwise that made life after college just as fun, if not more fun, than my time at Stanford, which I didn't think was possible!"

Anonymous Stanford Student

Bill Burnett offers the following advice.

We have been teaching the Designing Your Life course for over a decade and now we're sharing our (scientifically proven) Life Design movement with the world in our new book Designing Your Life. Our five mindsets will help you get started on your way to building a well-lived, joyful life."

The same design thinking responsible for amazing

technology, products, and spaces can be used to design and build your career and your life, a life of fulfilment and joy, constantly creative and productive, one that always holds the possibility of surprise."

Bill Burnett

The Stanford course stresses the following five points:
1. Be curious.
2. Try stuff.
3. Reframe problems.
4. Know it is a process.
5. Ask for help.

EXERCISE ONE

PERSONAL SWOT ANALYSIS

WHAT

The acronym SWOT stands for: strengths, weaknesses, opportunities, and threats. SWOT can be a useful tool to uncover and develop personal opportunities. A personal SWOT analysis will help you to identify your personal characteristics that can help you identify and achieve a successful goal. How to do your own SWOT analysis?"

Note: the author is not connected to Stanford University and these exercises do not reflect content taught at Stanford University.

1. Draw a two-by-two grid on a sheet of paper
2. At the top of the four boxes write the headings Strengths, Weaknesses, Opportunities Threats. One heading per box.
3. Work through the questions below and write the answers in the relevant boxes.
4. Show your answers to some friends, relatives or colleagues and refine the answers based on their perspectives about you.
5. Do the opportunities questions last.
6. Iterate refine and develop your answers.
7. Validate your current position.

8. Which skills and experiences should you emphasize?
9. What new skills should you acquire?
10. Brainstorm career directions.
11. Highlight opportunities
12. Identify possible threats.
13. Determine possible actions. There are four types of actions you could take:
    - Strengthening a specific skill or adding something to your strengths quadrant.
    - Minimizing or eliminating a weakness.
    - Pursuing or exploiting an opportunity.
    - Protect yourself from threats.
14. Revisit and update your SWOT chart each year.

LEARNING OUTCOMES
Your Personal SWOT Analysis will help you to understand the aspects of the four components of the SWOT analysis as it applies to you and to develop an action plan to achieve your personal objectives.

SOME QUESTIONS TO ASK YOURSELF WHEN CREATING YOUR PERSONAL SWOT

STRENGTHS
1. What do you do well?
2. What do you do better than others?
3. What are you most competent at?
4. What knowledge do you have that can help you?
5. What skills do you have that can help you?
6. What do other people say you do well?
7. 7. What is unique about you?
    - Your capabilities
    - Your competitive advantage
    - Your unique selling points
    - Your resources
    - Your assets
    - Your contacts
    - Your networks
    - Your experience
    - Your location
    - Your value
    - Your awareness
    - Your qualifications
    - Your values
8. Do you have good ways of monitoring your progress towards goals?
9. What is your education? What did you enjoy?
10. What could be useful resources to work towards your goals?
11. Does your education or experience give you a competitive advantage? What is that advantage?
12. What are your achievements?
13. What positive personal qualities do you have?

WEAKNESSES
1. What could you improve?
2. Where are you least efficient?
3. What don't you do well?
4. What knowledge and skills are you missing?
5. What should you avoid doing?
6. What could you do better?
7. How could you measure your improvement?

- What is holding you back?
- Gaps in capabilities
- Gaps in experience
- Gaps in education
- Lack of competitive strength
- Lack of reputation
- Lack of accreditation
- Presence and reach
- Lack of financial resources
- Lack of confidence
- Distractions
- Other vulnerabilities
8. What do you avoid doing?
9. What are the underlying causes of you failures? Identify some failures and ask why five times

OPPORTUNITIES

1. What real opportunities are present today?
2. Do you have a set of goals?
3. From which opportunities can you profit and how?
4. What could be done today that isn't being done?
5. What is missing in the market that you may be able to provide?
   - Market developments
   - New industry or lifestyle trends
   - Gaps in chosen areas
   - Weak competition
   - Technology
   - Innovation
   - Unique selling proposition
   - Internationalization
   - Business development
   - Information and research
   - Personal contacts
   - Networks
   - Productivity

- Economies
- Seasonal changes,
- Influences
6. Who can support you and how?
7. What trends do you see in your professional area?
   - What are the recent trends?
   - What type of people is getting hired?
   - What skills do they have?
   - Is it a growing field?
   - Can I obtain better education?
8. How can you get noticed?
9. How can you improve your networking?
10. What does your resume look like?
11. What does you Facebook profile say about you?
12. Is there a stepping stone
13. Can you start working half-time just because you like the job you are going to do?
14. Who can you learn from?
15. Who can introduce you to the right people?
16. Is there a person who can show you how to use your strengths in the best way possible?

THREATS

1. What obstacles do you face in achieving your goals?
2. Who might cause you problems in the future and how?
   - What Is The Competition Doing That Might Cause Difficulties For You?
   - Political
   - Legislative Changes

- Market Forces
- Environmental Factors
- New Technologies
- Heavy Competition;
- Poor Market Demand
- Bad Contracts And Dishonest Partners
- Unexpected Obstacles;
- Loss Of Key Colleagues
- Loss Of Financial Backing
- Local And International;
- Seasonal Threats

3. Who/what may get in your way? –
4. Who are your biggest competitors and what are they doing?
5. Are there training or educational requirements that are required?
6. Is technology changing my professional field?
7. Is technology changing the future of my industry?
8. How do I stay ahead of that trend?
9. Are you marketable?.
10. Changing market requirements and their impact on you.
11. Changing professional standards that you don't meet.
12. Reduced demand for one of your skills.
13. Evolving technologies you're unprepared for.
14. The emergence of a new competitor

EXERCISE TWO

ADDRESS A NEED IN YOUR LIFE

WHAT

Follow this design thinking process to address something in your life that you would like to change. Depending on what you select the time frame may be longer than a typical class exercise.

PROCESS

15. List five problems in your life that you want to address.
16. Select one problem that truly interests you and that you'd like to resolve soon. Select an actionable problem.
17. Describe the problem in one sentence.
18. What do you already know about the problem?
19. What do you not know about the problem?
20. What solutions have you tried?
21. What are your assumptions?
22. Define the problem with a sentence "How might I...?"
23. Reframe the problem in five different ways with five different "How might I...?" sentences.
24. Select the frame that you feel best represents your challenge at this point.
25. ,Answer the question"Why do I want to meet this challenge?" in one sentence.
26. ,Answer the question""What's stopping me from meeting this

challenge?" in one sentence.

27. Brainstorm at least 10 potential solutions to meet this challenge.

28. Keep your ideas simple and concise. Begin each statement with a verb to emphasize action. Deliberately create radical ideas that you can build upon.

29. What new ideas might a friend offer? What ideas might a competitor offer? What ideas might your mother suggest? What would your worst enemy suggest?? What other points of view might you take to generate even more ideas?

30. Circle the four best solutions.

31. List at least 15 potential criteria that you might use in

32. Measuring the worth of these selected solution ideas. Remember that useful criteria must be specific, clear and simple. Extend your effort to think of a wide range of criteria; don't be too quick to home in. When you think you've finished, try to add five more potential criteria to your list.

33. From your criteria list, circle four that you feel are most important. Make sure you know exactly what your selected criteria mean.

34. Now write down your final selection below at the beginning of step 6 as your solution for action.

35. What new problems might this idea create?

36. Where might you encounter difficulties with this idea?

37. Who might be negatively affected by this idea?

38. Who would benefit from this idea?

39. How might you introduce this idea?

40. When might be the best time to introduce this idea?

41. Let's diverge further. Putting aside your judgment, quickly list at least 10 simple steps that you might take.

42. Write down each thought as it occurs to you. Prompt yourself with questions like, Whom could I call? What could I buy? Where could I go? What would I need?

43. From this list of possible actions, circle the one you believe you should do first. Make sure it starts with an action work and is simple, clear and specific.

44. "When," write down a specific date and time for taking this action. Then under the heading "Where," write down the specific place in which you plan to take the action.

45. You'll likely think of further action steps that should be carried out either just before or just after

46. your first step. In either case, repeat the procedure above. Perhaps you can nail down only a few action steps right now.

47. Whose support might you need?

48. Write down whatever you think might prevent you from taking the first step in your action plan.

49. Circle the most important impediment, then list at least three ideas for overcoming it.

18
VISUALIZATION METHODS

PROCESS FLOW DIAGRAM

WHO INVENTED IT?
Frank Gilbreth, American Society of Mechanical Engineers,1921

WHY
1. To represent a flow of process or decisions or both.

CHALLENGES
1. Use standard symbols.
2. Arrows should show the direction of flow.
3. A junction is indicated by two incoming and one outgoing line.
4. The two most common types of boxes are for a process step and for a decisions.

HOW
1. Define the process boundaries
2. Complete the big picture first.
3. Draw a start box.
4. Draw the first box below the start box. Ask, 'What happens first?'.
5. Add further boxes below the previous box, Ask 'What happens next?'.
6. Connect the boxes with arrows
7. Describe the process to be charted
8. Review.

RESOURCES
Pen
Paper
White-board
Dry erase markers.

BAR CHART

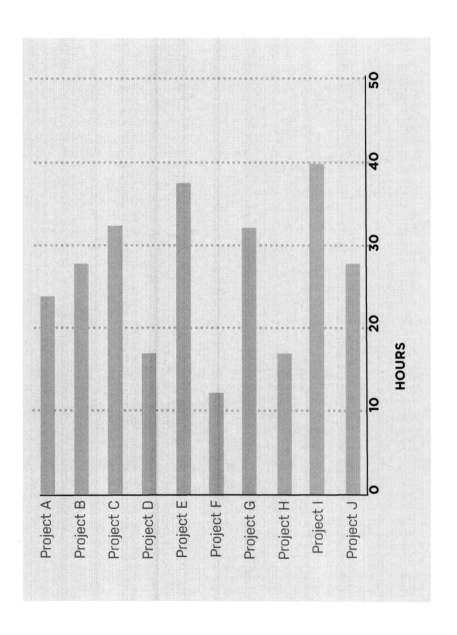

BAR CHART

WHAT

A simple bar chart is useful to present information for a quick problem or opportunity analysis. It provides a comparison of quantities of items or frequencies of events within a particular time period.

WHO INVENTED IT?

The first bar graph appeared in the 1786 book The Commercial and Political Atlas, by William Playfair (1759-1823)

WHY

1. To display a "snapshot" comparison of categories.
2. To depict the relationship between variations over time.
3. To illustrate process variability or trends.
4. To indicate a potential problem area (high or low frequencies).

CHALLENGES

1. Care should be taken not to insert more than five bars or cover more than five time periods. This would make the Bar Chart cluttered and difficult to interpret.

HOW

1. Collect data from sources
2. Draw the vertical and horizontal axes.
3. Decide on the scale
4. Draw a bar for each item.
5. Label the axes

RESOURCES

Pen
Paper
Graph paper
Computer
Graphics software

"

We are visual animals. Over 80% of the information processed by our brains from our senses comes through our eyes. Here are some tools that you can use to visually communicate the relationships of complex data."

LINKING DIAGRAM

OBJECTIVES	WEIGHTING		RESPONSIBILITY
Reduce SKUs by 25%	10		Industrial Design
			Engineering
Establish new factory in China	8		Transportation
Decrease returns by 25%	6		Human Resources
			Manufacturing
Increase sales by 25%	7		Quality
Establish distribution Network in China	7		Marketing
			Sales
Increase speed to market by 30%	4		Sourcing
Reduce manufacturing costs by 25%	9		Management

LINKING DIAGRAM

A linking diagram is a graphical method of displaying relationships between factors in data sets.

WHY

To analyze relationships of complex data

RESOURCES

Pen
Paper
White-board
Dry erase markers

HOW

1. Select a problem to analyze.
2. Team brainstorms two lists of factors that relate to the problem such as outcomes and actions.
3. Team rates the items by importance. 1-10, 10 being most important.
4. Draw lines between related items in each list.
5. Review and refine
6. List insights
7. Take actions based on the insights.

ONION MAP

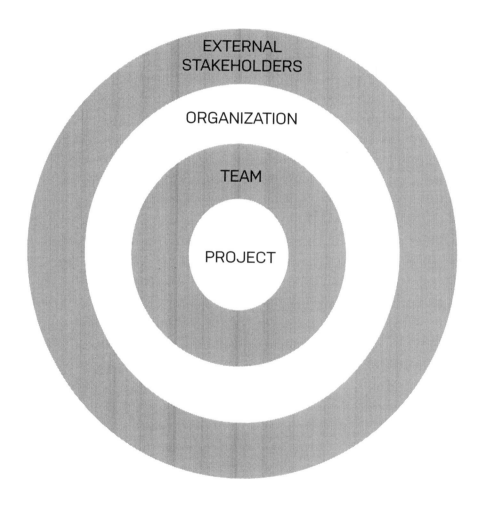

ONION MAP

WHAT

An onion map is a chart that shows dependencies of a system. The items in each circle depend on the items in the smaller circle.

WHO INVENTED IT?

Onion models have been used for centuries to indicate hierarchical levels of dependency. Peter Apian's 1539 Cosmographia used an onion model to illustrate the pre-Copernican model of the universe.

WHY

1. It is an effective way of describing complex relationships
2. It provides a focus for team discussion and alignment
3. It is fast
4. It is inexpensive.

HOW

1. Define the system to be represented by the onion diagram.
2. Create a circle to define the innermost level of dependency
3. Create concentric circles around the inner circle to represent progressively higher levels of dependency
4. Name the levels.

RESOURCES

Pen
Paper
Software
Computer
White-board
Dry-erase markers

RADAR CHART

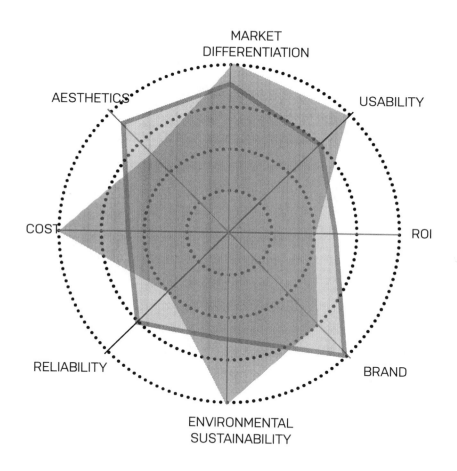

MARKET
DIFFERENTIATION

AESTHETICS

USABILITY

COST

ROI

RELIABILITY

BRAND

ENVIRONMENTAL
SUSTAINABILITY

RADAR CHART

The radar chart is a star shape chart that allows information to be logged radially for a number of variables. The radar chart is also known as a web chart, spider chart, star chart, star plot, cobweb chart, irregular polygon, polar chart, or kiviat diagram.

WHO INVENTED IT?
Georg von Mayr 1877

CHALLENGES
1. Radar charts may not provide information for trade off decisions.

WHY
A spider diagram is a way of displaying a great deal of information in a condensed form,

HOW
1. Draw a circle on a flip-chart paper
2. For each item to evaluate draw a line from the center to the circle.
3. Write the item on the intersection between the line and the circle.
4. Draw spider lines from the inside to the outside of the circle (see photo).
5. Gather the participants around the flip-chart.
6. Ask them to put one dot for each item: If highly ranked the dot should be close top the center; if poorly ranked the dot should be close to the circle.
7. Present and discuss the result with the group.

RESOURCES
Paper
Pens
Computer
Graphic software

VENN DIAGRAM

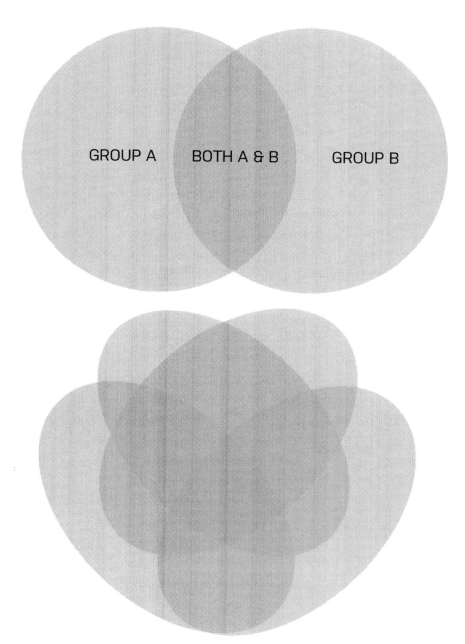

GROUP A   BOTH A & B   GROUP B

Venn's four-set diagram using ellipses

VENN DIAGRAM

....

WHAT

A Venn diagram is an illustration of the relationships between and among groups that share something in common. Venn diagrams show intersections. Venn diagrams normally are constructed from overlapping circles. Circles represent groups of things with a shared attribute. The interior of the circle and the areas of overlap symbolically represents the elements of discreet sets.

WHO INVENTED IT?

John Venn 1880

WHY

1. A useful tool for simplifying and communicating data related to user populations and design features
2. Explaining systems of taxonomy
3. Displaying organizational systems
4. Exploring different classes of items

HOW

Decide what you want to map.

1. Pick two classifications.
2. Draw a circle for each classification.
3. Fill up the circles with items that are in each classification.
4. Establish what overlaps.
5. Redraw your circles but this time overlap them
6. Fill in each circle with the items in that classification which are not in both classifications
7. Fill in the overlapped section with the items in both classifications,
8. Add a third classification in the overlapping section
9. Fill in that section with the items that are in both of the previous classifications.
10. Name the third secrtion.

RESOURCES

Paper
Pens
Colored markers
Software

19
TEMPLATES

STORYBOARD TEMPLATE

PROJECT _____

NAME _____

DATE _____

DIALOGUE _____

ACTION _____

DIALOGUE _____

ACTION _____

DIALOGUE _____

ACTION _____

PROJECT _____

NAME _____

DATE _____

DIALOGUE _____

ACTION _____

DIALOGUE _____

ACTION _____

DIALOGUE _____

ACTION _____

PROJECT _____

NAME _____

DATE _____

DIALOGUE _____

ACTION _____

DIALOGUE _____

ACTION _____

DIALOGUE _____

ACTION _____

635 BRAINSTORM TEMPLATE

PROBLEM STATEMENT:		
	IDEA 1	**IDEA 2**	**IDEA 3**

	IDEA 1	IDEA 2	IDEA 3
1			
2			
3			
4			
5			
6			

CONTEXT MAP TEMPLATE

Trends	Uncertainties	Technology	User needs	Economic	Political	Trends

COMPETITOR MATRIX

Brand	Brand A	Brand B	Brand C	Brand D
Brand Statement				
Value Proposition				
Target Customers				
Business model				
Technology				
Environmental Performance				
Key Differentiation				

PERCEPTUAL MAP TEMPLATE

SPIDER DIAGRAM TEMPLATE

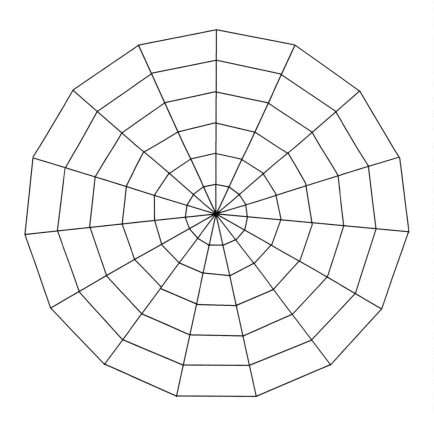

STAKEHOLDER POWER INFLUENCE MAP

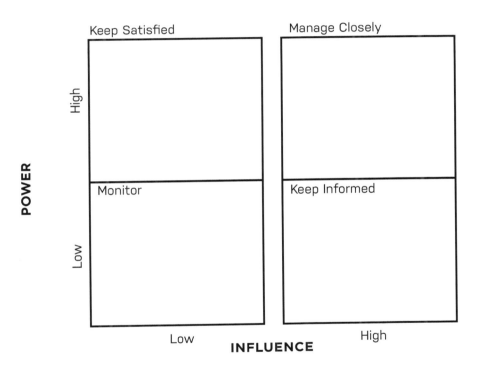

DESIGN THINKING SCORING RUBRIC

LEVEL SCORE	EXCEEDS EXPECTATIONS 6	STRONG 5	EFFECTIVE 4	DEVELOPING 3	EMERGING 2	NEEDS TO IMPROVE 1
AMBIGUITY	Comfortable when things are unclear	Comfortable when things are unclear	Limited comfort when things are unclear	Limited comfort when things are unclear	Uncomfortable when things are unclear	Uncomfortable when things are unclear
EMPATHY AND HUMAN VALUES	Sees and understands others point of view. Focuses on user needs	Sees and understands others point of view. Focuses on user needs	Has limited understanding of other points of view	Has limited understanding of other points of view	Sees only own point of view	Sees only own point of view
COLLABORATIVE	Collaborates effectively with people from other disciplines with different backgrounds and viewpoints	Collaborates effectively with people from other disciplines with different backgrounds and viewpoints	Collaborates with people from other disciplines with different backgrounds and viewpoints in a limited way	Collaborates with people from other disciplines with different backgrounds and viewpoints in a limited way	Cannot collaborate with other. Sees only own point of view.	Cannot collaborate with other. Sees only own point of view.
CURIOUS	Is interested in things that are not understood and seeing things with fresh eyes.	Is interested in things that are not understood and seeing things with fresh eyes.	Shows limited interest in things that are not understood and seeing things with fresh eyes.	Shows limited interest in things that are not understood and seeing things with fresh eyes.	Is not interested in things that are not understood and seeing things with fresh eyes.	Is not interested in things that are not understood and seeing things with fresh eyes.
HOLISTIC	Balances perspectives of business, human values, the environment and technology	Balances perspectives of business, human values, the environment and technology	Considers the perspectives of business, human values, the environment and technology in a limited way	Considers the perspectives of business, human values, the environment and technology in a limited way	Does not consider the bigger context focuses on only one aspect such as business profitability	Does not consider the bigger context focuses on only one aspect such as business profitability

	Crafts ideas with no judgment of the idea or idea creator	Crafts ideas with no judgment of the idea or idea creator	Some judgment of ideas and other idea creators	Some judgment of ideas and other idea creators	Extensive judgment of ideas and other idea creators	Extensive judgment of ideas and other idea creators
NON JUDGMENTAL	Crafts ideas with no judgment of the idea or idea creator	Crafts ideas with no judgment of the idea or idea creator	Some judgment of ideas and other idea creators	Some judgment of ideas and other idea creators	Extensive judgment of ideas and other idea creators	Extensive judgment of ideas and other idea creators
OPEN MINDSET	Is able to tackle problems regardless of industry or scope. Out of the box thinker	Is able to tackle problems regardless of industry or scope. Out of the box thinker	Can address problems over a number of industries and a limited range of scope	Can address problems over a number of industries and a limited range of scope	Can only address problems in a single industry of limited scope	Can only address problems in a single industry of limited scope
BIAS TOWARD ACTION	Creates prototypes and physical embodiments of ideas and actions that effectively move project forward	Creates prototypes and physical embodiments of ideas and actions that effectively move project forward	Creates some prototypes and progress but in a limited way	Creates some prototypes and progress but in a limited way	Talks about ideas but does not create physical prototypes or move project forward through actions	Talks about ideas but does not create physical prototypes or move project forward through actions
EXPERIMENTAL	Embraces experiment as an integral part of work	Embraces experiment as an integral part of work	Experiments in a limited way	Experiments in a limited way	Does not experiment	Does not experiment
COMPLEXITY	Creates clarity from complexity	Creates clarity from complexity	Limited ability to address complex problems	Limited ability to address complex problems	Cannot address complex problems	Cannot address complex problems
PROCESS	Is mindful of process	Is mindful of process	Follows process in a limited way	Follows process in a limited way	Has no process	Has no process
SHOSHIN	An attitude of openness, eagerness, and lack of preconceptions even when at an advanced level	An attitude of openness, eagerness, and lack of preconceptions even when at an advanced level	Some openness, and eagerness. Some preconceptions	Some openness, and eagerness. Some preconceptions	Lack of openness, and eagerness. Many preconceptions	Lack of openness, and eagerness. Many preconceptions
ITERATIVE	Makes improvements with prototyping feedback loops and cycles regardless of design phase	Makes improvements with prototyping feedback loops and cycles regardless of design phase	Limited ability to refine or improve ideas through iterative user feedback and prototyping	Limited ability to refine or improve ideas through iterative user feedback and prototyping	No ability to refine or improve ideas through iterative user feedback and prototyping	No ability to refine or improve ideas through iterative user feedback and prototyping

CRITICAL THINKING SCORING RUBRIC

LEVEL	EXCEEDS EXPECTATIONS	STRONG	EFFECTIVE	DEVELOPING	EMERGING	NEEDS TO IMPROVE
SCORE	6	5	4	3	2	1
SUMMARIZES THE PROBLEM	Clearly identifies the challenge and relationships of the design problem	Clearly identifies the challenge and relationships of the design problem	Summarizes the issue. Some aspects are incorrect or confused	Summarizes the issue. Some aspects are incorrect or confused	Summarizes the issue. Some aspects are incorrect or confused	Fails to identify the challenges and relationships of the design problem
CONSIDERS CONTEXT	Analyzes the design problem with sense of scope. Identifies the influence of context.	Analyzes the design problem with sense of scope. Identifies the influence of context.	Explores context in a limited way. Relies on authorities.	Explores context in a limited way. Relies on authorities.	Explores context in a limited way. Relies on authorities.	Analyzes the problem with bias of own context. Fails to justify opinion
COMMUNICATES ORIGINAL PERSPECTIVE	Demonstrates own perspective supported by experience and unassigned sources. Integrates contrary interpretations	Demonstrates own perspective supported by experience and unassigned sources. Integrates contrary interpretations	Presents own perspective. Addresses other views inconsistently	Presents own perspective without addressing other views	Single view simplistic position adopted with little consideration. Fails to justify opinion	Single view simplistic position adopted with little consideration. Fails to justify opinion

SUMMARIZES THE PROBLEM	Examines evidence and questions bias accuracy and relevance	Examines evidence and questions bias accuracy and relevance	Selective use of evidence. Discerns fact from opinion. May not recognize bias.	Selective use of evidence. Discerns fact from opinion. May not recognize bias.	Repeats information without question. Does not distinguish between fact and opinion	Repeats information without question. Does not distinguish between fact and opinion
CONSIDERS CONTEXT	Considers context, assumptions and evidence. Ideas are qualifies. Considers ambiguities	Considers context, assumptions and evidence. Ideas are qualifies. Considers ambiguities	Conclusions consider evidence. Present implications that may impact other people.	Conclusions consider evidence. Present implications that may impact other people.	Fails to identify conclusions. Conclusions are absolute and from an external source.	Fails to identify conclusions. Conclusions are absolute and from an external source.
COMMUNICATES ORIGINAL PERSPECTIVE	Addresses divers perspectives to inform analysis. Justifies own view while respecting views of others	Addresses divers perspectives to inform analysis. Justifies own view while respecting views of others	Integrates multiple viewpoints in a limited way. Some evidence of self assessment	Integrates multiple viewpoints in a limited way. Some evidence of self assessment	Presents single perspective. Fails to recognize other perspectives	Presents single perspective. Fails to recognize other perspectives

SAMPLE INTERVIEW CONSENT FORM

Research should, be based on participants' freely volunteered informed consent. The researcher has a responsibility to explain what the research is about and who will see the data. Participants should be aware that they can refuse to participate; confidentiality, and how the research will be used.

The information contained within this book is strictly for educational purposes. If you wish to apply ideas contained in this book you are taking full responsibility for your actions. There are no representations or warranties, express or implied, about the completeness, accuracy, reliability, suitability or availability with respect to the information, products, services, or related graphics contained in this book for any purpose. Any use of this information is at your own risk.

Purpose of the research
The purpose of this project is [purpose]. *Provide a brief, usually one-paragraph, explanation of what the research is about and state why the subject is being asked to participate [e.g., inclusion/exclusion criteria]*

What we will ask you to do
If you agree to be in this study, you are asked to participate in a recorded interview. The interview will include questions about [topic] , The interview will take about [duration] minutes to complete. With your permission, we would also like to tape-record the interview.

Risks and benefits
There is the risk that you may find some of the questions about [topic] to be sensitive. *[Describe any possible benefit to the participants or others that may reasonably be expected from the research; then describe any reasonably foreseeable risks or discomforts to the participants, or state "there are no foreseeable risks," if none are identified.]*

Compensation:
There will be [amount of compensation] [type of compensation] compensation. *[Specify whether participants will be compensated and if so, the amount. If amount will be prorated for any reason, state this.]*

Taking part is voluntary
Taking part in this interview is completely voluntary. You may skip any questions that you do not want to answer. If you decide not to take part or to skip some of the questions, it will not affect your current or future relationship with Cornell University. If you decide to take part, you are free to withdraw at any time.

Your answers will be confidential

The records of this project will be kept private. In any sort of report we make public we will not include any information that will make it possible to identify you. Research records will be kept in a locked file; only [who] will have access to the records. [Regarding the storage of the tape, who will keep it, where will it be stored, after the transcription is done?] If we tape-record the interview, we will destroy the tape after it has been transcribed, which we anticipate will be within [duration] months of its taping.

If you have questions: [contact]

If you have questions

The researchers conducting this study are [researchers]. Please ask any questions you have now. If you have questions later, you may contact [name] at [email] or at [phone].

Statement of Consent

I have read the above information, and have received answers to any questions I asked. I consent to take part in the project. In addition to agreeing to participate, I also consent to having the interview tape-recorded. I understand the information presented above and that: My participation is voluntary, and I may withdraw my consent and discontinue participation in the project at any time. My refusal to participate will not result in any penalty.

You will be given a copy of this form to keep for your records.

Interviewee Signature ....Date ....
In addition to agreeing to participate, I also consent to having the interview tape-recorded.

Researcher's Signature ....Date ....
This consent form will be kept by the researcher for at least [duration] years beyond the end of the project and was approved by the [Organization] on [date].

This consent form will be kept by the researcher for at least [duration] years beyond the end of the project and was approved by the [Organization] on [date].

TESTING SCRIPTS

RECRUITMENT SCRIPT

Hello, may I speak with X We are looking for participants to take part in a research study evaluating the usability of the X Product. There will be $xx payment for the hour long session, which will take the X Building located downtown. The session would involve one-on-one meeting with a researcher where you would sit down in front of a computer and try to use a product while being observed and answering questions about the product. Would you be interested in participating? If not: Thank you for taking the time to speak with me. If you know of anyone else who might be interested in participating please have them call me, at xxx-xxx-xxxx

SCREENING SCRIPT

I need to ask you a couple of questions to determine whether you meet the eligibility criteria— Do you have a couple of minutes? If not: When is a good time to call back? Keep in mind that your answers to these questions to not automatically allow or disallow you take part in the study—we just need accurate information about your background, so please answer as

well as you can.
Have you ever used X product?
If yes:
How long have you used it for? [criteria: at least 1 yr.]
And how often do you use it? [criteria: at least 3 times a month]
If no:
Have you ever used any data processing products, such as [list competitor or similar products]? [criteria: Yes]
If yes: How long have you used it for? [criteria: at least 1 yr.]
And how often do you use it? [criteria: at least 3 times a month]
Self-identify participant gender via voice and name and other cues.

SCHEDULING

If participant meets criteria: Will you be able to come to the X Building located downtown for one hour between May 15 and 19? Free parking is available next to the building. How is [name available times and dates]? You will be participating in a one-on-one usability test session on [date and time]. Do you require any special accommodations?
I need to have an e-mail address to send specific directions and confirmation information to. Thanks again! If participant does not meet criteria: Unfortunately,

you do not fit the criteria for this particular evaluation and will not be able to participate. Thank you for taking the time to speak with me.

PARTICIPANT RECRUITMENT SCREENER

The usability test of the X Product requires 12 participants from 2 user groups.

User type experienced
Product users
Number 6
Characteristics current product users/customers who have used x product
For at least 1 year and use it at least 3 times a month
3 males, 3 females

User type New product
users
Number 6
Characteristics People who have no prior experience with X Product, but do have at least 1 year's experience using similar products (e.g. data processing tools).
3 males, 3 females

THINK OUT LOAD SCRIPT

When you are doing the testing there may be times that you become frustrated or confused, but you do not say anything,
We want you to say it out loud so we can see the problem and improve the design. We only can recognize what you tell us is a problem. Let us know what you are thinking. There here are no wrong answers. We're looking for your genuine impressions. Your comments will help us improve the design.

Source: Usability Testing Basics. An Overview

20
GLOSSARY

GLOSSARY

In this short glossary I have brought together a collection of terms used in Design Thinking, service design and user-centered design.

These fields are emerging areas of design and I believe will become the most significant areas of design this century. There are many terms that are used and these terms are still evolving.

At the back of this work you will find a list of my other publications if you would like more in-depth information about any of these fields.

I hope that you will find this collection useful.

A-B TEST
Testing technique where a percentage of site visitors are shown an alternate version of a design. The effectiveness of the two designs is then compared.

ACTOR
A person involved in the creation, delivery, support, or use of a service.

AFFINITY DIAGRAM
A tool used to organize a large number of ideas, sorting them into groups based on their natural relationships, for review and analysis

AFFORDANCES
The qualities of a design or material that affects or suggests how it can be used. For example, the affordances of a hammer (weight, handle and and grip, scribed head, etc) suggest it should be used for striking objects. Looking at affordances is especially useful when analyzing how designs or materials prompt certain behaviors. (eg. "When all you have is a hammer, everything looks like a nail."
Source dSchool Stanford

ANALOGOUS SITUATIONS
An analogous situation is a situation from another area or industry that may relate to an area of focus for a design and may suggests ways to improve it.

ANALYTIC INDUCTION
A qualitative research method that begins with a rough hypothesis, which is modified through the examination of cases that don't fit the hypothesis.

ANALYTICS
A broad term that encompasses a variety of tools, techniques and processes used for extracting useful information or meaningful

patterns from data.

ARTIFACTS
Physical service touchpoints. For example the New York Underground map

BACKSTAGE/ BACKOFFICE
Backstage activities are those taken by the service delivering company employees that are not visible to the customer. Backstage actions are actions that impact customers. Backstage actions are separated from onstage service delivery by the line of visibility. Activities above the line of visibility are seen by the client while everything below it is invisible. On an aircraft, the taking of an order for a meal is an onstage or front-stage action, and the preparation of the food is a backstage action if it is not seen by the traveler.

BETA LAUNCH
The limited launch of a software product with the goal of finding bugs before final launch.

BIAS
A one-sided viewpoint, inclination or a partial perspective. An interviewer might inadvertently bias an interviewee's answers by asking a "loaded" question, in which a desired answer is presupposed in the question.

BODYSTORMING
Prototyping method,

Service situations are be acted out,for example for example at the hotel reception. The design team cast the roles, practice the situation. often with the input of end users The purpose is to prototype and test interactions to better understand and refine them.

BRAINSTORMING
Brainstorming is a group or individual creativity approach where design solutions are generated by members of the team in a collaborative session.

A method for generating ideas, intended to inspire the free-flowing sharing of thoughts of an individual or a group of people, typically while withholding criticism in order to promote uninhibited thinking.

CARD SORTING
A technique using either cards or software, whereby users generate an information hierarchy that can then form the basis of an information architecture or navigation menu.

A technique to investigate how users tend to group. The users are given a set of cards containing individual item names and are told to sort them into related piles and label the groups. Card sorting provides insight into the user's mental model and suggests the structure and placement of items on a Web site.
Source: Human Factors

International

CAUSATION
A relationship between an event (the cause) and a second event (the effect), where the second event is a consequence of the first event.
Source: Human Factors International

CHANNEL
A medium for communication or delivery. Most services use more than one channel. For example phone, email, in-store or web site.

CLOSED QUESTIONS
Questions that elicit a yes/no response.

CO-DESIGN
Process in which the design team directly engages end users to assist in the design to access knowledge that is crucial to develop successful design solutions.

The designers should provide ways for people to engage with each other as well as instruments to communicate, be creative, share insights and envision their own ideas. The co-design activities can support different levels of participation, from situation in which the external figures are involved just in specific moments to situations in which they take part to the entire process, building up the service together with the designers.

COGNITIVE DISSONANCE
A PET technique in changing impression. Cognitive dissonance refers to the discomfort caused by holding two or more conflicting (dissonant) beliefs at the same time. People seek to reduce the discomfort by changing one of the beliefs, thus returning to a state of 'consonance'. So, for example, someone holding the belief that "I am a smart consumer," may be faced with the dawning realization that "I paid too much for that car." The two beliefs are in conflict (dissonant) and therefore uncomfortable, so one of the beliefs must change. To avoid undermining positive self-belief, and because it is difficult to get a different car, the user's attitude about the car will change, so that it is seen as more valuable, and therefore worth the price paid.
Source: Human Factors International

COMPARISON TESTS
Usability test that compares two or more designs. Examples might be comparing alternative wireframes, comparing before and after designs, or a comparing a design against competitor designs.
Source: Human Factors International

CONCEPTUAL MODEL
A model constructed by the users in their mind to understand the working or the structure of

objects, based on their mental model and previous experience, to speed up their understanding. Also called mental model.
Source: Human Factors International

CONFIRMATION BIAS
The tendency to search for, notice, and interpret information in a way that confirms one's beliefs or opinions.
Source: Human Factors International

CONTEXTUAL INQUIRY
A semi-structured field interviewing method based on a set of principles that allow it to be molded to different situations. This technique is generally used at the beginning of the design process and is good for getting rich information, but can be complex and time consuming.

CODE
a word chosen to represent an idea, topic, or event that is an important theme of the interviews. After these words are decided on, they are connected to colors or symbols used to mark passages of the transcripts.

CODING
The process of marking passages of the interview's transcript that are about the same thing. By same thing we mean-the passages have the same phrases repeated in them or they talk about the topic in the same way. These passages are marked with a name, the code, which is usually connected to a longer explanation of what the passages have in common. Codes stress what themes run through the interview or the collection of interviews.

COLLABORATIVE DESIGN
Inviting input from users, stakeholders and other project members.

COLLECTIVE INTELLIGENCE
Collective intelligence is shared knowledge that comes from the collaboration of a group of people and is expressed in consensus decision making. Collective intelligence requires openness, sharing ideas, experiences and perspectives.

CONTEXT
Context
The world the service belongs to. The context is the specific frame in which the service takes place. Exploring and defining the context means setting the project boundaries in terms of limits but also opportunities. Context is external elements that surround and influence design. These items can be physical and non-physical and cultural. The environmental context relates to the time, the day, the location, the type of place and any other physical aspect that could influence your design. The surrounding context influences the success of design.

CONTEXTUAL INQUIRY

Interviewing users in the location that they use the product or service, to understand their tasks and challenges.

CONVERGENT

Process of Narrowing down ideas through synthesis.

CROSS-DISCIPLINARY COLLABORATION

Combines the wisdom and skills of different professional disciplines working in close and flexible collaboration. Each team member requires disciplinary empathy allowing them to work collaboratively with other discipline members. Design teams can include anthropologists, engineers, educators, doctors, lawyers, scientists, etc. in the innovative problem solving process.

CULTURAL PROBE

Cultural probes are sets of simple artifacts (such as maps, postcards, cameras, or diaries) that are given to users for them to record specific events, feelings or interactions in their usual environment, in order to get to know them and their culture better. Cultural probes are used to uncover aspects of culture and human interaction like emotions, values, connections, and trust.

CUSTOMER JOURNEY

The customer journey is a graphical representation of how the customer perceives and experiences the service interface over time It often also shows the phases before and after the interaction with the service. A customer journey map is a tool to explore, visualize, understand and refine an end user experience.

DECOY STRATEGY

A PET technique in changing impression linked to the Contrast Principle. People want to compare things before making decisions and like to make easy comparisons. So you can persuade them to select one of a small number of easily compared choices by introducing another choice that can't easily be compared. For example, you are more likely to get people to purchase a front loader washing machine, if you give them two front loader choices (easily compared) by contrast to a third choice of a top-loader (less easy to compare). In another example, you can increase sales of an item, by offering a similar, but inferior item at about the same price. It's easy to compare them, recognize the contrast in quality, and conclude that the better quality item represents exceptional value.
Source: Human Factors International

DEDUCTIVE ANALYSIS

A type of analysis that begins with theoretically derived hypotheses then tests them with data that were collected in accordance with the theoretical context.

DIARY STUDY
Asking users to record their experiences and thoughts about a product or task in a journal over a set period of time.

DIVERGENT
Expansive idea generation and exploration of ideas.

EMPATHIZE
This term is sometimes used to encompass the Understand and Observe steps or as a replacement for them. The use of this emotional term helps remind designers that they must always consider the human experience of real people. It's more than just seeing it from their perspectives, it's about understanding how they feel about it all and what it means to them.
source: dSchool Stanford

EMPATHY
Principle in the Design Thinking process and human- centered design, in which the user's perspective is always represented.
Source: Libraries Toolkit

ENTRY POINTS
Position of access to a service, where people are able to engage the service as customers, providers, or stakeholders.

ETHNOGRAPHY
The process of gathering information about users and tasks directly from users in their normal work, home or leisure environment.

EVIDENCE
Service evidences are touch-points that represent parts of a service experience.

EVIDENCE-BASED DESIGN
Evidence-based design is the approach of basing design decisions on credible research to achieve the best possible outcomes. Evidence-based design emphasizes the importance of basing decisions on the best possible data for the best possible outcomes. The design is not based just on the designer's opinion.

EXPERIENCE DESIGN
The application of design processes with the goal of creating an appropriate experience for the person interacting with the product. This process begins with understanding the needs and wants of the user. Analysis focuses on cognitive, emotional and motor aspects of the interaction and is completed when the quality of the experience is measured with the developed product.
Source: Human Factors International

EXPERIENCE PROTOTYPING
Service experiences have components that are intangible, and change over time and have multiple touch-points. Services are prototyped different ways then physical products. Experience Prototype is a representation, that

is designed to help us understand, explore or communicate what it feels like to engage with a product, space service or system.

EXIT POINTS
Point of disengagement of a service, by stakeholders.

EXTREME USER
A person who lies at the periphery of a group of users. Extremes can can include age, ability, occupation, experience, etc. Rather than designing for a composite or "average" user, a design team will oftentimes look to extreme users for surprising and actionable insights. Focusing on extreme users can lead to more innovative solutions, more profound insights about a group of users, and new, untapped markets for a product or service. *Source: dSchool Stanford*

FIELD STUDY
A field study is a general method for collecting data about users, user needs, and product requirements that involves observation and interviewing. Data are collected about task flows, inefficiencies, and the organizational and physical environments of users.

FIVE WHYS
An analysis method used to uncover the root cause of a problem.

Example of the method:

A patient had the wrong leg amputated
1. Why: Patient gave consent for amputation the night before the proposed surgery to Registrar (who was not going to undertake procedure).
2. Why: Amputation site marked with a biro (wrong leg).
3. Why: Registrar unaware of hospital policy on amputation sites being marked with a skin pencil and with bodily part being fully visible to Doctor.
4. Why: The department had no induction procedures for new medical staff working in the department.
5. Why: Because "we've never been asked to". *Root Cause Analysis Tool Kit. NHS*

FOCUS GROUPS
A direct data gathering method in which a small group (8–10) of participants are led in a semi-structured, brainstorming session to elicit rapid feedback

FORMATIVE EVALUATION
Formative evaluation is a type of usability evaluation that helps to 'form' the design for a product or service. Formative evaluations involve evaluating a product or service during development, often iteratively, with the goal of detecting and eliminating usability problems.

FREE LISTING
Free listing is a technique for

gathering data about a specific domain or topic by asking people to list all the items they can think of that relate to the topic. It can be used to gather data in large group settings or in one-on-one interviews.

FRONTSTAGE/ FRONTOFFICE
These are face-to-face between customers and employees. These are separated from the customer by the line of interaction.

GAMBLER'S FALLACY
The mistaken belief that if an event has occurred more frequently than normal, it will happen less frequently in the future, and vice-versa.
Source: Human Factors International

GAP ANALYSIS
A technique used to determine the difference between a desired state and an actual state, often used in branding and marketing. Gap analysis may address performance issues or perception issues.
Source: Human Factors International

GESTALT PRINCIPLES
Set of principles developed by the Gestalt Psychology Movement that established rules governing how humans perceive order in a complex field of objects. Gestalt principles of visual organization state that objects near each other, with

same background, connected to each other, or having similar appearance are perceived as belonging to a group.
Source: Human Factors International

GROUNDED THEORY
A qualitative research method in which theory is developed after data has been gathered and analyzed.

GROUPTHINK
Groupthink is consensus of opinion without critical reasoning or evaluation of consequences or alternatives. Employees may self-censor themselves for fear of upsetting the status quo.

HCI
Human Computer Interaction involves the study, planning, and design of the interaction between people (users) and computers.

HEURISTICS
Best practices, principles, or rules of thumb. Established principles of design and best practices in interface design, used as a method of solving usability problems by using rules of thumb acquired from human factors experience.
Source: Human Factors International

HEURISTIC EVALUATION
A usability evaluation method in which one or more reviewers, preferably experts, compare a

software, documentation, or hardware product to a list of design principles, referred to as heuristics and identify where the product does not follow those principles. Evaluating a website or product and documenting usability flaws and other areas for improvement.

HICK-HYMAN LAW
Demonstrates the relationship between the time it takes someone to make a decision and the number of possible choices he or she has. More choices will increase decision time.
Source: Human Factors International

HIGH-FIDELITY PROTOTYPE
A prototype which is quite close to the final product, with lots of detail and a good indication of the final proposed aesthetics and functionality.

HORIZONTAL PROTOTYPE
Prototypes that display a wide range of features without fully implementing all of them. Horizontal prototypes provide insights into users' understanding of relationships across a range of features,
Source: Human Factors International

HOW MIGHT WE?
A positive, actionable question that frames the challenge but does not point to any one

solution.
Source: Libraries Toolkit

HUMAN-CENTERED
An approach to design that adapts the solution to the end user through understanding the end user. The understanding is developed through engaging the end user and testing a variety of possible solutions through an iterative design process.

INDUCTIVE ANALYSIS
a type of analysis that begins with collecting and analyzing data, after which hypotheses are made.

Putting the user and user's perspective at the center of a solution. Human-centered or people-centric design requires having empathy with the user to solve for their specific needs. This philosophy involves starting with people and desirability first, before moving on to feasibility and viability.
Source: Libraries Toolkit

INTERACTION DESIGN
(IXD) Sometimes referred to as IxD, interaction design strives to create meaningful relationships between people and the products and services that they use.

INSIGHTS
Ideas or notions expressed as succinct statements that interpret patterns in your research and can provide new understanding or perspective on the issue.
Source: Libraries Toolkit

INTERCEPT
Spontaneous, casual and brief conversations with users in a natural context. Unplanned interviews that garner live feedback for your mini-pilot.
Source: Libraries toolkit

INTERVIEW GUIDE
A list of questions to direct conversation and make sure key issues get discussed. The guide should be flexible to move with conversation but at the same time its main purpose is to keep the interview on topic.

INTERVIEWER BIAS
the influence of the interviewer on the interviewee, which affects responses

I-SHAPED PERSON
Someone who has deep skills and knowledge in one area but not a broad competency across other areas.

ITERATIVE CONSULTATIVE PROCESS
An iterative consultative process is a design process of inviting diverse stakeholders to review a design and give feedback in order to improve the design from their point of view.

ITERATE
The act of repeating a process with the aim of approaching a desired goal, target or result. Each repetition of the process is also called an iteration.
In Design Thinking it refers to the cycles of prototyping, testing and revision.

ITERATIVE DESIGN PROCESS
Iterative design is the process of prototyping testing and refining a design in a series of repeated steps.

JOURNEY MAP
A visual representation of a particular person or persona's experience with a service. The experience is documented over time and often shows multiple channels.

LEADING QUESTION
a question that is phrased in a way that suggests to the interviewee an answer that the researcher prefers.

LEARNINGS
The most basic level of information you record from your research, including direct quotes, anecdotes, first impressions, notes on the environment, notes on what was most memorable or surprising, and more.
Source: Libraries Toolkit

LIKERT SCALE
A type of survey question where respondents are asked to rate the level on which they agree or disagree with a given statement on a numeric scale, e.g., 1–7, where 1 = strongly agree and 7 = strongly disagree. (Also see Rating Scale.)
Source: Human Factors

LINE OF VISIBILITY
In a service blueprint this is a line that separates face to face customer employee interactions from customer employee interactions that are remote or not face to face.

LOADED WORD
a word that has positive or negative connotations and can influence the interviewee's response to a question.

LOW-FIDELITY
PROTOTYPE A quick and easy translation of high-level design concepts into tangible and testable artifacts, giving an indication of the direction that the product is heading. Prototypes that are simple, focused on one or two features. Low resolution prototyping allows a team to make their ideas tangible and gather feedback.

MASLOW'S HIERARCHY OF NEEDS
A theory of motivation, in which individuals' needs are described as a hierarchy, often illustrated as layers in a pyramid. Needs at each level must be met prior to an individual aspiring to the next level. Maslow's theory describes five levels: Physiological, Safety, Social, Esteem and Self-actualization. In PET we can design to meet needs at one or more of these levels. For example, a mobile phone may meet people's safety ('I need to contact you in an emergency'), social ('I like to keep in touch wherever I am') and self-esteem needs ('Look at my cool phone'), with somewhat different design considerations applying to each of these levels.
Source: Human Factors International

MINIMUM VIABLE PRODUCT
A minimum viable product is a simple version of a new product which allows a team to learn the maximum amount about customers with the least effort. The goal of an MVP is to test fundamental business hypotheses as efficiently in the real world as possible.

MODERATOR
A person that works with a group to regulate, but not lead, a discussion. Whereas a facilitator might take charge of a discussion to shepherd it in a specific direction, a moderator remains passive, without explicitly leading the process or driving a desired outcome. A moderator takes the lead from the participants, listening and intervening only when necessary to encourage further discussion or ask for clarity for other participants or audiences.

NEEDS
A necessary function or condition. There are a wide variety of human needs such as

food, shelter, security, affection and self fulfillment.

OUTSIDE-IN PERSPECTIVE
This is the perception that people outside of an organization have of the organization and it's products and services such as customers and other stakeholders.

PAPER PROTOTYPE
Paper prototyping is the process of creating rough, often hand-sketched, drawings of a user interface, and using them in a usability test to gather feedback. A rough, often hand-sketched, drawing of a user interface, used in a usability test to gather feedback. Participants point to locations on the page that they would click, and screens are manually presented to the user based on the interactions they indicate.

PARADOX OF CHOICE
Limiting choice is a PET technique in changing impression. Paradoxically, people think they want many choices, but can, in fact, be overwhelmed by the complexities too many choices introduce to decision-making. So, people are more likely to be persuaded to make a purchase (or other decision) if you limit their choice to a small number, often no more than three or four.
Source: Human Factors International

PARTICIPATORY DESIGN
An approach that involves stakeholders such as clients, end users, community members in the design process to ensure that the design meets the needs of those it is serving as well as generating buy-in. A type of social research in which the people being studied have significant control over and participation in the research.

PERSONA
A persona is a fictitious identity that reflects one of the user groups for who you are designing. A representation of a user segment with shared needs and characteristics. In user-centered design and marketing, personas are archetypal characters that represent different user segments that might use a product or service in a similar way.

PLACEBO EFFECT
A PET technique in changing impression. In medicine, for example, you can achieve health improvements just by giving the impression you are treating patients with a drug, even if you are giving them a 'placebo', a neutral substance with no known medical properties. There is evidence that the more expensive patients think the drug to be, the greater the placebo effect.
Source: Human Factors International

POINT OF VIEW OR POV
In Design Thinking, a POV

means the point of view of a very particular person. Creating a point of view involves synthesizing the data gained in the Understand and Observe phases in order to create a common reference/ inspiration for later ideation and prototyping. The idea is to focus on a real person, with many of the concrete details found during the Understand/Observe phases. One approach is to develop one or two concise sentences that express User+Need+Insight. Good: "Mark is a shy, recent college graduate who needs a way to stay connected with the college community because he feels that his life could be more exciting. Alumni newsletters and college reunions need not apply." Bad:"Mark needs a website to share pictures and news with the people he met in college because he feels lonely."
Source: dSchool Stanford

POWER OF EXPECTATION

A PET technique in changing impression. Presenting goods or services in a way that raises the expectation that they will be good, results in users perceiving them as better. A wellformatted report, for example will be seen as better written than a scruffy one, even if the text is exactly the same. Similarly, a well presented meal will not only be more tempting than the same food just thrown on the plate, but will also taste better (as every good chef knows!). So, in PET, if we design to give the expectation that goods

and services will be good, they are more likely to be experienced as good.
Source: Human Factors International

PROBES

Areas you want to go more in-depth in an interview.

A technique used during in-depth interviews to explore the interviewee's emotions about the topic we're researching. The 'probing' questions asked gently nudge the interviewees to disclose their feelings and beliefs. For example: "How do you feel about shopping on-line?"
Source: Human Factors International

PROTOTYPE

A prototype is a model built to test a concept with end users in order to learn from. Prototyping helps understand real, working conditions rather than a theoretical conditions.

QUESTIONNAIRES

A research instrument consisting of a series of questions and other prompts for the purpose of gathering information from respondents.

REFRAMING

Reframe to create different perspectives and new ideas.

How to reframe:
1. Define the problem that you would like to address.

2. There is more than one way of looking at a problem. You could also define this problem in another way as."
3. What if a male or female used it?
4. What if it was used in China or Argentina?
5. "The underlying reason for the problem is."
6. "I think that the best solution is."
7. "You could compare this problem to the problem of."
8. "Another, different way of thinking about it

RETURN ON INVESTMENT (ROI)

A monetary evaluation of benefits relative to the effort or expenditure invested; a measure of how much return, usually measured as profit or cost savings, results from a given use of money. In the context of usability, ROI is the monetary (or other) benefit gained as a result of an investment in good usability design.
Source: Human Factors International

REVERSE CARD SORT

A usability testing technique, opposite to that of a card sort, where participants are given a list of items to see if they can figure out where to find them. Their success validates the self evidence of the navigational structure of a design. Categories have already been made and labeled appropriately
Source: Human Factors International

ROLE-PLAY

Assign roles and act out scenarios with props and end users feedback to refine your design.

SATISFACTION SYSTEM

The satisfaction system is the system of how the products or services satisfy the customer's needs. It includes the product or service and its related products or service. It involves understanding how related products add value to the main product. Customers are interested in the entire system beyond the individual product.

RULE OF RECIPROCATION

The technique is built on a social rule where people given a gift feel compelled to give something back. For example: You give your customer a small gift. Later, they're likely to consider signing up for your new service.
Source: Human Factors International

SCALE

Service design considers micro and macro scales ,detailed interactions, and holistic overviews of an experience.

SCENARIOS

A scenario is a hypothetical narrative illustrating an event or series of events. It is a method of imagining a user experience in the real world.

Use scenarios are a method of prototyping ideas in order to explore and refine them.

Scenarios are short stories about people and activities that describe typical usage and focus on goals, actions and objects.

Scenarios evoke reflection in design and provide a common reference point. Scenarios help express the requirements of the different stakeholders in a format that can be understood by the other stakeholders. They can be written, illustrated, acted or filmed. Scenario generating aims to predict how people could act in particular situations.

A concrete, often narrative, description of a user performing tasks in a specific context sufficiently detailed that design implications can be inferred. Source: Human Factors International

SENSORIAL DESIGN
Sensorial Design is a term used to include the presentation of an experience in all senses. For example, Visual Design only covers visual expression and presentation to the visual sense. Audio Design includes the creation of music, sound effects, and vocals to communicate and entertain in the aural sense (hearing). Likewise, all of the other human senses (touch, smell, taste, etc.) are elements of an experience that can be designed.

SERVICE DESIGN
Design for experiences that reach people through many different touch-points, and that happen over time.
British Standard for Service Design: BS 7000 -3, BS 7000 -10,BS EN ISO 9000

Service designs can be both tangible and intangible. Service design can involve artifacts, communication, context and behaviors. It should be consistent, easy to use and have the strategic alliance.
Gillian Hollins, Bill Hollins, Total Design: Managing The Design Process in the Service Sector

SERVICE ECOLOGY
A service ecology is a system of people, objects and the relationships between them that form a service.

System in which the service is integrated: i.e. a holistic visualization of the service system. All the factors are gathered, analyzed and visualized: politics, the economy, employees, law, societal trends, and technological development. The service ecology is thereby rendered, along with its attendant agents, processes, and relations. *Mager 2009*

Ultimately, sustainable service ecologies depend on a balance where the actors involved exchange value

in ways that is mutually beneficial over time.
Live/work 2008

SENSUALIZATION
Sensualization is the approach of considering the experience to be the total of the individual experiences of the five senses.

SERVICE
An exchange of value, involving tangible and intangible elements A system of products spaces human interactions and experiences.

SERVICE MOMENTS
Discrete points of interaction between a user and a service, often mapped out in a user journey. An example of a service moment is a patron placing a hold on a book, which can be done at home via the website, in the library via the website, or at the reference desk.
Source: Libraries Toolkit

SERVICE SYSTEM
The ecology of relationships, interactions, and contexts of a service. channels, resources, and touchpoints, internal and external, that facilitate the delivering of a service.

STAKEHOLDER
A person, group, or organization directly or indirectly involved or affected by a product, service or experience.

Stakeholders include any

individuals who are influence by the design. Specifically, the project team, end users, strategic partners, customers, alliances, vendors and senior management are project stakeholders

Possible stakeholders
1. Employees
2. Shareholders
3. Government
4. Customers
5. Suppliers
6. Prospective employees
7. Local communities
8. Global Community
9. Schools
10. Future generations
11. Ex-employees
12. Creditors
13. Professional associations
14. Competitors
15. Investors
16. Prospective customers
17. Communities

Why involve stakeholders?
1. Stakeholder analysis helps to identify:
2. Stakeholder interests
3. Ways to influence other stakeholders
4. Risks
5. Key people to be informed during the project
6. Negative stakeholders as well as their adverse effects on the project

SWIMLANES
An approach used in service design involving arranging descriptive boxes into rows (the "swim lanes") to provide additional context about how

the steps are related. Work flow is represented over time and is usually read from left to right.

SYNTHESIS
The sense-making process in which research is translated and interpreted into insights that prompt design. Useful frameworks for synthesis include journeys, Venn diagrams, two by twos and maps.
Source: Libraries Toolkit

STAKEHOLDER MAP
A visual representation of the stakeholders in a service and the relationships between them.

SERVICE DESIGN
Service design is a form of conceptual design which involves the activity of planning and organizing people, infrastructure, communication and material components of a service in order to improve its quality and the interaction between service provider and customers.
Service design - Wikipedia, the free encyclopedia, https://en.wikipedia. org/wiki/Service_design (accessed March 20, 2016).

SOCIAL DESIGN
Design done for the social good or top positively impact society.

STRATEGIC DESIGN
Design that focuses on big picture systematic problems in order to increase an organization's future innovative and competitive advantage.

STORYBOARD
A storyboard is a graphic sequence of illustrations, words or images for the purpose of communicating a user scenario or experience. Storyboarding, was developed at Walt Disney during the early 1930s. A storyboard is a tool inspired by the film-making industry, where a visual sequence of events is used to capture a user's interactions. Depending on the audience, it may be an extremely rough sketch, purely for crystallizing your own ideas.

SUMMATIVE TESTING
Testing done to measure the success of the design in terms of human performance and preference.
Source: Human Factors International

THINK-ALOUD PROTOCOL
A direct observation method of user testing that involves asking users to think out loud as they are performing a task. Users are asked to say whatever they are looking at, thinking, doing, and feeling at each moment. This method is especially helpful for determining users' expectations and identifying what aspects of a system are confusing.

TOUCHPOINTS
A touchpoint is any point of contact between a customer and the provider of a service, product or experience. A touchpoint is where a potential customer or customer comes in contact with your brand before, during and after a transaction.

Identifying your touchpoints is an important step toward creating a journey map or a service blueprint. Each touchpoint is an opportunity to create a better customer experience. A touchpoint can be a physical, virtual or human point of interaction. Chris Risdon from Adaptive Path defines touchpoints in this way. 'A touchpoint is a point of interaction involving a specific human need in a specific time and place.' Laura Patterson of VisionEdge defines a touchpoint as " any customer interaction or encounter that can influence the customer's perception of your product, service, or brand."

TRANSCRIPTION

The process of turning audio or video recordings into a typed format.

T-SHAPED PERSON

A person who has deep competency in a particular subject area and broad knowledge and skills across a range of disciplines.

TWO BY TWO

A type of framework with opposing axes showing a spectrum along a particular dimension on each axis. This framework is used to organized ideas within the four quadrants, or to demonstrate mappings of ideas across several dimensions.
Source Libraries Handbook

UNIQUE SELLING PROPOSITION

An exclusive message that concisely describes a product against its competition, and which the business or brand can use consistently in its advertising and promotion to achieve a cutting edge in the market.
Source: Human Factors International

UNMET NEEDS

Six principles that will ensure a design is compatible with user needs:
1. The design is based upon an explicit understanding of users, tasks and environments.
2. Users are involved throughout design and development.
3. The design is driven and refined by user-centered evaluation.
4. The process is iterative.
5. The design addresses the whole user experience.
6. The design team includes multidisciplinary skills and perspectives.

Some Questions to ask:
1. Who are the users?
2. What are the users' tasks and goals?
3. What are the users' experience levels?
4. What functions do the users need from the design?
5. What information will be needed by end-users?,
6. In what form do they need it?
7. How do users think the design should work?

USABILITY

Is the ease of use and learnability of an object, such as a book, software application, website, machine, tool or any object that a human interacts with.

USABILITY ROUND-TABLE

A meeting in which a group of end users is invited to bring specific work samples and discuss the validity of an early prototype.
Source: Human Factors International

USE CASES

A use case is a list of steps that define the interactions between a user and a system. Use cases, especially when used as requirements for software development, are often constructed in UML, with defined actors and roles.

USER-CENTERED DESIGN

A design process during which the needs of the user is considered at all times. Designers consider how a user is likely to use the product, and they then test the validity of their assumptions in real world tests with actual users. Design that responds to user needs that is developed through engaging and understanding the point of view of users.

USER JOURNEY

The step by step journey that a user takes to reach their goal.

USER PROFILING

Based on research of user groups develop different character profiles to represent your users. These are also called personas.

USER VALIDATION

Process of testing to determine if the user's needs or requirements have been met

VALUE EXCHANGE

A service provider makes a promise to the service recipient in exchange for some form of value. The movement of value from the service provider to the recipient is the value exchange.

VANITY METRICS

Data that make you feel good, but is not very useful or actionable such as new users gained per day or number of downloads. Vanity metrics do not reflect the key drivers of a business.

VERTICAL PROTOTYPE

Prototypes that display just a few complex features of a product and almost completely implement only these features. Vertical prototype tests provide insights into users' understanding of the complexity, issues, and problems of a specific feature.
Source: Human Factors International

VISUAL HIERARCHY

Refers to the overall page layout and its ability to lead the users' attention through the page elements. Effective visual hierarchies create an appropriate balance in composition that draws users to top levels of the hierarchy while optimizing visual access to important page level elements
Source: Human Factors International

WICKED PROBLEM

A wicked problem is a problem with contradictory, and changing requirements. The term 'wicked' is used, not in the sense of evil but rather its resistance to resolution.

Wicked problems are characterized by:
1. The solution depends on how the problem is framed.
2. Stakeholders have different world views and frames for understanding the problem.
3. The constraints of the problem and the resources needed to solve it change over time.
4. The problem is never solved definitively.

wicked problem : definition of wicked problem and synonyms http://brevard.ifas.ufl.edu/ communities/pdf/SF_Wicked_ Issues_Background_Defined_ (accessed March 20, 2016).

WIREFRAME

A rough guide for the layout of a website or app, either done with pen and paper or with wireframing software. The wireframe depicts the page layout and shows how the elements work functionally. It focuses on what a web interface does, not what it looks like. Wireframes can be sketches or computer images.

WIZARD OF OZ

A user-based evaluation of unimplemented technology where, generally unknown to the user, a human or team is simulating some or all the responses of the system.

WORKAROUND

A user's personal solution to a problem with a service or product, that circumvents the standard procedure. It is often temporary or makeshift. Observing these behaviors often leads to fruitful advances in insights and inspiration.
Source: Libraries Toolkit

21
INDEX

INDEX

I

IBM 434
icebreaker 176, 181
idea 81, 90, 111, 149, 152, 169,
170, 213, 214, 232, 256, 277,
278, 310, 314, 321, 335, 346,
347, 389, 390, 391, 392,
394, 396, 397, 400, 403, 411,
425, 429, 434
idea advocate 401, 403
ideation 277, 296
IDEO 16, 27, 28, 73
imitate 411
implementation 283
improvement. 294
indirect observation 242
inductive analysis 519, 519–557
information 108, 112, 117, 214,
223, 224, 227, 228, 231,
232, 255, 330, 391
inhibition 213, 278
innovate 131
innovation 26, 27, 98, 131, 132,
377, 557
innovation diagnostic 131
innovative 75, 90, 410, 417, 429
insight 326, 424
insights 76, 108, 109, 177, 206,
213, 214, 221, 224, 228, 229,
231, 232, 234, 242, 243,
244, 245, 246, 247, 248, 251,
264, 296, 302, 314, 401, 412,
429, 431, 433, 437, 469, 519
inspiration 406, 407
in-store 302
integrative thinking 25, 26
intellectual property 152, 375,
391
intent 75
interact 219, 428, 433, 441, 461
interaction 440
interaction design 519
interactions 108, 288, 294, 297,
314, 424, 425, 440

intercept 520
interviewer bias 520
interview guide 520
interviews 100, 109, 117, 149, 209,
210, 214, 223, 224, 227, 228,
229, 230, 231, 232, 233,
234, 235, 324, 325, 327
interviews 555–557
investment 134, 170, 283, 411,
424
I-shaped person 520
Ishikawa, Kaoru 21
iteration 81, 152, 404, 441, 503
iterative consultative process 520
iterative design 520

J

J. Muller, Michael 432
John Venn 19
Jones, John Christopher 22
journey 252, 253, 294, 301, 314,
315, 347, 528
journey map 252, 253, 294, 298,
314, 520, 528
judgement 503

K

Kahn, Herman 20, 412
Kaoru Ishikawa 317
Kawakita, Jiro 21
Kelley, John f. 461
Kimbell, Lucy 17
Kipling, Rudyard 255, 401
Klein, Gary 407

L

laddering 228
Lawson, Bryan 17, 22, 26
leading question 520
Leifer, Larry 16, 26
Levinson, Jay Conrad 24
Lewis, Clayton 434
life cycle 381, 382

SWOT analysis 21, 169
synectics 417
synthesis 264, 527
systems 94, 332

T

table 214, 278, 302, 303, 305, 307, 309, 312, 334, 349, 397
tablet 302, 332
tacit knowledge 177, 223, 227, 230, 231
talk 229, 248
target audience 300, 336
task 434
tasks 201, 205, 210, 215, 224, 228, 230, 232, 284, 412, 425, 433, 434, 437
taste 279, 289, 399
team 90, 107, 149, 213, 214, 219, 272, 274, 278, 289, 297, 303, 326, 327, 338, 347, 352, 389, 390, 391, 392, 397, 400, 411, 412, 425, 429
team members 156, 401, 416
teams 81, 90, 132, 557
technique 218, 228, 234, 327, 330, 335, 390, 391
techniques 97
technologies 131, 170
technology 297
telephone 235
test 90, 114, 152, 243, 244, 245, 247
testing 428, 432, 461, 464, 469, 472
the environment 377, 392
themes 277
think 108, 279, 288, 290
think aloud 434
think aloud protocol 527
think and feel 291
thinking 96, 111, 112, 114, 213, 278, 297, 298, 299
thinking out loud 434

time 108, 117, 205, 213, 214, 220, 224, 229, 231, 238, 255, 289, 302, 303, 307, 309, 312, 314, 326, 340, 390, 391, 392, 440, 528, 557
Titchener, e.b. 19
title card 440
Tolman, Edward 20
tools 108, 227, 294
touch 214, 399
touchpoint 100, 110, 297, 302, 305, 314, 348, 352, 527, 528
toxic 381
Toyota 218
transcription 528
tree 162, 165
triangulation 115
tripod 301
T-shaped person 520
TV 302, 332, 345

U

understand 97, 99, 100, 212, 248, 256, 294, 299, 300, 310, 325, 326, 347, 425
understanding 97, 99, 234, 297, 314
unique selling proposition 528
unmet needs 528
usability 207, 412, 446, 450, 460, 463, 464, 509, 513, 529
use cases 529
user 100, 110, 224, 228, 229, 230, 231, 232, 248, 277, 301, 326, 327, 330, 425, 440
user-centered 464
user centered design 17, 529
user experience 186, 428
user journey 452, 529
user needs 277
users 108, 110, 206, 221, 224, 227, 229, 294, 310, 326, 327, 330, 347, 425, 440
user validation 529

ux charette 144

V

W

22

DCC ON-LINE PROGRAMS
DCC WORKSHOPS
OTHER DCC TITLES
ABOUT THE AUTHOR

DCC ON-LINE COURSES

https://dcc-edu.org

OUR MISSION

Through our on-line programs, workshops and publications we provide skills to fulfill evolving work roles and to to create better solutions in a new economy. We provide quality education which is better value, more accessible, more flexible and more relevant for working global professionals. On-line live, interactive continuing education courses that you can access from home, from work or anywhere with an internet connection.

ABOUT US

Our programs are for working designers and anyone seeking design and management training. Our on-line programs are presented direct from Los Angeles by some of the most experienced design professionals in the world. We offer introductory courses, five-week certificate programs and eight-week advanced certificate programs that meet once per week. The courses are delivered at a number at different times to fit your schedule and time zone.

Our books have been specified as texts at many design and business schools including the University of California, Art Center Pasadena, Parsons Graduate Program, and Purdue University. We can present a custom program in your location anywhere in the world. We can tailor an on-line program to your schedule and needs. Contact us at info@curedale.com.

WHO HAS ATTENDED OUR COURSES?

Past participants in our on-line programs have included thousands of executives, design managers, designers from all design disciplines, architects, researchers, social scientists, engineers and other decision-makers from the following organizations including the following organizations. Tesla Motors, NASA, Kaleidoscope, Speckdesign, Intel, Nike, MillerCoors, Radiuspd, Gensler, Herman Miller,Trek bikes, Catalystnyc, Sylvania, Whipsaw, Berkeley University, Stanford University, Pininfarina, Inscape, Newbalance, MIT, Rhode Island School of Design,Tufts, Nokia, Steelcase, Mayo Clinic, Ocad, California State University Santa Barbara,University of Michigan,In Form, RIT,Honeywell, Columbia University,Nissan, Volkswagen, Sony, Nestle, Kraft Foods, Otterbox, Henry Ford Museum, Samsung, Ammunition, Siemens AG, Group, frog Design, Ziba Design, Plantronics, Luxion, Philips, Method, Visteon, Texas Instruments, Cisco, Mindspring, Hasbro, Dow Corning, Bressler Group, Reebok, Logitech, HP,CCS, Praxxis Design, Levi Strauss, NCSU, Design & Industry, Kensington, Symantec, Canberra University, Australian Government Department of Defence, Maya, Karten Design, Autodesk, Barco, Shutterstock, Lucid, Colgate, Starbucks, Sunbeam, Seimens.

DESIGN THINKING

DESIGN THINKING PROCESS AND METHODS MANUAL 3RD EDITION
Author: Robert A Curedale
Published by:
Design Community College Inc.
August 21, 2016
Paperback: 690 pages
Language: English
ISBN-10: 194080549X
ISBN-13: 978-1940805498

DESIGN THINKING PROCESS & METHODS GUIDE 2ND EDITION
Author: Curedale, Robert A
Published by:
Design Community College, Inc
January 2016
Paperback: 422 pages
Language: English
ISBN-10: 1-940805-20-1
ISBN-13: 978-1-940805-20-7

DESIGN THINKING PROCESS AND METHODS MANUAL 1ST EDITION
Author: Robert A Curedale
Published by:
Design Community College Inc.
Edition 1 January 2013
Paperback: 400 pages
Language: English
ISBN-10: 0988236214
ISBN-13: 978-0-9882362-1-9

DESIGN THINKING POCKET GUIDE 2ND EDITION
Author: Curedale, Robert A
Published by:
Design Community College, Inc
Jun 01 2013
Paperback: 228 pages
Language: English
ISBN-10: 098924685X
ISBN-13: 9780989246859

DESIGN THINKING QUICK REFERENCE GUIDE
Plastic laminated
Loose leaf one page
Author: Curedale, Robert A
Published by:
Loose Leaf: 1 pages
Publisher: Design Community College Inc.; 1st edition (2015)
Language: English
ISBN-10: 194080518X
ISBN-13: 978-1940805184

DESIGN THINKING TEMPLATES & EXERCISES
Author: Curedale, Robert A
Published by:
Design Community College, Inc
2016
eBook 51 pages
Language: English
ISBN-10: 1-940805-16-3
ISBN-13: 978-1-940805-16-0

MAPPING METHODS

EXPERIENCE MAPS
JOURNEY MAPS
SERVICE BLUEPRINTS
EMPATHY MAPS
Author: Curedale, Robert
Published by:
Design Community College, Inc
March 2016
Paperback: 402 pages
ISBN-10: 194080521X
ISBN-13: 978-1940805214

SERVICE BLUEPRINTS
Author: Curedale, Robert
Published by:
Design Community College, Inc
March 2016
Paperback: 152 pages
ISBN-10: 1940805198
ISBN-13: 978-1940805191

JOURNEY MAPS
Author: Curedale, Robert
Published by:
Design Community College, Inc
March 2016
Paperback: 152 pages
Language: English
ISBN-10: 1940805228
ISBN-13: 978-1940805221

EMPATHY MAPS
Author: Curedale, Robert
Published by:
Design Community College, Inc
March 2016
Paperback: 152 pages
Language: English
ISBN-10: 1940805252
ISBN-13: 978-1940805252

AFFINITY DIAGRAMS
Author: Curedale, Robert A
Published by:
Design Community College, Inc
March 2016
Paperback: 128 pages
Language: English
ISBN-13 978-1940805269
ISBN-10 1940805269

MAPPING METHODS: FOR DESIGN AND STRATEGY
Author: Curedale, Robert A
Published by:
Design Community College, Inc
April 2013
Paperback: 136 pages
Language: English
ISBN-13 978-1940805269
ISBN-10 1940805269

SERVICE DESIGN

SERVICE DESIGN
PROCESS & METHODS
2ND EDITION
Author: Curedale, Robert A
Published by:
Design Community College, Inc.
Edition May 2016
Paperback: 589 pages
Language: English
ISBN-10: 1-940805-30-9
ISBN-13: 978-1-940805-30-6

SERVICE DESIGN
250 ESSENTIAL METHODS
Author: Curedale, Robert A
Published by:
Design Community College, Inc.
Edition 1 Aug 01 2013
Paperback: 372 pages
Language: English
ISBN-10:0989246868
ISBN-13: 9780989246866

SERVICE DESIGN
POCKET GUIDE
Author: Curedale, Robert A
Published by:
Design Community College, Inc.
Edition 1 Sept 01 2013
Paperback: 206 pages
Language: English
ISBN-10:0989246884
ISBN-13: 9780989246880

DESIGN METHODS

DESIGN METHODS 1
200 WAYS TO APPLY
DESIGN THINKING
Author: Robert A Curedale
Published by:
Design Community College Inc.
Edition 1 November 2013
Paperback: 396 pages
Language: English
ISBN-10:0988236206
ISBN-13:978-0-9882362-0-2

DESIGN METHODS 2
200 MORE WAYS TO
APPLY DESIGN THINKING
Author: Robert A Curedale
Published by:
Design Community College Inc.
Edition 1 January 2013
Paperback: 398 pages
Language: English
ISBN-13: 978-0988236240
ISBN-10: 0988236249

50 SELECTED DESIGN
METHODS
Author: Curedale, Robert A
Published by:
Design Community College, Inc.
Edition 1 Jan 17 2013
Paperback: 114 pages
Language: English
ISBN-10:0988236265
ISBN-13: 9780988236264

DESIGN RESEARCH

DESIGN RESEARCH METHODS 150 WAYS TO INFORM DESIGN

Author: Curedale, Robert A
Published by:
Design Community College, Inc.
Edition 1 January 2013
Paperback: 290 pages
Language: English
ISBN-10: 0988236257
ISBN-13: 978-0-988-2362-5-7

INTERVIEWS OBSERVATION AND FOCUS GROUPS

Author: Curedale, Robert A
Published by:
Design Community College, Inc.
Edition 1 Apr 01 2013
Paperback: 188 pages
Language: English
ISBN-10:0989246833
ISBN-13: 9780989246835

INTERVIEWS OBSERVATION AND FOCUS GROUPS

Author: Curedale, Robert A
Published by:
Design Community College, Inc.
Edition 1 Apr 01 2013
Paperback: 188 pages
Language: English
ISBN-10:0989246833
ISBN-13: 9780989246835

INNOVATION

30 GOOD WAYS TO INNOVATE

Author: Curedale, Robert A
Design Community College, Inc.
Edition 1 November 2015
Paperback: 108 pages
Language: English
ISBN-10: 1940805139
ISBN-13: 978-1940805139

DESIGN FOR CHINA

CHINA DESIGN INDEX THE ESSENTIAL DIRECTORY OF CONTACTS FOR DESIGNERS 2014

Author: Curedale, Robert A
Design Community College, Inc.
Edition 1 2014
Paperback: 384 pages
Language: English
ISBN-13: 978-1940805092
ISBN-101940805090

BRAINSTORMING

50 BRAINSTORMING METHODS

Author: Robert A Curedale
Design Community College Inc.
Edition 1 January 2013
Paperback: 184 pages
Language: English
ISBN-10: 0988236230
ISBN-13: 978-0-9882362-3-3

BRIEFING CHECK LISTS

PRODUCT DESIGN
BRIEFING CHECKLIST
Author: Curedale, Robert A
Published by:
Design Community College, Inc.
Edition 1 2016
Paperback: 54 pages
Language: English
ISBN-10: 1940805317
ISBN-13: 978-1940805313

WEB DESIGN
BRIEFING CHECKLIST
Author: Curedale, Robert A
Published by:
Design Community College, Inc.
Edition 1 2016
Paperback: 90 pages
Language: English
ISBN-10:
ISBN-13:

FURNITURE DESIGN
BRIEFING CHECKLIST
Author: Curedale, Robert A
Published by:
Design Community College, Inc.
Edition 1 2016
Paperback
Language: English

ABOUT THE AUTHOR

Rob Curedale was born in Australia and worked as a designer, director and educator in leading design offices in London, Sydney, Switzerland, Portugal, Los Angeles, Silicon Valley, Detroit, and Hong Kong. He designed or managed the design of over 1,000 products as a consultant and in-house design leader for the world's most respected brands. Rob has three decades experience in every aspect of product development and design research, leading design teams to achieve transformational improvements in operating and financial results. Rob's design scan be found in millions of homes and workplaces around the world and have generated billions of dollars in corporate revenues.

DESIGN PRACTICE

HP, Philips, GEC, Nokia, Sun, Apple, Canon, Motorola, Nissan, Audi VW, Disney, RTKL, Governments of the UAE,UK, Australia, Steelcase, Hon, Castelli, Hamilton Medical, Zyliss, Belkin, Gensler, Haworth, Honeywell, NEC, Hoover, Packard Bell, Dell, Black & Decker, Coleman and Harmon Kardon. Categories including furniture, healthcare, consumer electronics, sporting, housewares, military, exhibits, and packaging.

TEACHING

Rob has taught as a full time professor, adjunct professor and visiting instructor at institutions including the following: Art Center Pasadena, Art Center Europe, Yale School of Architecture, Pepperdine University, Loyola University, Cranbrook Academy of Art, Pratt, Otis, a faculty member at SCA and UTS Sydney, Chair of Product Design and Furniture Design at the College for Creative Studies in Detroit, then the largest product design school in North America, Cal State San Jose, Escola De Artes e Design in Oporto Portugal, Instituto De Artes Visuals, Design e Marketing, Lisbon, Southern Yangtze University, Jiao Tong University in Shanghai and Nanjing Arts Institute in China.

AWARDS

Products that Rob has managed the design of have been recognized with IDSA IDEA Awards, Good Design Awards UK, Australian Design Awards, and a number of best of show innovation Awards at CES Consumer Electronics Show. His designs are in the Permanent collection of the Powerhouse Design Museum. In 2013 Rob was nominated for the Advanced Australia Award. The Awards celebrate Australians living internationally who exhibit "remarkable talent, exceptional vision, and ambition." In 2015 Rob was selected with a group of leading international industrial designers to provide opening comments for the international congress of societies of industrial design conference ICSID in Korea.

Made in the USA
Columbia, SC
23 December 2017